25/12/01

THE COLD WAR YEARS
Flight Testing at Boscombe Down, 1945–1975

Tim Mason

First published in Great Britain in 2001 by
Hikoki Publications Ltd
Ashtree House, Station Road, Ottringham, East Yorkshire, HU12 0BJ
Tel: 01964 624223 Fax: 01964 624666
E-mail: hikoki@dircon.co.uk
Website: http://www.hikokiwarplanes.com
© 2001 Hikoki Publications

All rights reserved. Apart from any fair dealing for the purpose of private study, research, criticism or review, as permitted under the Copyright, Design and Patents Act 1988, no part of this publication may be reproduced, stored in a retrieval system, or transmitted in any form or by any means, electronic, electrical, chemical, mechanical, optical, photocopying, recording or otherwise, without prior written permission. All enquiries should be directed to the publisher.

ISBN 1 902109 11 2

Edited by Barry Ketley
Artwork by David Howley
Design by Sue Bushell
Printed in Great Britain by
Ian Allan Printing, Hersham, KT12 4RG

Distribution & Marketing
in UK & Europe by
Midland Publishing
(a part of the Ian Allan Group)
4 Watling Drive, Sketchley Lane Industrial Estate, Hinckley, Leics, LE10 3EY
Tel: 01455 233747 Fax: 01455 233737
E-mail: midlandbooks@compuserve.com

Distribution & Marketing
in USA & Canada by
Howell Press Inc
1713-2D Allied Lane, Charlottesville, Virginia 22903-5336, USA
Tel: (001) 804 977 4006 Fax: (001) 804 971 7204
E-mail: HowellPres@aol.com

Caption to photograph on title page: *Epitomising the years of the Cold War are the three V-bombers of the British deterrent seen flying together for the first time in May 1957. Vulcan B.1 XA892 with Victor B.1 XA918 on the left and Valiant B.1 WZ373 on the right were flown by B Squadron of the A&AEE. © Crown Copyright*

ALSO AVAILABLE

The Secret Years
Flight Testing at Boscombe Down 1939–1945
Tim Mason
ISBN 0 9519899 9 5

RAF & RCAF Aircraft Noseart in World War II
Clarence Simonsen
ISBN 1 902109 20 1

Condor
The Luftwaffe in Spain 1936–1939
Patrick Laureau
ISBN 1 902109 10 4

Stormbird
Flying through fire as a Luftwaffe ground-attack pilot & Me 262 ace
Hermann Buchner
ISBN 1 902109 00 7

Luftwaffe Fledglings 1935–1945
Luftwaffe Training Units & their Aircraft
Barry Ketley & Mark Rolfe
ISBN 0 9519899 2 8

Emblems of the Rising Sun
Imperial Japanese Army Air Force Unit Markings
Peter Scott
ISBN 1 902109 55 4

Eyes for the Phoenix
Allied Aerial Photo-Reconnaissance Operations in South-East Asia 1941–1945
Geoffrey J. Thomas
ISBN 1 9519899 4 4

Shadows
Airlift and Airwar in Biafra and Nigera 1967–1970
Michael I. Draper
ISBN 1 902109 63 5

Luftwaffe Colours 1935–1945
Michael Ullman
ISBN 1 902109 34 1

Forever Farnborough
Flying the Limits 1904–1996
Peter J Cooper AMRAeS
ISBN 0 951899 3 6

Forthcoming
KG 200 – Geheim Geschwader
Geoffrey J. Thomas
ISBN 1 902109 33 3

CONTENTS

FOREWORD
By Sir John Allison 4

INTRODUCTION AND ACKNOWLEDGEMENTS 5

THE ESTABLISHMENT 6

FLYING 23

THE ASSESSMENT DIVISIONS AND SECTIONS 41

INTRODUCTION TO THE FOLLOWING CHAPTERS 71

BOMBERS AND MARITIME AIRCRAFT 72

FIGHTERS AND SINGLE SEAT STRIKE AIRCRAFT 109

HELICOPTERS 158

TRANSPORTS 190

MISCELLANEOUS TYPES 221

TRAINERS 233

CARRIER AEROPLANES 269

APPENDICES

APPENDIX 1
Commandants, Chief Superintendents, Superintendents and Establishment Secretaries 308

APPENDIX 2
Roll of Honour 309

APPENDIX 3
First Flights from Boscombe Down 310

APPENDIX 4
Flying Hours 311

APPENDIX 5
Electromagnetic Compatibility 311

APPENDIX 6
Abbreviations and Acronyms 312

INDEX OF AIRCRAFT 313

GENERAL INDEX 332
Names and places

FOREWORD
By Air Chief Marshal Sir John Allison KCB CBE FRAeS

In *The Cold War Years* historian and former test pilot, Tim Mason, picks up the story of flight testing at the Aeroplane and Armament Experimental Establishment at Boscombe Down where he left it—at the end of World War 2—in his earlier major work, *The Secret Years*.

This new book covers the next thirty years. It is, of course, a fascinating period, spanning as it does what is arguably the last great era of experimental test flying, before computers could be harnessed to pre-assess handling and performance with some accuracy and before mankind moved into space. Moreover, the early part of this ground-breaking time at Boscombe Down saw the transition from pistons to jets, from straight to swept wing and from subsonic to supersonic flight. It was also a period when the British aircraft industry still enjoyed great diversity and during which new designs and projects, all requiring testing and evaluation, abounded. Every military, or potentially military, aircraft of British origin during this rich period, plus most foreign designs destined for our armed forces, finds a place in these pages.

Also chronicled with clarity and unflinching candour are the difficult adjustments needed to move Boscombe Down from a wartime to a peacetime footing. This went far beyond adjusting to the massive draw down that always impinges upon military establishments of all kinds following success in major conflicts—most recently, for example at the end of the Cold War. We read how the close partnership between industry and the Establishment that had been forged in the crucible of war soon broke down under the commercial pressures that returned with peace. Thus there is human drama as well as technology between these pages. The reader can, for example discover how difficult the Establishment's position became in the face of political determination to bring the Swift into service to meet a pre-ordained timetable and without due regard to its state of development. It is clear that the independent role of the Establishment, and the integrity and objectivity of the testing, provided the only bulwark against Departmental folly.

This book is therefore an important historical work that not only records in meticulous detail the key facets of the flight tests themselves, but looks behind the scenes at organisation, structures, politics and human relations. It fills a significant gap in the published history of British aviation and is a worthy successor and companion volume to *The Secret Years*. I commend it to all who have an interest in military aircraft, and in their testing and development, and in particular to all military aircrew since 1945, every one of whom will have benefited from the dedication and expertise of those who served at Boscombe Down.

1: *Lightning DB XG310 in aerodynamic form of an F.3, seen in early 1963. The main external difference is the fin increased in area to 130%, but it still gave insufficient directional stability at high angles of attack at supersonic speeds. Half way along the fuselage is the notice "Keep clear of intakes when engines are running"—useful positioning as there is another by the intakes of the Avon 210 engines.*

INTRODUCTION AND ACKNOWLEDGEMENTS

The Aeroplane and Armament Experimental Establishment at Boscombe Down in Wiltshire had as its primary task between 1945 and 1975 the acceptance testing of aircraft weapon systems being procured for the Royal Navy, the Army and the Royal Air Force. The motto on the Establishment's badge and the armorial bearings is *"probe probare"*—"Properly to Test", aptly summarising its role in ensuring that the Services received equipment which met the requirements laid down by the Ministry of Defence (combining in April 1964 the Admiralty, War Office and Air Ministry). Soon after the end of the Second World War in 1945 another threat to peace emerged from the policies pursued by the communist bloc to which the Western nations responded by rearming. Military policy, and thus activity at AAEE, were dominated by the need to maintain adequate armed forces, equipped with the best weapons that could be afforded. At Boscombe Down, as elsewhere, these were "The Cold War Years."

This book is about the aircraft evaluated there after their makers' own tests, what the Establishment found, how it was organised, how it changed to meet altered circumstances and about some of the people who made it all happen. All aircraft for the British services were tested (with the exceptions of the American B-29 Washington and the AD-4W Skyraider) plus several civil and experimental designs. Over 2,100 aircraft are described with the aim of presenting as comprehensive a coverage of the Establishment's flight testing as space and surviving records permit. Preceding the section on the aircraft are three chapters on the Establishment, the Flying, and the Divisions and Sections which managed the tests. The task of condensing the work of 30 years by over 2,000 people (on average) into a book of manageable and saleable proportions has led me to be extremely selective in my choice of material for inclusion.

I am most grateful to the Defence Evaluation and Reseach Agency (DERA) at Boscombe Down for its assistance in making this History possible, in particular the use of the documents, mostly in the Information Centre. Extensive contributions have been made by current and ex-members of the Establishment, and by a generous group of enthusiasts. Many individuals have helped with information and photographs; first and foremost is Wason Turner whose long association with Boscombe is matched by his encyclopaedic memory and kindness in helping me. I also thank the following: John Gregory, Jenny Eburne, David Walton, Clare Wood, Wendy Gubbels, Lynne Ryland, Sarah Hutchinson, Chris Wheatcroft, Sharon Evans, Dudley O'Niell, Phil Cripps, Alex Wright, Naomi Read, Dan Seagrave, John Sharp, Robert Robertson, Phil Butler, Peter Gosden, Derek Collier-Webb, Rod Smith, Norman Parker, Terry Heffernan, Bruce Robertson, Philip Jarrett, Peter Green, Gordon Swanborough and Peter Allin. I offer particular thanks to Barry Ketley, my long suffering publisher, and to Sir John Allison for his kind Foreword.

Photographs marked © Crown copyright are published with the permission of the Defence Evaluation and Research Agency on behalf of the Controller of HMSO.

I have found it impossible to avoid some abbreviations and acronyms; a glossary is at Appendix 6. In general the word "Boscombe" is used, thus according with conversational convention in dropping the "Down." The word "Ministry" on its own means the same as "Headquarters," while "contractors/constructors/firm" and "industry" are usually interchangeable in this work.

2: Victor B.1A XA930 receives fuel from the long suffering Valiant WZ376 using its Mk 16 HDU in mid-1961; during the trial the Victor made one sortie of 12hr duration. © Crown Copyright

THE ESTABLISHMENT

War and Its Aftermath

The rolling downland of Wiltshire, home to mankind for over five millennia, had seen the arrival and expansion of a new kind of frantic activity at Boscombe Down in the middle years *anno Domini* of the twentieth century. Flight testing of military aircraft there by the Aeroplane and Armament Experimental Establishment (AAEE) started in 1939, reached a zenith in 1944, and had scarcely reduced in 1945 when World War Two ended. In the six years of conflict some 1,500 aeroplanes had passed through, most subjected to the Establishment's probing evaluation of their capabilities before being approved or otherwise for service with the Royal Air Force or Royal Navy. The prewar sloping grass aerodrome had by 1945 been sullied by 2,500 yd of concrete to form the first runway extending to the southwest, while the earlier six hangars and other buildings remained largely unchanged. A myriad of temporary buildings for domestic, office and technical purposes had sprung up together with more permanent structures for controlling flying, blowing air to simulate flight, and firing guns. The business of flying, testing, arming, servicing, administering and defending the aeroplanes gave employment to over 2,000 people, both men and women, the large majority serving in the RAF or Royal Navy, and most serving only for the duration of hostilities. As a unit of the Ministry of Aircraft Production, the conduct of tests was in the hands of civilian Scientific and Technical Officers, most on temporary engagements. The Establishment was from 1944 organised into three assessment Divisions—

3: A 1947/8 view of the airfield at Boscombe Down, showing the runway as originally built (2,500 yd long), the single central access track which caused a quagmire at its entry point, and the chalk exposed as work on the domestic site proceeds. © Crown Copyright

Performance, Armament and Engineering, together with sections for radio/radar, navigation and photography, all under the Chief Superintendent. Directly under the RAF Commandant was the Flying Division including four trials squadrons—known as A (fighters), B (four engines), C (naval) and D (twins and miscellaneous), together with its servicing support. The Empire Test Pilots' School left for Cranfield in October 1945 and, apart from noting that it returned in January 1968, is not considered further here. Similarly, the RAF Handling Squadron, a Lodger unit from April 1954, is omitted.

Following the defeat of Nazi Germany in May 1945 and the surrender of Imperial Japan the following August, the return of peace was marked at AAEE by a rapid reduction in both personnel and aircraft. Release to civilian life of service men and women started in June 1945 in accordance with plans drawn up to reflect national priorities, but which soon caused critical shortages at Boscombe Down where testing continued. In particular, armament specialists quickly disappeared. Equally serious was the rapid and large scale reduction in civilian scientific and technical staff. Those who remained and wished for permanent appointment were required to enter "The Civil Service Open Reconstruction Competition." Pay was static and low with little prospect of promotion. Morale remained low for some time. Aircraft numbers fell from 134 in August 1945 to a low of 51 in June 1947. Included in the total for January 1946 were three aircraft (a Boston and two Mosquito PR 34s) for meteorological research, a hang over from the High Altitude Flight. These three had departed by September 1947. Testing of alleged "rogue" aeroplanes, another wartime responsibility, ceased formally in October 1947. Primarily the reduction was due to the reduced requirement for trials coupled with the difficulty of the Establishment in supporting even the smaller number, and also due to the need to dispose of American aircraft supplied under Lend-Lease arrangements. There were 28 machines of American origin in August 1945; all had gone by early 1947. Partially offsetting the military contraction was the formation of a section to test civil aircraft and to consider appropriate operating criteria includng safety critical performance.

While these inevitable changes were occurring, the Headquarters changed from the Ministry of Aircraft Production to the Ministry of Supply on 1 April 1946. This further innovation did not *per se* cause difficulty at Boscombe, but did lead to more active consideration of the Establishment's future, already agreed in 1944 when Air Marshal Sir Ralph Sorley, Controller Research and Development, said, "It is intended to make [Boscombe Down] the shop window of British aviation ... with a lavish scale of building." It would be the country's main test centre for land aircraft intended for military or civil use. Plans were agreed for extensive building work on a scale which with the benefit of 50 years of hindsight seems incredible; in the event new building was restricted to the work detailed below.

Rebuilding

Aeronautical research and development was given high priority by the postwar Government, and, as if to compensate for the almost complete absence of construction work (other than laying the first runway) in the war when hundreds of other airfields were built, the AAEE received precedence in the early years of peace, at a time of national austerity and rapid retrenchment in the armed forces. However, the Commandant had to remind his masters at the end of 1945 of the urgency of further work, particularly in view of the unsatisfactory consequences of a single runway with quagmires at the access points. New runway and building work soon began thereafter, with the severe winter of 1946–7 adding urgency to the construction. The station official record (F 540) says about February 1947, "Hot water [was] obtainable through the means ... of coke brasiers *(sic)* in the wash houses." Warmth for the WRAF, too, almost! By 1950 nine new barrack blocks, each housing 100 airmen had been completed together with a new airmen's and an enlarged sergeants' messes, workshops, and a large administrative building (Building 456—the "Gin Palace", much to the joy of Technical staff who had endured years of wartime huts of dubious warmth). Work on a new Air Traffic Control Tower (completed in 1952), bulk fuel storage (192,000 gal in 1962) and bomb store had begun, as had construction of the first of four of the very large hangars. In the event, three hangars were never completed, and even the first was reduced in size by one bay, although when completed in 1954 it contained a weighbridge capable of determining the weight and both horizontal and vertical CG of machines up to 250,000 lb. This hangar, built on 400 ft of chalk, became known, inevitably, as "The Weighbridge." Other intended building became hostage to economy measures, and such facilities as the radio and radar sections soldiered on in old accommodation for many years; such wooden buildings continued to give the place a gloomy appearance. New buildings (Radex) for airborne radio trials were eventually ready between 1970 and 1972. Nevertheless, after the first postwar flush of construction, later building included A Squadron hangar (moved from High Post airfield in 1947–8), three other modest hangars (including C Squadron in 1955 and the heliport for D Squadron on the South side of the airfield), a new blower tunnel (1952) and various administrative buildings. By 1971 the only remaining hangar dating from the First World War was known as "Building 45", but had modern steel roof trusses. Plans were well under way in London by 1975 for the first batch of hardened aircraft shelters to be built at Boscombe for the use of USAF F-111 aircraft in wartime.

Two additional concrete runways together with the extension of the main runways and associated taxiways were laid between 1948 and 1950. Excavations for the North/South runway revealed evidence of Iron Age and Romano-British use and human occupation for 850 years

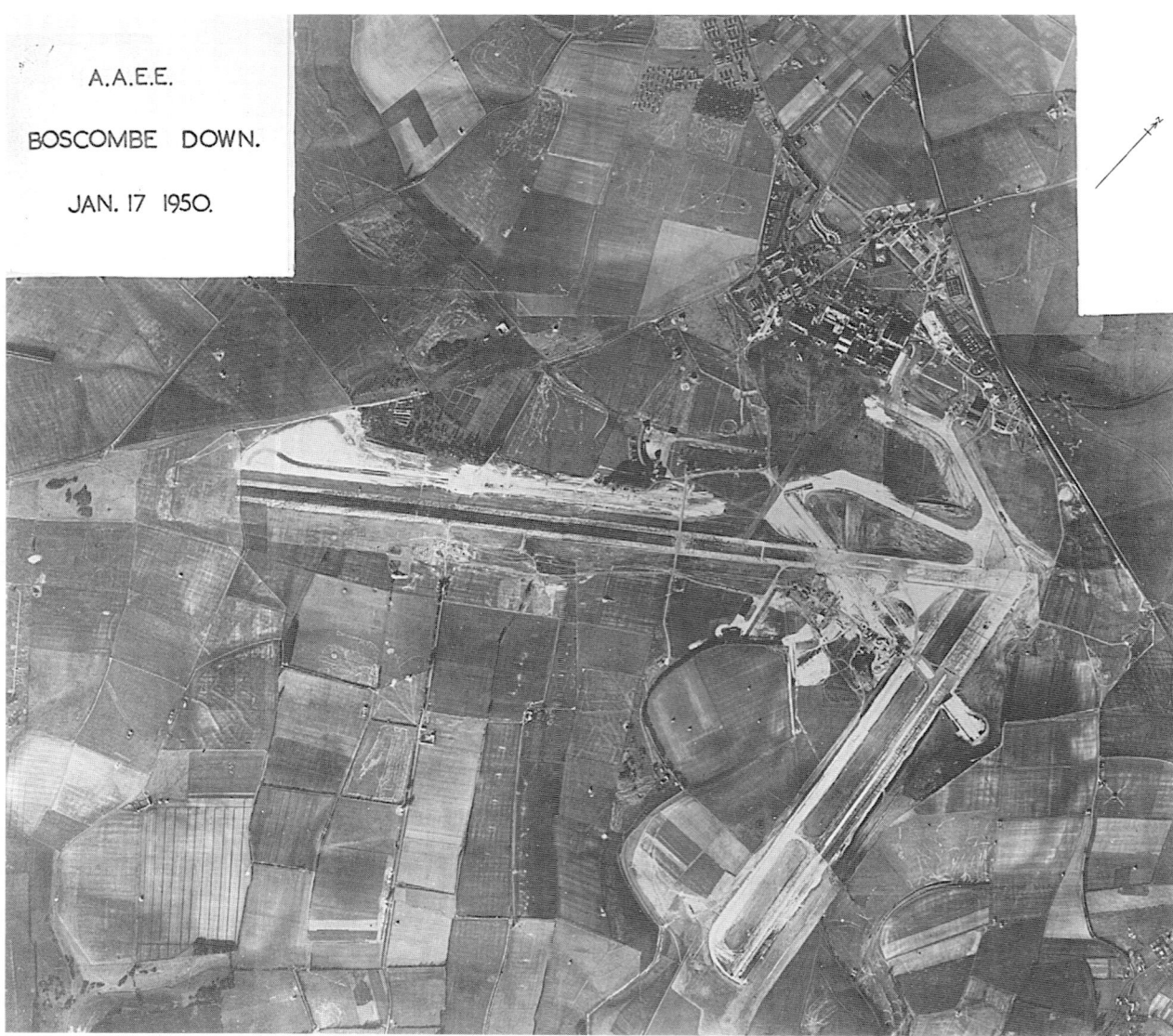

4: 1950 view of the airfield with the second and third runways almost complete, and the taxiway to the threshold of runway 06 under construction.
© *Crown Copyright*

up to 450 AD. In 1949 AD, the Ministry built dwellings in Salisbury for late Georgian/early Elizabethan Anglo-Saxon man toiling at Boscombe Down.

The Role of the AAEE

The demobilisation of personnel continued into 1946, and the Establishment reviewed its commitments, particularly taking into account the overlap and duplication that appeared to exist in the country for the testing of Service and civilian aircraft. Writing in May 1946, Mr E T Jones, the Chief Superintendent, commented, *inter alia*, that AAEE had recently (January) disbanded one flying unit (D Squadron), but was still required to undertake full acceptance trials on all military aeroplanes, including flying which contractors had previously done, or had omitted. A stronger and single Ministry point of contact at each contractor was suggested (via the Resident Technical Officer (RTO) organisation)

to help ensure that firms did properly what their contracts called for. On duplication, Jones said that Handling Squadron had extended its scope beyond that of writing Pilots' Notes, that some tests by the Airborne Forces Experimental Establishment (AFEE) repeated Boscombe's work, and that the Central Fighter Establishment similarly made assessments which AAEE had already done. While many of his recommendations fell to Headquarters for resolution, he made pleas for greater delegated authority for local purchase of instrumentation, the limit was a mere £50, and, more significantly, for a reduction in the scope of re-tests after even minor modifications had been made. On internal organisation, an amalgamation of the two groups of engineering people—one under the Superintendent of Flying for routine, and the other under the Superintendent of Engineering for major and experimental servicing was already under consideration, and implemented shortly thereafter. Jones omitted to mention the overlap of some trials between AAEE and RAE; duplication of handling at high Mach number was evident a few years later.

Other minor changes in the commitments of AAEE in the early postwar years concerned armament and radar. The armament expertise at Boscombe during the war had led increasingly to the resolution of problems, a development task not strictly within the Establishment's terms of reference. This anomaly was resolved by transferring the work to Farnborough, but on the other hand AAEE assumed responsibility for assessment of new radars and navigation equipment before being passed to the services for their own evaluation.

The peacetime role of the Establishment came under scrutiny within the newly formed Ministry of Supply, but it was October 1949 before the major policy document was produced by the Controller of Supplies (Air), Air Marshal Sir W Alec Coryton. He started by saying, "The Establishment exists for the purpose of conducting acceptance trials on aircraft and their associated equipment destined for use by the Fighting Services and the Civil Corporations." For military aircraft, intimate collaboration with the Design Firm was to be maintained in order to facilitate progress, and, where necessary, action was to be taken through the Ministry Headquarters for remedial action prior to final clearance for Service use. For civil aircraft acceptance testing was to be undertaken only for those types ordered by the Ministry, although Certificate of Airworthiness testing could also be undertaken by arrangement with the Air Registration Board. In addition, the Establishment was, "to maintain an adequate corpus of knowledge on the technique of flight testing ... to enable British representatives to speak with authority at International Conferences." Perhaps the first challenge to the policy came a few months after its introduction when the civil section (CATS) found itself rather sidelined by being denied the opportunity to work on the new turboprop and jet types. The main argument put forward for continuing to test the modern types was the risk of falling behind in their absence. CATS atrophied thereafter, (becoming more a corpse and than a corpus, perhaps), but the change to support flying was gradual.

Financial and functional control of the Establishment was exercised by the Ministry of Supply and its successors, while command and administration of RAF personnel were the responsibility for many years of Maintenance Command through the Air Officer Commanding No 41 Group. The Head of Establishment, the Air Commodore Commanding (ACC as he was known for a short time—but referred to in this work as the Commandant by which title he was commonly known for most of the period) was responsible for the efficient working and organisation of the Establishment, while the Chief Superintendent, of equivalent civilian rank, was to be responsible to the Head of Establishment for the technical work of testing. While access to Headquarters by the Chief Superintendent was formally limited to tests and civilian staff, in practice he carried equal weight in all matters, including the signing of documents on behalf of the Establishment.

The 1949 policy paper was given detailed consideration at Boscombe, and most of its directions implemented. The major disagreement concerned the Superintendent of Flying who continued to report directly to the Commandant, and not to the Chief Superintendent to whom all the remaining Superintendents, ie, of the trials Divisions, were responsible. In a parallel staff action, No 41 Group said, "Under agreement between the Air Ministry and the Ministry of Supply responsibility for the servicing of aircraft [at Establishments] rests with the Air Ministry." It followed that RAF servicing policy would apply, noting the special nature of the work, particularly where prototypes had no RAF (or RN) schedules; the Officer Commanding the Servicing Wing "must endeavour to produce a ... schedule." This policy for aircraft servicing remained unchanged with civilianisation in 1957–8. The two policy papers laid responsibility for safety *for* flight with the OC Servicing Wing, and for safety *in* flight with the Superintendent of Flying (S of F); there was no disagreement at AAEE on these fundamental responsibilities. The procedures for the latter to discharge his responsibility for safety were, nevertheless, reviewed; the need for his approval of every Trial Instruction was, for example, formalised. Thus the organisation originated in 1944 was, with the addition of the civil aircraft work, very largely maintained, and, with changes to reflect civilianisation in 1957–8, remained recognisable at the end of the period under review in 1975. The more important changes in the creation and renaming of Divisions are discussed later.

Notwithstanding the policy as laid down, it was rarely a simple question of pronouncing on the acceptability or rejection of a new aircraft. In forming recommendations for limitations to be applied in Service, the primary consideration was safety of flight, closely followed by operational capability. More often than not, it was then a matter of determining and weighing up shortcomings in performance and handling, and then either suggesting modifications or concessions that might be made for release to service. In the latter case, some limitations would be recommended for service use and only the air staff could decide on acceptability. The process eventually became a continuous dialogue involving the contractor, the Ministry project office advised by AAEE and other agencies, and the user service.

The relationship between AAEE and contractors underwent considerable changes. The wartime encouragement of all firms to share problems and advances with each other and with the Establishment evaporated with peacetime conditions and the prewar corporate jealousies resumed, and thus practice was at variance with the policy of, "intimate collaboration" decreed by CS(A). By the early 1950s, AAEE had only limited knowledge of the activities at firms, and frequently received aeroplanes without prior warning, even at times to the extent of absence of handling advice on new types.

Perhaps the most glaring example of this unsatisfactory situation was the Supermarine Swift. Performance Division and A Squadron had very little idea of the problems being found by Supermarine at nearby Chilbolton; this ignorance at AAEE was but one manifestation of more fundamental shortcomings in the contemporary procurement arrangements. First and foremost was the pressure imposed by the rearmament programme, for which the Swift was the chosen day fighter needed in service at the earliest moment. Ministers had told Parliament in 1951 and 1952 that the Swift had been ordered, and in mid-1953 that it would enter service that year. Thus the pressure was on from the highest political level, possibly clouding the view in the project office as to the bad news coming from AAEE where even the limited flying of the unrepresentative prototype and just two flights in the first production aircraft had revealed severe instability, tightening in turns and aileron buzz among the more alarming phenomena. It appears that Headquarters, ie Ministry of Supply (MoS), had a more sanguine view of the problems, preferring to believe the firm's optimism of successful resolution of them, and also to the extent of concurring in an RAF announcement that the first squadron would form by the end of 1953. The Establishment's request for at least a preview of the squadron-standard aircraft was refused. Just two months before the political deadline for entry into service. an instrumented aircraft was received but crashed fatally. Two further, but uninstrumented, aircraft arrived with the instruction to clear them rapidly to the absolute minimum standard to permit crew familiarisation. The first clearance was given at the end of January 1954; in the very brief time available the shortcomings remained abundantly apparent, and a very restricted flight envelope was reluctantly recommended, eg altitude limited to 25,000 ft. This situation was extremely unsatisfactory to all concerned, and AAEE flying then proceeded into the summer of 1954 in an attempt to broaden the clearance given, and included all four marks of the type. The range of aerodynamic problems was fully explored at last, and real improvements found in the Marks 3 and 4. However, the fundamental problem of lack of lift remained, and the powers-that-be were persuaded that Vickers-Supermarine had not produced the hoped for successor to the Spitfire. Had the AAEE been permitted to make earlier assessments of production standard aircraft, at least the RAF would have been spared the embarrassment of having a squadron of useless aeroplanes; however, such an assessment would not have prevented the construction of many unsatisfactory airframes, because the "Super Priority" scheme had ensured that production had proceeded well before the type had been demonstrated to be acceptable.

5: Vampire FB.5 VZ216 with two Smoke Curtain Installations (SCI) under the starboard wing ready for blowing at 180 kt in 1953. There appears to be a camera housing at the wing tip, probably for other trials. © Crown Copyright

The extent of lack of communication between the MoS and the Air Ministry, referred to above, became embarrassingly obvious to the AAEE test pilot attending the Central Fighter Establishment Annual Convention in 1954. It became clear that the Chief of the Air Staff, who was present, was unaware of the true position of the Swift's problems—a position reached only because of poor communication by MoS. To this damning indictment could be added the difficulty in obtaining Supermarine's flight test results, possibly exacerbated by the policy of "cost plus" contracts where the firms made more profit by spending more, and the denial of opportunities for early testing by AAEE of production aeroplanes. The Air Ministry's displeasure with MoS resulted in considerable revision of the latter's management practices, and the repercussions of the RAF's discovery of the type's unsuitability, due to the lack of communication from the MoS, were widespread. An interesting comment exists in the report made by Col W R Stark USAF at the end of his tour of duty at AAEE which spanned the Swift debacle; he was present to oversee the logistical interests of Strategic Air Command, but nominally in the post of Technical Assistant to the Commandant—a nice piece of cold war obfuscation. After giving fulsome praise to the capabilities of the staff of AAEE, his report included the suggestion that the Ministry of Supply should give up altogether its responsibility for the aircraft industry. He thought that the RAF/Air Ministry should have more direct control over its suppliers, and that the administrative and financial staff had too much sway over aircraft projects—in 1955!

Gradually, close working relationships were formed, and the results of contractors' tests became known to the Establishment in good time. The closely related problem of rearmament, with production under the "Super Priority" scheme being ordered "off the drawing board" before testing had started, coupled with the problems experienced particularly by the fighters involved, led to AAEE frequently being placed in an invidious position. On the one hand contractors struggled to achieve presentable aircraft but with concomitant delays, while on the other hand the Services pressed for early delivery of operational types. AAEE was, in the vernacular, *the meat in the sandwich,* for which a relevant example occurred in 1964 when the Establishment was being pressed by the RAF and Headquarters for early clearance of various bomb bay configurations of the Vulcan for operations at low level. Considerable effort went into preparing the details of the trial to ensure the most expeditious completion, but the promised aircraft was delayed, arrived late and then needed modifications including instrumentation before trials flying could begin. To the extreme irritation of the trials team at Boscombe, it was decided that the date fixed for the aircraft to return to the firm for the retrofit programme would be honoured, with the result that the trial could not take place and further delay—outside the control of AAEE—was incurred while a replacement was found.

The Swift story reflected little credit on MoS; AAEE suffered by association. Misunderstandings of the role and work of the Establishment have been a recurring theme over the years. Visitors, even at senior level, often expressed surprise at the extent of the facilities available, some even admitting, with a certain but misplaced logic, to the belief that Handling Squadron did the basic handling trials. In 1975 the Air Staff threatened to remove the Establishment's long-term Hercules on account of gross under-utilisation; its flying hours were, indeed, very low by RAF standards. The Air Staff was eventually persuaded that utilisation was, in fact very good, and that trial sorties were carefully planned to minimise flying time. 20 min was the shortest successful aerial delivery sortie with one dummy run at nearby Larkhill followed by the trial drop. An example of the lack of understanding at working level is provided by the record of an Establishment visit to a Bomber Command station as the Vulcan was entering service. The station had previously been given talks by Avro pilots who had claimed, among other things, that AAEE did not know that the bomber had flown at more than Mach 1; this and other comments led the RAF people to suggest that the presence of AAEE was superfluous, since a very good understanding existed between the Command and the manufacturer. The AAEE visitors explained the reasons for the apparent supersonic achievement. (Due to pressure errors in the airspeed system an Indicated Mach number of 1.0 was a True Mach number of 0.935), but refrained on this occasion from commenting that the "good understanding" could lead to the firm misleading the Service, and delivering unsatisfactory aeroplanes.

Areas of Special Expertise

The knowledge and facilities at Boscombe in the 30 years since WW II led to several areas of special expertise and capability, in addition to the primary responsibility of evaluating every military aircraft for its suitability for service. These included all aspects of deck operations, icing, its measurement and remedy on airliners in the 1940s, the continuous study of helicopter operation in snow and icing from 1959, an icing tanker from 1968, the evaluation of air crew escape facilities and other items in the blower tunnel plus dedicated aircraft for ejection seats, aerial refuelling with the probe and drogue method, airborne assessment of navigation and other avionics in flying laboratories, the environmental hangar, the radio environment simulator and aerial delivery of people and freight. A unique event in the postwar AAEE resulted in the Establishment team winning the Royal Aero Club's competition for the design of a light single seat racing aircraft; the "Shriek" as it was named looked remarkably like the German Heinkel 162 Volksjager.

More discussion on these topics is given in Chapters 2 and 3.

6: Arsenal 5501 69 (developed from the German V-1) at Aberporth where the AAEE team evaluated its auto flight capabilities as a target. It was not a success. © Crown Copyright

7: How NOT to do pressure error measurements using the tower fly-past method. The camera, which has the calibrations visible, photographed the subject aircraft while the aircrew recorded the accurate readings on board—a comparison was then made and the aircraft's error determined. In this case in Vulcan B 2 XL361 in 1975, the pilot, Sqn Ldr T (Tim) Mason, was too low and liable to induce errors from ground effect, ie, flying within half a span of the surface ... but great fun! © Crown Copyright

Administration and Control

The 1949 policy perpetuated the arrangements which, since the earliest days at Martlesham Heath, gave the Establishment, in effect, two masters. These arrangements gave rise to a few difficulties, but nevertheless continued throughout the period under review, being adapted as required during the gradual change from service to civilian manning, principally in the strengthening of the section for civilian administration. By 1951, some interesting manifestations of this pragmatic approach included the accounts section, run on RAF lines but passing bills to the Ministry for payment; stores equipment and motor transport were obtained from Service sources where possible and operated in accordance with RAF procedures, but to meet Ministry requirements for AAEE's task. With the evolving structure of Ministries[1] to oversee defence procurement (one civil servant told the author that he had been in five Ministries and worked in the same office in London throughout) the more significant implications for AAEE came later. In the early 1970s, following the creation of the Procurement Executive, the responsibility for ordering the trials (Controllerate of Aircraft -CA) became separated from responsibility for the provision of the wherewithal to do them (Contollerate of Establishments and Research—CER).

The critical resource to conduct the trials at AAEE was always regarded as professional scientific and technical manpower, known as White Paper Grades (WPG). By 1950, the Establishment's annual report included a summary projection over five years of WPG effort needed to meet forecast tasks. However, the accuracy of the forecasting was subject to the changing requirements of Headquarters where the project offices had little understanding of the impact of their demands, with the result that manpower priorities had to be altered at short notice, and some tasks failed to be completed in times of high workload, ie, usually. Increasingly, the Establishment made a comprehensive assessment of new commitments before accepting them in an attempt to match resources to tasks. While available manpower determined what testing could be undertaken, the costs of doing so received separate treatment—largely for the benefit of Headquarter's financial branches to add to annual estimates (Long Term Costings). AAEE's costs were minute in terms of the overall sums involved in aircraft and weapon projects. By 1962, a very comprehensive breakdown of the cost of every aircraft was made on a monthly basis. An analysis of the annual costs for the financial year 1963-4 showed a total of £9,978,000 (approximately equally divided between "cash" and "non-cash"). Of the total, 49.4% was for aircraft in service, of which the Buccaneer S.1 had the largest single share. A projection for the following year gave a similar total, with 53.8% for in-service aircraft, and the Vulcan B.1 and B.2 together taking the greatest share.

By the end of the period covered by this work, regular major reports were made for the annual review by the Controller, Aircraft, of AAEE programmes. That for 1975 gives a comprehensive picture, and is summarised here. The ability of the Establishment to fulfill its obligations was determined by the number of Senior Scientific Personnel (SSP—a term including serving officers, but otherwise similar to the earlier WPG) available for the tasks imposed by the nation's military aircraft programme. The paper concluded that the existing total of 258 SSP was appropriate. Of this number, some 190 were regarded as "deployable" on projects, while the balance filled management and central staff positions. Employment on major projects included the Jaguar (34 SSP) and other new types (53.4) at AAEE; the MRCA (Tornado) (16.5) had yet to arrive. Some 12 types of aircraft (25.3 SSP) already in-service were also tested. Continuing tasks included helicopter operations in snow and ice, aerial delivery of men and stores, and equipment trials unrelated to specific aircraft, for example four new radio altimeters, and a rotor head camera system developed by the Photographic Division for icing trials on helicopters. Aircrew and industrial grades of staff gave the managers fewer headaches, although skilled electronic tradesmen were difficult to recruit. The reduction in the authorised number of industrial grades to 1310 at the beginning of 1975 merely reflected the number of people currently employed. Finally, the report expressed disappointment that only 14 applicants were considered suitable for training as apprentices; facilities for 24 per year had been created at the start of the scheme in 1969.

Some Significant Developments 1945–1975

The thirty years following the Second World War saw aerospace develop at an ever increasing pace, and nowhere were the effects more pervasive than at AAEE. Indeed, many advances in trial management, test techniques, instrumentation and understanding of aircraft behaviour followed work at Boscombe. Whether the initiative for change came from an internal or external source, a summary of the major developments as they affected AAEE is given here; the following two chapters give a more detailed account of the resulting effects within Divisions.

In spite of the welcome return of peace, and the unwelcome departure of many key staff, both service and civilian, the business of testing continued for several years from 1945 much as before, but on a greatly reduced scale. With peace came calls for higher standards, from handling to maintainability, much requiring extra work of

---

[1] Ministries of Aircraft Production, Supply, Aviation, Technology, Aviation Supply, Defence (Aviation Supply) and Defence (Procurement Executive).

evaluation. In some cases, however, as with the Spitfire Mark 18 and its longitudinal instability with full fuel, the wartime standard was not remedied as early replacement was planned. Prewar practices resumed to a limited extent with civil aircraft testing and also with deck operation by C Squadron in trials managed by Performance Division, and there were also a few competitions between rival designs—for trainers and a Naval anti- submarine type.

The first major change at Boscombe followed events on the world stage when the West felt threatened by the policies behind the Iron Curtain where the Communist bloc had maintained its armed forces at the wartime level. The catalysts of the Berlin blockade and the Korean war led very rapidly to national rearmament including a crop of new military aircraft, soon arriving in such numbers that AAEE's meagre resources were stretched to the limit. Of equal significance to the volume of testing was the challenge of the problems posed by aerodynamic and associated advances in performance; the details are discussed later. Speaking to the Royal Aeronautical Society in 1999, Mr H W (Wason) Turner (Chief Superintendent 1974–75) said, "As one who was there in the thick of it I can say without fear or favour that the Establishment acquitted itself well." One result of the frantic activity in the early 1950s, and of great significance to this history, was the shortage of time for report writing; for example, many results of tests on the early swept wing fighters are now recorded only in an abbreviated form, written long after the event. The backlog of unwritten reports grew and grew, and much trials work was never written up. Thus a large volume of technical information, obtained at not inconsiderable cost, languished in job files, never to see the light of day, and much is now lost.

Intense effort involved weekend and public holiday working as the norm, and included, in addition to the trials themselves, meetings, letter reports (not preserved from that early period) and growing intercourse at all levels between AAEE, the Ministry, the Services and, after the Swift experience, industry. While the pace of activity and the problems revealed were stimulating, the fighters in particular were disappointing, and suffered in comparison with the earlier experience at AAEE of the F-86 Sabre which had few of the handling shortcomings of the first British swept wing aircraft. (It is an interesting coincidence that crew comfort of the first Shackletons was roundly condemned just as the relatively luxurious Neptune was entering service.) This level of activity coincided approximately with the decade of the 1950s, and also led to the hastening of a scheme to reduce the overload at Boscombe whereby much pure performance measurement was delegated to approved contractors under the supervision of AAEE. The post of External Trials Co-ordinating Officer (ETCO) was established to oversee this work and much effort went into checking the adequacy of firms' capabilities; Mr R K (Roger) Cushing was the first ETCO. The working of the scheme has, however, been difficult to determine. It is clear that AAEE itself made but few checks of manufacturers' results, and equally clear that Pilots' Notes and later Operating Data Manuals nevertheless included performance and cruise data promulgated by Headquarters (PPAN). It is the consensus of those involved that the information supplied by manufacturers was often based on a minimum of actual flight tests and that much data came from little more than estimates. One manifestation of the unsatisfactory arrangements for disseminating performance information occurred in 1956 when the Operational Requirement branch of the Air Ministry complained of the large discrepancy between the figures for take off distances in Pilots' Notes and those obtained by squadrons. The matter was investigated as AAEE was held to be blameworthy; it was discovered that AAEE figures (which were comparable to the squadron figures) had not been incorporated in the Notes which were based on early manufacturers results. On the other hand, the Victor figures in the performance manual, which were published before any relevant flying by AAEE were later found to be accurate. Whatever the actual basis of the figures, it seems that the scheme did not operate as intended, and ETCO's role gradually changed to the administration of overseas trials—taking over some of the work of the Flying Division.

By the end of the 1950s, a further sea-change had been put in train with the 1957 White Paper on Defence; the intended abandonment, *inter alia,* of further manned fighter and bomber aircraft had far reaching consequences, not least at Boscombe. Initially, the White Paper had little effect, but gradually the extension of the operational lives of existing types gave rise to continued testing of new roles and modifications. In the longer term, fewer British-made types appeared than would have otherwise have been the case, and to some extent had to be replaced by foreign-made, ie American, types. In parallel with the policy on manned aircraft was the continual series of Defence Reviews, each followed by a reduction in national commitments and inevitable scaling down of military procurement. AAEE's work reduced accordingly, most noticeably from about the late-1960s

An event of more immediate impact followed completion of much of the planned rebuilding when the Airborne Forces Experimental Establishment (AFEE) moved from Beaulieu in the New Forest to Boscombe Down in September 1950, thus implementing a decision taken in 1947 to return the former site to the Verderers. The heterogeneous group of 17 flying machines making the move by road and air included a Tempest target tug, sundry transports, gliders, and, most significantly, helicopters. Incorporated into AAEE as the Airborne Experiments Division (formally promulgated in December) under Mr W G Jennings, it formed D Squadron with two Flights—Airborne Forces and

8: What might have been! "B" Squadron aircrew pose with the squadon's TSR.2 in early 1966. Seated (left to right): Flt Lt T (Tim) Mason, Flt Lt B (Barny) Platt, Flt Lt J I (Dusty) Miller, Flt Lt Alan Fisher, Sqn Ldr J (John) Waterton (senior pilot), Gp Capt A D (David) Dick (Superintendent of Flying), Wg Cdr G R K (Geoff) Fletcher (O C B Squadron), Sqn Ldr E D (Ned) Frith (senior pilot designate), Sqn Ldr D L (David) Bywater, Flt Lt R L (Bob) Beeson, Flt Lt J (Jim) Watts-Phillips and Flt Lt J (John) Bell—all pilots—probably unsteady when standing! Standing: M Eng Doug Allen, M Eng (Gillie) Potter, Flt Lt (Steve) Stephenson, Flt Lt F (Fergus) Robertson, Flt Lt G (George) Moore, Flt Lt J (Jim) Newbery, Flt Lt Vic Rollason, Flt Lt (Dinty) Moore, Flt Lt L (Les) Darlow, Flt Lt M J (Mike) Cull, Flt Lt J E (John) Bussey, Flt Lt P H R (Pete) Singleton, M AEOp (Jim) Fell, M Sig P (Pete) Leigh. Absent were Flt Lt A S (Tony) Cottingham and Flt Lt BP (Pidge) Holme.

Helicopter. The Hoverfly helicopters were soon joined by British designs. The remnants of the Marine Aircraft Experimental Establishment were absorbed into AAEE on arrival from Felixstowe on 4 July 1956.

Long before all the policy changes worked through, the increasing range of avionic equipment led to the forming of Navigation and Radio Division in 1956. The growing need for assessment of camera installations created the Photographic Trials Section in about 1954, which together with the existing facilities section, formed the Photographic Division. Above all, vastly expanded flight envelopes of jet powered aircraft brought problems of stability, control, weapon release and engineering. While the straight and swept wing fighters of the early 1950s presented challenges mainly for Performance Division (not forgetting Flying Division!), early guided weapons stretched the expertise and resources of Armament and Navigation and Radio Divisions and the V-bombers of the late 1950s introduced new complexities for all divisions. In 1961 Mr R P (Reg) Dickinson outlined his views on the implications of the air weapons system concept. He saw the need for avoiding duplication of effort by a logical and co-ordinated system of testing by all the disciplines involved. The internal organisation was immediately thereafter strengthened by the creation of Weapons System Division (re-titled Trials Management Division from 1966) to co-ordinate all areas of AAEE's testing of the more complicated aircraft and systems, beginning with the V-bombers/Blue Steel and Skybolt missiles, Lightning Mark 3, Buccaneer and TSR2. Misgivings in the existing Armament Division were only slowly overcome. The Division also included the Instrument Research Section and a Maths Services Section serving the whole Establishment, and introduced management data techniques for more effective control of trials effort.

On the international scene, the formation of NATO led to assessments by AAEE in the 1950s of trainers and strike aircraft in an attempt to achieve common equipment of air forces; some assessments were made by the Establishment alone and normal reports raised. Others were made as part of a NATO team as in 1957 for evaluation of five types of competing light strike fighters; a brief report concluded that the Fiat G-91 was most suitable. NATO groups for the study of research and development, were keenly supported—as typified by the 1954 paper for AGARD[2] by W G Jennings on helicopters.

2 Advisory Group for Aeronautical Research and Development

Next to the fundamental change occasioned by the advent of weapon systems, perhaps the most significant single development affecting flight test work was that of data gathering; advances in instrumentation and recording continued throughout the period under review. The kneepad and filmed records of special instrument panels had given way to paper trace recording of transmitting sensors and voice-recording on wire (Oh! how easy it was to unleash miles of tangled wire by mistake). The first Wirec was used in a Tudor II in July 1946, and ground recording of pilot's running commentary from a spinning Tempest the following November. By the 1960s these had yielded to continuous recording on magnetic tape of many parameters and even to transmission of the data to ground stations. A 1965 report explained the abilities of a machine to change digital magnetic tape into the punched paper tape required by the Establishment's Pegasus computer. All flights, whether devoted to handling and performance or to another duty, could gather valuable data; equally important, this information could be analysed more readily than the earlier tedious manual trawling through endless paper traces. The Establishment's range of test instrumentation expanded to meet the changing demands; a report, many pages thick, was produced as a reference for other test centres throughout the Western world of the range of instruments available. In the mid-1950s AAEE had probably the most comprehensive collection anywhere, but, even so, at the end of the 1950s the photographing of the auto-observer panel remained in vogue, and, on the ground, the slide rule reigned supreme at a time when many contractors had analogue computers. By 1975, the amount of flying to explore a type's basic envelope had very significantly reduced. However, diverse weapon loads and roles, updates and modifications all combined to demand considerably more test flying of individual types than previously. Also adding to the work was the Services' continuing requirement for world wide operations and thus the need of clearing aircraft in hot and cold climates. In June 1955 support of the overseas trials in diverse locations led to the formation of the Air Transport Flight, later forming Support Squadron, and finally subsumed by the new E Squadron in January 1964.

Two other developments were apparent by 1975 namely, international co-operation in aircraft procurement, well underway on the military side for 10 years with France on the Jaguar and helicopters, and also the concentration and increasing reliance on the handful of capable contractors for work previously done at Boscombe. Both had the effect of reducing AAEE's flying tasks at Boscombe, while increasing travelling and general inconvenience. Close working relationships were formed with French and later German and Italian testing centres, the last two in preparation for the MRCA (Tornado). One noteworthy side effect of the international collaboration on the MRCA was the gift to AAEE of a Sea Fury target tug on its retirement from service in Germany.

Relationships with Other Nations

The wartime links with flight testing in the United States were strengthened in the early years of peace with formal visits to Edwards Air Force Base and to "Navy Pax"—Patuxent River, as part of the Establishment's remit to keep abreast of developments for acceptance testing in other countries. Much was gained thereby, not least by the pilots who flew most of the latest fighters and bombers of both Air Force and Navy. For example, in September 1949 two pilots flew 15 types in a four week period in North America. These and later visits were duly written up, but have not been included in this work. Visits stopped after 1951 as a team could not be spared, until a trip to the U S Navy in 1957. and another to the USAF in 1959. On the latter visit, the performance of thin wings, reheat and advanced systems of new types favourably impressed the team; the aircrew emergency equipment did not do so. Reciprocal visits by U S test pilots included a team in 1957–8 who flew the V-bombers. In 1959 the Americans generously made available four types of "Century Series" fighters at Edwards Air Force Base for assessment by a team including Sqn Ldr H A (Alan) Merriman as preparation for Lightning testing.

With the peacetime re-emergence of French aviation, exchange of information and visits to test centres were soon established and co-operation on the civil Concorde later underway. By January 1958 a team visiting France was able to fly the Fouga Magister, Dassault Mystere IVA, the Sud Aviation Vautour and the Sud Est Baroudeur. In the 1960s Anglo-French (or should it be Franco-Anglican ?) collaboration on a trio of helicopters (the French Puma and Gazelle with the British Lynx) reached the practical flying stage in early 1966 when Cdr L G (George) Locke (OC D Squadron) and Mr J (John) Gregory of Performance Division made the initial assessments of the French machines. There then followed more than a decade of constant communication and travel between Boscombe and France for work on the helicopters and the Jaguar project.

The Establishment's involvement with the MRCA (Tornado) began well before the first flight in 1974, by which time cordial working relationships had been established with the German and Italian test centres.

People—Service and Civilian

In June 1948, there were 69 White Paper Grade staff plus 12 assistants, and a year later at the end of the post war rundown the total number of people of all grades on the strength of AAEE was 1,400 (including only about 100 civilians), the lowest recorded number up to 1975. It is a dichotomy that as the extensive building programme was underway stressing the importance of the future of the Establishment, so the disappearance of manpower seemed to be indicating an opposite emphasis. The manpower situation soon changed with the arrival of the Airborne Forces personnel, and with recruiting for the extra work of rearmament. In March 1956, there were 132 RAF and 23 Royal Naval officers, plus 1,620 other ranks, and 817 civilians of whom 149 were scientific and engineering grades—a total of 2,592 giving the greatest number in the history of AAEE. (Handling Squadron is excluded). It is interesting to note that the peak in aircraft numbers (110[3]) occurred in August 1954; it could be said that it took eighteen months to approve and recruit the people needed for the extra work. After the doldrums of the immediate post-war period, the rapid increase in test work from about 1950 transformed the morale of both service and civilian personnel. The national rearmament effort on the air side had a natural focus at Boscombe Down, the importance of aircraft testing was self evident, and the challenge of working on the latest military designs with rigidly enforced security restrictions added to the sense of purpose. A young scientific graduate considering his future in the 1950s decided to join the Establishment on seeing the level of activity, and "the wall-to-wall aluminium" created by the aircraft out on the hardstandings. The high morale was sustained into the 1960s and beyond; for all, whether aircrew, trials officers or groundcrew there was always something new, interesting and challenging—it was the nature of the job.

Civilianisation

Civilianisation would probably have occurred earlier but for two factors. First was the impact of a Cabinet ruling that users (ie the Armed Services) should be represented in acceptance of all equipment made for them by the MOS. Second, under discussion in 1949, was the difficulty in offering sufficient permanent positions to attract the large number of new employees needed.

A visitor returning to Boscombe Down in 1975 after an absence of 30 years would undoubtedly have been struck by the new buildings, the smaller visible number of aircraft, (48 AAEE aircraft in late 1975) but particularly by the infrequent sight of servicemen. Over the years, civilians took over much of the work previously done by servicemen, the most rapid changeover occurring progressively from early 1958 when all aircraft servicing (apart from the Naval C Squadron) became a civilian responsibility. Between April 1957 and August 1960 some 936 RAF posts had been abolished, with a further 118 in prospect by April 1961. An earlier anomaly was thus removed; in 1946–49 at least, civilians worked a 5-day week while their RAF colleagues worked 5½ days. A new Division, Technical Services, formed soon after 1958 to reflect the new arrangements. One indirect result of the changed manning was that the disciplinary powers of a Commanding Officer[4] were transferred in November 1959 from the two group captains (Superintendents of Flying and Armament) to the wing commander of the newly created "RAF Unit Boscombe Down" who added this responsibility to the administration of the remaining servicemen. On 16 March 1970, when the RAF post was downgraded to squadron leader, the powers were vested in the Commandant whose position regarding disciplinary authority in the intervening 11 years appears somewhat anomalous.

Overseas Testing

From 1944 a small team from AAEE was based at Khartoum in the Sudan for testing the adequacy of engine cooling in a hot climate; the work soon expanded to include some performance measurements, cabin and equipment cooling and the effects of sand. The following year the unit was graced with the title of "Tropical Trials Unit, Khartoum," and later, "Tropical Experimental Unit"; it provided the base for performance, engineering, radio and navigation trials to meet the world wide operating clearances required in military specifications. With the advent of airliner testing, the need for hot and high performance measurements led to the frequent use of Nairobi in Kenya at an elevation of over 5,000 ft. A steady flow of aeroplanes arrived from Boscombe, including trainers which rarely strayed beyond the shores of the UK in later service, but for which an overseas role had originally been foreseen. Among the hazards to flying were large birds including buzzards, a risk becoming more significant as aircraft speeds increased with concomitant difficulty in avoidance and risk of damage from collision. Serious damage occurred in February 1954 to a Canberra PR7 when Flt Lt J D Price made a skilful landing at Khartoum after a large bird inconsiderately removed all the starboard tail plane at 434 kt. In 1954 the unit moved to Idris, South of Tripoli in Libya, where, in 1959, the Commanding Officer, Sqn Ldr Ron Bowers was particularly noted for his efficiency. Winter, and even summer, temperatures sometimes failed to rise to the extremes needed, and the short runway became a limitation. Alternative locations were sought, fortunately found at nearby USAF Wheelus, Tripoli, where the 11,000ft runway gave reassurance for take offs requiring unusual lengths of concrete. With the political changes in Libya, coupled with a reduction in the number of tropical trials required, the TEU was disbanded at the end of 1966. Other venues were then arranged on an *ad hoc* basis, and included Khormaksar in Aden, Singapore and, in the USA, Edwards and Yuma. Hot weather airfield trials of Naval machines were included, but occasional deck trials of fixed wing aircraft also took place in the tropics, as in 1966 when the Buccaneer, a particularly critical type at launch even with

---

[3] A Sqn—30 aircraft, B—18, C—25, D—24 and CATS—13.

[4] Powers of a Commanding Officer carried well defined legal responsibilities in the RAF.

9: "C" Squadron foursome in March 1957. Hunter WT556 was flown by Lt Julian, Meteor XF274 by Lt (Block) Whitehead, Sea Balliol VW599 by Lt Reynolds and the Seamew XE186 by Lt Hedges; Lt Davies flew the photographic Sea Balliol WN526. © Crown Copyright

10: The first telemetry at Boscombe Down was housed in this van, and used for a spinning trial of Scimitar F.1 WW134 in April 1959. It proved particularly useful as the Scimitar had unusual recovery characteristics, and soon showed that the best technique was for the pilot to let go of the stick. © Crown Copyright

11: *Canberra PR.3 VX181 at about the time of the start of its lengthy stay at AAEE from November 1951. The only point to remark is the small temperature probe just ahead of the "Entrance" notice; otherwise it looks as it did 20 years later.*

12: Three Hastings flown by Air Transport Flight in about June 1972 with WD496 (a C.2 allocated to Navigation and Radio Division) leading and the two overseas support aircraft (TG500 to left in photograph and TG502 with lowered tailplane—both C.1As) behind. © Crown Copyright

13 below: C Squadron in March 1963 with two each of Sea Vixen FAW.1s (XJ560 left and XN700 right), and Buccaneer S.1s (XK523 probably and XN924 "115-E" right), and Hunter GA.11 WT721. © Crown Copyright

Spey engines in conditions of high temperatures and low wind speed over the deck, flew from the deck of *HMS Victorious* off the Philippines. The aircraft failed to gain climbing speed and crashed; Lt Cdr J D (Dave) Eagles ejected successfully. The positive result of this accident was the adoption of a safer trim setting for launching, and eventually an improved shape of underwing tank. Between 1945 and 1975 several hundreds of aircraft made journeys to all points of the compass for their behaviour to be observed. Chapters four to ten note some of the more interesting characteristics found, notably a common absence of effective cockpit, cabin and avionics cooling in the early years, particularly on the ground.

At the opposite end of the temperature spectrum, Canada and Norway played host to AAEE cold weather trials; the winter trials were on a far smaller scale than the tropical. There was no permanent detachment, although AAEE had a permanent representative at Namao, Canada after taking over from the Ministry the responsibility for cold trials. Mr W (Bill) Aynsley was the last AAEE resident, leaving in 1959 when the RAF detachment departed. Fort Churchill, Manitoba then joined Uplands, Ottawa as the delightful locations. After several years of use involving many hours of hovering helicopters in the rig at Uplands, it was decided that the results were of limited value as the icing produced was unrepresentative of actual conditions in forward flight.

Teams arrived from Boscombe for each trial under arrangements made on an annual basis with Canadian hosts.

Community Relations and Press Visits

AAEE was, perhaps, regarded as secret and remote to all but a small number of farmers and local residents, with even Amesbury in the valley two miles away somewhat removed from the activity up the hill. The goings-on there were until late in the period not generally mentioned in the press, and the few noise complaints included the incensed inhabitants of nearby Allington when a visiting squadron of Naval Sea Vixens

14: A nice aerial view of the technical area probably in 1959. Among the aircraft seen are: Hastings, Anson, Canberra, Javelin, Shackleton, Valiants but little of A and C Squadrons. The nearest hangar became the sole remaining First World war representative by 1975, but having a modern roof.

15: What happened when the pilots found that the engineers had rendered serviceable one aeroplane of each type on "A" Squadron in May 1967. Led by Wg Cdr A H (Alan) Merriman and Flt Lt Brian Bullock in Javelin FAW.2/7 XA778 (it alone had both VHF and UHF radios), the Hunter FR.10 XF426 had Sqn Ldr Hugh Rigg aboard, P1127 prototype XP980, Flt Lt Derek Parry and Jet Provost T.3 XM352, Flt Lt Dick Foster, struggling to keep up with the big boys. The Lightnings (all DB—from the nearest), XG313 with Flt Lt Robin Hargreaves, XG336 Flt Lt Graham Andrews, XG329 Capt Einar Enevoldson (USAF) and XG307 Flt Lt Andy Jones. © Crown Copyright

practised low level circuits over their houses for several evenings. The resident aircraft rarely ventured into the dark air. An accident to a Brigand in July 1952 caused great distress in a housing estate in the Bemerton area of Salisbury where five prefabricated dwellings were destroyed. Engine failure led to the aircraft crashing, killing the crew, injuring nine civilians and rendering 34 people homeless, 14 of whom were subsequently accommodated at Boscombe. Tea supplies to the rescuers had to be suspended when the tea ration was used up. Local reaction to this tragedy ("yet another crash" said the local paper) appears to have been subdued although the local MP raised a question in Parliament. Mr V Oxford, a builder, was commended for his attempts to extricate the crew while sustaining burns to his hands. Similarly, the efforts of Mrs Pat Harvey of Bridport were recognised by the award of the Queen's Commendation for Bravery in trying to save the crew of the Canberra which crashed in May 1970. In general, local residents and community leaders maintained only limited personal contact, but were, more formally, invited to the annual cocktail party to commemorate the Battle of Britain.

Press visits, taboo throughout the war, started in July 1945 with a demonstration of armaments at Boscombe and the following day at Larkhill. The next was in the mid-1950s, followed by a promotional facility for the Press and TV in November 1968, and in 1971 by the Royal Visit. The growing importance of community relations was recognised by the appointment in 1968 of Mr T H J (Terry) Heffernan as Public Relations Officer—a job he undertook in addition to his primary and other duties, which included for a time chairmanship of the Amesbury Council.

Use by Industry and as a V-Bomber Dispersal

The prewar annual Contractors' Dinners resumed on 8 November 1946; 143 people filled the Officers' Mess Dining room. Similar numbers attended subsequent years—although from 1968 the format was changed to reflect the graduation of the ETPS courses. In view of close relations between the contractors and the Establishment evident in these social gatherings from the earliest postwar years, it is surprising that the grave lack of communication described earlier occurred.

One result of the extensive building programme and in particular the creation of a 3,500 yd runway, was the use of Boscombe by British firms in the 1950s and 1960s; Sir Ralph Sorley would have been gratified by this use of "the shop window." Many types made their first flights there; Appendix 3 has a list. At least two aeroplanes fell off lorries getting to Boscombe—the Gloster GA1 (No SM809) in July 1947, and in September 1964 the second TSR2 (XR220). Avro established a flight test team in the

Special Fittings hangar to conduct tests on the quartet of 707 delta wing prototypes in the early 1950s. Other users included Fairey with a Rotodyne rotor and flying controls ground test rig in 1957, and Avro with the Stentor motor of the Blue Steel guided bomb. Avro's rig caught fire, and the tests cancelled before the good citizens of South Wiltshire were subjected to the shattering noise of the rocket firing. Industrial firms, both British and foreign, used the radio environmental simulator (REG), the environmental hangar and blower tunnel on a regular basis.

As a dispersal for four V-Bombers, a site on the south side was prepared, and used on exercises by the Victor B.1s of No 15 Squadron and later by Vulcan B.2s of No 27 Squadron.

Ceremonial

After the unsuccessful bid in late 1970 for "Royal" to be added to "AAEE," it is particularly pleasing to record at the end of this chapter that 50 years after the adoption of the word "Establishment" in the title of the unit, Princess Anne (deputising for the Queen who was indisposed) made a formal visit and presentation of Armorial Bearings on 19th March 1971. A rather less well publicised ceremony had taken place in London in 1951 when Mrs Attlee, the Prime Minister's wife, presented the Inter Unit Farms and Gardens Trophy to the Commandant; the success was repeated at least in the following year. Whether farming, flight testing the latest aircraft or entertaining royalty, AAEE's achievements were outstanding.

16: A C Squadron three-ship formation led by Sea Balliol T.21 WL732, with Sea Vixen XJ582 and Buccaneer S.2 XN974 on 21st October 1964. © Crown Copyright

FLYING

The business of the Aeroplane and Armament Experimental Establishment can be summarised in two words: 'aircraft' and 'flying'. Without aircraft there would have been no AAEE—without flying there would have been precious few trials; flying had been at the heart of the Establishment since its earliest days as the Experimental Flight at Upavon in 1914, and pilots were there to work the flying machines. Aviators always formed a small and privileged group within the organisation, and in January 1946 numbered about 50 of a total of about 1,600 at Boscombe; there were 43 pilots, a number reaching a nadir of 38 in 1947. Test pilots arriving post war had the benefit of professional training at the recently formed Empire Test Pilots' School. All were servicemen, apart from the two civilians in the civil aircraft section. In March 1961 there were 60 RAF pilots plus about 10 RN with 14 RAF NCO aircrew. AAEE flying was uniquely varied (over 200 types were flown between 1945 and 1975, covering every role of all three services plus some extras such as airliners, and in temperate and intemperate climes), sometimes routine, often challenging and occasionally exciting at or near the limits of performance and control. Risks were involved and the well tried "step-by-step" approach employed to minimise them. This chapter contains many accounts of the vicissitudes of exploring the flight envelopes of high sub- and trans-sonic aircraft at a time before the effects of compressibility were properly understood and remedies incorporated into new designs. And yet accidents, some fatal, happened particularly frequently in the early years of jet propulsion, even when ejection seats were available. An American wag called this, "The period of destructive [flight] testing."[1]

The 1950s were especially bad, due not only to the novel designs, but also to their profusion and above all to the pressure of getting them into service in the shortest time. All the evidence seen and heard by the author indicates that the Establishment's standards of acceptability never faltered, and that the pilots' views, given their unassailable position, carried the utmost weight in deciding acceptability.

Organisation

The Flying Division remained under the command of an RAF group captain responsible to the Commandant throughout the 30 years of this history. Its composition reflected the changing needs of the aircraft under test, with squadron organisation determined in most cases by the category of machine flown. Thus in August 1945 there were A Squadron (RAF Fighters), B Squadron (four engined craft), C Squadron (Naval machines), D Squadron (RAF twin engines), and Communications and Special Duties Squadron (CSDS)("Special" for the Porton Down Establishment) with a separate Flight for intensive flying. D Squadron disbanded in January 1946, followed by CSDS at the end of February; the Intensive Flying Development Fight (IFDF), organisationally part of Engineering Division, joined them on 22 November 1948, but continued as the Intensive Flying Section into the 1950s. The work of the three defunct units was

17: A good example of four squadrons co-operating in January 1966. The Argosy C.1 XN814 was "owned" by E Squadron, piloted by B Squadron with an E Squadron engineer, refuelling a C Squadron Sea Vixen FAW.2 XN685, while an A Squadron pilot flew the chase aircraft. © Crown Copyright

[1] A remark made later when structural integrity checks on the ground were made using ultra sonic, magnetic particle and other methods, or "Non Destructive Testing."

absorbed into the remainder, which were joined in December 1950 by a reformed D Squadron under Wg Cdr Gibson, having A Flight (fixed wing) and B Flight (rotary wing) for the airborne forces trials on transfer from Beaulieu. The Civil Aircraft Testing Section formed as a separate flying unit in January 1947 (the servicing element started three months earlier), and formally disbanded in November 1960 when its remaining tasks transferred to Support Squadron.

This organisation of four squadrons served well enough throughout the 1950s during the period of intense activity. The Air Transport Flight, formed in June 1955 to support overseas trials, was joined in November 1960 by the fixed wing, ie Airborne Forces, element of D Squadron to form Support Squadron in which the third Flight operated the Meteors on training, rating, target and other tasks.[2] D Squadron became the helicopter unit. There were no fewer than 27 aircraft in the three flights of Support Squadron in March 1962 of which 14 flew on trials and the remainder purely on supporting tasks such as photographic chase, overseas ferrying, training and communications. A further change in 1964 reflected the increasing number of new transport types under test and E Squadron formed with two flights, trials and air transport, the latter including the remaining Meteors from Support Squadron which disappeared. Fixed wing Naval aviating declined after the granting of a badge (motto, "Ex Caligine Veritas—Truth out of Obscurity) in 1961 and C Squadron disbanded on 7th March 1971 although the remaining testing of Phantoms and Buccaneers continued initially in A squadron. In March 1974, E Squadron's task was effectively over and it also disbanded; its remaining trials and support tasks reverting to B Squadron. Such rivalry as existed between the squadrons sometimes descended into noisy gestures, as in the early 1960s when the Mark 2 Vulcans of B Squadron, parked outside A Squadron, would use the deafening power of one engine a high power to start the others by cross feeding. Such activity could be self-defeating, as the fighter squadron claimed on more than one occasion that a B pilot could have flown one of their machines, but the phone call making the offer was drowned out by noise of the Vulcan! The flying of other squadrons' aircraft broadened the professional knowledge of test pilots and was actively encouraged until the late 1960s when single-seaters became more complicated; there remained, however, the "common user" Meteors and Hunters for training. The use of "visiting" co-pilots in two-pilot aircraft continued.

For launching trials of the Blue Steel guided nuclear weapon, the AAEE supplied the scientific staff (Mr Wason Turner and Mr Brian Ramsdale) and an armament specialist (Flt Lt Les Sykes) to No 4 Joint Service Trials Units (JSTU) in Australia, culminating in the actual firings after drops from V-bombers in 1964. Another pair of JSTUs were based at Boscombe and, although functionally controlled by the Air Ministry/Ministry of Defence, the flying was regulated by AAEE, the aircrew were mostly from C Squadron with some from A Squadron and the aircraft maintained within the squadrons. The units were No 13 (Red Top air-to-air missile) at Boscombe from 1 February 1962 to 14 July 1967, and No 22 (Martel air-to-ground missile) formed at Boscombe on 1 January 1966 and disbanded on 31 December 1974. The work involved weapon configurations which had no Service Release, and AAEE flying arrangements overcame this procedural problem. A further team of one (ie Mr John Moakes) had started work in the USA on the Skybolt air launched ballistic missile at the time of cancellation in 1962.

Support

By 1960 the airfield had modern landing aids and lighting, the longest military runway in the country (and ipso facto possessing the greatest aid to flight safety) and for high level control its own radar controllers at nearby Sopley. Flying activity could be intense with seven or eight disparate aircraft in the circuit—maybe some short of fuel—possibly using two runways—all traffic and radio handled with aplomb by the calm ATC controllers. Just as most servicemen and many civilians considered their tour of duty at Boscombe to have been the most stimulating of their professional lives, so pilots found the ATC to be a revelation on first encounter. Nevertheless, in an early incident in January 1952, a visiting American B-36 landed in bad weather a mile before the beginning of the runway when the pilot was confused by the differences between UK and US approach and runway lighting. The frozen ground prevented the aircraft from sinking, and after minor repairs it flew back home. The pilot arrived a lieutenant colonel and, it is said, left as a passenger ... as a lieutenant! No doubt he felt that summary justice had a wintery chill to it. Three other B-36s landed satisfactorily.

The fire and rescue services kept pace with the increase in aircraft fuel and weapon loads, and by 1975 had an up-to-date fleet of fire engines to meet the requirements of the most demanding type.

The Role of Test Pilots and Aircrew

The role of the test pilot at Boscombe Down was to decide on acceptability of a new aircraft, modification, equipment, technique or role. His training prepared him for this work, while the breadth of his experience of many types of aircraft was of the greatest importance in making sound judgments. Having made his test flight, the

---

[2] In December 1954, 11 Meteors served all five flying units: A Sqn—2, B Sqn—2, C Sqn—1, D Sqn—3, CATS—3.

pilot then had to tell others of his experience and what he thought of it; a verbal debrief would usually be followed by a formal written report to the trials officer. It has always been a bone of contention among pilots that their reports never left the Establishment, but were paraphrased into the main report. The test pilot played an increasingly important part in activities other than flying—from early involvement in the design, particularly cockpits, of new types, to deciding remedies and further investigations following test flights of recalcitrant machines. In between were the more routine discussions of the results of flights; in cases of unexpected or poor behaviour the pilot's experience was unique. Explanations of aircraft behaviour were often elucidated by examination and analysis of instrumentation records. Some aircraft types, particularly the early swept wing designs, made their characteristics abundantly clear—and the pilot's task was then to convince others of the problems. Sooner or later a great meeting would be arranged to discuss the matter, and it could be a frustrating business as the pilot, probably the only person present who had actually flown the aircraft under discussion, was also the most junior of those attending. An extreme example of the uphill battle experienced by an AAEE test pilot occurred in connection with the Swift (see p. 10 above) where Sqn Ldr P D (Peter) Thorne had not only to explain the Establishment's findings in the face of sceptical officials, but, infinitely worse, was accused of misleading the meeting as the firm's pilots told a different, and less damning, story. The situation was exacerbated because the officials (ie the Headquarter's project office) had seen fit to restrict the amount of Swift flying available to AAEE. Eventually, the type's unsuitability as a fighter was acknowledged and the A Squadron pilots' views vindicated.

Another instance of a test pilot's influence concerns the Buccaneer Mark 1, with woeful catapult launching capabilities, due largely to inadequate engine power. Following the fatal loss of an AAEE aircraft on leaving the catapult, the whole future of carrier operation of the Buccaneer was put in doubt. Cdr R M Crosley, OC C Squadron, with the active encouragement of Mr Dennis Higton, the C Section Leader in Performance Division and the Chief Superintendent, Mr Handel Davies, fought a long battle with the powers-that-be in obtaining modifications and approval for a further trial; Crosley's technique of keeping the hand clear of the stick was among the innovations. Following trials at RAE Bedford (for which Dennis Higton made the first launch as observer), 40 successful launches were made at sea. On this occasion the pilot's views, doggedly maintained, played a key part in saving the operational career of the early Buccaneer; the clearance for the Mark 1 version for catapulting was the more significant as it paved the way for approval of the more powerful Mark 2. The Lightning exhibited several characteristics calling for the pilots' opinions. Slight longitudinal instability at supersonic speed was considered acceptable, as was the straightforward operation of the radar which reduced the adverse impact of the auto-pilot which failed to achieve its specified performance. Pilots of A Squadron considered that even in the single seat environment, the aeroplane, its radar and weapon firing would be within the competence of the front line pilots. Less acceptable in the early development Lightnings was the position of the stick near its rearmost position on the approach making the landing flare problematic; changing to plain flaps in production gave a fortuitous nose up trim change on lowering thus producing a more central stick position for landing. Directional characteristics at high speeds involved much investigation, by both the firm and AAEE; the initial increase in fin size (to 130%) failed to cure problems of trim change with speed. More important, however, the Establishment contributed to the understanding of the phenomenon known as roll/yaw divergence.

These three stories are but examples of a trend where test pilots had increasingly to present the results of their flying to a critical and often sceptical audience. Preparation for flight was another area where standards changed over the 30 years. At one extreme, preparation could start many months ahead of related flights when staff of relevant Divisions of the Establishment, including the project pilot, liaised with the Air Staff and the manufacturer of a new type. At the other extreme, preparation could be at short notice on a familiar type when a pre-flight briefing sufficed. There may have been a grain of truth in the popular image of the 1950s that test pilots jumped from one aircraft to another, and it was certainly true that briefing of pilots new to type sometimes left much to be desired. As late as 1952 the Commandant directed that pilots were to be given dual instruction or a demonstration on types new to them; this followed a fatal accident to a Brigand in which an engine failed during the pilot's first flight on the type. The pilot had been flying Valettas in which a single push and release on the button resulted in the propeller feathering; the drill in the Brigand required the button to held in continuously to achieve full feathering. By the 1960s, aircrew made use of Service training facilities for types new to them, and, where available, used flight simulators in familiar types for periodic practice of emergency drills; this trend reflected the dearth of new types, the longevity and complexity of those in service, and the need to achieve the highest professional standards of operation.

So much for preparation. After flight activity ranged from extensive debrief and a lengthy written report (usually covering a series of tests) of handling investigations at one extreme, to ticks on a flight test card from a sortie dropping weapons as planned. In multi-seat aircraft, the pilot, who was invariably the captain, was assisted by other crew members in operating instrumentation and making notes. For tests with an unusual degree of risk, the crew was reduced to the minimum needed for safe operation, eg three in a V-Bomber instead of the normal five. In addition to qualified

18: Sqn Ldr A E (Arthur) Callard, the pilot, with Flt Lt E A J Haskett (navigator—right) and A J R Robson (signaller—left) of B Squadron in February 1951 when they broke the record Westwards across the Atlantic in Canberra WD932 on delivery to the USA, taking 4hr 37min for the 2,100 miles to Newfoundland. Leather helmets, goggles and pressure waistcoats were de rigueur.

19: "A" Squadron in 1950/1. Left to right: Sqn Ldr R A (Ray) Watts, Flt Lt A D (Alan) Woodcock, Flt Lt Polly Perkins, Flt Lt D (Chalky) White, Sqn Ldr PL (Peter) Parrot, Flt Lt B G (Bill) Aston, Flt Lt J W L (John) Innes and Sqn Ldr E J (Red) Roberts. Photo H W Turner

20: A "fag" break in Khartoum in 1948 during hot weather trials of Hastings C.1 TG509. Standing (l to r) Jack Lodge, Don Evans, Ben Fortes, John Cotton; squatting Stan Sleeman and Fred Matthews.

21: Flight Sergeant Cowan, the highly regarded SNCO of A Squadron, meets Sqn Ldr M E Blackstone after a Vampire trip in the Summer of 1948.

22: The aircrew of A Squadron in January 1974, the normal complement of eight pilots and two navigators was enhanced by two Jaguar armament specialists. From left to right: Flt Lts Russ Pengelly, Guy Woods, Colin Cruikshanks, Bob Cole, Sqn Ldr John Lumsden, Flt Lt Pete Frieze, Sqn Ldr Nick Warner (Senior Pilot), Wg Cdr Mike Adams (OC A Squadron), Lt John Leng, Flt Lt Mick Hindley, Sqn Ldr Keith Mills. Flt Lts Tony Forster, Peter Orme and Bert Loveday. Immersion suits (Pengelly and Leng) give the flavour of the flying clothing of the period; anti-g connectors are visible on Pengelly, Cole and Orme. © Crown Copyright

23: The Commandant and Superintendents in 1974: back, left to right—Gp Capt Alan Merriman (CO ETPS), Mr Brian Ramsdale (Trials Management), Mr Harry Plascott (Engineering), Gp Capt Bertie Ward (Armament), Mr Bob Shields (Photographic), Mr Donald Lang (Performance) and Gp Capt John Wilkinson (Flying); front—Mr Pop Popham (Navigation and Radio), Mr Frank Brown (Chief Superintendent), Air Cdre Geoff Cairns (Commandant), Mr John Bennett (Technical Services) and Mr Keith Hodges (Secretary).

24: *Futher evidence of the hard life at Boscombe Down. Wg Cdr R L (Roger) Topp, OC A Squadron, demonstrates great style at skittles in the Silver Plough at Pitton in 1963.*

25: *Flt Lt D C (David) Scouller at sausage with Sqn Ldr G (George) Cannon at the rear left and Flt Lt R deV (Bob) Bolt to right—also at the Silver Plough in Pitton.*

service aircrew, the pilots could call on civilian Flight Test Observers (FTO) drawn from the scientific and technical staff, ideally those involved with the management of the trial. The preparation of FTOs for their aerial activities underwent a fundamental change during the 30 years of this history. In 1945 the wartime practice of a last minute 'phone call to a Technical Office usually resulted in a frantic rush to the aircraft by an unsuspecting junior who found that in extreme cases the engines were running as he arrived having grabbed a parachute *en route*. Instruction on his duties and on safety matters were overlooked. Improvements in safety briefing occurred gradually, and matched the comprehensive briefings given by the scientific staff to the aircrews. A formal training programme based on the aircrew equipment section (see page 61) and later renamed The Aeromedical and Survival Training School) was established. All aspiring bird men, service and civilian, in AAEE and elsewhere in British research and development flying who came under the regulation of the Director of Flying were obliged to attend the School periodically, the better to breath oxygen, bale out or eject if necessary and survive in the wilds of Wiltshire and further afield; the training given varied according to the maximum altitude to be flown by the individual. This more professional approach was long overdue, and coupled with the thorough briefing for every flight, whether or not FTOs were in the crew, went a long way to improve flight safety.

It seems to be in the nature of things that the more outrageous behaviour in aviating circles belonged to the aircrew—pilots in particular. The Officers' Mess was always a convivial meeting place on formal and not-so-formal occasions. In the late 1940s and 1950s in particular, the constant flow of firms' pilots, many with previous experience at Boscombe, enlivened the proceedings. Among memories of survivors is Sqn Ldr P P C (Paddy) Barthropp, noted for his desire to make up for time lost as a prisoner of war, who decided that a flare path was just what the Officers' Mess corridor needed. Unfortunately, his oral attempts at lighting up were too successful and he was badly burned. Even group captains were caught up in the fun—Gp Capt R C Dawkins introduced a stallion to the dining room—others, it seems, failed to join in the horse play. Gp Capt T B Cooper had a reputation for pressing on and for paying scant regard to the opinions of subordinates; he died in the Meteor accident mentioned below. In spite of the best attempts by earlier generations, the Mess survived to less boisterous times when the more serious business of flying was also treated in a more disciplined and professional way—a trend throughout military aviating.

Excitement and Surprises

There can have been few flights more exciting than the Lightning's ultimate test of the AI23 radar's "lock-follow" capability at very high closing speeds—25 nautical miles per minute. A head on interception at 1.7M against a Javelin at 0.95M was carefully planned

26: Holders of the world speed record for helicopters between London and Malta—Wg Cdr C B (Cyclops) Brown and Flt Lt G (Gordon) Smith posing in front of a Belvedere in 1959.

27: The Comandant, Air Cdre Geoff Cairns presents the Legion of Merit medal to Major John Blaha USAF, the exchange pilot with "A" Squadron in 1974. His British AFC was presented to him on return to the USA, and he became an astronaut, spending some time in Russia. © Crown Copyright

28: Victor K.1 XA918 in its third configuration at AAEE in July 1967 (first as a bomber, then as a two point, and finally as a three point tanker). The Canberra B.2 WH876 is being used to give pilots training in flight refuelling; on this occasion the training fitted in between trials of other receivers. © Crown Copyright

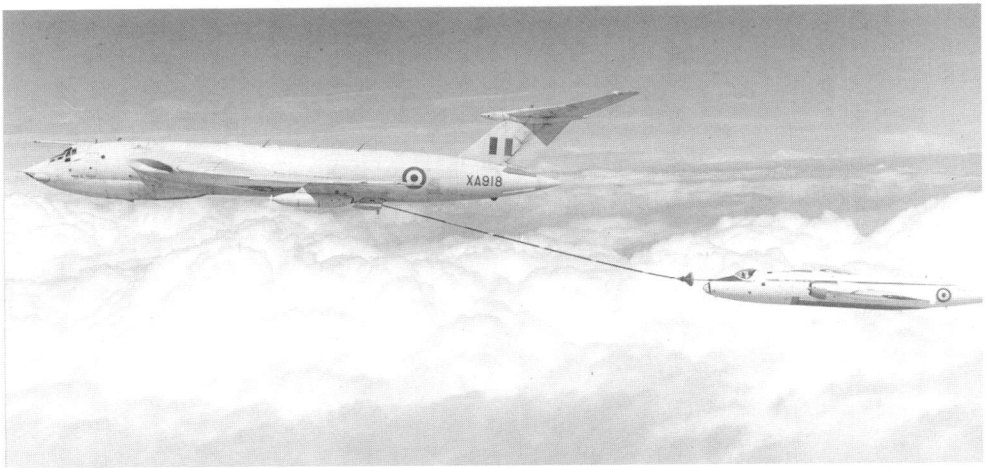

29: Anson Mk 1 AX403 in use at Khartoum to blow sand into the intakes of Meteor F.3 EE336 in 1946. © Crown Copyright

30 and 31: Two views of a typically instrumented cockpit of the 1950s—in this case, that of Athena T.2 VW891. Letters indicate the special fit:
A—stick force control
B—anti-spin parachute release
C—accelerometer
D—VG recorder cock
E—radiator flap desynn
F—control for auto observer
G—Barnes accelerometer transmitter. © Crown Copyright

and flown under ground control. The AI radar performed very well, and the pilot, Sqn Ldr H A (Alan) Merriman slid past (his words) with 200 yd separation. Blinking was not allowed (author's words)! The Javelin pilot felt a massive jolt as the shock wave hit him. Later, another Javelin calibrated for measuring pressure errors received an even more alarming jolt from a Concorde as it "slid past" during calibration at over Mach 2. Helicopters had their own way of concentrating the minds of pilots—for example, the Sea King had an Automatic Flight Control System (AFCS) which was required to be flown at maximum speed at 100 ft above the surface. In view of the possibility of a nose down runaway when under automatic control, intrepid D Squadron pilots made the investigation—flying downwind to ensure the highest ground speed. The real excitement came in delaying manual recovery—"to simulate the delay of an unsuspecting service pilot." The question of how long the delay should be on trials of malfunctions of automatics was hotly debated. No doubt self preservation carried the day—and night—on these trials as no untoward incidents were recorded. Other trials involved eye watering experiences when flight with cockpit canopies removed needed investigation. The Canberra was an early jet in 1951 to be so flown, and the Gnat Trainer, probably the last, in the mid—1960s; for the latter, the junior pilot, Flt Lt J Mayes, was "volunteered", partially because he alone retained his goggles from an earlier era. This pilot later took a Lightning to Wheelus (near Tripoli) where the engineers examined its response to the heat. A battery change during refuelling proved ill-advised as the fuel transfer valves were left unpowered and fuel surged out of vent valves onto the wings and gushed onto the crew underneath giving them a shower of hot Avtur.

Large aircraft also produced surprises, as with the Belfast after a period in the intense cold of Fort Churchill in Canada. On the climb there was a loud bang, the pressurisation failed and it was seen that the seals around the doors had perished. While attempts were being made to provide some sealing with rags in the gaps, the door flew out into space, threatening to suck the flight engineer, Roy Elliott, into the void. Quick action by Les Dix, a ground crew man who spread himself on the floor, got a hold on Elliott who was pulled to safety; Dix was awarded the MBE for this action.

Earlier surprises included the Vampire night fighter prototype which happened to cross the Porton range just as guns were fired on the ground, hitting the nose section; the aeroplane landed and the slight damage apparent was repaired. On the next flight, Sqn Ldr L W F Stark and the observer, Mary Bolter, had just dived, as planned, to within one knot of the limiting speed when, to their horror, the whole nose section flew off, hitting the wing, fins and rudders. Control was maintained with difficulty and a safe landing achieved; the pilot received a Green Endorsement in his log book. Lt Cdr R M Orr-Ewing was similarly rewarded for landing a Wyvern after the port wing tip was lost, as was Sqn Ldr D White for forced landing a Provost which had suffered a fractured propeller. A green log book endorsement was also given to Warrant Officer A Baskerville after engine failure in a Vampire and a safe landing.

As part of a demonstration to a visiting Soviet delegation in November 1945, Sqn Ldr J (Jan) Zurakowski gave the low show in a Vampire, including a slow fly past which actually struck the ground and he slid to a halt. First on the scene was a party of German prisoners of war working on the runway who attempted to rescue the uninjured Zurakowski; as a Pole, he had a great dislike of "Huns", and refused most vehemently to be helped until the crash crew arrived. Two months later, another Pole, Flt Lt A R (Tony) Majcherczyk, was awarded a "Good Show" for successfully landing a Tempest following engine failure. His family joined him from Poland after a long separation, just days before he was killed in July 1946 when his Meteor failed to recover from a spin. This cruel twist of fate was particularly tragic as the anti-spin parachute had been deployed, but broke off immediately. Among incidents which ended without serious injury was a braking test for which a fleet of bowsers flooded the runway. In short order Sqn Ldr C A (Tommy) Tomlinson wound up the Valiant to test speed, then closed the throttles and applied the brakes. The ensuing sideways skid looked most ominous to the runway caravan controller who made a sharp exit just before his cosy "office" was wrecked.

For unwelcome excitement, the catapult launches of the under-powered Buccaneer Mk 1 took some beating; the steam catapults were themselves scarcely equal to the task. The first trial was curtailed in January 1960 by problems with *HMS Victorious*. Ten months later, two aircraft flew for further trials on *HMS Ark Royal* off Malta. Cdr RM Crosley, Officer Commanding C Squadron, who flew on this trial commented that flying off the catapult, sinking to sea level and watching the airspeed barely rise was very unpleasant; however, the experience of watching the launches of his colleague was even more frightening. Deck landings gave fewer heart-stopping moments—but approaches remained tricky on account of poor thrust/boundary layer control characteristics. In August 1961 Lt O (Ozzie) Brown and Terry Dunn were killed on further catapult launches using *HMS Hermes* in which deliberate overtrimming had been set to determine the hands-off launch technique; the aircraft pitched up and stalled without the crew being able to escape. The Inquiry found some evidence which obscured a positive explanation for the tragedy. The subsequent concern about the viability of Buccaneer Mk 1 carrier operations was resolved, as described above, and a fourth set of 40 deck landings and catapultings were made successfully from *HMS Hermes* in May 1962, followed by a further 85 from *HMS Ark Royal* in February 1963.

As with the Belfast incident described above, sharp bangs in aircraft usually indicated that all was not well. Flt Lt R W (Ray) Bray in the first Shackleton Mk 3 was to drop bombs in Lyme Bay on a cold day needing the use of the fuel burning heater in the cabin. As the bomb doors were opened for the first time there was a loud explosion and a nasty burning smell; no damage could be found, but the heater had stopped heating. On landing, the cause was found to have been due to a momentary drop in pressure as the bomb doors were opened causing the heater to switch off and then on again with a build up of fuel inside; the damage was extensive, and due to repositioning of the heater intake to cater for the nose wheel configuration of the mark. The second prototype Valiant was used for high Mach investigation, terminated by extremely violent buffeting described as, "like being inside a boiler undergoing pneumatic rivetting." Some years later, the same aircraft was chosen to make rocket assisted take offs at maximum weight and after one of them there was a heavy jolt and a muffled explosion. Some ill fitting panels were noted from an airborne inspection but no other symptoms were apparent and the aircraft landed. The rear spar had split; a strengthening modification had not been incorporated, and it was believed that the split was a long term manifestation of damage from the earlier "hammer" buffeting. In June 1966 a Canberra B15 at a weight beyond the designer's intentions needed over 9,000 ft (of the available 11,000 ft at Wheelus in Libya) to leave the ground before giving up the ghost following a sharp crack and loss of aileron control on a later trip. It fell into the Mediterranean Sea and Flt Lt B P (Pidge) Holme and the author were fortunately dressed for bathing under their flying overalls—a matter of great amusement to the USAF Base Commander who watched their arrival by helicopter after rescue. Sometimes the noise of breakage occurred before leaving the ground, as happened to Flt Lt Bernie Noble in a Javelin. On pressing the starter button there was a massive explosion and concussion throughout the aircraft. A smart exit was hampered by the rapid disappearance of the groundcrew, apart from one brave soul who, however, remained transfixed holding the step ladder some distance from the cockpit. The damage proved irreparable.

Flying Training of Civilian Staff

A scheme had started in 1940 for technical staff in the Ministry of Aircraft Production to be given flying instruction at RAF schools; in 1944 the scheme was broadened so that the training could be undertaken at the Establishments. At AAEE two Magisters arrived, changed after the war to Tiger Moths and then a Harvard. Initially tutelage was by local pilots on a casual basis, one of whom was Sqn Ldr K J (Pop) Sewell whose empathy with his students appears to have been nil; from mid-1945 onwards an RAF qualified instructor came on strength. The pupils included Mr F H Beer, the Superintendent of Engineering by 1949, whose aviating is recorded in a series of mishaps in AAEE aircraft, starting with a breakage of a Tiger Moth on landing in 1949, retraction of the undercarriage of a Meteor on the ground in 1954, and flying into the ground short of the runway in an Anson in 1959 during a radar approach in good weather. The second accident put a stop the flying of trials aircraft by non-professional pilots, and the third stopped all such flying. The scheme for teaching civilians stopped in 1949 as an economy measure,[3] but it had been useful in other ways. For example, Flt Lt D W E (Dave) Allum had the indignity of being told to undergo special instruction after writing off a Mosquito in a cross wind take off. A scheme of financial grants continued, however, thus enabling technical staff to obtain private pilot's licenses elsewhere.

Flight Safety

The RAF established a Directorate of Flight Safety in 1946, and a specialist post for flight safety in the Directorate of Flying R&D within MoS was soon created. At AAEE the subject was handled in accordance with RAF procedures by the headquarters of the Flying Division One bizarre effect of the new focus on the subject was the compilation of statistics on a monthly basis. Three major accidents (a Firefly and a Vampire with undercarriage problems and another Vampire with a fire in the tail boom) occurred in December 1946 during which 92 trials sorties were flown, extrapolated into a rate of 326 per 10,000 sorties. While the number of accidents in the first decade or so post war was, indeed, awful, the basis of the statistics makes meaningful comparison difficult; however, the Establishment rate for 1970 was 1.1 per 10,000 hours. Assuming the 1946 sorties were of an average duration of one hour, then the reduction in the rate of accidents over 24 years from 326 to 1.1 is a statistical nonsense—nevertheless reflecting a considerable improvement in flight safety. AAEE had an accident record similar to the Services. Given the nature of the flying of new types to the limits of their performance coupled to the extremely short duration of some early jets, it is, perhaps, surprising that the Establishment's record was not worse. The reasons are largely unchanged from earlier times, viz, flying was carefully controlled, risks approached in a step-by-step fashion with experienced and specially trained aircrew, the maintenance staff were skilled and the flying needed weather better than that suitable for other military operators, and, for UK flying at least, operations were from a long wide runway with outstanding air traffic controllers.

The accidents chosen for inclusion here are from the extensive records retained for posterity—existing

---

[3] Even after this purge, Ministry aircraft (known as the CS(A) Fleet) numbered some 545 machines in 1953.

records of skilful handling where accidents have been avoided are far less comprehensive; but a balanced view of the Establishment's achievements may be obtained by considering this chapter in the light of the vast amount of flying reflected by the contents of chapters 4 to 11.

Some accidents in the early post war years almost beggar belief with the benefit of half a century's hindsight. In July 1946, Wg Cdr J C Mann (OC B Squadron) took off in a Lincoln to investigate airspeed errors during yaw; he had two civilian FTOs, but no flight engineer, nor other qualified aircrew. A minute after take off all engines failed and a forced landing made on Porton Range without injury to the crew. The engine cut off switches had been left in the cut off position and operated of their own volition as air pressure built up. Had a qualified flight engineer been carried this oversight would, most probably, not have occurred; a modification was soon made to the cut out operating system of the Lincoln. Another of the same type crashed in July 1948 while investigating asymmetric handling at 3,500 ft; two engines were giving maximum power when a spin developed with insufficient height to recover. All four aboard were killed; the tragedy was compounded by the unique nature of the aeroplane which had been extensively modified for radar trials. The Board of Inquiry made two significant observations: that the pilot had insufficient experience on type for the trial, and that he should have conducted the asymmetric work at a considerably higher altitude. Perhaps the most surprising folly was perpetrated by Gp Capt T B Cooper (Superintendent of Flying) who took off in March 1949 into extensive cloud cover up to 20,000 ft, without an instrument rating[4] and with one of two vacuum pumps, which drove the gyroscopic instruments, unserviceable. He also lacked recent instrument flying practice. Nine minutes after take off he was killed when the aircraft crashed near the airfield.

On a slightly more positive note, one benefit of the increasing emphasis on safety in the RAF and at Boscombe was demonstrated in November 1952 when a Venom and Valetta collided in low visibility. Although the Venom pilot was killed, all 12 aboard the transport survived with only two serious injuries, in spite of landing port wing first under little control. Rearward facing seats had recently been installed; in addition, a jeep broke out of its restraints but had been placed ahead of the troops and caused no injury.

In 1955–6 the Establishment assisted in making the Canberra safer after Bomber Command had suffered several fatal accidents attributed to the electric tailplane trimmer "running away." Flt Lt G R K (Geoff) Fletcher had the task of investigating the many palliatives suggested, tested by trimming nose down and delaying

[4] The Instrument Rating Scheme had recently been introduced for all Service/RAF pilots. The first examiner at Boscombe was Wg Cdr C D Brown, OC D Squadron.

response for two seconds. He became well acquainted with the Wiltshire countryside which filled the front window as the aircraft pitched nose down. The Command limited speed in service to 250 kt.

The Ultimate Solution

Escapes by parachute feature throughout the period. The first occurred in May 1947 when an engine fell out of the wing of a Sea Hornet leading to the rear fuselage separating followed by a spin; Lt K R (Ken) Hickson suffered minor injuries after baling out from the inverted position. Another followed control failure in April 1956 in a Whirlwind helicopter in which parachutes were worn only for certain flights. The pilot and two flight test observers baled out, but only the pilot, Flt Lt M H Beeching survived; the FTOs, plus a third who did not manage to leave the aircraft, were killed. Ejection seats earned a very poor reputation at AAEE in the early years, on account of extreme discomfort in normal flying, and unreliability when used for abandonment. Seats by Vickers (in the E.10/44 Attacker on its first visit), and Malcolm (known also as the ML and in the first Wyverns) were soon replaced by those by Martin Baker. All three makes were treated with great suspicion by pilots—and all were flown without the firing cartridge (ie inert) at least until 1949. Lt Cdr T J A King Joyce was killed in June 1948 in an Attacker fitted with a Martin Baker Mk 1A seat—but it seems certain that it was inoperable. In June 1951 the first ejection by the Establishment ended fatally for Lt Cdr D K Hanson when the canopy of a Wyvern detached, striking the fin and leading rapidly to the break up of the airframe. He ejected at 1,500 ft, but his leg was almost severed by the control column, thus rendering him unconscious and unable to operate the manual separation lever to deploy the parachute; he died on ground impact. All Wyverns were grounded pending remedial action. Equally grievous was the ejection in July 1955 from the Supermarine 525 when it entered a flat spin. The pilot, Lt Cdr T A Rickell had, the Court of Inquiry deduced, to remove his helmet to reach the seat firing handle and then he had to penetrate the toughened canopy which had failed to separate. He left the aircraft at 200 ft—too low for parachute deployment—and was killed. The board noted that the anti spin parachute had not been operated. Two years later, the canopy of a Hunter also failed to jettison when Wg Cdr D F Dennis (OC A Squadron) could not recover from a spin. However, the seat shattered the perspex satisfactorily, but faulty rigging led to a tangled parachute and he was seriously injured. In February 1958 incorrect servicing of the top (securing) latch was found to have been the cause of an involuntary ejection of Flt Lt R S May during inverted flying of a Javelin. He was killed because the parachute could not deploy due to the abnormal sequence of events, while the navigator, Fg Off J M V Coates, also died after the drogue snagged the aircraft and thus failed to pull out the parachute. In October 1958, Kano in Nigeria hosted an AAEE Sea Vixen flown by Lt J A (John) Neilson and W H (Willie) Stewart. At 450 kt a vulture was ingested into the port engine causing a fire and loss of control some 50 nm from Kano. Two difficult ejections followed. Incorrect rigging of Stewart's rip cord damaged his parachute and the seat failed to separate, causing extensive bruising on his descent as it banged against him. On landing, Stewart's troubles were not over. His rescuers put him on a donkey, but failed to secure him adequately with the result that he fell off. Transfer to a poorly sprung vehicle for the remainder of the journey added to his woes—and ensured that bruising extended over his entire body. Neilson had to bend forward to pull the firing handle, and damaged his sternum on landing; their injuries were classified as minor. In the seven years covering the above accidents, there was but a single completely successful ejection; it occurred in December 1955. Sqn Ldr A D (David) Dick left a Javelin spinning in a flat mode not seen previously and which was impervious to all recovery actions tried, including streaming the anti spin parachute. The pilot's broadcast commentary of his sequence of actions prior to ejection has become a model of calm reporting under great duress.

It is gratifying to record that nine accidents involving ejections between 1959 and 1975 led to 15 successes and only two fatalities, the latter most probably caused by use outside of the seat's design limits. Perhaps the most disorientating conditions of these nine accidents occurred in November 1974 during wind up turns of a two seat Jaguar with a large centeline store. On the last, an uncommanded pitch up was followed by inertia coupled rolling involving extremely violent and rapid variations in roll (50° to 130°/sec), yaw (over 20°/sec) and pitch (20°/sec nose up and down)—figures from the digital recorder—A Squadron pilots couldn't count that quickly! Recovery from this oscillatory motion proved impossible, and Flt Lt C J (Colin) Cruikshanks, almost unconscious in the front seat managed to eject himself and Wg Cdr C C (Clive) Rustin blacked out in the rear seat. Both landed without injury. Colin Cruikshanks later became Commandant.[5]

Apart from King Joyce's, all the accidents described above occurred with Martin Baker seats. The Folland (Saab) seat appeared in the Gnat, and its only employment at AAEE proved fatal to Sqn Ldr E J Roberts in October 1958. Control of the fighter was lost (due to a seized control relay) and he ejected, but the automatic separation device failed to function, and he was killed before he was able to effect separation manually.

---

[5] The eighth "old boy" from A Squadron to do so; B Squadron have managed one (after the period of this work), other Squadrons and Divisions—nil

The lessons to be learnt from accidents were always considered carefully, and policy, procedures or aircraft altered as necessary. The most important consequence of accidents was in modifications to the aircraft which might otherwise have gone unremarked in trials or other flying, or which had been considered minor criticisms for later improvement. It was decided following the Javelin's spinning accident that pilots needed positive warning before the stall, and thus avoid a spin with its problematic recovery. An effective two-stage warning was introduced in which operation of the second required immediate recovery action. The activities following the loss of the first Victor Mark 2 in 1959 were the most wide ranging of any AAEE accident. Recovery of the wreckage took a long time and resulted in relatively minor modifications to the aircraft. Preceding that, the whole business of conducting flight tests was examined, including briefing procedures and detailed warning of ATC of the area of operations. Of assistance to the Victor Board of Inquiry was a copy of the detailed briefing for the crew; it helped in determining the most likely flight conditions prior to the loss of control. A minor example of changes after an accident was the introduction of an organised method of informing pilots of the modification state of individual aircraft following loss of a canopy from a Sea Hornet flown by Lt H C N (Nic) Goodhart when the speed limit was inadvertently exceeded because a strengthening modification had not, as he had assumed, been incorporated.

If this section appears unduly pessimistic, the reader should bear in mind that the book covers 30 years of flying of many untried aeroplanes, often at the forefront of technology, and at the limits of their capabilities. Many thousands of hours were accumulated in test and support flying without mishap. It is worth repeating that records for skilful flying are scant; those for accidents are complete.

Some Interesting Tests and Flights

Spinning and Stalling

By 1963 a system had been installed in a hut behind Air Traffic Control for displaying information relayed by telemetry from a spinning aircraft; by 1965 an improved ground station had been installed in a purpose-built hut near A Squadron. The spinning of fighters and pilot trainers continued throughout the 30 years of this history—"fighter" embracing all single seat warplanes. The Javelin spin has been described above, while the Gnat Trainer proved difficult to clear on account of the three distinctly different types of spin—all well shown to those watching in the telemetry hut. The RAF's (ie Flying Training Command's) desire to have one foolproof recovery technique for all spins was eventually met after fitting roll direction indicators on the instrument panel to ensure that the pilot was not confused as to the direction of spin. The two-seat Lightning, on the other hand, had consistent spin behaviour from all types of entry, but the RAF considered that its squadron pilots should practice spinning on a Jet Provost with an instructor. The Scimitar had an inconsistent spin and caused the odd moment of puzzlement as various recovery actions were tried; it was later decided that the most consistent recoveries followed release of the stick while persisting with opposite rudder. Larger aircraft produced their share of surprises, usually limited to stalling. The Shackleton in its Mark 3 form (and still looking like the Lancaster of 15 years earlier) had a stall detector on only one wing with widely differing warning margins between left and right turning stalls. This was considered unacceptable, particularly in the attack configuration with bomb doors open and radome down when, without warning, there was a sudden snatch on the ailerons and the aircraft rolled onto its back. The Establishment insisted that a stall detector should be fitted to both wings. During subsequent tests by the firm to develop a satisfactory device, the aircraft crashed killing all on board. AAEE later approved a stick shaker which gave adequate warning to avoid a stall.

Compressibility

The effects of compressibility on handling had been experienced during the war, and scant improvement in behaviour was apparent in the straight wing designs of the first decade *post bellum*. Almost all the designs were assessed at AAEE, and by 1951 a unique and large volume of data had been accumulated, duplicated to some extent by the RAE at Farnborough. A paper was written for the Aeronautical Research Council summarising the results from 6 types (including 10 marks), which today makes instructive reading, giving a good idea of some of the perils of the time; many pilots of A, B and C Squadrons were involved. All aircraft tested at high mach number exhibited one or more of the following characteristics: heavying of control/s, pitching up or down, buffeting, snaking or dropping of a wing. Manual ailerons and elevators needed stick forces too high to prevent pitching or rolling and loss of control; low air speeds, ie low dynamic forces, meant that structural limits were not exceeded. For the Services, AAEE recommended maximum speeds below the critical figure, but noted that acceleration, ie application of g, caused unpleasant behaviour at lower speeds/mach numbers. The paper also remarked that the two swept wing types flown up to that time merely delayed the onset of the characteristics.

A little later, two recorded events served to underline the possible alarming behaviour resulting from high mach flying. In April 1951 the Venom Night Fighter prototype was dived to achieve M 0.86 when it pitched nose down and rolled to port; the controls were ineffective and speed built up to M 0.895 in a steep dive. Control was regained after some 20,000 ft had been lost, and Mach number reduced in the denser air. A year later a Meteor Night Fighter experienced fin stall during investigation into lateral and directional stability at 35,000 ft, and the aircraft entered a steepening dive. Application of opposite rudder set up a pendulum motion until, at a lower altitude, control was restored. Neither phenomenon had been experienced by the firms involved, and energetic discussions with them ensued.

Deck trials

In June 1946, a year after the first but inconclusive carrier landings by a Vampire of the RAE, C Squadron made another series of deck landings and unassisted take offs, also in a Vampire. These were completed without difficulty using *HMS Triumph*; earlier problems were absent. These trials were significant in that the jet engine and the nose wheel undercarriage received approval for deck operations, using a straight-in approach made possible by the pilot's uninterrupted view, and flying onto the deck without a flare. The AAEE Naval Squadron then became the authority for deck clearance of naval types. The first jet fighter for the Navy, the Attacker retained a tail wheel and made its deck trials from October 1947; on the prototype leading edge slats could be deployed by the pilot on crossing the round-down to ensure a positive wire engagement. The advent of heavily loaded carrier aircraft from the 1950s and tested by C Squadron always raised the pulse rates of those involved—whether in the aeroplane or goofing (watching). The Buccaneer Mark 1 was the most critical type on catapult launches, as related above, but even the Scimitar with ample thrust had its moments as on one occasion when establishing the minimum speed for launching at high weight; two 500 lb bombs were loaded. On leaving the catapult, the aircraft sank lower and lower towards the sea; the pilot (Lt Maurice Hedges) was a mite alarmed but with great devotion to duty and a steely nerve he saw the speed very slowly rise and then he climbed away. After landing-on (having jettisoned the bombs) it was discovered that 1,000 lb bombs had, in error, been loaded. The pilot's conversation with the armourers is not recorded. The adequate power of the Scimitar's two Avons had been further demonstrated on a free (ie, uncatapulted) take off from *HMS Ark Royal*; the parking brake remained on, yet the aircraft became airborne—leaving black marks visible on the deck for many-a-day.

Other notable events included the flying of six types by C Squadron and others onto the 876 ft long deck of *USS Antietam* on 2 July 1953; a distinguished audience saw the angle deck in use for the first time—having paid 4/= (20p) for a dry lunch! Later that year, the first mirror landings were made by a Wyvern on *HMS Illustrious*.

Flight Refuelling

B Squadron pilots joined in aerial refuelling trials at Boscombe on two Valiants under the management of Vickers from May 1957. The early design and strength of the hose and drogue left much to be desired as learning and testing went hand-in hand. A particular problem was

32: Javelin FAW.1 XA561 after it failed to recover from a spin; Sqn Ldr A D (David) Dick ejected on 8 December 1955. It evidently landed with little or no forward, or backward, speed; the large "slug" appears to be a burnt out tree. Behind the elevators are rails for their protection in the event of streaming the anti-spin parachute; the 'chute was deployed, but failed to effect a recovery. Also visible underneath the fin is a tubular "A" frame to which the parachute was attached. © Crown Copyright

33: Vulcan B.2 XH538 in a good refuelling position behind the Establishment's resident tanker in early 1961. The low refuelling speed coupled with the adequate thrust of the Vulcan's Olympus 201 engines meant that without the additional drag of the extended air brakes engine response made formating difficult. It was also found that reducing cabin pressurisation differential made throttle movement easier since the linkage passed through seals in the bulkhead. © Crown Copyright

34: Operation "Floodtide" with an F-101B taking on fuel from AAEE's tanker in 1961. The American aircraft is fitted with a probe having a British Mk 8 nozzle. No serious problems were reported. © Crown Copyright

35: The rig on the South side of the airfield for testing the unique rotor of the Fairey Rotodyne using a single engine; later a second engine was added.

36: Buccaneer S.2 XN976 on board the USS Lexington on trials. Points of interest are the drooped ailerons and the frantic work under the rear of the aircraft to fix the tie back, and the wooden deck which splintered under the onslaught of the jet blast from the engines.

37: Buccaneer prototype XK523 on HMS Victorious in May 1960.

38: Buccaneer S.1 ready for launch—demonstrating the extreme nose up attitude adopted during these critical investigations with wing tanks.

39: AAEE test Scimitar F.1 about to be accelerated into the air.

the unreliability of seals leading to very close encounters with the tail of the tanker as the receiving pilots were blinded by fuel pouring on the windscreen. Nevertheless, very creditable progress was made by Valiant and Vulcan receivers and wet (fuel transfer) and dry contacts had been made by day and night by mid-June 1957. Extension of the clearance to the Vulcan Mk 1A took place in 1959, and two 12 hour sorties flown by Flt Lt P J (Peter) Bardon. General progress in refuelling was threatened several times by the unserviceability of the refuelling equipment; there were some 32 relays in the system, and to a varying degree each could spoil transfer. Flt Lt R W (Ray) Bray made a study of the problem as a result of which four key relays were duplicated with great benefit to reliability. In the meantime, in-flight refuelling was becoming widespread, and AAEE pilots of the early trials received instruction from the company involved (Flight Refuelling Ltd) using a probe equipped Canberra B Mark 2. Three pilots from each squadron was a typical number on a sortie with a resident expert, and after a demonstration the visitors played musical chairs to reach the driving seat and have a go; the confusion in the cramped cockpit during changeover during which the controls were unattended may be imagined. Getting the probe into the basket was a new skill acquired by most, with a few who decided that they were not cut out for it when they very visibly bent the probe.

A, B and C Squadrons became proficient, with B having the tankers—first a long serving Valiant and later a resident Victor with two and then three hoses. C Squadron cleared their own Sea Vixens, Scimitars and Buccaneers as "Buddy" tankers as required. E Squadron had, for a short period, an Argosy tanker and a receiver, but it was considered that the experienced refuelling team of B Squadron was more fitted to do the trials. Similarly, B Squadron helped with the refuelling of the Belfast and VC-10—the latter involving an overnight marathon during which the Superintendent of Flying caught up with his paper work on board. So easy was the VC-10 behind a Victor (and so smooth was Sqn Ldr E D (Ned) Frith the pilot!) that the gallant Superintendent almost missed observing the second refuelling!

Overseas Flights

Flights to distant locations, usually Khartoum until it closed, involved considerable flying time, and frequent refuelling stops for short range aircraft. Two examples illustrate the flavour. Two Provosts, one powered by a Cheetah and the other by a Leonides, were required to do tropical performance and engine cooling tests in 1951; to increase the range each machine had an extra 20gal fuel tank behind the pilots. Khartoum was reached in 11 stages on the sixth day having navigated by use of eyeballs, a Dalton computer, indifferent maps and usually silent radio. The two aircraft returned to Boscombe after eight weeks away having performed admirably; the modern Leonides powered the Provost in RAF service. Such trips leave vivid memories of such events as a furnace-like sand storm, spectacular lightning under thunderstorms in Kenya and beautiful colours in brilliant early morning flying over the Greek Islands, and were typical of the experiences of many crews.

Records, Trophies, Races and Medals

In 1960, the Belvedere helicopter was due to fly to Idris in Libya; the new interim standard power control system, in addition to an extra fuel tank, made such a prospect feasible. Enthusiasm gathered apace for this trip when D Squadron suggested that a helicopter speed record to Malta en route and attendant publicity were good ideas. Support at the two refuelling stops was to be provided by a team flying in the Valetta. Take off at 4:30 AM from a dank Gatwick, then four hours to Orange in Southern France, a 35 minute turn round, another refuelling at Pratica di Mare (the Italian "AAEE") and Malta was reached in twelve hours and ten minutes after departure. OC D Squadron, Wg Cdr C D (Cyclops) Brown, who piloted two of the three legs, said that he felt in no way over-taxed by the trip—he was duty-free, too, after work. No doubt Flt Lt Gordon Smith, the expert helicopter pilot who flew the middle leg, kept a wary eye on progress towards the record; he spent over 10 years on D Squadron.

Four earlier point-to-point records had been established by AAEE. In February 1951 a crew from B Squadron piloted by Sqn Ldr A E (Arthur) Callard delivered a Canberra to the USA, establishing an unofficial record of 4 hr 37 min for the 2,100 mi between Aldergrove, Northern Ireland and Gander, Newfoundland. In January 1953, after leaving the UK, another Canberra reached Australia in under 24 hr for the first time, crewed by Flt Lt Dick Wittington and Flt Lt J A Brown. C Squadron made two records; London to Amsterdam in 23 min 39.7 sec by Lt J R F Overbury flying a Sea Hawk in July 1954, and London to Malta by Lt Cdr D F Robbins averaging 588 mph in a Scimitar in June 1958.

Records involving altitude were the parachute drop by Sqn Ldr John Thirtle with four Parachute Jumping Instructors on 16 June 1967 fom 41,380 ft, falling freely for 39,180 ft from a Hercules captained by Sqn Ldr B J (Bernie) Noble. Thirtle was awarded the AFC for this feat. In January 1971, the climb of a Harrier took 2 min 22 sec to reach 45,000 ft flown by Sqn Ldr Tom Lecky-Thompson, establishing a record for jet-lift aircraft. It could have gone higher but the pilot needed extra oxygen equipment. Rolls Royce, the engine manufacturer, was horrified to learn that the higher temperatures normally available on take off with water injection had been used to coax a little more thrust from the Pagasus in the climb—but without the water. No damage was found.

Records for carrier flying included the first landings on board by a swept wing aircraft, a Swift (Supermarine

Type 510), on 8 November 1950; Lt Cdr D G Parker of C Squadron made several landings that day—but probably not the first. A few days later disaster was narrowly averted when only one (of two) rockets fired on take off, and the aircraft struck the ship's gun turret but remained controllable. On 24 May 1950 Lt Cdr J S Bailey made his 2,000 th deck landing; he went on to complete 2,282 such landings before being killed in a road accident.

In 1954, C Squadron won the Boyd Trophy for the greatest contribution to flight safety by a naval flying unit. The Squadron had given the eponymous Admiral Boyd his first jet flight in 1945 in a Meteor with a small seat behind the pilot in place of the ammunition.

Posing as front line squadron pilots flying standard aircraft, Sqn Ldrs Graham Williams and Tom Lecky-Thompson of A Squadron raced in Harriers from New York to London, and London to New York respectively in 1969. Among notable achievements Lecky-Thompson won the East-to-West race, and the London take off was the first by a jet from a city centre.

Each year a small number of awards of the Air Force Cross were made to test pilots, including naval aviators such as Cdr L G (George) Locke in 1971. Exceptionally, awards of a second (bar) AFC were made to Wg Cdr I H (Ian) Keppie (his first was at Bedford) in January 1972 and Wg Cdr E D (Ned) Frith in January 1973. Sqn Ldr P D (Peter) Thorne received a second bar to add to the two AFCs previously won in the RAF. The hazardous nature of the work of the parachutists was marked with awards of the Air Force Medal to Sgt P Keane in 1971, and to Flt Sgt P J Quinney the following year.

Perhaps the most notable record between 1945 and 1975 and made from Boscombe was achieved by the Fairey Company which flew the FD2 from the airfield; their pilot Peter Twiss made the necessary pair of runs to establish an absolute world air speed record of 1,132 mph on 10 March 1956, landing with insufficient fuel for an overshoot and a further approach. The aircraft used, WG774, was undergoing servicing when the press arrived some days later, and the other, complete, aircraft hastily had its fuselage number changed to that of the record breaker for the cameras.

40: *Lt J R F Overbury of C Squadron poses in July 1954 having flown a Sea Hawk in record time (23min 39.7sec) from London (Bovingdon) to Amsterdam.*

41: *Harrier pilots for the Daily Mail TransAtlantic Air Race in May 1969. Sqn Ldr G C (Graham) Williams (left) flew New York to London, while Sqn Ldr T L (Tom) Lecky-Thompson won the prize for the fastest time from London to New York. Flying clothing makes an interesting comparison with 17 years earlier; see photo 18.*

THE ASSESSMENT DIVISIONS AND SECTIONS

The management of trials fell to the Assessment Divisions and Sections, while the flying and servicing of the aircraft remained as support functions undertaken by Flying and, later, Technical Services Divisions respectively. Engineering had joined the long established Performance and Armament Divisions in 1944, and the work of AAEE became ever more diverse throughout the 30 years from 1945. Sections for radio and radar, for navigation and photography became increasingly important and were raised to Divisional status. From Beaulieu in 1950 came helicopters, aerial delivery and target towing to be added to the Establishment's repertoire. Co-ordination of the disparate but coincident trials on the more complex types became the responsibility of Trials Management (initially Weapon Systems) Division. An intersting example of the distinction made between "Assessment" and "non-Assessment" Divisions concerns the report by Sqn Ldr R

42: A posed loading of a 500lb bomb under the wing of Brigand B.1 RH798 in 1947/8. © Crown Copyright

H (Roger) Beazley, a pilot of A Squadron, who appraised the American F-15 Eagle in October 1975. Because he was in Flying, a support, Division, his report could leave the AAEE (and then after an eight month delay) only after being paraphrased by Mr G Langton who had no part in the actual flying during the assessment.

Most of the work of the Assessment Divisions and Sections is described in Chapters four to ten ; this chapter outlines the organisational changes, some of the people involved and the more important and interesting events.

Performance Division

In 1945, Performance (a term embracing stability and control in addition to pure performance) Division had some 38 trials officers and 51 assistants manning sections for each of the flying squadrons, and for engines, methods and research. The Superintendent, Mr S Scott-Hall, had two deputies, the Senior Performance Technical Officer, known familiarly as "Spito", and the Senior Handling Technical Officer, who was also known familiarly. With the creation of the post for running external trials (ETCO), the duties of the two deputies were combined into the Senior Aircraft Technical Officer; Mr H J (John) Allwright became the first incumbent. The importance of these posts lay not only in determining policy for testing, but also in ensuring consistency in the opinions expressed in reports on behalf of the Establishment. Newcomers sometimes found this hierarchy a little bureaucratic. Peacetime atrophy reduced the fighter Section (A Per²) to two trials officers in January 1946. By the time that the many new types with their attendant problems appeared from about 1950 there had been a small increase in professional trials officers, but the greatly increased volume of work threatened to swamp the inadequate staff, particularly in this Division. The staff gradually expanded and, in common with Engineering Division, the number of trials sections maintained parity with the flying squadrons, ie up to five in the late1960s.

Limitations

Among the Division's responsibilities was the promulgation of aircraft limitations, eg speed and acceleration—"g", for all trials, and as a general rule AAEE flew figures just below the aircraft's maximums (typically 95% of design speed which the manufacturer should have demonstrated). The Establishment then recommended lower limits for the Services, partially to allow for inadvertent overstepping the mark in, say, combat. The subject and its philosophy are extensive, but two examples of exceptions are the Vulcan and Phantom. The Vulcan was restricted to 350 kt at low level (250 kt for training), a figure consistent with the general rule; Bomber Command then required the highest speed for wartime operations and, after trials, the AAEE recommended clearance to 417 kt—the design maximum (V_D) for a once only dash to the target. The Phantom was intended to enter British service with the same limitations as the American version, adjusted as necessary for the Spey engine. AAEE was involved in the philosophical discussion as to the merits of the American system of clearing military aircraft to the absolute maximum attainable and permitting the Service to set its own limits. However, as AAEE trials of the type were limited to systems, the opportunity of recommending alternative limitations did not arise.

Modus Operandi

The business of the Division was dominated by work undertaken on behalf of the Aircraft Project Offices in the Ministry for the evaluation of new types and their modifications; there was also work on methods of performance measurement, formulation of standards of flying qualities and related topics. This latter activity was initially on behalf of the Directorate of Research, but gradually reduced in scope to collating information on phenomena as they occurred in routine clearance testing. Nevertheless, among the Research Section's work in 1946 was a comparison with American test methods which were similar to AAEE's, but in the USA firms did more of the testing. A heartfelt comment was that the scale of testing and the resources over there were vast—how much more was the gap to widen over the following decades! The Section's work included an investigation into the effects of compressibility on a Spitfire in rectilinear flight (no less) which showed that the zero lift angle of attack changed by $1/2°$ between sea level and 40,000ft. Jet climbing techniques were changed to take account of the energy height concept and times to height reduced by 10% thereby. Over a longer timescale was the investigation of calibration of pressure instruments at high altitude. Acceptable ($\pm$3mph) results could be achieved using a ground radar (AA No3 Mk7 sited on the airfield), but the large number of runs required for accuracy rendered this method impractical at first, and progress had been delayed in May 1946 when the Army removed its radar servicing team at short notice. By 1949 the use of radio communication to keep the aircraft on track improved the situation, and the method was used as a routine until 1952. In that year a calibrated Meteor pacer gave $\pm1^{1}/_2$ knots accuracy when tried at both high and low levels. Formation became the method adopted, later using a Venom and then a succession of Javelins and latterly a Phantom. The second Javelin gave an accuracy of $\pm$ 10ft at 10,000ft altitude and $\pm$50ft at 50,000ft; the third Javelin with a trailing static cone achieved $\pm$15ft accuracy up to 515 kt and 50,000ft.

Other performance work of a research nature included the great simplification of take off analysis with the advent of a concrete runway enabling a fixed position for the camera to be established. The F47 camera was replaced by an Eclair type in 1960. Large constant speed propellers of the turbojet engines (turbo props) gave poor power response to throttle movement at first; then, in 1950, a new controller gave very good results in tests of the Python of a Wyvern. Further refinement incorporated automatic limitation of the engine temperature although tighter control was needed in 1953 tests. Theoretical study of the means of reducing the amount of performance flying indicated that precise knowledge of engine thrust was needed; unfortunately, the trial of a pitot rake in the exhausts of a Meteor and a Venom proved insufficiently accurate at first. The topics for more fundamental research concerned performance reduction methods for turboprop types, the essential requirements of powered flying controls including feel and artificial stability, recommendations for the type and presentation to the pilot of warnings of malfunctions, and, later, development of the drag index concept for the wide range of external weapons on attack aircraft. The study of improving the amount and accuracy of data gathering and reduction methods were continuing tasks; for fixed wing aircraft the work was relatively straightforward—the advent of rotating wings in 1950 opened a new era of complexity.

Surviving research reports after 1950 are dominated by helicopter problems and their solution—from twin engines to stability, deck flying and definition of an unsafe flying zone (height/speed). In 1951 it was found that much information could be gleaned from two steady auto-rotative descents. The tandem Bristol 173 helicopter with a V-tail and three-blade rotor gave many months of fascinating work from which it was concluded that it had static and dynamic instability about all three axes; vibration and heavy controls added to the interest. Later work, including an H-tail and four blade rotor and power controls of the development, named Belvedere, made handling acceptable. The pioneering flying of helicopters was done by test pilots rapidly converted from fixed wing flying, while the more significant work of defining the criteria by which helicopters could be judged (having been developed over many years for conventional aeroplanes) fell to the scientific staff. Attention turned to more advanced problems of auto-hovering, and assessment of new instuments, such as an artificial horizon catering for the large pitch changes inherent in rotary wing flying.

Mr J Poole (Superintendent of Performance) reviewed in 1963 the helicopter work to date, including the introduction of turbine engines, rotor governors, autostabilisers and autopilots. The Establishment developed methods of testing these innovations. Performance measurements fell into five categories: power required at various speeds, partial climbs, ceiling climbs, range flights and vertical climbs. Stability proved difficult to assess, although experienced pilots made valuable judgments on acceptability of handling. Autopilot development was rapid—and the Mk 19 version[1] for the Wessex was a considerable advance—and together with the Mark 3 Flight Control System became a standard against which others were judged.

Meanwhile, for fixed wing machines, the advances in control and handling were eagerly adopted and equally eagerly tested at AAEE. It is surprising, however, that the transonic British fighters were presented for tests with features such as manual controls and fixed tailplanes some years after the Establishment had flown the F-86 Sabre which demonstrated the advantages of powered controls and other benefits. The results had been widely reported. After the peak of fighter work came the V-bombers offering a vast increase in performance, complexity and weapon capability. The aspects investigated by Performance Division revealed numerous shortcomings including aileron flutter in the Valiant, fuel "slosh" in all three types, and the need for artificial stability aids in the Victor and Vulcan. It is interesting that the Vulcan handling was considered poor at the prototype stage while the production aircraft had the benefit of stability aids from the first and thus considered acceptable, whereas the Victor preview on the prototype led to only minor criticisms while the first production aircraft revealed the need for radical improvement in handling. AAEE suggested to Handley Page that they should fit a Mach-trimmer similar to that already in the Vulcan; Avro's people were, for some reason, unhappy about this use of the device by a rival firm. Considering the advances represented by the V-bombers, it is surprising how limited was the time allocated by Headquarters to the previews, and AAEE found itself, as so often, having to work under extreme time pressure. The term "preview" was coined at about the time of the early V-Bomber flying. Previews became an integral part of the testing process, and were made by AAEE as early as possible in the programme of new types to assess, in particular, handling to discover any bad traits. New or improved features frequently received individual previews. Another task given to the Establishment was a consequence of the well publicised fatal accident to a Vulcan at Heathrow in 1956. Every British military aircraft type had a height limitation imposed, below which it was not permitted to continue a "blind" approach; the limitations were the result of work on every type by Performance Division.

Once established in service, the V-bombers continued to make demands on Performance Division as tactics changed and the roles multiplied.

In the mid-1960s automatic landing for V-Bombers and their supporting transports required considerable testing and much theoretical analysis. One problem was the undulating nature of Boscombe's main runway which made meaningful measurements very difficult, although the full leader cable and other equipment was installed; Bedford's flat and smooth runway was used. Early work involved the practical, including a para-visual display in the cockpit of a Meteor, and the theoretical, eg determination of acceptable tolerances of every component for a successful automatic landing; all aspects involved considerable discussion of the methods to be used for assessment. Actual landings of Argosies, Belfasts and Vulcans were made before the original scheme was abandoned in 1966. By this date vertical flight by the P1127/Kestrel/ Harrier also provided a great deal of food for thought, much of it devoted to the methods of clearing for service the jet-borne and partially jet-borne regimes of flight. One early conclusion was that for short landings, control of the approach was obtained more easily by the use of nozzle angle than by throttle adjustments.

One rather clandestine event in 1956 involved a party from Performance Division travelling to Heathrow to observe the landing and take off distance of the first visit by a Soviet Tu104; figures were obtained, but as the team had no knowledge of the techniques employed, the usefulness of the exercise was very questionable. It provides, however, a good example of the effort needed to learn about the "other side" in the cold war years.

Deck trials of naval aircraft evolved considerably between 1945 and 1975, but always needed a Performance Division trials officer (boffin). In the early days of free take offs (albeit often with rocket assistance)

---

[1] Most earlier marks related to fixed wing autopilots

the trials officer had merely to supervise preparation of the aeroplane, and note the factors affecting take offs and landings. The ship's routine was firmly in the hands of the sailors, but steam catapults, mirror landing aids and aeroplanes with very critical performance changed the emphasis. It became vital to the success of the trial that the "boffin" should control all aspects of the operation. This realisation followed the sea trials of the first naval Sea Vixen (which could not fold its wings) and the first Scimitar (which could not be catapulted) in 1956 when difficulties arose on board *HMS Ark Royal*, partly due to the setting of the mirror landing device. Whoever actually conducted flying trials on board, deck suitability trials of new naval aircraft were invariably given priority. Sufficient low speed handling and take off measurements were made to establish the feasibility of deck operations—not to mention giving the pilots a little practice for the thrills to come. These arrangements meant that any shortcomings at higher speeds and altitudes remained to be discovered after deck trials—however successful these may have been—the two designs for the N 17/45 by Fairey (later, Gannet) and Blackburn both needed considerable development after initial carrier work.

Civil Aircraft Testing Section (CATS)

Treatment of this Section here is longer than its activities warrant as a result of the lack of surviving reports of its work; there is little of CATS in later chapters of this book.

From 1943, the Brabazon Committee examined civil aviation in the UK post war including a forecast of classes of new passenger aircraft that would be required. Meanwhile, at Boscombe Down, complementary work started in 1944 when the Research Section (Messrs K J Lush and A K Weaver) considered modern operating and performance standards, and their application to passenger carrying operations. In early 1945, a Civil Aircraft Testing Section formed under Mr D (Donald) Fraser, charged, inter alia, with testing the civil aircraft ordered by the Government (the Brabazon types) to check compliance with specifications. The Section also played a major part in representing the United Kingdom at early ICAO[2] meetings. With statistical assistance from the Research Section, standards were established and the results played a major part in the formulation of ICAO documentation against which all types could be evaluated, and more immediately formed the basis of much of British Civil Airworthiness Requirements.

In July 1945 one aeroplane, a Fortress flown and serviced by B Squadron, started civil performance work, concentrating on the effects of engine failure at all stages of flight with a view to defining the safest repeatable techniques. Take off posed the most interesting phase of activity, and attracted the greatest attention. The Fortress,

with four engines and ample rudder control proved benign in its response to engine cuts, and was replaced by a twin engine Dakota. A Liberator proved useful in tests of emergency stopping on the runway. From these early trials came the concepts of gross and nett performance and the categorising of types by their ability to cope with failure of a power plant at any stage. Work continued throughout 1946, the year in which the first new types ordered by the Government appeared. The Avro Tudor Mark 1 came in April, followed by the Mark 2 in July, the Bristol Freighter and Miles Marathon in August and September respectively. Handling certification on behalf of the Air Registration Board of the Marathon was completed by January 1947, but trials continued on performance aspects. Other work included compilation of the civil Flight Test Handbook which made slow progress and appears not to have survived.

In January 1947, the status of CATS was raised to include its own aircrew and maintenance people, and headed by the Senior Civil Aircraft Technical Officer (SCATO), Mr J C K Shipp, who enjoyed equal status with his counterparts for performance and handling. Within Flying Division the arrival of Group Captain H A (Bruin) Purvis (retired and a wartime Superintendent of Flying) as Chief Civil Test Pilot, was shortly followed by Mr W (Doc) Stewart. Lettice Curtiss, who had achieved distinction during the war as a ferry pilot, was most disappointed in being refused a flying job at Boscombe, and accepted a post in the Technical Office. Civilian flight engineers, radio operators and a navigator joined in 1948, and aircrew from B Squadron continued to fly with CATS. The maintenance element, formed in October 1946, was rapidly recruited from mainly ex-service tradesmen; much later it provided the nucleus from which the civilian servicing sections were formed when civilianisation began in 1957. The first test flight took place on 1 January 1947 when Bruin Purvis flew a Bristol Freighter on carbon monoxide contamination measurement, the first of many such sorties on a variety of aircraft. He also flew his final sortie in an ex-CATS Comet in July 1963. After 13 years in the post, and 36 years of aviating, he became in 1960 only the second recipient of the Award of Merit of the Guild of Air Pilots and Navigators. He retired again in 1963 after a career ranging from the Avro 504 to the Swift. His only recorded "black mark" in CATS was in 1949 when the brakes failed on an Ambassador and two Tiger Moths were written off; he was held partially to blame for taxying too fast.

The 1944 decision to involve AAEE again in civil testing was logical—flying for Certifiates of Airworthiness (C of As) had been done pre-war, the Establishment had expertise on the latest performance and handling techniques, the Air Registration Board had been reduced in wartime to a small licence granting body, and AAEE had good relations with industry. However, while CATS expanded to discharge its reponsibilities, other forces were at work to remove civil aircraft testing from Boscombe.

---

[2] *The International Civil Aviation Organisation (ICAO)*

The earliest friction arose in 1945 from having two authorities for approval of civil machines—the Ministry (advised by AAEE) for the "Brabazon" types and the Air Registration Board for aircraft requiring C of As; each authority issued its own technical requirements,[3] and manufacturers were faced with two sets of standards, of which the Ministry's were the more stringent. The differences were gradually resolved—but not before causing an adverse effect on the first post-war British airliners. The two airline corporations had their own development units, and CATS worked periodically with BOAC's[4] Unit at Hurn, Bournemouth; BEAC[4], on the other hand formally asked for AAEE not to test its aeroplanes. One of the first and unfavourable reports by CATS concerned the Tudor. The maker, Avro, complained bitterly that the damning report had been sent to the Corporations—this despite the distribution being normal practice as directed by the Ministry.

The ARB position was that the contractors should do as much testing as possible, noting that many had airfield and other facilities below requirements. Within CATS another source of friction had been created because new types on test had their firm's servicing party, leaving the local team to look after only old and well known types. With these influences in play and ARB's increasing ability to undertake all CofA work, CATS role started to change in 1948 to the extent that by the end of the year the work in prospect appeared scant—with no plans for testing of the new turbine engine types. In 1950, insult was added to injury when CATS was acused of using military methods in assessing radios and navigation equipment for civil application. SCATO was moved to write, "All [at AAEE] ... are to bear in mind the peculiar susceptibilities of the [civil authorities and Corporations] who are so apt to disagree among themselves and to take advantage of any discordant signs elsewhere." By the end of 1951, following the refusal of BOAC to let AAEE test the Comet coupled with the improvements in contractors' airfields, the role of CATS changed to that of undertaking trials which had no natural home in a Squadron.

Among the more interesting trials flown by CATS were those for the Research section. In 1947, following a series of accidents to civil Dakotas and a plea for help from the ARB, a trial in three African locations concluded that the accident airfields had been unsuitable. At maximum weight, climb was reduced to a mere 340ft/min in the tropics, and with full flap a climb was impossible; height could not be maintained following failure of one engine. Another investigation concerned the causes of the significantly lower performanance of the Wayfarer following engine stoppage by fuel cut off when compared to rapid throttling. For three years from 1952, Mr G C Abel led a team on research into icing

using a suitably equipped Viking. The first requirement was for real icing—and the local meteorological forecasters proved adept. Test techniques were developed, and included the difficult measurement of the size of super cooled water droplets. The results contributed to an increased understanding of icing and thus to airline safety.

The many thousands of flying hours, in the main routine, produced their fair share of thought provoking moments, but there was only one fatality in the five years of CATS's original role. The prototype Marathon had adjustable fins. On 28 May 1948 the pilot, Flt Lt Brian Bastable had set the fins on take off to the correct position to assist handling in the event of a failure of an outboard engine; for cruising and higher speeds the fins were designed to be reset to avoid over stressing. The aircraft crashed killing the pilot and Miss Beryl Edmunds (Flight Test Observer); the fins were found to be at the take off setting.

In June 1951 the last airliner, a Hermes 5, finished its tests, although two Ashtons and the Nene-Viking were assessed later. CATS kept its name and became a unit for navigation and radio trials flying, with the DECCA navigation system as a major trial. Government-owned civil aircraft required no further testing, and, in any case, the Air Registration Board had become capable of doing all the work on civil machines. In 1960 the unit became Support Flight of Support Squadron.

Armament Division

Internal Organisation

The Division was headed by an RAF group captain throughout the 30 years to 1975, and the trials officers were almost exclusively RAF with a few from the Navy; however, civilians took over much of the armament servicing by the mid-1960s. The internal organisation remained for some years in its wartime form when the three sections for tests of bombs, guns and rockets were supplemented by the Armament Drawing Office, the Armament Research Section[5] and the station armoury. The first organisational change involved removal of gun development to RAE Farnborough in August 1950, leaving the Gunnery Section with five civilians and two servicemen; the Division then had 10 aircraft under test. Four years later, there were 12 under assessment plus 9 expected in the immediate future. This doubling of commitments, in particular the anticipated volume of clearance work for the forthcoming V-bombers led to a strong plea for more staff. Since the Division was manned by both servicemen and civilians, the case for an increase had to be made in two parts. That for the civilians is dated November 1954, and proposed an increase in

---

[3] The Ministry issued the first Civil Aircraft Design Memorandum on 28 Mar 1945.
[4] British Overseas Airways Corporation and British European Airways Corporation

[5] Armament Research and Development Section until 4 Mar 1946

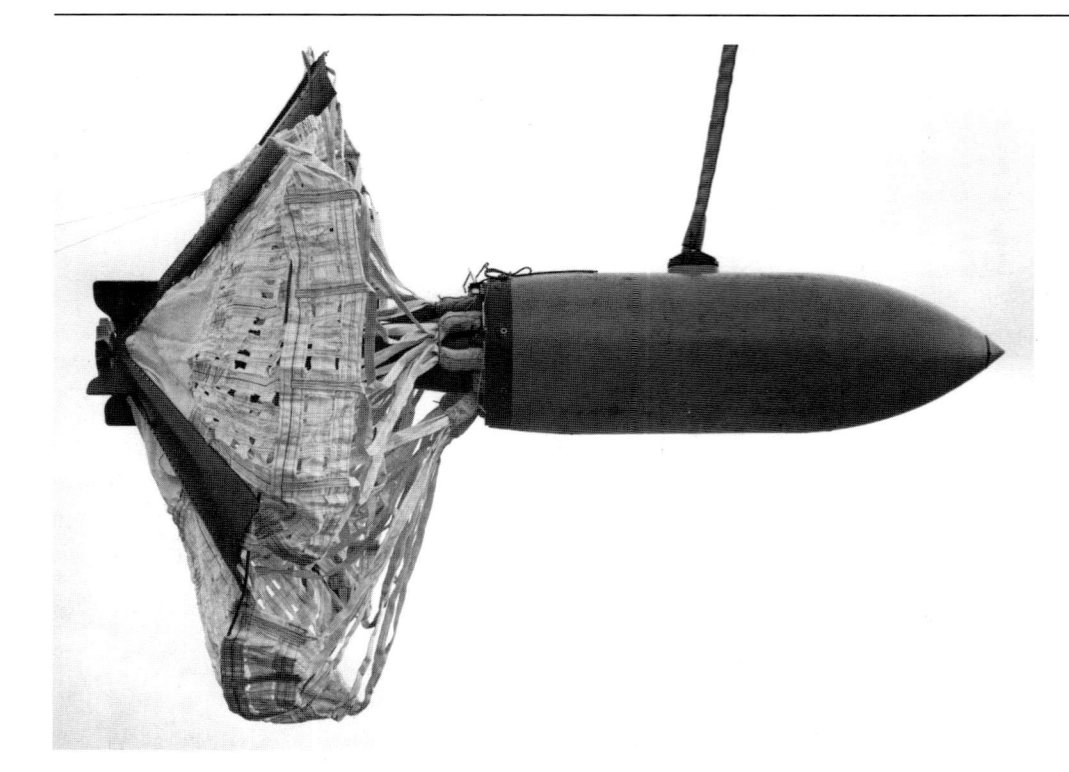

43: *A 1,000lb bomb with retarding parachute partially deployed in July 1967. © Crown Copyright*

44: *Sea Vixen FAW.1 jettisons a Bullpup missile cleanly from the port outer pylon in 1962. © Crown Copyright*

45: *Canberra B.15 WH967, jettisoning the starboard AS30 missile. © Crown Copyright*

46: Vulcan B.1A, XH478 doing 350 kt in 1968 dropping 1,000lb bombs (two retarded, one ballistic with 0.3sec spacing) at Larkhill; this aircraft, at the end of its life made trials to clear weapons for the Mk 2 remaining in service.
© Crown Copyright

47 and 48: A comparison of two bomb trolleys—British (right) and American (below right). Although the British examples had advantages, these were outweighed by the considerably greater virility of the American model.
© Crown Copyright

professional grades (scientific, experimental, engineering and technical) from 17 to no less than 41. As presented the case looked strong, as the Engineering division had 33 such posts, Performance 46 and Airborne Forces 22. Unfortunately, the parallel Service paper has not survived; no doubt the overall picture would show a less compelling case as the service element of the Division predominated—both before and after 1954. Nevertheless, substantial increases took place. In June 1955 a change followed the reduction in rocket projectile work, which by 1957 resulted in Sections for Bombing, Gunnery, Guided Weapons and Armament Test Research. A more fundamental reorganistion led to creation of Strategic Weapons (SW), Nuclear Weapons (NW) and Tactical Weapons (TW) Groups while retaining the Research Section. In September 1965 Gp Capt A H Bullock had Wg Cdr H C Flemons—SW Group, Wg Cdr J B Stonor—T W Group, and Wg Cdr M O Rayner—N W Gp.

The introduction of the Nuclear Weapons Group led to one of many examples of the increasing inter-Divisional co-operation when the safety aspects, so dominant with nuclear armament, resulted in the Division taking over REG—more properly "The Radio Frequency Environment Simulator". Known at its creation in 1962 as "Flight Deck Simulator", it produced a wide spectrum of radio frequencies in close proximity to the aircraft under test next to the stop butts. Armament Division ran REG on behalf of the Establishment, and extended the value of the facility by a lengthy investigation under Dr Byrne and using a Vulcan, to establish the ability to simulate the electro magnetic pulse (EMP) of a nuclear explosion. Appendix 5 lists a typical range of equipment and armament cleared for EMC.

The work of the Division generated 178 formal reports in 1970, falling to under 100 in 1975; this statistic reflects the reduction in trials experienced throughout the Establishment.

Armament Trials.
The work of the Division throughout the 30 year period may be considered in three categories: assessment for service use of the armament installation of every type of aircraft, secondly, evaluation of new weapons and equipment, and, thirdly, research into armament problems together with optimising test methods to obtain the data on which to make judgments. In this work the first and by far the largest category, armament of new aircraft, is treated as an integral part of the type's tests and thus described in Chapters 4 to 10. AAEE's function in this regard was investigation of loading/unloading, safety (that of nuclear weapons in conjunction with the Ordnance Board[6]), carriage, and release of stores; trials of all the possible loads of, for example the Shackleton, were nevertheless extensive and time consuming. The policy,

---
6 The Electrical Explosives Hazards (Nuclear) Sub-Committee

confirmed in 1950, for contractors to clear every store configuration before AAEE's trials was rarely, if ever, implemented in full. Certainly by 1965 new configurations were first flown as a matter of routine by AAEE.

The First Ten Years
Among the early research tasks on guns were instrumented recorders for barrel temperatures, identification of problems in the development of 20mm Hispanos, an "Explosimeter" to measure the concentration of gases in gun bays and, in 1949, an investigation into explosions in the bays of the Meteor and Seafang followed by development of palliatives. Early Meteors and Vampires suffered from directional snaking which affected aiming; an extensive trial with a Tempest for comparison and using gun sight cameras reached an inconclusive end in 1949 due, it was reported, to flying by too great a number of pilots, some of whom were inexperienced. A borrowed F-86 Sabre in 1952 revealed no additional wander as a consequence of its swept wings and powered controls. Other reports from the early 1950s cover topics such as structural stiffness, techniques for measuring recoil and run out of guns, bullet patterns, and methods of assessing the performance of Aden (30mm) guns. Contemporary evaluation of the Gyro Gunsight (GGS) Mk 4E/L for rocket firing showed significant improvement in accuracy. Theoretical studies of bomber evasion were confirmed in mock combats between two Vampires; without a margin of performance, the fighter had a slim chance of success. However, sighting times were considerably reduced if the slower bomber weaved.

In the Gunnery Section, one of the first significant evaluations concerned the HSS 804 and 404 20mm Hispanos for Dutch and Belgian Meteors. After comparative tests in a Vampire the HSS 804 was preferred. An accident occurred during these tests and an armament officer was killed clearing a stoppage. The report remarks, "a feasible method of clearing safely similar stoppages is suggested"—a very sensible suggestion! The HSS 804 then fired 38,178 rounds from Dutch, Belgian and a British Meteor, resulting in the need for only a few minor modifications. Later, an attempt to improve the rate of fire from 30 mm Adens of Hunters and Javelins using a new lubricant proved to be of little benefit. By way of a change, AAEE assessed as satisfactory the twin 20mm gun installation on an Air Sea Rescue launch; no flying was involved.

An interesting and lengthy investigation by J E H (Jack) Braybon of the aircraft attitude and actual flight paths during rocket attacks used a Mosquito; greater accuracy resulted. R Ps of the wartime variety were tested on many aeroplanes and fitted variously on the tips, centre and inboard wing positions, and, on a Meteor, the fuselage. Some 69 rounds of the 180lb-head rocket were successfully fired from Spitfires and a Tempest, but development seems not to have been pursued, probably on account of inaccuracy. Low voltage reaching the rockets of a Neptune caused initial failures; the Establishment developed a voltage detector and cured the problem.

In 1951 a Mark 2 Dive Bombsight in a Vampire produced indifferent results during trials frustrated by lack of range availability. Bomb fuses of various types came under scrutiny, including the Type 721 Mk II* and Mk III, the Type 893 modified for more sensitive graze firing, and, in 1952–4, variable timing (VT) Type 916 for 1,000lb bombs. Bomb trolleys continued to be developed; a trial in 1956 of an American Type MF-5 was favourably reviewed with its ability to raise stores 71 inches compared to the British maximum of 25½ inches.

Armament Division analysed results from the first quarter of 1953 and found that aircraft were unserviceable for 39% of the time, were unavailable for 10%, and the weather unsuitable for 16% of the time. As a result, the six trials on bombers produced 84 sorties in 258 working aircraft/days, and 19 trials on fighters produced 218 sorties in 683 working aircraft/days. The loss of flying due to winter weather was surprisingly low.

The Middle Ten Years
Guided Weapons, justifying their own Section in 1955, featured largely in the activities in Armament Division from the mid-1950s. Evaluations of Blue Jay (Firestreak) included application to the SR53 project in 1957, and firing in cold weather in Canada. Some work on guns and rockets, sights and recorders continued, as well as investigations into methods of assessing rocket accuracy, measuring combustible gases after firing Aden guns and evaluating the guns' special servicing equipment. In 1959 harmonisation of Hunter guns needed repeat attention, while in 1963 a Sea Vixen trial indicated that use of airstream direction (ADD) simplified calculations for weapon sighting.

The Third Ten Years
By the mid-1960s, and with the Radio Environment Generator (REG) fully operational electromagnetic compatability (EMC) became a popular trial (in the year to June 1975 some 59 EMC appraisals were made)—including investigation of the wide range of loads on the Naval Buccaneer and Sea Vixen, the compatibility of the Victor tanker with its many receivers, the smoke screen equipment on a Wessex, target equipment on the Canberra tug, and nuclear safety on several types of bomb and aircraft—among them the Wessex carrying the Bomb HE 600lb MC (WE177). The value of EMC testing had been demonstrated in 1966 when it was found that identified radio pulses could activate a fuse and arm the weapon in flight; over a year later the fuse, suitably modified, passed its test. Bombs, flares, missiles and guns remained the stock-in-trade of the Division, the work broadening to encompass the evaluation of crew procedures for dropping nuclear weapons. On the Buccaneer, for example, 16 separate actions by the crew, 10 by the pilot, six by the observer, were needed to release a live weapon; the investigation included the effect and significance of single failures of all parts of the equipment. Other work included conventional bombs with modifications to retard their flight after release at low level and high speed; many trials ensued on several aircraft, including the Vulcan, and encompassed tests of the associated practice bombs. A trial of a different nature took place in 1968 for the CDEE[7] at Porton: a spray system comprising a rig under the fuselage and a tank with controls in the fuselage was flown to simulate a chemical attack for training troops. The device was successfully flown under the Wasp, Wessex and Pembroke; attempts to use the Pembroke as an icing tanker proved of limited value. At the end of the period under review, nearly all work continued to be at the behest of the Director of Air Armament in Headquarters, the majority on CA Release including the Harrier (MATRA rockets and VT fusing of bombs), Nimrod (various sonobuoys), Jaguar (Various 1,000lb bombs, flares and gunnery), Buccaneer (BL755 and Martel), Phantom (XJ521 air-to-air missile and gun accuracy for air-to-air use) were underway at the end of the year—together with helicopter clearances on the Wasp, Wessex, Sea King and Lynx (MK44 and Mk 46 torpedoes and depth charges). Weapon assessments were also in hand, some with the Ordnance Board, and EMC of many types of aircraft continued.

Weapon ranges
The large range at Ashley Walk in the New Forest closed in 1946 and, after removal of debris and some restoration, handed back to the Verderers in 1948. Crichel Down was closed shortly after 1945, and approval of the area West of Boscombe for gun firing lapsed with the cessation of hostilities. Thus, of the wartime ranges, only Lyme Bay and Porton remained; both continued in use, the former assuming an ever-increasing importance as the Establishment's primary range, while the height and other retrictions remained limiting factors on the use of Porton. The AAEE area of Lyme Bay was small, but use of a larger area could usually be agreed with the Navy. Even so, high level and high speed required great care to ensure that bullets and spent cartridges fell in the prescribed areas. Inevitably, strays occurred—as on the day that a Hunter's cartridges fell on land, disturbing a gentlemen who told the ensuing Board of Inquiry that he had been seated in the "private outhouse" when he was surprised by a metallic clang on a tin bath hanging opposite, from a cartridge that had fallen through the flimsy roof.

The *ad hoc* arrangements for the use of Enford for rocket firing were soon replaced by more formal agreement for the use of Imber, both on Salisbury Plain. The latter also included bombing and was under the command of an AAEE squadron leader, and shared with the Army and the RAE; it had the advantage of radar

[7] Chemical Defence Experimental Establishment

49: The Australian IKARA M417 unmanned aircraft with a Mk44 torpedo, parachute pack and its Mattina motor in 1969 being subjected to "S" and "X" band radiation by the dishes behind, part of the Radio Environment simulator (REG). © Crown Copyright

50 and 51: A conventional 5,000lb HC bomb ready for loading into Canberra B.2 VX169 (below) which kneels to receive its load from the rear in late 1951. © Crown Copyright

52: Two Triplex (three standard rocket tubes) projectiles under the wing of Sea Mosquito TR.33 TS444 in July 1946. Firing up to 350 kt posed no problems. © Crown Copyright

53: An RP Mk 12 installation on Seahawk FGA.4 WF284 in late 1954. Accuracy was poor at first prior to modifications to the gunsight Mk 4E.

54: Four 4.5in flares, aircraft, reconnaissance 2 Mk 1 under the port wing of Harvard IIB KF183 in August 1953. The aircraft then persued less offensive activities for three decades at AAEE. © Crown Copyright

55: Target Drone U-120D XE725 at Aberporth undergoing autopilot assessment by AAEE in December 1953. © Crown Copyright

56: The Delmar target was the interest in this November 1962 photograph of Meteor TT.20 WD706. The winch (a Delmar DX4) next to the fuselage, the target outboard of the starboard engine and various fittings and safety cables are noteworthy. © Crown Copyright

57: Proof that the life of an AAEE test pilot was varied and arduous! Tiger Moth T7340 was towing Sedburgh TX.1 WB933 over one of the six White Horses North of Boscombe Down in August 1953. © Crown Copyright

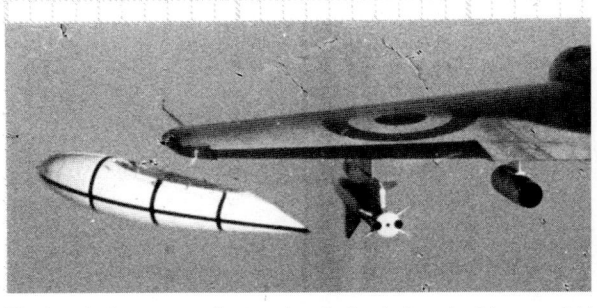

58: A typical sequence of separation during jettison, in this case a 244 gal tip tank from Canberra B15 WH967 at 37,000 ft at 0.77M, armed with AS30 missiles and MATRA rocket pods on 20 Dec 1965.
© *Crown Copyright*

and kinetheodolite coverage by 1952. Increasing use was made of the RAE's range at West Freugh in Scotland.

Engineering Division

Formed in 1944, the small Division grew slowly to make engineering and maintenance appraisals; it also took over some tasks of an engineering nature from Performance Division. On 16 May 1949, Engineering Test Section formed. For many years the Division was lead by Mr F H (Bertie) Beer, also an intrepid but careless pilot.

Blower Tunnel

Built during the war to test flame damping, and powered by Merlin aero engines, the blower tunnel (more accurately a nozzle) received use post war predominantly as a means of testing hood jettison characteristics and crew escape facilities. As can be seen from the accompanying illustrations, the arrangement of each subject fuselage in front of the nozzle involved its own engineering solution, including a method of catching the canopy. The original framework used the two uprights from the rejected Brodie suspension gear. Details of individual types are in Chapters 4 to 10, and at Appendix 3. Three, later four, alternative nozzle sizes could be fitted to give wind speeds of up to 330 kt. An innovation in 1959 was the introduction of water spray to simulate rain; the problem above 180 kt was the breaking up of water droplets on meeting the airflow. Ten years later the use of liquid nitrogen enabled icing conditions to be simulated. The supply of Merlin engines appeared at one time to be drying up, but in the 1970s a source was found in Spain (Merlin 500 series giving 30% more power than the existing motors), and a little later Farnborough's tunnel closed yielding its engines to Boscombe.

The first canopy jettison took place in late 1946 from the single seat Hornet, the test serving also to validate the facility for this work which rapidly expanded as types proliferated. In 1952 the first tests were made using live subjects from a dummy Valiant fuselage from which it was concluded that under favourable conditions the rear crew without ejection seats could escape. However, the Engineering Division was, if anything, more vociferous than the aircrew in condemning over many years the lack of assisted escape facilities in the rear of the V-bombers. The change to low level operations led to further work, but rear crew escape was enhanced only to the extent that their seats swivelled with a complementary boost from the seat cushion. A whoopee cushion really was no substitute for an 82ft/sec/sec ride on a bang seat.

Among other uses, the blower tunnel checked flow patterns behind Smoke Curtain Installations (SCI), the functioning of anti-spin parachutes, the jettison of tanks and missiles, and any equipment needing a good flow of air. Once the icing facility was ready, it was possible to

59: A 5cwt jeep, 75mm howitzer and six CLE III containers are loaded on Hastings C.1 TG500 in 1950 prior to dropping. © Crown Copyright

60: A "shape", ie a dummy Little E nuclear weapon known as "Bomb 1,650lb MC". It was dropped, as were six others, by Canberra B(I).8 WT347 in loft manoeuvres (LABS) in late 1960; this trial cleared the 124° release—known to crews as "over the shoulder". © Crown Copyright

61: The Blue Steel mounted in Vulcan B.2 XH534, showing how the trolley offered up the missile. © Crown Copyright

62 right and 63 below right: *Stages in obviating damage on firing the guns of Meteor F.8 VZ467. Armament Division played a key, developmental, role in the final, successful, modification in May 1950.* © *Crown Copyright*

64: *A 1,000lb bomb with variable timing (V/T) fusing 916 undr the wing of Sea Vixen FAW.1 XJ526 in early 1960. Release characteristics, including operation of the fuse, were acceptable up to 550 kt.* © *Crown Copyright*

55

65: *A typical mixed load in Canberra B.6 WH952 in late 1958, comprising three 1,00lb target indicators and four 4.5in reconnaissance flares.* © Crown Copyright

66: *The prototype Boulton Paul Type "N" gun mounting (sometimes known as the Type "N" turret) in Shackleton MR.2 WG530 in 1953. This last UK aircraft free-gun mouting was unsuccessful at first due to sight vibrations on firing plus excessive CO gas.* © Crown Copyright

obtain some idea of the latest proposal for helicopter anti-icing prior to departure for colder climes.

Air-to-air Refuelling

Aerial refuelling became a major new task for AAEE from the late 1950s, with both the Royal Navy and RAF requiring clearance for their aeroplanes. At AAEE, all assessment divisions made contributions—but Engineering took the lead as their interests predominated. Notes on individual types are in Chapters 4 to 10, and piloting aspects in Chapter 2.

In May 1957, two Valiants arrived at Boscombe for Vickers trials, but including AAEE pilot participation. In November 1960 the benefits of co-operating with the USAF led to exercise Floodtide involving a USAF KB-50 tanker and Valiant and Vulcan receivers, and then a Valiant tanker and three American receivers—B-66B, F-100F and F-101A. The American aircraft were adapted for the British probe and drogue technique using the current Mark 8 equipment; the contacts were at 28,000ft by day and night, and made between 230 and 250 kt. From these and national trials over many years Engineering Division made a great contribution to the integrity, practicality and safety of the system. The types of British service aircraft involved in AAEE refuelling up to and including 1975 are noted below.[8]

Environmental Hangar

In mid-1968, the Environmental test Hangar came into use, and immediately justified its existence in the savings in the cost of some tropical trials which were not needed. For example, in 1973 the first Bulldog spent a month inside and was, as a result cleared for operations in ambient temperatures up to 35°C; Ethiopian Canberras and Saudi Arabian Strikemasters were similarly examined for their manufacturer. The hangar had a floor area of 9,500 square feet, a height of 18 feet, and could maintain a temperature 75°C above ambient, while increasing humidity to 100% up to 35°C.

Aircrew Equipment Assemblies

Staff from MAEE, including Mr Vince Drake, formed a nucleus of the Section and introduced the decompression chamber (given an explosive decompression facility in 1959) and water tank for training and testing sea survival equipment. The first task of the Section in the mid-1950s was to ensure that the correct high level oxygen equipment was available for AAEE's own test flying; this naturally led to assessments of the kit, and very soon to consideration of the escape facilities of new aircraft. Thus the advent of ejection seats, high altitude oxygen eqipment and, later, anti gas masks were subject to the appraisal of this section prior to entry into service. By 1963, known as the "Parachute and AEA

[8] Tankers: Argosy, Buccaneer, Scimitar, Sea Vixen, Valiant, Victor Marks 1 and 2; Receivers: Argosy, Belfast, Buccaneer, Canberra, Harrier, Jaguar, Javelin, Lightning, Phantom, Scimitar, Sea Vixen, VC-10, Valiant, Victor and Vulcan.

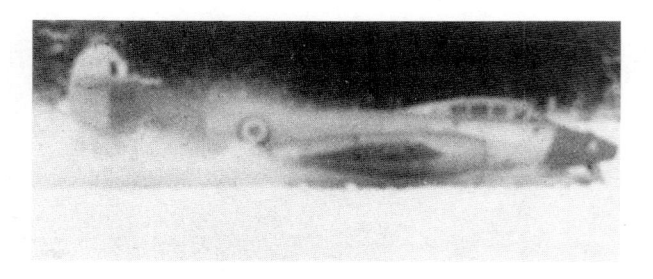

67: Meteor T.7 WA690 passing through (from top): natural slush, water (nose wheel), water (main wheel) and synthetic slush—all at 60 kt ground speed, between 1962 and 1965. The synthetic slush involved copious use of Polycell mixed in a cement mixer. The camera windows on the nose and the explosive warning triangles are unusual; the aircraft was also used briefly for ejection seat trials. © Crown Copyright

Test Facility at AAEE," it had five dedicated aircraft—an Argosy, Beverley, Canberra, Meteor and Valetta, plus chase aircraft, dummies and use of the blower tunnel.

A major task in the 1950s involved assessment of the new P-type oxygen mask, finally cleared in April 1958, and later the ML and the Taylor partial pressure helmets; the Taylor helmet was marginally preferred, but both had poor radio quality, donning was laborious, the Taylor tended to blow oxygen into the eyes, while for some aircrew the mouth opening aligned with the nose. It was felt that with very careful fitting and improved ventilation, Canerra PR.9 crews would find them acceptable. Pressure helmets met fierce resistance later in service on account of their discomfort and limitation of view. A Meteor was modified with limited success for ejection seat firing from the back; it was soon replaced by a Canberra with the ability to fire two seats from the rear. By the end of 1972,

68: *Hornet F.1 PX 218 in the Blower Tunnel in 1946, the first of many aircraft to blow their tops in the name of flight safety.* © *Crown Copyright*

69 left and 70 below left: *Two 1949 versions of flame damping for the Firefly AS Mk 5 VT477. Probably the last flame damping trial at AAEE.* © *Crown Copyright*

71: Short SB.5 WG768 undergoing canopy jettison tests in the blower tunnel, minor modifications were recommended. © Crown Copyright

72: French Ouragon 105 ready for canopy jettison trials in the Blower Tunnel in December 1950; separation was exceptionally clean. © Crown Copyright

73: A Rushton target stowed on a winchpack containing eight miles of cable on Canberra TT.18 WJ632 in 1968. © Crown Copyright

74: *Halifax C VI LV838 in the penultimate appearance of the type at AAEE in October 1945; the fan inside the cowling gave significant cooling when combined with opened gills, but at a penalty of 13mph in speed. © Crown Copyright*

75: *An early application of a roller conveyor, seen here inside Hastings TG500 with the wind baffle for aerial delivery. On the ground, a wary eye was needed on the motion of the store being loaded onto the sloping floor. © Crown Copyright*

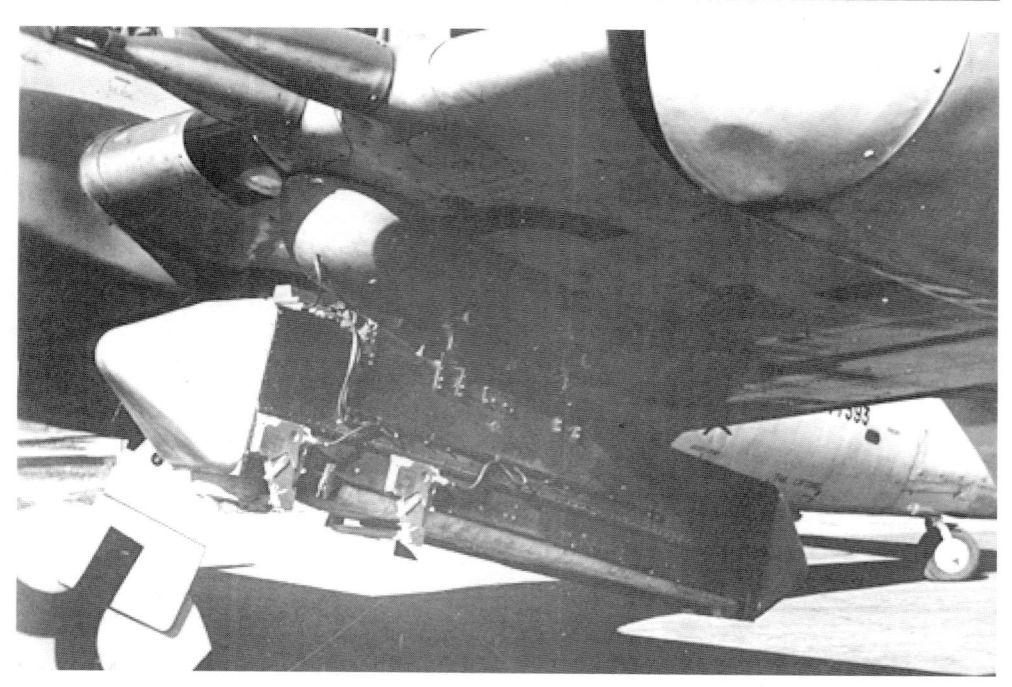

76: *Many types of aircraft were cleared for carriage and release of Air Sea Rescue gear Type G, shown here in May 1949 mounted on Firefly Mk 5 VT393. © Crown Copyright*

the Canberra had made over 200 firings, nearly all over the Larkhill range. To assist pilots finding the required track to fly on the range, some large "unmissable" dayglo boards had been erected; unfortunately, boards for other purposes were also "unmissable" and to avoid confusion smoke flares were lit on the correct boards. Needless to say, the flares had a habit of burning out just before they were of use. Of such frustrations were many trials made. In 1972, 20 surplus Mark 3J ejection seats were acquired and used as required; an incidental finding from a series of trials with them was the inadequacy of much flying clothing for ejection at high speed.

Aeromedical and Survival Training School

The advent of special oxygen equipment for very high level flying resulted in AAEE aircrew visiting the Institute of Aviation Medicine (IAM) at Farnborough for fitting. Local facilities were soon created at Boscombe by Mr R (Bob) Gigg on arrival from MAEE in 1956, and the ASTS grew to give training to all flight test aircrew in industry and the Establishments and who flew with oxygen or ejection seats. By 1975, several hundred people had been trained in the joys of anoxia, being dragged by a parachute harness and dinghy drill with one hand tied up.

Towed Target Section

This Section under Sgt Don Betts came from Beaulieu with a Mosquito and a Tempest with the job of testing new towed targets and providing targets for Armament Division; assessing the towing capabilities of new aeroplanes came a little later under Mr Don Evans. Firms involved in target manufacture initially had no aircraft of their own and it fell to the Section to undertake development trials—using several aircraft including a dedicated Meteor and then a Canberra.

The types of target were banner (or flag), sleeve, winged and reflective. Development and use of the various banner targets continued throughout the 30 year period; sleeves, of small size when packed, received a small fillip when AAEE developed a target exchange system for use in flight, and winged targets of four types attempted to meet an RAF requirement but were too fragile and difficult to operate when tested between 1951 and 1953. The reflective type developed into a sophisticated device, towed up to eight miles behind the tug. The Section tested, and made improvements to, the various winches (up to Type H), a miss distance indicator, and particularly to the Dart Mark 3 target; a snatch pick up technique was refined and frequently demonstrated by a Canberra.

Among trials were snatch pick up of the Mark II target by a Sea Hawk and a Scimitar; later a Canberra towed an American Trident model. The Flight Refuelling company (FRL) gradually predominated in the target business, making among others, the Delmar winch and special target tested on a Meteor. FRL received its own Canberras and the Section's development work reduced dramatically. The Canberra in its RAF target towing role had the ability to stream 40,000ft of cable and needed approval for Service use; the behaviour of the Rushton target at the far end needed observing and chasing was a most demanding task.

Airborne Experiments Division (Airborne and Helicopter Division from 1 October 1955)

From September 1950 the helicopters, airborne forces and target towing remained organised much as at Beaulieu before the move to Boscombe. The Division had its own flying unit—D Squadron—and in December 1951 had 21 aircraft (the peak for the Division) of which eight were helicopters, five were for airborne forces (described below) and the remainder on target towing. The Division disbanded on 1 September 1961; the engineering aspects of helicopters under Mr W A Hibbert transferred to Engineering Division and the remainder to Performance under Mr J Poole.

Airborne Forces

The work in the quarter century 1950–75 was almost entirely concerned with parachute delivery of people or stores. Apart from a single successful attempt to snatch a Horsa glider with a Valetta, normal clearance for service of the Valetta and Hastings attracted most early attention and details are in Chapter 7.

The interruption to trials caused by the move from Beaulieu appears to have been minimal—at least reporting continued without a break. Included were research subjects such as measurement of the forces exerted on both human and inanimate objects by the opening of parachutes, but most work concentrated on the practical problems of loading and dropping stores and minimising the risks and delays of troops leaving aircraft. A new life saving jacket and new parachutes for troops (Back Type B5 MkII in 1951 and later a Type R), all needed minor modifications. Two years work was needed to achieve a satisfactory reserve parachute. A new Valise was cleared for dropping from the Valetta, Dakota and Hastings, while other developments included the dropping of increased weights of stores (ie, bigger wicker baskets) from inside, and vehicles from outside the aeroplane. Work on many specialist loads, parachutes and techniques continued into the 1960s and 1970s; on the aircraft roller matting floors proved a great boon from the first tests in 1959. In 1963 attention turned to determining the maximum speed and minimum height for dropping.

With the Beverley of 1954, delivery by parachute of heavy stores became a practical proposition, and the extensive trials reinvigorated the Airborne team. Testing of all the combinations of medium and heavy platforms and other loads continued over many years. Dropping from the ramps of the Andover and Argosy included the Gemini rubber boat (inflated), followed by its crew. Six one ton containers dropped in a stick from the Andover

77: *Argosy dropping nine one-ton containers illustrates the type of recording made from the ground of every trial release.* © *Crown Copyright*

78: *Hercules C.1 XV178 has its load extracted after an ultra low level airdrop (ULLA); the wheel height was critical to the integrity of the load on arrival.*

79: *A stressed platform is extracted from a Beverley C.1 by the small parachute while the main has just started to deploy. The shields (air deflectors) at the open rear door were later removed at the request of Transport Command.*

gave interest as the pilot had to push the stick fully forward when the load travelled over the ramp—thus giving a CG well beyond the aft limit—fortunately for a few seconds only. Many combinations of the distribution and separation of one-ton containers were made to minimise the risk of tipping up in the air, and to recommend to the RAF a safe and repeatable technique.

The Beverley remained in use until 1971 and the Argosy until after 1975, the latter mainly for paratroops.

The Hercules dominated the dropping trials after the late 1960s and started with an extensive programme to measure floor angles at various speeds and flap settings. Twelve one-ton containers slid smoothly towards the opened freight door of the Hercules once their restraints had been released, giving the pilot practice at pushing the stick well forward. The versatile aircraft extended the weight of the Heavy Stressed Platform to 35,000lb; after despatch, some improvement was needed to reduce the swing of the load. Two other developments further demonstrated the Hercules's abilities. In 1967 a team of five well equipped parachutists were dropped from over 40,000ft, opening their parachutes after falling free for over 39,000 ft. Closer to the earth, ie 15ft, was a technique known as Ultra Low Level Airdrop (ULLA); the Beverley was used for initial experience by E Squadron crews. The Hercules, suitably instrumented with a large scale radio altimeter dial in front of the pilots, carried on the work by day and then by night. After the initial method of extracting the load by a hook dragging along the ground had been discarded, the method preferred of streaming a small parachute involved much team work on the flight deck. Later trials from 1968 using mainly the Hercules repeated the drops of the Gemini boat followed by the crew for covert operations. The eager Special Forces team wanted to parachute already seated in the Gemini, but film of the boat turning upside down on despatch illustrated the foolhardiness of the idea. Also tested were reefed mains extraction for lower drops, and development of the canopy first technique.

Navigation and Radio Division

Radio/Signals Section

The small section for radio and radar testing and maintenance was decimated by the end of 1945, leaving just a single junior, Mr H (Henry) Maidment as the sole trials officer of the radar team for over nine months. Fortunately, trials were limited to IFF in a Spitfire and AI Mk10 in a Mosquito, and he had time to liberate much test equipment left behind by the repatriated Americans; such kit had previously been unobtainable. His other tasks included recovery (from a disused Welsh coalmine!) and preparation of the automatic gun laying radar for the rear turret of a Lincoln bomber; the protracted flight trials owed their limited success to his taking along a test set for airborne calibration. Following the arrival of Mr C (Cyril) Withers as section leader, activity picked up somewhat, and included a trial of ASV 13 in a Brigand. The set caught fire a few minutes after take off and Henry Maidment remembers vividly his frantic efforts to extinguish the conflagration—his actions spurred by the strong smell of petrol fumes from a leaking valve. Some months later the aircraft crashed fatally.

Known as Signals Test Section, it created much flying, a significant amount arising from the need for all new radios, aerials or changes to aircraft shape to be checked; Alf's Tower, a prominent feature 20 miles West of Boscombe was used as a datum. Usually 36 headings had to be measured by transmissions to Radex at Boscombe—each one exactly over the tower, and the polar diagram established. In 1959, OC B Squadron complained that a Victor on a number of urgent trials actually spent over 35% of its flying time on polar diagrams.

Experimental Navigation Section

With about 30 members, the Navigation Section finished the war with a lot of expertise on astro navigation, sextants, compasses and single position line navigation. Much of the expertise disappeared with rapid demobilisation.

However, the Experimental Navigation Section, as it became known, manned by RAF navigators most of whom

80: What the properly equipped parachutist wore in May 1967 for jumping from over 40,000ft. He has additional telemetry apparatus in the box under the parachute which is shown undergoing check out from the power supplies on the ground. © Crown Copyright

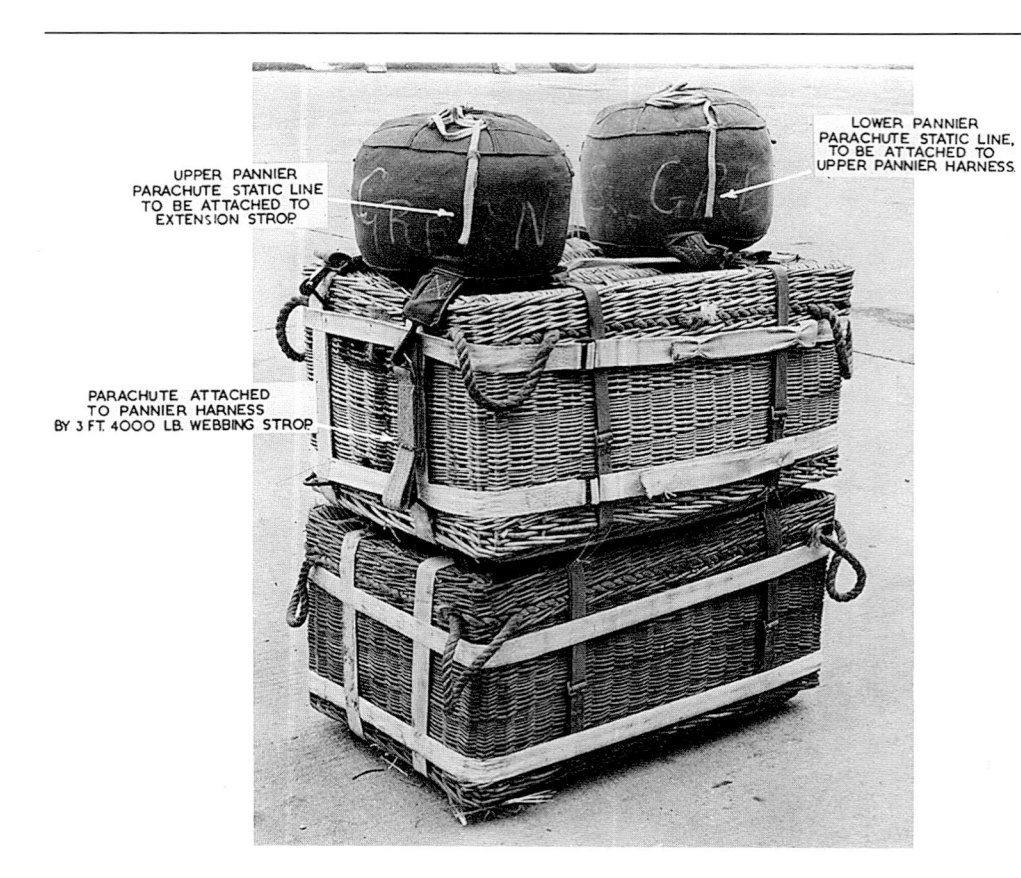

UPPER PANNIER PARACHUTE STATIC LINE TO BE ATTACHED TO EXTENSION STROP

LOWER PANNIER PARACHUTE STATIC LINE, TO BE ATTACHED TO UPPER PANNIER HARNESS

PARACHUTE ATTACHED TO PANNIER HARNESS BY 3 FT. 4000 LB. WEBBING STROP

81 and 82: *Hastings C.1 TG500 being loaded in 1950 with a tier of two panniers with their parachutes. Wicker baskets seem to have been ubiquitous in aerial delivery for a number of years. © Crown Copyright*

had the "Specialist Navigator" qualification, continued to evaluate new equipment and to examine the navigation facilities of aircraft undergoing tests; it was led by an RAF Wing Commander (in 1948 Wg Cdr Revell). In April 1953, a minor reallocation of responsibilities involved transfer of bombsight equipment (but not the sighting head) from Armament to Navigation Division. The Section had a Wellington at first, followed by a Hastings, an Ashton, a Hunter and Canberras. A Canberra was modified with the navigator's station turned into an "auto observer" which photographed the relevant parameters once every 10sec throughout the flight down a calibrated track using the Decca Navigator chain as datum. Another filmed record was made, also at 10sec intervals, using the sun for accurate heading reference. The post flight work involved extremely tedious and lengthy analyses of thousands of datum points. Having determined the accuracy of the new kit under controlled conditions, long range flights to Khartoum followed; the problem of assessing the performance of new eqipment continued to receive much attention. A major trial in the early 1950s concerned Green Satin, a doppler equipment giving very accurate drift and groundspeed from which a precise position could, with a suitable compass, be derived. A little later, a similar doppler in the Scimitar gave repeated errors of two to three miles; finally it was discovered that the navigation charts were at fault! Other navigation equipments, of which there were a great many in the 1950s, had to be similarly measured and analysed; they included Ground Position Indicators Mk 4 and 6 for the V-bombers, Blue Devil (T4) bombsight (both using inputs from the doppler), an improved periscopic sextant, and TACAN for fighters. Such extensive expertise led to requests for trials of civil navigation aids, most notably the DECTRA long range aid principally for use over the North Atlantic. Twelve crossings were made by a Valiant, and the auto observer (one frame per minute for the entire trip) was augmented by two navigators taking precise LORAN[9] fixes every two minutes. The analysis effort surpassed even that required by the doppler trial. The team under Sqn Ldr E W F Hare was awarded the Johnson Memorial prize of the Guild of Air Pilots and Navigators for this work. Another navigation expert, Sqn Ldr D F H (Pinky) Grocott later became President of the Institute of Navigation.

A Division At Last

With navigation rapidly becoming a science involving black boxes possessing innards more akin to radar, and with both disciplines assuming an increasing significance in military aeronautics, the logical decision was taken to amalgamate the two and Mr A (Pop) Popham arrived in September 1956 to head the new Division. He demurred at first on the title proposed, which became instead "Navigation and Radio Division", and his acronym "SNR". He found the alternative "SRN"[10] to be *infra dig*, and retired in 1974. Integration was to be a long process, and the two sections of radio/radar, predominantly civilian, and navigation, mainly servicemen, ploughed lone furrows for some years.

The effort given to the V-bombers from the 1950s dwarfed earlier work of the Division. In 1958 a review was made of six years evaluation of the Navigation and Bombing System (NBS Mk 1) including the radar (H_2S Mk 9), compass, doppler, wind finder, radio altimeter and computer. The trial culminated in flying the whole caboodle in Valiants and Vulcans. It was concluded that from 45,000ft, the average radial bombing errors were 500yd, and that navigation errors of 1.24% of the distance travelled could be achieved without position fixing en route. One weakness of the Green Satin doppler was its tendency to unlock at even small pitch and bank agles. The compasses also had shortcomings which became critical later in the Vulcan for the Skybolt missile (in contrast to the accurate inertial navigator of the Blue Steel missile which could be also used to navigate the aeroplane prior to launch). Much effort went into defining the accuracy required, and then in evaluating the resulting Heading Reference System in a Vulcan and the Division's Comet. Cancellation of Skybolt led to HRS Mk 2 without astro tracking; accuracy remained within $1/2$ degree.

By the early 1950s combat aircraft routinely arrived at AAEE lacking their radar which remained to be fitted at Boscombe. The ensuing work and subsequent ground and air testing coupled to the plethora of aircraft types appearing throughout the decade occupied much of the time of the Radio/Radar Section. The radars themselves were frequently early development models made by firms new to the work, and, apart from dubious reliability, the new equipment had unexplored capabilities Thus assessment became more a development task than one of evaluating compliance with specification.

Orange Putter, the tail warning radar intended for flying at 45,000 ft in the Canberra, illustrates some typical vicissitudes of early radar. The workings were in a sealed container to maintain internal pressure at the operational height. The seals leaked, and the test aircraft, a Lincoln, took over an hour to reach 29,000ft. The results were that the radar did not work at altitude, and that on the more rapid descent the container collapsed around the delicates. Improved seals prevented depressurisation, but range of detection remained poor. Other problems, widespread with valve radars, incuded the adverse effects of gun firing and the dissipation of heat; both occupied much time and effort. The Hunter and Javelin were the first types to include temperature measurements in radar bays as a matter of routine. Valve technology reached its zenith in the Air Interception radar (AI Mark 23) for the early Lightnings and the interception technique used the time honoured attack from the rear of the target, although assessing the abilities of the analogue computer to determine the optimum interception profile stretched the Section's resources. It was felt that the pilot would be very

---

[9] *LORAN an earlier long range aid*
[10] SRN—State Registered Nurse

83: *An early anti-sand intake on Wessex HC.2 XR503. © Crown Copyright*

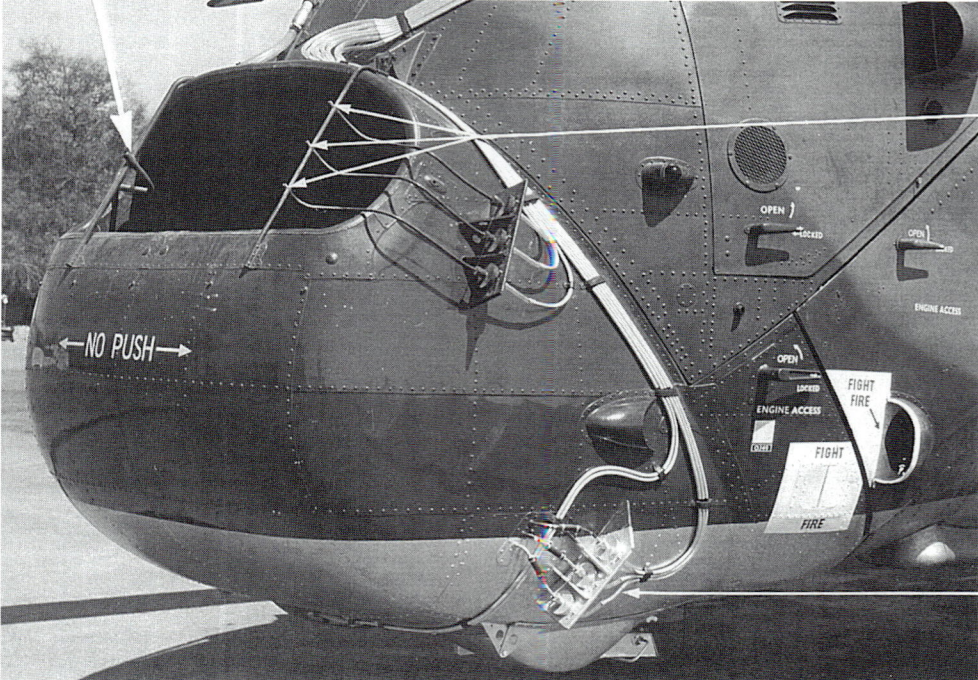

84: *A momentum particle sand separator on Wessex HC.2 XR503 in August 1966. The extensive work of instrumentation is readily apparent, but the first engine failure occurred after only 1hr 40 min of flying in the sand. © Crown Copyright*

busy, but the Air Staff had already taken the decision to make the Lightning a single seater. The Lightning Mark 3 (AI Mark 23B plus Red Top) with its head-on interception at closing speeds of up to 2,000mph was a significant advance for both the trials team at AAEE and later the RAF. The tasks of assessing interception geometry, missile slaving and launch characteristics were daunting, and required manpower and computing resources beyond those available within the Division. As a result BAC (formed in 1960 and subsuming English Electric) at Warton was persuaded to assist with its digital computing facilities, and thus was established the first joint avionic trial in the UK. The Lightning investigation involved probably the first use of rigs and modelling as trials tools. The test aircraft retained A13-type trace instrumentation, laboriously converted to punched tape for analysis. The productive working relationship with Warton blossomed with trials during the development of the RAF's nav-attack system in the Jaguar, and was further cemented in the early days of the MRCA (Tornado).

Position fixing in the first Comet laboratory aircraft relied largely on photography when cloud cover permitted. The laborious post-flight analysis of finding the exact position and comparing it with the position derived from the HRS inputs led to urgent investigation of more rapid but equally accurate datum sources, and eventually to the new Comet in 1964 which served for over quarter of a century. It was nearly ideal as a flying laboratory, but lacked an auxiliary power unit, thus making starting awkward on its many overseas trips. Perhaps the most valuable feature of this Comet was the extensive array and integration of position fixing aids to provide a datum against which new equipment under test could be assessed. The datum information (known as Highway) was recorded digitally and transferred in the aircraft onto drums of punched tape for analysis on the ground. Ground analysis was done by the computer section—slide rules had definitely had their day. Of the hundreds of avionic equipments tested, a few must serve as examples—Airborne Decca Loran (ADL 21) in 1960s for trans Atlantic use of the Loran C ground transmissions, including 56hr in a Vulcan giving accuracy of $1/2$ mile within 700nm of the transmitter, various Marconi Dopplers produced continuous groundspeed and drift for an early analogue computer to integrate with heading to give a ground position, a sun or star sight (GL161) for determining accurate heading for use with inertial systems, HARCO for coupling a Decca Navigator into the autopilot system, and many inertial navigation systems. The Division's task broadened constantly to encompass evaluation of the complex tactical systems and sensors of the Nimrod, testing the navigation/attack systems of the Harrier, Jaguar and Phantom, and assessing the performance of the Terrain Following radar of the V-bombers. The Division pioneered the introduction of computer modelling for weapon aiming, following the introduction of the many and varied operational attack profiles of the Buccaneer.

Photographic Division

By October 1952 a Photographic Trials Section was in existence for work on the Canberra PR 3, but there is some evidence that the Trials Section was set up in 1950 for new aircarft cameras. In any event, from 1954 Mr G MacLaren Humphreys was in charge and his responsibilities broadened to encompass the Photographic Division having some 48 staff in 1968. There were then four Sections for trials of new cameras and photographic equipment, and air camera installations in aircraft prior to service use, plus provision of photographic and optical services, metal photography and printed circuits. In the 1960s, trials included a compact casette allowing more film to be carried, and automatic exposure controls for the F96 camera, both proving advances. The F49 Mk 4 survey camera was tried in a Dakota, Canberras, Valiant and Victor with gradually improving results, but was less successful with colour and infra red film. The decade finished with a fan of three F 95 Mk 7 cameras in the nose of a Scimitar, and an F 126 camera in a Canberra and then a Nimrod, both trials giving good pictures. 1970 saw remarkable results from an American KB-18A camera in a Phantom; in good weather the images were sharp from horizon to horizon while travelling at over 450 kt at low level. The challenging environment for cameras at over 40,000ft was overcome successfully in a Canberra having a 48in lens to its oblique F 96 camera with a novel but acceptable mounting.

Weapon Systems Division

Weapon Systems, the last Division to be created, was the logical outcome of Mr R P (Reg) Dickenson's 1961 paper on the subject. He was the first Superintendent, and his staff drawn initially from Performance and Engineering Divisions. Of the first five projects taken over on formation, two were cancelled (Skybolt and TSR 2), but three (Blue Steel, Buccaneer and Lightning Mk 3) were fully tested and entered service. Other projects followed including the Nimrod, Anglo-French helicopters and the Harrier, but the work of actual testing fell to the other Divisions.

A Mathematical Section and later Computer and Instrumentation Group (CIG) formed part of the Division. In the late 1960s CIG, under Mr Derek Haines, had instrumentation in 60 aircraft—and the business of designing, fitting, checking, calibrating, rectifying and maintaining this vast array overwhelmed the small staff available until aircraft numbers were reduced. On the computing side, theoretical studies were made, including an assessment of the probiblity of hits on a target aircraft from the Lightning's battery of 2 in rockets, fired in a single pass; scatter was found to be excessive, and the system was not adopted for service.

85: A Wessex HC.5 shows its "mod 1051" intake in 1969. © Crown Copyright

86: Wessex HC.5 at Uplands, Ottawa with a pre-mod 1051 nose door plus ice guard. © Crown Copyright

87: Sea Vixen FAW.1 XJ488 calibrating the ice build up behind the icing Canberra in 1967. © Crown Copyright

88: Canberra PR.7 WT509 after over 20 years RAF service returned in January 1975 with modernised avionics. It is seen here in the Environmental Hangar with a heater box round the rear fuselage. © Crown Copyright

89: *The large camera crate mounted in Victor SR.2 XH675 in late 1962. The crate could fit a fan of eight F 96 Mk 2 cameras (lens up to 48in) for day work or five F 89 Mk 2 cameras (up to 36in) for night oprations.* © *Crown Copyright*

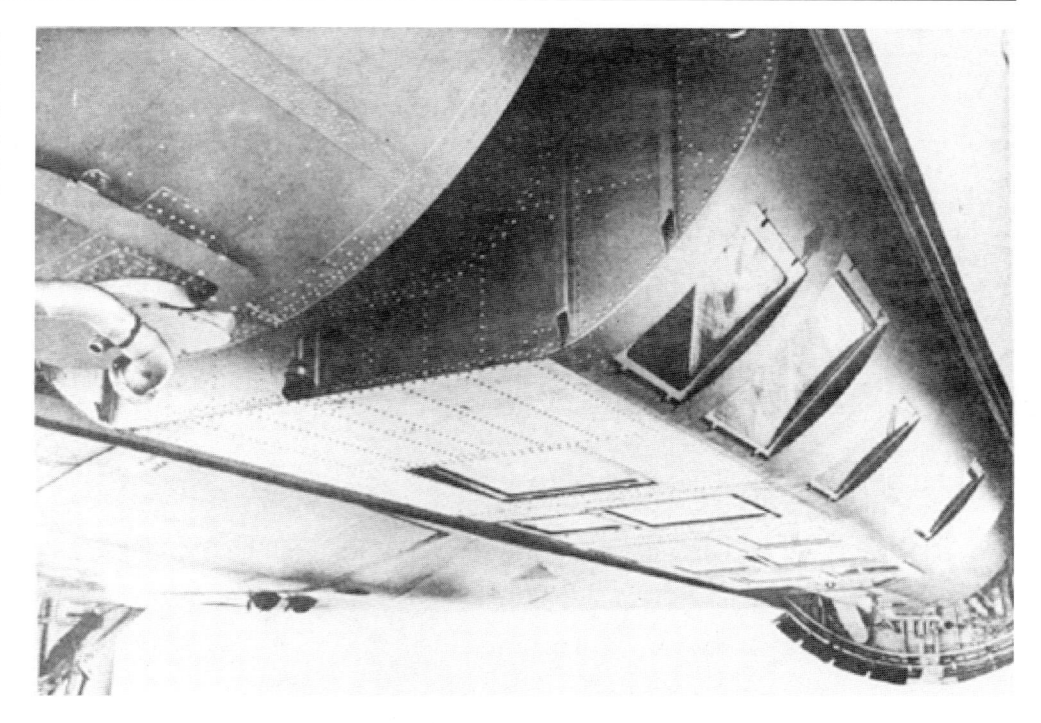

90: *The Blue Knights in July 1974; this display team was formed by the trials parachutists of AAEE. Left to right: Sgts Peter Keane, Tony Cadiz (hopefully he didn't jump with his hat backwards), Bill Cook, Flt Lt Alan Jones, Sqn Ldr Norman Hagget, Sgts Gordon Flint, Harry Parkinson and F S Peter Quinney. Among the many awards made to the team was the AFM to Peter Keane—the first at Boscombe to a serviceman who was not qualified as aircrew; he was also in the team that jumped from over 40,000ft.* © *Crown Copyright*

91: *A four-ship formation unique to AAEE. The icing Canberra discharging water which became supercooled and iced the Nimrod while the Argosy waited its turn; The chase is probably a Meteor. The reason that the Canberra's wheels were down was probably to increase drag, thus requiring a power setting in the more responsive range for this slow formation.* © *Crown Copyright*

92: Venom NF.2 WL857 after completion as a pressure error datum aircaft in 1958. The only visible evidence of its role are the duplicated pitot/pressure heads on port wing tip and fin, and temperature probe under the fuselage. Its accuracy was checked over three years by a variety of methods; its performance quickly proved inadequate for formation with faster aeroplanes. © *Crown Copyright*

93: Damage to Javelin F(AW).4 XA725 following an explosion on start up.

94: Hunter F.6 XE601 showing the starboard RFD target and its container under the wing © *Crown Copyright*

INTRODUCTION TO THE FOLLOWING CHAPTERS

2150 Aircraft in Seven Chapters

These seven chapters aim to describe the tests on, and purpose of, every aircraft known to have been on the strength of, or flown by, AAEE between 1945 and 1975. Apart from the constraint of space, descriptions are limited by the available documents—either because formal reports were not written or have not survived (or have not been found). Enough remains, however, for a reasonably comprehensive picture to emerge. It is a formidable canvas, encompassing every type of land and shipborne type used by the British armed services (apart from the Washington and Skyraider), plus many others which appeared in prototype form only, and including, in the early years, civil types, and later some of foreign origin. Some 200 types are described in varying detail. The details included are those which the author considered important or interesting; much routine testing, such as weighing and pressure error measuement, is omitted.

During the period under review (1945–75) the Approved Firm scheme started in the 1950s where performance was measured by the firm and checked by

95: Canberra B.2 WD954 with Mount Kilimanjaro as a spectacular backdrop during overseas trials in July 1952. The report concluded after flying from Aden that a cold air unit on the ground was not warranted—one of the Establishment's rare mistakes! © Crown Copyright

the AAEE. In practice little checking was done and therefore, from 1950 or so AAEE reports, on which this section is largely based, contain few performance figures.

Allocation to chapter is somewhat arbitrary, eg Mosquito appears in "Bombers" (Chapter 4), and includes all roles of the type. Carrier aircraft omit helicopters, which have their own chapter; types which had significant service use in land and sea based versions are in the appropriate chapters. Non-carrier naval aeroplanes, eg Sea Devon, are included with the land based version. The index gives the location of all aircraft by type and serial number/registration.

Where speed is quoted in relation to handling, eg stalling or take off, the figure refers to indicated air speed; *other performance is in true height, speed and climb rate, and take off distances are corrected for still air in standard sea level conditions, except where otherwise stated.* Powerplants are given by type and mark/series, and omit output as individual engines varied, limitations changed with time and affected the ratings, and modification state/build standard could also affect output.

The order within chapters in general reflects the chronology of receipt of the first of the type, ie the main report number until the reference system changed in about 1974.

BOMBERS AND MARITIME AIRCRAFT

Vickers Wellington

B and T Mark 10. Investigations, using NA724, into mis-set trimmers and failure of the flap/trimmer interconnection continued until September 1945; in the latter event, pilots were advised not to use flap for landing. Next month, a stiffened elevator on DF609 reduced the reversal of stick forces in dives up to 320mph. In 1948 RP589, with modifications for training two navigators, received a damning report on account of the lack of space, poor layout, negligible downward view and impossibility of astro-navigation. Two years later tests on PG420 at Hullavington showed that astronomical observations could be made using a new platform in the fuselage.

Short Stirling

Mark III. EF517 lay dormant prior to removal at Christmas 1945.

Mark V. Some unreported cabin heating trials may have taken place on PK136 during its brief visit at the end of 1945.

Handley Page Halifax

B Mark III. LV999 completed some more tests on the rear turret, a Boulton Paul Type D, including shortened ammunition feed tracks for the troop carrying version, before departure early in 1946. HX246 spent some time from mid-1949 in the blower tunnel as part of an evaluation of two types of thermocouples, and later with CATS on heated de-icing.

B Mark VI. NP849 and NP924 both departed in mid-1946 having been de-instrumented after performance and cooling research work respectively. Wartime attempts to achieve acceptably low cylinder temperatures on LV838 (four Hercules 100) resulted in post-war tests of cooling fans behind the propellers; opening of the gills to maintain acceptable temperatures in weak-mixture cruising was still necessary, and reduced speed by 12 mph.

Armstrong Whitworth Albemarle

Mark II. V1743, a platform for air-to-air photography, left by December 1945.

96: Lancaster ASW.3 SW289 in February 1946. The lifeboat reduced range but made little difference to pressure errors (the static vent is under "SW" of the serial number), but reduced range. The front turret appears to be armed. © Crown Copyright.

de Havilland Mosquito and Sea Mosquito

FB Mark VI. TA547 completed its work on the 800lb incendiary and drop tanks before departure early in 1946, while TA501 made a lengthy investigation into dive angles in an attempt to improve RP accuracy. The latter machine was extensively instrumented, and firings were photographed from a chase aircraft, but apart from showing that a Range Computer Type A was useless, the trial appears to have been inconclusive; results depended on the skill of the pilot.

B and PR Mark XVI. The photographic NS624 soon disappeared in 1945. The bomber ML994 made some tests of the metal under wing tanks by early 1946, and RV300 then completed work on the 800lb incendiary.

FB Mark 26. Both KA104 and KA201 arrived from Canada in October 1945, for gunnery and bombing respectively, and both proved the equal of the home built Mark 6 fighter bomber.

TR Mark 33. LR387 returned in August 1945 with folding wings, arrester gear, four-bladed propellers and a larger horn balance to the elevator; the last gave satisfactory longitudinal handling for the naval torpedo/reconaissance role. Production TR.33s arrived first in November 1945; TW227 made unreported handling flights with a torpedo, and TW229 cleared the radio/radar equipment. The rocket installation on TS444 for 16 three inch rockets with 25 or 60lb heads, or four rockets of the triplex variety with 350lb heads caused no problems up to 350 kt. A limit of 300 kt was imposed with bombs or other external stores. Large and inconsistent airspeed errors were attributed to the radome on the nose; a pair of interconnected static vents on TS449 in 1948 cured the worst errors.

PR Mark 34. Three wartime aircraft, RG176 (performance), RG182 and RG183 (both meteorological research) departed early in 1946. VL623 in 1946 and RG231 the following year are annotated in servicing records for periscopic sextant trials; any report has not been found.

B, PR and TT Mark 35. This multi-role mark included TA638, a bomber, from wartime performance testing subsequently used to investigate pressure error measurement by formation at high altitude. Cluster bombs and pyrotechnics occupied TK650 in 1949–50 and led to some operating restrictions; VR793, also a bomber, appeared for a short visit in 1953. Cameras (F52-day, F61-night and K19B-night) worked well in TK615 from April 1951, but night results were spoilt by poor illumination from the 4.5 in photoflashes; smaller photoflashes discharged from the starboard engine nacelle gave better pictures. Chief criticisms were of the poor cockpit layout of the controls for the extensive radio/radar fit, and interference on VHF from the Gee-H radar; a landing accident in March 1953 curtailed further flying. Cable breakages kept TK634 under investigation in 1951 until replaced by RS719. Towing of the four feet diameter sleeve target was straightforward, but the starboard engine tended to overheat in UK summer temperatures.

NF Mark 36. Capable of being loaded to 21,000 lb all up weight, this Mark was assessed as being hazardous as a night fighter on account of poor single engine performance when tested in RL136 in 1949; the Establishment recommended a limit of 19,000 lb by reducing fuel (which meant, *inter alia,* leaving the 63 gal fuselage tank of this Mark empty). 3,000 rpm/plus 12 psi was normal take off power; it was recommended that plus 18 psi should be used following engine failure—provided that control could be maintained. Normal power gave a safety speed of 175 kt in RL114, with the added complication of the feathering controls being placed for the right hand, ie, the pilot had to change hands at a very critical time. The AI Mark 10 seems to have worked well.

TR Mark 37. This Naval variant was represented from 1946 by TW240 with one "Uncle Tom" carrier under each wing. Deck approaches were made at an indicated speed higher than expected due to over-reading of the airspeed indicator by 7-8 kt.

NF Mark 38. Similar in role to the NF36, the NF38 also had similar performance and handling—the three inch higher canopy and AI Mark 9B producing no measurable effect. In 1949 a major benefit was the placing of the feathering controls for the left hand in VT706 and VT658 in 1949. VT654 had new hydraulic pumps acting at double standard speed; the undercarriage lowered in 17 sec (30 sec previously) as a result, but an accumulator system was considered to be preferable. VT651 (1948) and VT657 (1950) made month-long visits.

TT Mark 39. Pressure errors were small in PF489, and, in late 1948, handling in the target towing role was similar to other Mosquitoes, but it had a pronounced swing on take off, poor single-engined performance and a restricted view. PF606 checked the radios.

Avro Lancaster

B Mark I, B and MR Mark III. General purpose bombing did not detain HK543 long after 1945, and pressure error measurements on NG384 with a modified vent were also soon over; a new (24 way) bomb distributor in ND899 received comprehensive use throughout 1946. Porton made brief use of ME570 in early 1946. Assessment of braking propellers on LL813 (Merlin 24) took less than three months at the end of 1945 following several ground loops as pilots

97: *Wellington T.10 RP589 had severe shortcomings as a navigation trainer for which it was tested at the end of 1948. The lack of space and difficulty in moving about limited its usefulness.*

98 and 99: *Comparative views in August 1949 of Mosquitoes—NF.36 RL136 (upper) and NF.38 VT706 (lower). The three inch higher canopy of the Mk 38 can be discerned, but performance was little different. Single engine performance was considered unacceptable at night at high weight, and the maximum recommended to be reduced from 21,000lb to 19,000lb. The Mk 36 was on loan from 29 Squadron.*
© *Crown Copyright*

100: Mosquito NF.38 VT654 on arrival in May 1948. The radar nose is unpainted, the propellers are wide chord. © Crown Copyright

101: Sea Mosquito TR.37 TW240 in December 1947 with four bladed propellers, a radome and under wing fittings for Uncle Tom rockets. © Crown Copyright

102: Sea Mosquito TR.33 TS444 in December 1946. When the radome was fitted to house the radar, large and inconsistent errors occurred from the single static source on the nose; adding a second source on the opposite side cured the problem. © Crown Copyright

employed the familiar technique of opening a throttle on the inside of a swing to keep straight; in reverse pitch this action aggravated the situation. Evaluation of new compasses, using RF147 for over two years, included the acceptable Sperry Gyrosyn, and the unacceptable Admiralty Transmitting Compass Type III with large turning and acceleration errors. The perennial quest for an efficient Flare Chute met with success in its Mark VIII form in PA367 in 1949; the Shackleton was intended as the beneficiary. TW923 of the RAE put in a short appearance in early 1949. A single example of the Air Sea Rescue conversion (SW289) spent over a year from November 1945 completing pressure error, performance and other tests both with and without the lifeboat under the fuselage. In 1951, RE206 had strengthening modifications permitting successful firing of rockets with flare heads (RP Mark 8 installation) from under the wing tips of the maritime version.

Mark II. LL619, a general purpose bomber, departed in early 1946.

Mark VII. Trials of the FN82 tail turret were completed in NN801 by April 1946.

Consolidated Liberator

Mark VI. EW126 continued in use until late 1946, and amassed lots of data on engine temperatures, fuel flows and related topics, sometimes on trips to Kano, while the re-emerging BOAC benefitted from range measurements and techniques jointly developed with AAEE's flying of KL632 in 1946–7 to Nairobi.

North American Mitchell

Marks II and III. Three of these American light bombers remained in use at the end of the war—FV984 (stability research), FW151 (use by Porton) and HD347 (T1(b) bombsight); all had gone by mid-1946.

Douglas Boston

Mark III and IIIA. The long serving W8315 continued on various tasks, mostly for Porton, but after a bombing flight in October 1945 the nosewheel collapsed causing extensive damage which was not repaired. BZ274, an alleged rogue, soon disappeared, while of the three meteorological research aircraft, BZ286, BZ315 and BZ320, the first departed in 1945 before relevant modifications had been completed, and the latter pair continued flying well into 1946.

Boeing Fortress

Mark III. To this aircraft, KL835, goes the distinction of undertaking the first work on post-war civilian airworthiness requirements (later BCARs). A considerable amount of flying was completed on defining acceptable handling and performance on take off, particularly following engine failure. After creating much data, it was decided that its benign behaviour in critical stages of flight was unlikely to be representative of many types, and that a twin engined machine should be used; it left in mid-1946.

Short Sunderland

GR Mark 5. In 1956, an Establishment team tested PP127 after IFF Mark 10 and SARAH homing equipment had been fitted; the aerials of the IFF needed repositioning, but no retesting was done.

Vickers Warwick

Mark II. Concurrent trials on HG362 in late 1945 confirmed that the new position of the DR compass was acceptable, and that, with slightly reduced throttle settings, cooling of the Centaurus VII engines would be satisfactory in the tropics.

Mark V. LM777 made the DR compass tests on the Mark V, while PN760 proved a single cell flare chute needed several modifications. All Warwicks had left Boscombe by early 1946.

Avro Lincoln

B Mark I. The prototype, PW929, had made a favourable impression late in the war and remained to complete tests of the Flare Chute Mark III before departure late in 1945. It was found easy to contain the yaw created by rotation of the tail turret in RE227, but the heating of RE232 was inadequate at 20,000ft using hot air drawn from the inner engines. The latter machine was severely damaged when the undercarriage was retracted on the ground in April 1950.

B Mark 2. The first of this Merlin 68A-engined version, RF337, arrived in mid-1945 for 324 hr of intensive flying during which the opportunity was taken to assess the Type P generators (satisfactory), constant speed propeller units (Type AY203A replaced earlier unsatisfactory units), carbon monoxide (satisfactory) and intercooler blanks (charge temperatures remained acceptable). Guns in the Boulton Paul D tail turret of

103: Mosquito TT.39 PF606 showing the position of the IFF (front) and VHF radio aerials in 1949. © Crown Copyright

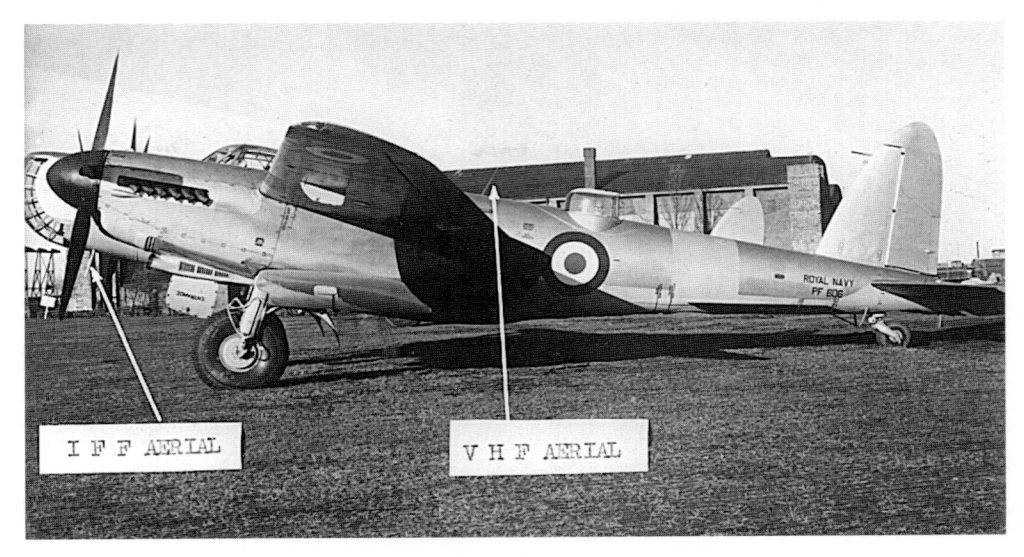

104: Mosquito TT.35 RS719 in July 1951 standing on pierced steel planking; location is not Boscombe Down. The winch is just visible between the undercarriage legs with the wire guide behind it. A small frame protects the tailwheel, while for the elevator and rudder there is a wire attached to the fin running to a small fixture inboard of the horn of the elevator. © Crown Copyright

105: Lancaster GR.3 RE206 with wing tip RP Mk VIII installation in August 1951. Three inch rockets with flare heads were successfully fired. © Crown Copyright

106: Lincoln B.2 RF561 in the configuration tested by AAEE; the extended nose for radar testing produced little change in handling. © Crown Copyright

107, 108 amd 109: Lincoln B.I RE227 showing the extent of rotation of the turrets to illustrate the handling report; the aircraft yawed in the direction of rotation, but control remained easy. The nose turret is a Boulton Paul Type F.1 (two 0.303 in guns), the upper a Bristol B.17 (two 20 mm guns) and the tail a Boulton Paul Type D.1 (two 0.5 in). © Crown Copyright

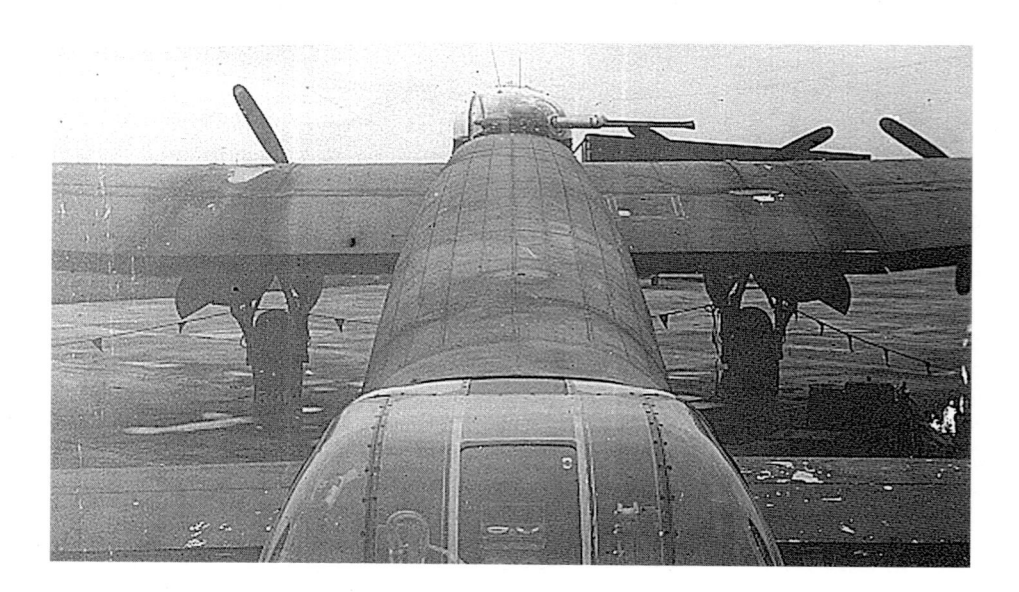

110: Warwick GR.II HG362 in October 1945, continuing its wartime compass and engine cooling tests. This view reveals no clues as to its work. © Crown Copyright

111: Lincoln B.2 WD123 in August 1953 at the end of its time at Boscombe. The capacious bomb bay is visible, as is the radome for the H_2S Mk 4 radar. © Crown Copyright

112: Brigand B.1 RH798 in July 1948 fully loaded with two 500lb bombs under the outer wings and a pair in tandem under the fuselage. © Crown Copyright

RF368 were heated electrically, but the gunner remained cool (1947 usage); indeed, cabin heating was again criticised. No such comments were made following tropical trials in RF370 starting late in 1945. Turret tests in RF354 (1948–9) and RF399 (1957) have left no surviving records, nor have the pressure system measurements in RF383 (1946) and RF504 (1948) with a new pitot position. Further investigation into unusual loss of airspeed when yawing came to a halt when RF401 crashed on take off in July 1946. A specially modified Lincoln (RF560), known as "Zephon", having Merlin 85A engines and lengthened nose and tail fittings, crashed fatally in July 1948 on asymmetric tests. It had been intended to fit radar to this aircraft for TRE trials. Similarly modified, RF561 completed the tests in 1949 following its sibling's demise. Minor modifications to RF519 met Porton's requirements for four years until early 1954; WD123 then took over for a further two years, following various icing and navigation work including tests of the ubiquitous E2 standby compass, and a lengthy evaluation of matching the radar returns with maps.

The tail warning radar (Orange Putter) gave disappointing results in RF329 at first with ranges limited to 1.6 nm on a Mosquito target; later interference from the aircraft electrical system masked any improvements in the radar. Brief trials of the homing aid SARAH on RF554, and of IFF10 on RF564 were completed in 1955.

Bristol Brigand

Last in a series of twin-engined aircraft, the Brigand suffered from changing operational requirements and structural weakness. Existing reports do not distinguish between the different versions, and supporting documentation is scant.

Mark 1. MX991, a prototype with Centaurus VII engines, arrived during the wartime period and was free from unpleasant handling characteristics for the "Fighter/Bomber/Torpedo/Rocket strike role"—single role!; no dive brake tests were made. Cockpit layout and 26 engineering improvements were recommended, but the four nose mounted 20mm guns (Hispano Mark V*) fired without residual CO gas. With modifications incorporated in production, RH750, RH752 and RH796 (Centaurus 57s) nevertheless revealed structural weakness in the wings and also damage to secondary structure from gun firing during trials lasting until February 1948. Pressure error tests had hardly started on RH745 (with third fin) when it landed wheels-up in November 1946 and RH752 crashed fatally in July 1947, possibly due to structural failure. Handling remained satisfactory with a Torpedo Mk XVII fitted with a monoplane tail (MAT Mk V) on RH746 in 1946. With standard fittings for the bombing role, but no bombs, RH800 weighed 26,093 lb (tare) and 40,310 lb (loaded) in mid-1948 with 10,000 lb (1,389 gal) of fuel. Similarly loaded but with three drop tanks, RH798 weighed 40,500 lb and required gentle handling in manoeuvres to avoid excessive stresses; airbrakes proved effective. Performance trials included oil cooling measurements on MX994 in 1946–7 when the need to keep the gills open reduced top speed by three percent. Engine cooling measurements followed at Khartoum in 1948 on RH753 with flared propellers having root fairing, later removed because of cracking; removal resulted in cylinder temperatures becoming too high at maximum power. Metal propellers afforded some improvement to cooling later, and also increased range and performance. At Khartoum, with the crew suffering from inadequate ventilation, take off distance to 50ft was 1,010yd at 38,000lb with the gills shut; reduced power (from 9½ to 6½ psi boost) for the climb with gills open/ gave a ceiling of 23,600 ft after 40.8 minutes. Back at Boscombe at the same weight, but with some fuel replaced by 1,000 lb bombs, it reached its ceiling of 24,400 ft after just 19 minutes thanks to lower ambient temperatures and metal propellers. In July 1952, the aircraft crashed tragically after a few flights towing a target in 1951. Maximum permitted speed was raised to 300 kt after modifications to the elevator proved effective in increasing stick forces in VS860, while corded trailing edges to the ailerons gave further improvement to handling. The outcome of the intensive flying of RH773 is not known, but followed hood jettison trials in 1947. RH763 spent 22 months from February 1948 on unreported handling at high altitude with Saunders control bearings.

Bombing and rocket trials occupied MX991, RH750, RH754 and RH796 intermittently from late 1945. RP Mark VIII Type 6 eventually became acceptable in mid-1948 after improvements to alignment, scatter, struts and other weak areas. The Gyro gunsight Mark IVC was satisfactory for rocketing. RH742 made three short visits to clear the jettisoning of bombs and fuel tanks. In 1950 and 1951, VS860 was approved for combined bomb and RP carriage and release including a two-tier arrangement on Mk 3A beams, but with some speed limitations.

Met Mark 3. Weighing up to 39,296 lb with two 90 gal and one 200 gal external fuel tanks on arrival in October 1948, VS818 required a run of 725 yd to unstick. The high altitudes at which this version was to fly meant extended sorties in RH763 at 25,000 ft using oxygen. Maximum acceptable Mach numbers for various configurations were determined, eg 0.54M with dive brakes open carrying a 200 gal tank, and up to 0.7M with dive brakes closed when clean. Roller bearings in all control runs reduced stick forces to an unacceptably low figure at aft CG, so the spring tabs were rendered inoperative, making forces too high at forward CG. In late 1949, an investigation into dive recoveries followed cases of wing buckling in the RAF; VS818 was used during intensive flying and recoveries made with very light stick forces. Handling suggestions followed, together with a

113: Brigand 1 MX991 in August 1945 in the multi purpose role, but lacking airbrakes; The handling of this aircraft seems to have impressed pilots during a short stay as hostilities ceased; later trials on it revealed shortcomings in gun armament. © Crown Copyright

114: Brigand TF.1 RH754 probably in mid-1947 used for rocket firing trials during which a strut broke necessitating repair by the firm; the RP.VIII installation was eventually cleared in 1948. It had a torpedo when photographed.

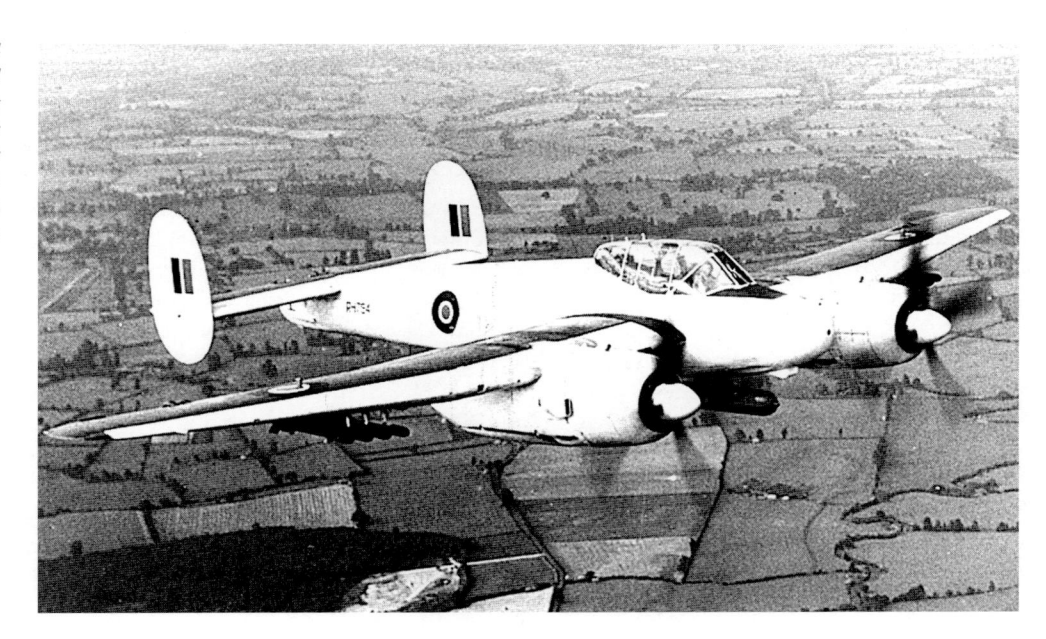

115: Brigand TF.1 RH746 with a torpedo Mk.XVII plus a monplane tail (MAT) Mk.V. Handling trials gave no cause for concern in mid-1946.

recommendation that accelerometers should be issued (but not too many—two per squadron!). The 1950 report on the type concludes with the damning remark, "This aircraft will never be efficient in the meteorological role with ASV13B [radar] ... for cloud identification."

T Mark 4. RH798 returned in 1950, suitably modified for the training of operators of the AI10 (SCR720B) radar. Full radar trials were made and changes to layout suggested.

T Mark 5. The work on IFF 10 and the radar AI21 (re-designed American APS-57) fitted to WA565 in 1954 resulted in clearance for the radar only; the aerials needed relocating.

English Electric Canberra

Introduction

The Canberra was a phenomenon when first flown at Boscombe Down; the outstanding performance is the more remarkable as its maker, English Electric, had not designed an aircraft for over two decades. Such was the sparkling speed, climb and ceiling that this bomber attracted the accolade from the Establishment on its first visit in 1949 that it should be developed as a fighter. Indeed, compared with the contemporary Meteor and Vampire fighters, the Canberra offered a considerable advance. Performance measurements at 50,000 ft in 1951 were novel—little wonder that over 50 years after its first flight the type remains in service. This account of the AAEE trials is in four parts: bomber, interdictor (including Marks 15 and 16), photographic reconnaissance and, finally, trainers with tugs. It is remarkable that the Establishment did not experience tail trim "runaways" that so plagued Bomber Command in the early years; investigation of various palliatives was, however, extensive.

Bomber Variants

B Mark 1. This designation applied to VN799 (Avon RA2) for a month of preview handling from October 1949. No specific performance measurements were made but the report, covering take-offs at 39,500 lb, reflects the enthusiasm of both the pilots and the Establishment. The stability was good about all three axes, it was very manoeuvrable and generally pleasant to fly. The only significant criticism concerned the uncomfortable seating on the Martin Baker Mk 1 ejection seat, which also obstructed full aft movement of the stick. There was no carbon monoxide detected in the cabin.

B Mark 2. VX165, the first with a movable tailplane, suffered the indignity of a recalcitrant nosewheel shortly after arrival in November 1950. The damage was soon repaired, and flying at 39,660 lb confirmed the earlier findings, although this more searching trial revealed the excessive heaviness of the elevators below 480 kt. Stick force per g varied from 35 lb at the aft CG to 67 lb at the forward; the latter was too high. High Mach behaviour remained acceptable up to 0.83M when buffetting increased with rapid dropping of a wing. At extreme forward CG touch down speed needed to be at or above the ideal figure since the stick hit the seat pan. Cockpit lighting and a reduction in misting on descent were improvements, but the airbrakes were considered to be inadequate at high speed; tip tanks were jettisoned cleanly on another trial. The inner windshield, while assisting flight up to 400 kt with the canopy removed gave a dangerously poor view at night. The remedy was tested at Warton in WD956 in December 1951 where a deflector replaced the windshield; with the canopy removed speeds up to 450 kt were satisfactory and ejections considered possible up to 400 knots. Meanwhile, VX165, retaining the Avon RA2s, received scant comment on asymmetric behaviour apart from a note to the effect that following engine failure the ensuing yaw caused the ASI to under-read by as much as 35 knots. At 40,000 ft, using maximum continuous power, 0.82M could be maintained without tip tanks, while at economical power setting, 1.18 anmpg were achieved—a very creditable figure in 1951. Further measurements were curtailed by the aircraft crashing on the approach following asymmetric engine response; the crew was slightly injured. VX169 (Avon RA2) confirmed the marked vibrations, both vertical and lateral, found on its sibling with bomb doors open; the effects became pronounced in the nose position. Wing tip tanks or cameras fitted to record armament releases were responsible for an increase in stalling speeds; at 31,500 lb threshold speeds of 100–105 kt were thus recommended, some 10 kt above the clean figures. This aircraft flew 155 sorties over a year from May 1951 to clear the existing range of bombs up to the 5,000 lb HC Mk 1, which required the nosewheel to be retracted for loading.

The first of many records made by the Canberra occurred on 21 February 1951 when WD932 crossed the Atlantic in 4 hr 37 min (Aldergrove to Gander), crewed by B Squadron. Minor discomfort was reported. Testing of production aircraft at Boscombe started in December 1951 some seven months after entry into RAF squadron service. WD945 repeated some earlier handling points without surprises; opening the bomb doors, although improved, produced buffet above 25,000 ft and at speeds greater than 0.73M. A partial remedy was a seal between the fuselage and tailplane on WH715 in late 1954. On WD945, at aft CG, nose-down travel of the tailplane was insufficient, but single-engine cuts from full power could be handled safely above 140 kt. Ram air for cooling the cabin at low level gave little comfort; otherwise pressurisation was satisfactory. In mid-1955, using the favourable weather at Habbanya, the T4 bombsight (for the V-Bombers) gave excellent results when fed with doppler drift and ground speed; average errors of 200 yd were achieved from 40,000 ft. The well equipped WD945

116: Canberra B.2 VX165 in the snow in December 1950. There appears to be a second pitot head on the nose, plus the intriguing notice, common to all Canberras—"Entrance Other Side"; the author is unaware of any aircrew having difficulty in finding the way in—but no doubt others did! © Crown Copyright

117: Canberra B.2 WK121, probably in 1968, resplendent in white finish and light blue trim but spoilt by red dayglo on wing leading edges. © Crown Copyright

118: Vulcan B.1A XH478 and Canberra B.8 WV787 return to Boscombe in February 1968 having investigated the suitability of the spray pattern for the Concorde behind the Canberra. Wg Cdr J (John) Wilkinson flew the Vulcan and Flt Lt Jock Wingate the Canberra. Mr R (Robbie) Forrester-Addie took the photograph from Meteor NF.14 WS838. © Crown Copyright

119: Canberra B.15 WH967 in December 1965 with colourful AS30 missiles under the wings, plus a replacement rudder. © Crown Copyright

returned in 1958 as escort for short range aircraft flying overseas. Meanwhile, WD954 completed tropical tests at Nairobi and Aden from which it was concluded, "the sun awning alone is sufficient to keep cabin temperature (on the ground) at a comfortable level ... except for servicing purposes." Generations of aircrew would disagree with that conclusion, but would concur in AAEE's comments on the need for more heating in the cabin at high altitude where lift and thrust boundaries were determined. Lift was abundant, ultimately limited by violent aileron snatching, but lack of power made attainment of the potential turning performance impossible in level flight.

From September 1952 additional armament clearance in WD958 included 250lb target indicators, 4½ in reconnaissance flares and a pair of 4,000 lb bombs. Indifferent results with an F24 camera prevented acceptable photographic evidence of the results of bombing at night. WH640, during a brief loan from No 109 Squadron, investigated various tails fitted to 1,000 lb target indicators. Trials of similar indicators fitted on an Avro triple carrier on WJ565 were interrupted in August 1953 when the nosewheel failed to lower for landing. CS(A) clearance for later bomb/mine/photoflash loads was made by analogy to previous work, and thus required no flying. Cockpit lighting was improved in WD959, but 2-position airbrakes gave no advantage in making a rapid descent from high altitude due to adverse Mach effects. Standard radio/navigation checks revealed the need for improvements to Orange Putter, the tail warning radar. Very good results followed the fitting of Green Satin (doppler) and GPI 4 (ground position indicator) equipment in WH638, except that a calm sea state caused the doppler to unlock; production equipment in late 1954 performed equally well.

Three trials in 1954–5 presaged later developments. WJ565 reappeared with a gun pack under the fuselage and containing four 20 mm guns; gun movement led to the firing circuit being broken and thus to intermittent firing. WD937 had a powered rudder assessed by the engineers as of "sound design", while WJ730 spent a year on low level night photography.

In 1956 WJ678 went to Namao in Canada for cold weather trials; it probably had modifications for the interdictor role. A contemporary was WK123 engaged on Blue Study blind bombing, 50 bombs dropped from 40,000 ft fell 891 ft from the target on average. Later trials, in 1961, included replacement of the VHF radio by UHF which required more cooling at low level, and the addition of TACAN navaid in WJ611 and in WE121 in 1963/4. The so-called "Silent Target" role of WJ567 needed only a few weeks to clear the radio modifications in 1968. A final radio modernisation of this mark produced WH919 in 1971, when the Establishment called it a B Mark 2(T); this aircraft had previously been exposed to the blower tunnel in 1961 and cleared operation of the frangible hatch over the navigators.

Seven Canberra B.2s played their part supporting other work. Perhaps the most interesting was WV787 with most of the features of a B Mark 8, including Avon 109s, but with further extensive changes to the nose, bomb-bay and rear fuselage with a detachable spray rake. Intended in 1966 for work with Microbiological Research Establishment at Porton, whose requirement for 50 ft at high speed at night was rarely used, its main task became that of an icing tanker over the next 10 years. WJ638 arrived in 1962 and ejected scores of anthropomorphic dummies on development and proving tests, usually over the Larkhill range; skilful pilots avoided ejecting themselves. WJ723 arrived in 1959 as a target for Sea Vixens, to be replaced after three months by WK121; the latter then spent 13 years on a large variety of chase, target, communication and training jobs. Of even greater longevity, WK164 still helped with odd jobs 16 years after arrival in 1959, including test of a double (30 ft by 12 ft) banner in 1970. A third long server was WH876 which later added flight refuelling training (non-functioning probe) to its repertoire. WJ643 looked like a pointed B(I).8, and in late 1958 gave A Squadron pilots experience of the AI23 radar for the Lightning.

B Mark 6. The need for handling trials of this mark was reduced by its similarity to the PR Mark 7 which came first. WJ754 was severely damaged three weeks after arrival in April 1954, and replaced by WJ755. Criticisms echoed those of the PR.7, and safety speed on take off with the Avon 109 engines was similarly determined at 175 kt; the Maxaret (non-skid) brakes were liked, while the two position airbrakes and the two tailplane trimmer operating speeds were felt to be advantages. At 54,000 lb, the take off roll took 1,500 yd, and 50 ft reached 2,685 yd from brake release when measured on WJ764. WT370 made a brief visit in 1958, possibly to check trim speeds. Bomb loads already cleared on the similar B 2 did not need further work, but in 1959–60 several new loads flew in WH952, notably mixed stores, including bombs combined with a long range fuel tank, followed by bombs and flares with clusters, and then 4.5 in flares with 1,000 lb bombs. In addition, the Avro Type 262 twin bomb carrier was found to offer advantages, but 1,000 lb flares persistently hit the sides of the bomb doors. WH952 continued with target towing for several years. Finally, at the end of 1974, came WT305 with a large dustbin-like growth, housing ZABRA equipment, on top of the fuselage; intended for RAF service, this unique modification was examined from a handling point of view at AAEE.

Photographic Reconnaissance Variants
PR Mark 3. Powered similarly to the B.2, the first PR.3, VX181, demonstrated slightly inferior handling at forward CG but indistinguishable behaviour at the aft loading; 0.85M true was achieved, all with tip tanks fitted. However, at aft CG without tip tanks, lateral and directional characteristics were significantly worse— attributed to fuselage flexing from the additional fuel in

it. As a consequence photography, first tried in North Africa, was not easy as straight and level flying required undue attention and the perennial problem of excruciating seating limited sorties to 2½ hours. The survey role, even with the advantage of the Mark 9 autopilot, was subject to short period oscillations and wandering with concomitant inaccuracy of the area recorded. Similar results attended day (F52 camera with 20 or 36 in lenses) and night (F89 with the same lenses) trials, with the extra phenomenon of vibrations making night results unacceptable. A mounting type 46 reduced the effect of vibrations in 1956. VX181 spent most of its working life from 1951 to 1969 at Boscombe, undertaking many photoflash, camera and camera bay tests for later versions in the role, in proving a stable platform (FSP100) for the TSR2, in quantifying the accuracy of the STR43 radio altimeter, and testing other avionic equipment including three further radio altimeters (STC Mk 7, APN-141 and AM-221) carried together for comparison. Production standard handling on WE137 from late 1952 was marginally better than the prototype, while the cockpit contained many features in need of improvement, including vital changes to the escape facilities. 1954 saw WE135 with experimental toe brakes and an internal rudder lock; both were praised. WE167 came in 1956 to try out a new wing tip discharger with 1.75 in flares. UHF radio and updated radio compass proved satisfactory in WE173, as also was a new HF radio on WE174—both in 1960. After completing its survey camera trial over North Africa in 1957, WE146 returned for a period in store until 1966. Replacing the prototype for general tests, WF922 included Lindholme sea rescue gear, F49 camera and gyro platform among its achievements between 1968 and 1975.

PR Mark 7. The first four months of 1954 sufficed to accept, weigh, instrument and investigate the handling of WH775. Although similar to earlier marks, shortcomings were more pronounced, viz: heavy ailerons, poor airbrakes, aileron snatch at the stall and instability at high mach numbers. Unexpected buffeting occurred at normal approach speeds, and, most serious of all, was the discomfort of the ejection seats. The more powerful Avon 109 motors were less prone to surging, although handling needed care at height on cold days. Increased inertia in roll and yaw caused lateral oscillations greater than on the PR.3, but were acceptable with use of the Mark 9 autopilot with a phase advance damping unit. With minor modifications the radio and navigation fit was satisfactory. Tropical trials at Khartoum on WH792 came to an abrupt halt in September 1954 when, at 434 knots, a large bird removed the complete starboard elevator and tailplane; a skilful landing was made.

The F89 Mark 2 camera (8 in lens) needed several improvements after tests in WT507 early in 1958. Six months later further modifications were recommended in a Mark 3 version following evaluation in WH780 which also tried modified plastic tip tanks. UHF radio and Decca 8 with log in WT503 were cleared for service, followed in 1963 by greatly improved heating of the cameras in both forward and rear bays. The new standard V/UHF (PTR175) in WT527 passed without further changes, but a more integrated avionics suite (known as SRIM[1] 3799) needed extensive work in three phases. The first involved WT519 with part fitted in mid-1973 followed by WT509 in late 1974 with a comprehensive fit, and ending with WJ815, flown by a 39 Squadron crew, on a hot weather trial in Malta.

PR Mark 9. The most radical of Canberra developments created the PR9 with powered ailerons and rudder, a 4 ft wing extension and 50% more thrust than other versions. In mid-1956 the first, WH793, demonstrated its prowess at 56,000 lb and was generally well liked. Satisfactory handling at 56,000 ft, and at high Mach number was followed by timed descent to 40,000 ft taking under two minutes, thus inside the limitation imposed by the safety equipment in the event of pressurisation failure. Asymmetric handling posed no difficulty—safety speed was determined at 150 kt; lack of inboard flaps necessitated a higher approach speed than was felt desirable.

In mid-1958, a dummy fuselage revealed the need for changes to the escape facilities during tests in the blower tunnel. XH134, flown at Boscombe initially by its maker, was assessed in 1959–60 by AAEE as having an efficient workplace for the navigator ("At last," in the report), but the viewfinder misted internally, and cumbersome flying clothing made life uncomfortable. Earlier, crews had found the Type D headpiece (pressure helmet) to become increasingly oppressive. Low flying, without the headpiece, could also be uncomfortable as the lightly loaded wings reacted vigorously to even slight bumps. The report on the autopilot of XH130 in 1960 has not been found; the pressure errors found by Shorts in the same year on XH132 were accepted by AAEE. In 1963 the original TACAN had proved to be acceptable in XH135, but the new miniature TACAN (ARI 5877) of 1963 in XH131 was unacceptable as it caused interference to three other equipments

Photographic developments kept XH133 busy, mostly at Boscombe, for over eight years from late 1959. The first clearance covered the F96 Mk 1 (up to 48 in lens), two F49 Mk 2 and two F95 Mark 2 cameras at all heights from 250 up to 56,000 ft; modifications were needed to clear the accompanying 8 in photoflashes. Tropical flying to test the bay heating for F96 cameras resulted in some condensation at low level after a lengthy period at height; oblique use of these cameras was accepted, but with some operational limitations. A development known as a micro-environment (ie, sealed camera heating and humidity) gave good results in 1966, and, the following year, acceptable aircraft stability

---

[1] SRIM—Service Radio Installation Modification

permitted clearance of the F49 Mark 4 stereoscopic survey camera. During a detachment to Aden, two disparate results are recorded. At ambient temperatures of over 50°C the radios under test overheated, and after prolonged flight at high altitude (minus 70°C) the fuel, Avtur without anti-icing, waxed (ie, became almost solid) causing pumps to fail. The ensuing double flame out was safely handled and another trial mounted in 1965 from which revised fuel handling drills were evolved to minimise chilling. Accurate control of temperature and humidity in a self contained box containing the cameras, known as System III, was progressively improved in XH134 over 18 months from early 1972.

Remaining use of this mark included XH164 in the blower tunnel for 10 days in 1961, XH176 in 1965 to clear the PTR175 radio and radio altimeter 5A; the latter had poor accuracy. XH174 had the improved radio altimeter 7 plus other modernised equipment including a roll damper, while XH175 underwent EMC checks of the combined operational avionic fit—both in 1968.

Interdictor Variants

B(I) Mark 6. Four 20 mm guns in a pack under the fuselage characterised this variant. Initial trials of WT307 included take off at 56,000 lb in early 1956. The first firings at AAEE, also on WT307, from mid-1957, suffered from gun bounce and thus intermittent firing as the micro switches repeatedly broke contact. The installation was cleared later on the B(I).8. Use of 25 lb bombs for toss bombing (LABS) training occupied WT312 on trials for 11 weeks at the end of 1958, but the EMC of the whole installation took place on WT311 only in 1962. Navigation at low level in this Mark was enhanced by Blue Silk doppler and ground position indicator (GPI 4A) equipment; Decca Mark 8 was a secondary benefit. All worked satisfactorily in WT322 from mid-1959. A second aerial for UHF was fitted after tests in 1962. After a warm up period of 15 minutes Decca/doppler in WT319 produced accurate and consistent results.

B(I) Mark 8. From May 1955 the prototype VX185 spent much time in front of the blower tunnel; The navigator's escape was assessed as being feasible below 180 kt, and the pilot's at any speed provided he wasn't killed in the process—the report says, "... the use of explosive bolts for hood jettison is deplored." Intensive flying of WT326 in November 1955 took place from Idris. Early in 1956 WT328 had barely started before it crashed fatally and was replaced by WT364. The navigator's position left much to be desired as it was inefficient with haphazard location of instruments, switches and lamps, and offered a poor crash position. WT333 arrived in March 1959 for armament work, concentrating at first on rocket firing; the Microcell battery of two inch missiles could be fired in dives between 15° and 30° provided, the report states, that maximum trim speed was not exceeded. The aircraft flew to Australia in 1966. Clearing bomb loads required three visits of WT347 from early 1959 to cure bomb bay buffeting. At the end of the following year an acceptable baffle permitted seven releases of the 1,650 lb (dummy nuclear) bombs in releases at 124° in loft manoeuvres. Reconnaissance flares separated cleanly from WT330 in 1962, but some modifications were recommended. Similar results attended XM272 and XM275 in 1963 when Lepus flares were dropped. EMC of the nuclear capability involved XH209 early in 1962, and EMC was also checked on WT346 a little later; neither trial included flying. Further changes to the avionic equipment, tested in XM265 (updated radio compass and weapon response simulator), necessitated more EMC checks, this time on XK952 in 1963. With a navigation fit similar to the later B(I).6, XM245 produced very good results with the Decca Mark 8, provided that extensive pre-flight preparations were made.

B(I) Mark 12. WT329 for New Zealand had an autopilot, an inertia weight in the elevator circuit to reduce control forces, the aileron spring tab was simplified and a cut-in switch introduced to prevent elevator trim runaway. All these changes were prompted by experience and were approved by AAEE in 1959; the Indian B(I),58 was similar. Blue Silk doppler and a T4B bombsight gave good consistent results as did the comprehensive radio fit. New Zealand navigators found the exit door too small.

B Mark 15. Much clearance work on this version devolved on WH967 during 11 visits from 1960 until carelessly dropped into the Mediterranean Sea by the author six years later. Retaining the third ejection seat, the normal crew was expected to be two. Three phases of armament work began with release of bombs from wing pylons, firing two inch rockets in batteries of 37, dropping 25 lb bombs from the bay to simulate 1,650 lb and 2,000 lb nuclear weapons and dropping the latter (dummies) in toss (LABS) manoeuvres. The next phase involved handling and firing Nord AS30 radio-guided rockets. Cleared weight was increased to 55,000 lb, and safety speed raised to 185 kt. Then, in 1965 came the so called "dual role" combining rockets, AS 30 bombs and tip tanks, thus increasing weight to 60,000 lb. Safety speed was 175 kt, and the time from unstick to reaching this figure exceeded 20 seconds. Take off run was 3,000 yd in tropical temperatures and distance to 50 ft not measured as the camera could not follow the aircraft with sufficient accuracy. WT205 arrived in 1963 for continuing armament work, including modified carriers for bombs and flares, assessment of a DX47 device to simulate nuclear weapon procedures, and dropping/firing/releasing all the dual role items. The pressing need was for a single switch to drop all wing stores in an emergency. Later a SFOM 83 gunsight was tried for low level release of 1,000 lb retarded bombs. EMC of the dual role was felt to be of marginal validity as the modification states of individual B.15s were so diverse; nevertheless, WT210 was cleared. WH966 came in 1966 for minor tests in the dual role. In 1970, WH972

120: Canberra PR.3 WE137 in March 1953 during brief handling checks to confirm some unsatisfactory features found on VX181; the port elevator and tip tanks spoil the paint job. The small fixed aileron tabs are visible. © Crown Copyright

121 right: Canberra B.8 WV787 making smoke (from oil in the white tip tanks introduced into the jet efflux) and spray from the nozzles (probably water/ice) in September 1967. Very much a "one-off"; the engines, basic fuel system and cockpit layout and canopy made it a B.8 from the pilots' point of view. © Crown Copyright

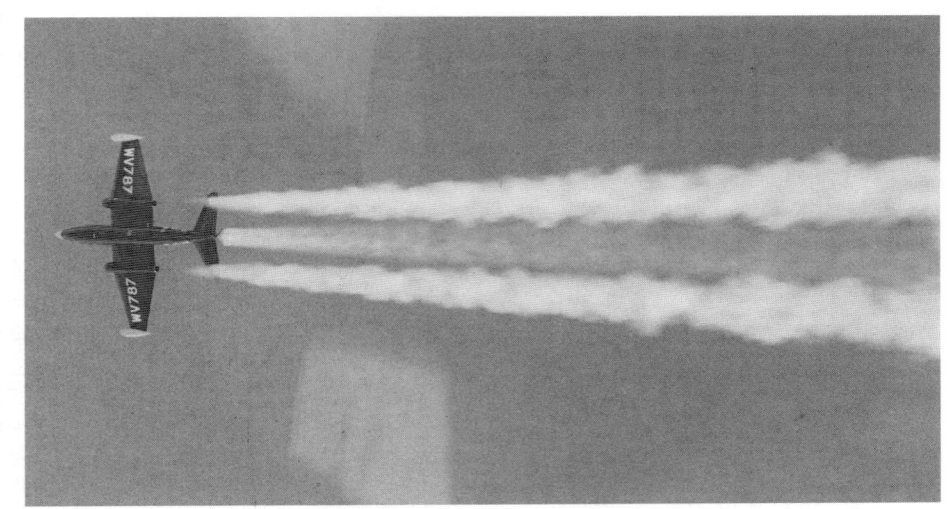

122 below: Canberra T.17 WJ977 on arrival in mid-1966. Visible features are the window dispensers looking like tip tanks, bulges under the wings for the bleed air turbines, the radome infested nose and the pressure head on the port wingtip. This very well equipped aircaft had a limited range. © Crown Copyright

relieved of all weapons quickly gained acceptance in the flight checking role.

B Mark 16. A single example, WT302, of this updated B.6 with Blue Shadow—side looking radar—revealed few problems with a bomb release safety lock (BRSL), the PTR175 radio and a G90 cine camera. The Air Staff called for a second navigator for the marking role; AAEE commented on the absence of an ejection seat for this man.

B(I) Mark 58. Bombing trials for India followed assessment of the T4 visual bombsight in a B(I)8 aircraft, XH232, using the existing Green Satin inputs. WT338, upgraded to B(I)58 standard with Blue Study and autopilot, stayed at Warton for AAEE's investigation. Both aircraft went to the Indian Air Force.

Training and Target Towing Versions

T Mark 4. Side by side seating for two pilots, without ejection seats at first, characterised this version with Avon 1 engines. WN467 was generally found acceptable after arrival in late 1955, but minor problems with the view, blocked by the direct vision panel, and difficulty in locking the right seat (which swung back to allow the navigator to mount) spoilt the effect. Principal criticism concerned the "very bad" escape facilities for the pilots, ie, through the door. Changes to the aileron gearing kept control forces to comparable figures with the smaller control wheel of the T.4. Unreported checks of trim tab settings were made on WJ878 in 1956, while modifications on WH844 were tested in the blower tunnel in 1960. UHF radio and Decca navigation needed a few modifications following tests in WH840, but earlier examination of the LABS changes to WJ880 were unremarked, as was the installation of Cossor 1520 HF radio in WH841. In 1967 WH854 (the last T.4 without ejection seats for the pilots) arrived, joining the ETPS machine WJ867 for training and odd jobs for the Establishment.

T Mark 11. WJ734 spent six months on clearance of the AI17 radar (as fitted to some Javelins) and associated changes; interference with radio equipment was cured by re-routing the radar cables. The radio altimeter, however, remained unacceptable.

T Mark 13. WE190 for New Zealand spent nine months at Boscombe, seven of them unserviceable waiting for approved ejection seats.

T Mark 17. Comprehensive jamming kit powered by bleed air turbines in this mark required careful trials planning to avoid blacking out large areas of the country's radar. Nevertheless, trials in the UK and Singapore on WJ977 were successfully achieved, although this mark suffered from very short range due to the bleeds. In the Far East the high temperatures caused no major difficulties with the equipment but the crew found ways of minimising time on the ground—the pilot's position soon reached 48°C and the navigator's 54°C. Pressure errors of the wingtip mounted pressure head remained unmeasured until WF916 appeared in 1970. WH863 cleared the rapid blooming window fired from the wing pods.

TT Mark 18. With two types of winch and two types of cable up to 50,000 ft in length, the TT 18 offered a great advance on the Meteor in the role. The first, WJ632 in 1968, lost several targets at the greatest tow length, and 35,200 ft was adopted as a maximum; even so, chasing the target was a demanding occupation. With the object of desire some six miles behind the tug, and thousands of feet below it, the target had a mind of its own—reacting to turns some seconds after the tug, then slowing and falling before racing off in a new direction. Production tugs, WK122 and WH718, joined the team and the required towing configurations were cleared for service, together with the associated radio and navigation facilities on board. WJ639 came in mid-1971 for further banner towing work.

T Mark 22. With the Navy's Buccaneer radar (Blue Parrot) this conversion of the PR.7 retained three F95 mark 4 cameras in the bays. WT510 in 1973 had a surprisingly high stalling speed, even allowing for the pressure errors in the wing tip pressure head, and light stick force per g at aft CG.

Avro Shackleton

MR Mark 1. The first Shackleton to arrive, the second prototype VW131, started a long association with AAEE in February 1950. At 72,000 lb it was found pleasant to fly, although tiring in bumpy conditions and tricky to taxi in a strong crosswind. Criticisms included the heavy rudder which overbalanced at large angles even at take off speeds, the high noise level at the pilot's station in the plane of the contra-rotating propellers, and the lack of a positive stall warning; it was considered that the flight engineer should have his own set of engine controls as the pilots found difficulty in making precise power settings. On the power of the port engines alone (2,750 rpm plus 9 psi), the rudder force was light and a minimum speed of 105 kt achieved. Take off (2,750 rpm plus 25 psi) at 86,000 lb using 17° flap, needed 910 yd to unstick, and 1,240 yd to reach 50 ft. Landing at 72,000 lb needed a minimum ground run of 1,100 yd but 1,260 yd from an instrument approach. The usable CG was limited by the heavy and unresponsive elevator on landing (forward CG) and the extreme push force needed on overshooting (aft CG). Tropical trials in Khartoum revealed the desirability of extra oil cooling, "dry" take off run of 1,635 yd, and with water methanol (wet) the run was 1,180 yd; climb rate in the heat became 655 ft/min compared to 940 in standard conditions. VW126

129: Canberra B.6 WT305 shortly after its 1975 trials at AAEE. The large "dustbin" housing ZABRA equipment produced no major surprises.

130: Nondescript Canberra T.13 WE190 which was delayed at Boscombe awaiting ejection seats for the two pilots prior to transfer to the Royal New Zealand Air Force.

131: Shackleton GR.1 VW131 seen on the South side of the airfield in early 1950. This aircraft bore the brunt of the type trials—the only visible evidence of its status being the probe on the nose for the yaw and pitch vane. The pilots' position was accurately placed in the plane of the contra rotating propellers; many pilots who flew the type suffered long term hearing loss. © Crown Copyright

132: Shackleton MR.2 VW126, actually an MR.1 aerodynamically representative of the later version. The nose looks like an add-on, but otherwise the craft appears unchanged; handling had been slightly improved, but it retained the directional wander among other shortcomings. © *Crown Copyright*

133: Shackleton MR.2 WB833, a conversion from a Mk 1, made tests of the new radio gear with the ASV13 radar, plus long flights which emphasised the extremely noisy and uncomfortable working conditions. © *Crown Copyright*

134: Shackleton MR.3 WR970 at the time of its AAEE trials in September 1956 with test probe on the nose and tip tanks seen here. The stall of this mark could result in rolling almost inverted, and occurred without natural warning; after return to the firm for the fitting of an artificial warner, it crashed fatally.

135 above: Shackleton MR.3 WR973 at Woodford during the AAEE preview flying in July 1965, of the Phase 3 with Viper jet boosters. With external power connected, cowlings removed, Viper doors open and the overwing door open, the total lack of activity defies a guess as to what's going on. © Crown Copyright

136 right: Shackleton MR.3 WR989. This Phase 3 aircraft is seen undergoing an icing trial of the Viper boosters in the outboard nacelles. The stream of freezing water behind the Canberra tanker was narrow, and judging the offset distance required skill; the chase pilot could give help. © Crown Copyright

137: The largest complete aircraft to grace the Blower Tunnel. Shackleton AEW.2 WL793 in August 1973. © Crown Copyright

made a visit in 1950 for the CO contamination check, followed by satisfactory assessment of a spring tab rudder in place of the earlier geared balance tab; noise had been reduced by fitting a ducted manifold to replace the original stubs. Meanwhile, VW135 with full operational equipment made flights of up to 15½ hours attracting the comment, "yaw, noise and vibrations render the aircraft unacceptable for long range maritime operations." Strong words indeed, partially echoed in November 1951 after long flights in VP263 when the grossly inadequate toilet arrangements afflicted the crew of 13. During these trips the directional wander was measured in two modes—up to 4° in five second cycle and another with a period of 35 to 70 seconds; use of the Mark 9 autopilot made little difference. The navigator's table vibrated continuously making plotting untidy in an atmosphere of noise and "disorder"; all quatifiable data were outside the AvP970[2] limits for noise. Even heating, measured in WB835 in late 1952, was insufficient. Improvements tested included increasing both the elevator span by 20% and its balance tab ratio in VP261 early in 1951, and re-rigging VW131 in the middle of the year, together with a new rudder.

VP259 weighed 49,505 lb (tare) in operational standard, reaching 85,739 lb with 3,292 gal of fuel and 5,500 lb of armament; range was calculated as 2,670 nm, thus meeting the specification. Increasing cruising speed from 140 kt to a more comfortable 160 kt reduced range by six to nine per cent; on three engines the reduction was similar.

The distance between the airframe and bullets fired from the B17 Mark 6 upper turret was too small and, in VP255, the gunner could not gain access to it in full flying kit. VW135 cleared all the bomb bay configurations from 1,000 lb to 11 lb bombs, and the radios and radar, including the ASV Mark13 in 1950–1. Three years later modifications by the Establishment allowed approval of the auto-flame float launcher; the flare chute successfully launched ASR apparatus Type F in 1954. Torpedoes, depth charges and sonobuoys were added to the repertoire of VP255 in 1956, and Lindholme rescue gear in 1959. VP254 cleared the IFF 10 and SARAH after defects had been remedied.

From mid-1955, VP285 fitted with Blue Silk (doppler) and GPI 4a and then GPI 6 (ground position calculator) did an extensive investigation over all types of terrain.

M R Mark 2. VW126, aerodynamically modified to Mark 2 form, returned in May 1952. The first report concerned the new wheel brakes and lockable tailwheel—both were liked although the air supply to the brakes was soon exhausted. Disappointing initial handling at both aft and forward CG disclosed no significant improvement in directional behaviour, nor in stall warning, although turbulence was less bothersome. Equally disappointing were the high noise level and vibration coupled with noisome toilet. In the approach configuration, stalls induced large wing-drops; an artificial warning device was strongly recommended. WB833 with the CG further aft was unacceptable as control forces reversed prior to the stall; the original CG limit was thereafter retained. More encouraging aspects included the well laid out cockpit, the interrupter gear for the B17 upper turret and improved oil cooling attributed to the piston oil jet tried in WG530. Nevertheless, slight overheating occurred at Khartoum, but the smaller oil cooler flap opening thus required gave an improvement of about 200 ft/min in rate of climb. Further cooling trials, in Aden, occupied WR964 in mid-1954. In 1953 WG530, with leading edge spoilers, had a reduced wing-drop at the stall with power on, but, at idle, there remained no warning and a stick shaker thus recommended. WG532 investigated accelerations on recovery from dives; 1.8g was the highest figure. It was found possible to throw out a wounded aircrew on his parachute from either exit of the aircraft—no doubt discipline improved on board thereafter. The remaining trials over several years of this mark in its primary anti-submarine role were concerned with armament and radio.

WG530 bore the brunt of early armament testing, including sonobuoy chutes of the mark 9 and 11 variety, and a new Boulton Paul Type N nose "turret" with unacceptable sight vibration on firing. By 1958 the ASV21 with other aids such as LORAN hyperbolic navigation aid became available for tests in WB833, and in 1960 UHF radios and TACAN for navigation. IFF 10 had a poor range in WR968 and aerial position was critical for the new radio compass in WR953. Weapon diversification at least matched that of navigation. WR962 included checks of combining three Mk 30 torpedoes with an oxygen crate in the bay, WG558 had a new flare chute (1961), WR965 checked an armament modification (1962), WL759 dropped Mk 44 torpedoes (1963–4) while WL785 evaluated sonobuoy parachutes.

Modernisation led to the Phase 3. WG556 had extensive new radios and radar for operation world wide which attracted only minor comment in late 1965; two years later the Radio Altimeter 7B of WL738 received attention. Equally extensive were changes to the weapon capability leading to two years' work on WR960 to cover all the possible combinations. Performance work on the Phase 3 aircraft employed WL737 in 1966 and WR955 to check landing distances in 1971.

AEW Mark 2. The Airborne Early Warning role gave the Shackleton a new lease of life with old American AN/APS 20F/I radar in a dome under the nose, an interrogator and several extra radios. The Establishment's resources in target aircraft were stretched to the full

---

[2] AvP970. The document which laid down acceptable standards for all military aircraft from basic handling to limitations of tyre temperatures.

during assessment. Trials starting late in 1971 on WL745 with just 7,385 flying hours to its credit demonstrated handling characteristics similar to the basic Mark 2, and thus acceptable using earlier standards; weight had increased to 96,000 lb. The only additional limitation (top speed 300 kt) was imposed by the strength of the radome; it was found that a similar limit was needed to avoid the risk of excessive sideslip from the vigorous use of the rudder. Much performance work was done at Akrotiri in Cyprus. UHF aerials proved in need of repositioning on WL757 in early 1974; WL793 paid a brief visit in August 1973 to check escape paths for the crew.

MR Mark 3. The firm flew WR970, the first MR.3, at Boscombe from September 1956 with some participation by B Squadron; it crashed in November flying from Woodford investigating the unsatisfactory stall. WR971 and WR972 arrived in December 1956 for CA Release performance and then armament tests lasting until mid-1958. The capacious bay could carry all the stores for catching submarines, CLE Container Mk 3 and/or an oxygen crate unconnected with submarines, although its presence required additional re-testing of the various offensive stores. One comment on the crate (also tested in Canada and at Idris in WR974) appears quaint even in its 1959 context, "Both aircraft were [flown] in the Colonial role." No early handling reports have been found of this nose wheel variant, but the radio, navigation (in WR973) and operational facilities were praised for comfort and general efficiency; the only exception was the poor layout of the bomb aimer's position. Tests of modifications in 1958 on WR972 also found favour, except over-reading of the Radio Altimeter 5; further changes to the aerial reflector box improved accuracy and may have been tested on WR985 in 1959. XF701 had a new AD712 radio compass in 1962. By 1961 the range of stores carried and dropped extended to the Lindholme Mark 3 rescue gear, and American markers dropped via the chute with the radome up and then extended.

With modernised avionics and revised crew layout WR974 and XF702 became Phase 3 aircraft for trials in 1964–5. While the tactical team approved of the efficiency achieved in 120 hr of flying, the weight increased to 106,000 lb in XF711 and pilots found take offs, which included over 50 with an engine cut before rotation, a matter of skill to achieve safely. A technique suitable for Service use was evolved giving slightly longer distances, but achieving consistency and safety. The heartfelt plea was for more power to add to the Griffon 57As, already using water; Viper jet engines in the outboard nacelles was the answer—to give the RAF its first six-engined aircraft. In 1965 a team visited the firm at Woodford to evaluate the new configuration, and flew WR973. Performance was enhanced at critical times, and handling acceptable; dealing with emergencies became increasingly a matter of management rather than skill. It took one year from April 1964 to drop all the possible weapon loads from WR982, which then returned in 1967 to investigate the effect on performance of the Viper jets windmilling. Short trials were made on XF703 (Honeywell radio altimeter in 1968), and XF705 (stall warning checks in 1969).

T Mark 4. Converted from the Mark 1, this trainer version passed rapidly through its clearance tests, starting with VP258 in early 1957 and continuing with VP293 and WB858 in 1959 by which time avionics and armament more representative of front line aircraft had been fitted. Minor shortcomings were soon rectified.

Vickers Valiant

Prototypes. The first "V" bomber to fly, and the first to be tested by AAEE, was a substantial advance on existing types in service; initial Release to Service appears to have been based on only very meagre experience of the two prototypes at Boscombe Down. The preview was held at Hurn in September 1951, with the intention of identifying areas in need of improvement on WB210 (four Avon RA3). The permitted flight envelope restricted the investigation to 42,000 ft and 0.8M, while weight was unrepresentative at 90,000 lb for take off. Stalls at 83,000 lb (a low figure never seen in service later) were straightforward with buffet followed by the left wing and nose dropping at 80 kt (flaps and undercarriage down); minimum engine speed restrictions made even this exercise of limited value. In simulated take off conditions with one engine at idle, the aircraft could be controlled down to a speed 10 kt above the stall. However, at all aircraft speeds the powered ailerons were crisp, the rudder light over small angles and the elevator a little too heavy, although with good response. In the cockpit, the pilots were too cramped for comfort, and they considered long flights up to 15 hr an unrealistic objective. Next came a dummy fuselage from which four live jumps from the crew door onto netting were made as the blower tunnel produced a 300 kt wind; escape under favourable conditions was considered feasible, but the AAEE condemned the lack of ejection seats for the rear crew. The next recorded flying is one flight in WB215 (four Avon RA14) on 11 July 1954 during which six dives to 0.905M caused severe buffet resulting in damage to the wings and undercarriage and return to the firm for repair. The severity of the "hammer" buffeting (described as "very scaring" by the crew) had not been experienced by Vickers, and was found to be due to the 10% increase in weight flown by the Establishment. This had the effect of a small but very significant increase in C_L at the maximum Mach number, creating flutter from shock wave effects. Vortex generators on the strengthened wings cured the problem some two months later, and then 13 days of tests, still with operating limitations in force, completed the clearance flying. Both elevator and ailerons were heavy, pilots' seating extremely uncomfortable, the nosewheel shimmied, and

138: The very first V-bomber—Valiant B.1 WB210 seen here as tested by the visiting B Squadron crew. The shiny metal nose contains no radar, and the aeroplane is equipped to a minimum standard for early flights. © Crown Copyright

139 and 140: Two photographs of Exercise Floodtide. That on the left shows Valiant B.1 WZ376 receiving from KB-50J 48-118, a three point tanker in January 1961. The B-50 appears to have a method of stowing the hose in its extended tail; the hose has a 8A basket. Markings on the B-50 are interesting. This Valiant had features of the bomber, photographic reconnaissance and tanker versions. The lower left photograph shows the Valiant in a generous light as it gives fuel to B-66B 55-302, in November 1960.

141: Valiant B.1 WP199 undergoes loading evaluation of the Blue Danube nuclear bomb—in this case a dummy. The "Bomb, 10,000lb, aircraft, MC" as it was euphemistically designated, required the services of the hoisting gantry. The black item at the extreme rear of the bomb bay is a baffle, lowered to produce acceptable airflow on release at altitude. Under the tail can be seen a "Houchin" ground power trolley, familiar to generations of air and groundcrew. © Crown Copyright

142: *The extensive camera fit on Valiant B(PR).1 WP205 can be seen in this image, taken in September 1955 of the special bomb doors with the camera covers open © Crown Copyright*

143 right: *Vulcan B.1 VX777 ready for testing in June 1955. There were pressure heads at each wing tip and a temperature probe under the nose; the visual bomb aiming window appears to be blanked off and the captain alone had a windscreen wiper. There was no radar. All these were to change in later aircraft as was the straight leading edge of the wing. © Crown Copyright*

144 below: *The Vulcan in the smoke of the Canberra's port engine. Not visible in the view is the Vulcan's cockpit clear of the smoke in order to keep safe separation. The silver tip tanks contained diesel fuel for injection into the jet efflux. © Crown Copyright*

cockpit layout condemned. Handling in manual control became progressively more difficult as atmospheric turbulence increased. The Service received initial clearance to fly the Valiant up to 120,000 lb and 360 kt and down to the onset of buffet; bomb door opening was not initially allowed. In a later trial with Super Sprite rockets to boost take off of this prototype, the starboard wing rear spar web failed in April 1957 with a violent lurch as the rocket packs were jettisoned; a safe landing was made.

B, B(PR), B(PR)K an B K Mark 1. The report of a cockpit assessment of WP204 in 1954 said, "[This aircraft] falls far short of the level expected ... in respect of crew comfort and detailed grouping and location of various services." In particular, the Martin Baker Mk 3 ejection seats were extremely uncomfortable. The large underwing tanks of WP210 increased weight to 167,000 lb in 1956 with concomitant decrease in cruise ceiling and rearward shift in CG; fitting vortex generators on the wings restored some of the lateral stability and gave satisfactory handling up to 0.85M provided the yaw damper was functioning. Take off run at the increased weight was 1,700 yd and distance to 50 ft 1,850 yd; cutting an engine at 110 kt on the ruway extended these figures to 2,265 yd and 3,250 yd respectively. Stalling at 133,000 lb in the landing configuration occurred in severe buffet at 113 kt—nearly 50% faster than on the light prototype. The aircraft then made six trans-Atlantic crossings in 1957 on behalf of the CAA to assess the first DECTRA ground station at Gander, Newfoundland. Other trials included a new doppler and radar altimeter. Performance measurements at Idris using water methanol were completed on XD872 in 1957–8. WP202 was progressively updated from early 1955 to a representative standard of navigation equipment; layout and comfort received the strongest criticism as the equipment itself worked to an acceptable standard. WZ373 made a good platform for astro navigation in 1957, but its main role was as part of the long term evaluation of NBS Mk 1, including navigation and bombing with the autopilot Mk 10 coupled. In 1958, the new T4A visual bombsight gave accurate results

While handling appears to have been somewhat briefly reported, the armament of the bomber version involved five aircraft at AAEE over the life of the type, starting with WP199 (four Avon RA14) in late 1954; the large bomb bay carried bombs up to 22,000 lb with ease, although loading large stores, including the 10,000 lb nuclear weapon, involved lowering the nose. The first armament report included a description of the two wing bomb cells capable of carrying a total of 10,000 lb—provided the store had a diameter of no more than 16½ in; in service the wing pods carried only fuel. Further tests of the T4 bombsight were made at Wittering on WZ367 in 1956 during six hours of flying. WP203 did not fly and made itself useful on ground trials of loading, unloading, release, EMC and nuclear safety checks for

three years from mid-1958. WP208 made complementary flying trials after further work in late 1958 investigating rear crew escape up to 360 kt using dummies with the escape/entrance door removed and the shield extended. Armament flying then started in early 1959 and weapon loads included up to twenty one 1,000 lb MC Mk 6 bombs, which could be released satisfactorily up to 310 kt, 1,000 lb target indicators, flare clusters, 2,000 lb mines, practice bombs, and any combination, generally cleared to 350 kt. WP208 also cleared the aircraft destructor system, which evidently did not function inadvertently! Following the introduction of low level operations in the RAF, WP219 checked the release of 25 lb practice bombs in 1963. An unknown aircraft had the topographical map display driven by the GPI 4 to assist low level navigation; its usefulness was limited by unsuitability for radar matching. In early 1956 WZ383 flew from Wisley at low level with an AAEE crew.

Evaluation of the secondary roles began with photographic reconnaissance in WP205 (four Avon 204) in 1955 with day flying over North Africa using F49 cameras (6 and 12 in lens) and F52 (20 in lens); the camera window gave good results, but the high airspeed spoilt resolution with the F49 (12 in). Four years later very good survey photographs were taken with the F49 camera with six inch lens. Ground equipment and loading arrangements for up to 28 eight inch photoflashes were approved; several modifications to the fins and fusing of the stores improved release up to 320 kt. Closed circuit television lacked resolution for reconnaissance. Following successful trials of Decca/Doppler in 1962–3, WZ383 had a Litton inertial navigation (IN) system (LN3-2A) and revised bomb bay heating for the F52 (20 in) oblique and F49 Mk 2 survey cameras; the IN gave impressive accuracy, but the distribution of the ample heating air needed further work. Trials by night and from Aden and Idris were included. New U/VHF radios and a new radio altimeter featured in WZ379, and the TACAN navaid in WP209 in 1963–4. The radio counter measures role featured at AAEE in 1959 with a fleeting visit by WP214.

Tanking, the third of the supplementary roles, involved WZ376 at Boscombe over eight years from 1959, although its last flight was in December 1964 when all Valiants were grounded. Trials started with checks of the extra radios and air-to-air TACAN, continued with air-to-air refuelling. XD814 had the Collins STR18B HF radio in 1964

Avro Vulcan

The delta wing was Avro's solution to the requirement for a high level (over 45,000 ft), high subsonic speed nuclear strategic bomber. Early aerodynamic and power shortcomings involved progressive development to the Mark 2, which

145: Vulcan B.2 XM606 over Canada in March 1967 shortly before descending for tests of the terrain following radar for which the scanner radome is just visible under the nose probe. © Crown Copyright

146: Vulcan B.2 XH533 with full airbrake extended about to land on runway 24 at Boscombe in 1963. All eight elevons are raised as the pilot, or the autopilot, starts the flare for landing. This is the first production Vulcan B.2 and it enjoyed a long association with AAEE. © Crown Copyright

represented an almost new type when first tested at AAEE some seven years after the first flight.

Blower tunnel. A dummy fuselage in the blower tunnel in early 1954 proved satisfactory separation of the pilots' hood; live jumps from the entrance door also used as an escape exit were made using copious mats and netting. The Establishment had doubts about the chances of survival of the rear crew, as the two navigators and air electronics officer were known. In 1958, flight trials of XA892, using dummies, led to the conclusion that provided the undercarriage was retracted and speed below 350 kt, successful escape should be possible.

Prototype. Avro flew the first prototype VX770 from Boscombe for a period after its maiden flight. In May 1955, (some 33 months after the first flight) the 2000 yd of available runway (reduced by resurfacing work) restricted weight for the preview flying of VX777 (four Olympus 101) to 130,000 lb. With low engine power and the original straight wing, there were serious deficiencies in handling above the cruise Mach number, including poor pitch damping, aileron oscillation and a low buffet boundary. At low speed, down to 72 kt at 90,000 lb, there was uncontrolled yaw, while engine handling left much to be desired. The low ceiling was attributed to the unrepresentative early engines. The maximum speed of 1.005 M indicated was 0.95 M true.

B Mark 1 and 1A. Some 26 sorties, mostly on XA889 (four Olympus 101 and kinked leading edge to the wings), from March 1956 were sufficient for the initial CA Release, and included investigation of the effect of failure of the recently installed stability aids (including the first auto-mach trim) on the prototype. Two actual failures of the auto-mach trim occurred—one causing a nose-down pitch recording minus 0.5g; this excursion beyond the limit caused no structural damage—but the rear crew were not amused! Natural damping remained very low, but the flying qualities were "safe and adequate"; full up elevator at 100,000 lb (mid-CG) occurred at 102 kt and defined the stall. Engine power still limited performance; 43,000 ft over the target could be achieved at 0.85M, and with a 10,000 lb bomb the radius of action of 1,500 nm left a 20% reserve of fuel. XA889 returned in 1958 with Olympus 104 engines, and again in 1962 for five years of armament work (including twenty one 1,000 lb bombs HE, MC Marks 6,9,11 and 12), then navigation and finally ASV21 radar tests. 1956 assessment of radios, radar and navigation kit of XA890 gave mixed results, with the G4B compass proving unstable, thus ruining astro navigation; the aircraft ended its days in 1969 on ground EMC work at AAEE. The Operational Reliability Trial held in 1956 in conjunction with the Vulcan OCU produced a very critical report. XA895 was generally well engineered, but rear crew escape received great opprobrium, the navigation and bombing system (NBS) was rarely serviceable and the autopilot, de-icing and bomb bay heating, among other items were lacking. With so little equipment working, it seems unsurprising that there was not much mutual interference during EMC checks. By 1958 the autopilot and de-icing had been rendered operative in XA894 for trials which included a trip to Malta. The need for a routine 100 hr servicing check, coupled with changing all four engines of XA899 delayed assessment of the flight instrument system in 1958. In the same year XA896 spent two months at Boscombe with Avro's servicing while the aeroplane remained on charge of 230 OCU. The limited range of weapons required initially by Bomber Command were 25 lb practice and 1,000 lb bombs, and the 10,000 lb nuclear store It took until mid-1959 to clear them; later, 1,000 lb target indicators and No 38 clusters were added to the offensive load. With the indicator moved from the pilot's to the AEO's position, the rear warning radar (Orange Putter) received approval in XH478 during 1958 and three years later 12 hr were flown as receiver behind a Valiant. This aircraft returned after squadron service to AAEE as a Mark 1A in 1966 for armament trials, including parachute retarded 1,000 lb bombs of five versions dropped at low level.

The change in the role of the Vulcan to operation at low level led to two short trials at AAEE in 1963, both on Mark 1As; XH475 investigated the handling and XH499 was used for determining weapon release parameters and the effect on aircraft systems.

Perhaps the most unusual Vulcan trial involved XA903 in 1976 when the Establishment's expertise and facilities were employed with the firms involved in firing the Mauser 27 mm gun in the half fuselage containing an RB199 engine; this was the only gun firing from a V-Bomber, and took place in the stop butts.

B Mark 2. With the arrival of XH533 (four Olympus 201) in May 1959, the CA Release trials were immediately given high priority. After initial performance, including take off measurements, XH533 returned in 1963 for a protracted period of auto-land trials to compile the necessary statistical data for reliability validation; it was calculated that an accident would result once in every 3,190 landings. By 1967 testing of individual aircraft at RAF Scampton had scarcely begun when the auto-landing requirement was cancelled. Following some handling tests on arrival in January 1960, XH534 was dedicated to carriage and release of the Blue Steel guided missile weighing some 15,897 lb in its Type 102A form. Releases from 50,000 ft and up to 0.95M had been made when a taxying accident with a Gannet in mid-1962 caused extensive damage. XL317 built to production standard had already done work on the Blue Steel at Boscombe, then a brief test on 617 Squadron's XL320 in1962, while XH539 made the first Vulcan live firing at Woomera in October 1963. From January 1960, the evaluation of the navigation/bombing system occupied XH536, and included a Decca Mk 4 roller map, not subsequently used in service; later, the heading reference system—HRS Mk 1 for Skybolt—proved greatly superior to the earlier compasses used in the flight system. Nuclear safety checks of the 2,000 lb, 6,000 lb and 7,000 lb weapons took three months and were followed by preview handling with two Sybolt missiles on XH537, all in 1960, the same year in which XH557 was borrowed from Handling Squadron for streamings of the brake parachute. Radio, radar and ECM occupied XH535 in 1961; Rapid Blooming Window tests had just begun as a joint trial with the firm when the aircraft crashed fatally for the rear crew in May 1964. Three disparate trials were made on separate visits by XH538 from 1961; flight refuelling as receiver, then equipment for the low level role including radio altimeter 7B, and finally ECM, including an X-band jammer and Red Steer tail warning radar. A long range tank type A in the bomb bay created a new configuration and required loading, carriage and release of the WE177 nuclear weapon and other bombing configurations to be re-examined in XJ784 in 1964–5. A major evaluation of Vulcan operations at low level employed XL391 (four Olympus 301) intermittently for four years from May 1963., and included a trial in Aden in 1964. Much work on evolving the most suitable flight profile for "popping up" to release, and escape from, a nuclear weapon was done, and also performance/range measurements. In order to reduce the risk of over stressing the airframe following a failure of the elevator artificial feel system when flying at high indicated airspeeds, the Establishment recommended a switch to isolate the system. Similarly concentrated flying of XM606 in the UK, Middle East and Canada proved the operation of the terrain following radar over all types of surface, including snow. The radar was degraded by precipitation; over severe terrain the radar made demands for manoeuvres beyond the pilot's capability to follow. Another very serious concern was the effect of low flying on the life of the airframe; in extreme conditions 1% of the life could be consumed in one hour's flying. The RAF needed no encouragement to train at slow speeds in favourable weather, and closely to monitor consumption of fatigue life. In 1968, XM612 had a failure monitor of the air stream detector, and XM649 (four Olympus 301) tried the Decca/doppler 72 in 1970; apart from loss of tracking with the undercarriage down the new kit gave accurate results with GPI Mk 6. Another major trial from 1968 resulted from the RAF's need for information on a double engine failure on take off; AAEE's remit previously had been to examine only single failures. In this case, it was considered that experience had shown that a single, catastrophic failure of one engine could cause failure of the adjoining motor. XH539 (four Olympus 202), ultimately loaded to the maximum weight of 204,000 lb, made double engine-cut take offs from Boscombe and in the heat (and 5,000 ft elevation) of California with repeatable results. One recommendation was for a pitot head unaffected by the large sideslip angles generated during dynamic engine cuts. Three other short trials were completed during the period under review, all concerning avionics. XH563 tested a new HF radio, making flights to Gan (Indian Ocean), Canada and Norway in the process during 1969 and XM597 had a successfully revised radar warning receiver in 1972–3. XL361 needed checking in 1975 for pressure instrument errors after two minute aerials had been placed in front of the cockpit canopy for new Blue Saga radar warner; high level checks against the datum Phantom showed the effect to be insignificant.

Handley Page Victor

Prototype. The firm brought WB775 (four Sapphire SA6) by road to Boscombe for its maiden flight in 1952, and again in March 1955 for a preview, limited to 100,000 lb all up weight, 248 kt and 2.25g. Handling received fulsome praise, "light and effective controls with [good] aircraft response, and excellent, infinitely variable, air brakes." It was considered to be suitable as a high level bomber with autostabilisers in use, although some flexing of the airframe was apparent at high Mach numbers—up to 0.98M indicated. The crew worried about structural integrity near the stall on account of very severe buffeting. Low engine power and the restricted view were criticised.

B Mark 1, B Mark 1A, B(K)Mark1 and K Mark 1A. The team that went to Radlett to fly XA917 (four Sapphire 201) in June 1956 found additional features of concern from its more searching evaluation. The two unacceptable handling items were—the longitudinal stability which became neutral at aft CG, and lateral oscillations which were naturally divergent at all CGs. The latter was controlled by a single channel yaw damper, but duplication was considered essential in view of the catastrophic consequences of a single failure. Other very desirable improvements were needed to the engine handling, the feel system and reliability of the braking parachute. Calculations of performance expected in service gave a target height of 46,500 ft at the cruising speed of 0.85M. The report contains the comment, unusual for the Establishment to make, "rate of development must be increased." From early 1957 trials for the CA release were underway, principally on XA920 (four Sapphire 202), and concentrated on the benefits of the automatic leading edge flap to counter pitch up, the effect of single failures of other automatic stability aids, and the suitability of the control characteristics for the role. Handling with the benefit of vortex generators on the outer wings and an automach trimmer was acceptable at weights up to 158,000 lb and speeds up to 0.95M, but many flight limitations were recommended to cover the various degradations of behaviour which would follow failure of the aids. Criticisms were relatively minor, and included lack of the autopilot and anti-icing, flash misting of the windscreen on landing and poor presentation of pitch information.

147: Victor B.2 XL233 in about July 1963. It has fixed droop leading edges to the outer wings, vortex generators behind them, Kuchman "carrots" containing window, and, in the tail cone, probably an anti spin parachute. An extensive stalling trial was completed satisfactorily. © Crown Copyright

148: Victor B.2 XH670 in January 1967 on fuel jettison measurements. The starboard under wing tank has a pink stain from fuel. Its configuration includes a flight refuelling probe, and is devoid of national markings on the underside. © Crown Copyright

149: Victor B.2 XL165 landing with the help of a braking parachute. © Crown Copyright

Later, after repairs following airbrake failure at 350 kt in May 1958, take off distance to 50 ft at 160,000 lb was measured at 1,730 yd. Radius (after take off at 170,000 lb) was calculated as 1,480 nm with 20% reserve of fuel; height over the target to release the 10,000 lb bomb, had reduced to 44,200 ft. Communications, radars, and bombing system fell to XA919 for initial testing, assisted by XA922 on loan briefly from Handling Squadron during repairs of XA919 following extensive damage caused by landing with the starboard wheel brakes locked on. Armament work centred on XA921 from 1957 to 1963; a special hoist was needed for loading the 10,000 lb nuclear store Blue Danube, successfully released above 14,000 ft at 350 kt and repeated at 0.95M (indicated). Other bombs of lower priority received approval progressively. In the case of the magnificent load of thirty five 1,000 lb bombs, success proved elusive at first, attributed to low voltage reaching the release units. A subsequent meeting of over thirty five 200 lb officials considered remedial action, resulting in effective modifications by the end of 1961. Later, many combinations of loads, including a long range tank in the bomb bay and American leaflet containers received clearance. Last of the aircraft involved in the first batch of trials was XA930 on operational reliability investigation; 187.5 hr flying, mostly by Bomber Command crews under the scientific control of AAEE, resulted in a list of 160 recommendations for improvements. Heating, gland material and several electrical items were included, with crew escape the main cause of complaint. With many of the improvements incorporated, plus a flight refuelling probe, XA930 returned as a Mark 1A in 1960 and prodded the AAEE's Valiant tanker; speeds between 220 and 240 kt up to 34,000 ft made life easy, and one 12 hr sortie was achieved. The vexed subject of rear crew escape received considerable attention in 1958; a fully equipped live crew reached the escape door (ie the entrance) at speeds up to 290 kt and acceleration up to 1.25g, but remained on board. Dummies leaving at higher speeds sometimes struck the engine intake lip; they never lived to tell the tale.

Four developments kept Victor Mark 1s at Boscombe until 1969. XH587 (four Sapphire 207), a Mark 1A, had extensive ECM in an extended tail cone tested from mid-1960, and assessment of modified avionics in XH667 required only 30 days in 1969. XA920 returned to investigate the various bomb bay loads (photoflashes, camera crate and long range tank) in connection with the forthcoming PR version of the Mark 2. The change to low level operations involved, first, preliminary handling and "pop-up" manoeuvres, then XH618 in systems analysis and dropping nuclear "shapes" (ie, dummy bombs), followed by a wing pod-mounted terrain following radar on XA933 (four Sapphire 202) and finally low and high level flying of XA940 with strain-gauged engines in 1967. The fourth development was as a tanker, starting in 1963 with XA918 equipped with two wing tip mounted pods (Mark 20B); handling remained normal, but at the increased weight of 185,000 lb buffet occurred on retracting the trailing edge flaps at 185 kt. The cure suggested was to fix the drooped leading edge flaps, already incorporated in newer aircraft.

With fixed droop, take off run increased but distance to 50 ft remained nearly the same. Extended trials were made with all British and some foreign receiving aircraft, and repeated when the Mark 17 hose/drum unit was operable in the bomb bay in 1965. Associated avionics tests were made on XA932 in 1964–5, and involved a trip to Cyprus. Full radio/ECM/radar compatibility tests took place in 1966 on XA937, a B(K) Mark 1[3] three point tanker (with bomb bay and two wing pod hoses). XH614, a K Mark 1A,[3] extended the cleared weight to 190,000 lb, and included measurements of climbing on two engines; the effect of autopilot malfunction during tanking was investigated using XH620 as receiver in late 1967.

B Mark 2. The preview of the first Mark 2 ended fatally on its first flight at AAEE when XH668 (four Conway 201) disappeared into the Irish sea in August 1959. The lengthy and painstaking investigation established conclusively that one wing tip pitot head had become detached at a critical time leading to irrecoverable loss of control. Preparatory trials for live firing of the Blue Steel in Australia included carriage of ballasted (sand and/or water) Type 100 and 102A missiles; the only release made in UK was from 51,000 ft at 0.84M in November 1961 from XH674. Meanwhile, handling trials were underway on XH672 (four Conway RCo11) with drooped wing leading edges from which evidence of longitudinal instability led to a restriction in the aft-most position of the CG. XH675 and XL233 also joined the trials, and the three aircraft completed the CA Release work both for the original build standard and for the retrofit condition (including Conway RCo 17 engines). One interesting phenomenon concerned the reversal of the aerodynamic derivative L_v (roll due to sideslip) at speeds above 0.94M (indicated); coupled with aileron jack stall at 36,000 ft when high Mach combined with high IAS, maneuvering became a dicey business. The effect in the worst conditions when trying to raise a wing would be for the pilot to find the ailerons of little help and he would instinctively try opposite rudder, only to find the bank angle increasing. Maximum Mach number in service was strongly recommended to be limited to 0.92M. Take off weight was increased to 206,000 lb and approaches to the stall very carefully flown in XL233 with an anti-spin parachute. (This test followed the crash of XL159 during slow speed investigation by the firm with an AAEE co-pilot who ejected safely). Reports of the tests on the following four aircraft have not been found. XL158's work on Red Neck (a high resolution

---

[3] An interesting use of designations; the B(K) Mark 1 retained a bombing capability, but the K Mark 1A had the bomb doors sealed—besides having the Mark 1A modifications

150: A "boomer's" eye view of a Victor B.2 from AAEE from a USAF KC-135 tanker; the hose fixed to the boom for the trial can be seen. This sortie was probably the only occasion on which a Victor refuelled from an American jet tanker.

151: Fuel jettison at seven gallons per second from a Victor K.2 was first tested in XL232 in 1974, and repeated with XL163 (illustrated). © Crown Copyright

152: Neptune MR.1 WX502 in March 1955 during trials of RP Installation Mk 13 carrying 32 rockets in two tiers. 25lb, 60lb or flare headed rockets could be carried; they could also all be fired once modifications had been made by the Establishment. Accuracy improved with a steeper dive. © Crown Copyright

reconnaissance system involving locking of the H_2S in the sideways position) started in 1961; the system was cancelled in 1962. In the same timescale, XL162 came under the scrutiny of the Nuclear Weapons Group of Armament Division, and XH673 confirmed the firm's performance figures at high weights. For two years from January 1961 extensive tests were made of the navigation/bombing system and ECM of XH671. In 1969 XL188 tested modifications to improve the reliability of the brake parachute. One heartfelt comment from bombing tests was the inability of the navigator to reach, and particularly to escape from, the prone visual bomb aiming position when wearing a back parachute and high level oxygen equipment. In 1965 use of this position was approved at lower heights where the more cumbersome flying clothing was not required.

The introduction of more capable jamming and other avionics required further checks of their compatibility with nuclear armament, and this was done at Wittering on XL511 in 1963. Low level trials in 1963–4 of the Mark 2 involved XL164 (equipment and aircraft performance, "pop up" manoeuvre and discharge of window), XH670 (high speed, wing tanks and airframe fatigue) and, at Woodford whither Victor development had been transferred, XH674 (Blue Steel). Optimum flying techniques for the safe release of the nuclear free fall (Yellow Sun) and powered and unpowered guided weapons were recommended for service use, together with suggestions for minimising the consumption of airframe life. The bombing system (NBS Mk 2) of XL164 had a sideways looking capability together with a rapid processing facility enabling a print out to be made on board; over complicated controls were included in the list of criticisms. Terrain following radar tests followed, but the requirement was cancelled before completion

B(SR) and SR Mark 2. XH675 continued tests in 1962–3 of its combined bombing/ photographic roles; 190 hr of flying over UK, the Mediterranean and Australia, gave generally acceptable results up to 55,000 ft from the fan of eight F96 Mk 2 day and five F89 Mk 2 night cameras. The increase in all up weight to 216,000 lb was cleared in 1963. However, survey trials using XL165 (a retrofitted SR Mk 2 aircraft) in 1965–6 of the new F49 Mk 4 cameras (each weighing 140 lb with 500 ft of 9.5 in wide film) in UK and Canada revealed the need for more accurate heading data. The compass problem was traced to the wing flexing and misaligning the pendulous detector units installed near the tips. After some shortcomings in the camera crate heating of XM718, XL165 had a completely redesigned and satisfactory system tested in UK, Canada and the Persian Gulf.

K Mark 2. After the many changes to role, upgrades, retrofits and rectifications which continuously reduced the number of Victors available to the front line in their few years of service, the final change to the tanking role gave relatively long service. AAEE trials started in July 1973 with the arrival of XL231 (four Conway 201) having reduced wing span, ailerons rigged three degrees up, two MK 20B wing pods and ballast in place of the bomb bay hose unit. Weight increase to 223,000 lb, and later 238,000 lb (XL232 with Mk 17B hose drum unit and two 1,915 gal tanks in the bomb bay), required full investigation, including fuel jettison at 3,200 lb/min from the tail cone. At the higher gross weight take off run was 1,970 yd and 50 ft reached after 2,315 yd; at 200,000 lb, landing from 50 ft needed 3,230 yd including 2,230 yd on the ground with the parachute streamed. A climb of 235 ft/min on two operating engines could be achieved at high weight The minimum control speed on two engines of 131 kt only became significant at much lower weights; the ample performance made test techniques interesting. The normal Victor aerodynamic warning before the stall occurred in three intensifying levels of buffet, and in spite of aileron jack stalling at high IAS, the specified rates of roll were achieved. Satisfactory results from tests of all single failures considered possible, plus engineering and avionic evaluations, were followed by many sorties tanking for all the receiving types using all three hoses together or singly.

Lockheed Neptune

MR Mark 1. Following earlier noise and vibration trials on an unknown aircraft, WX502 had a Mark 13 rocket installation in 1954 armed with a pair of tiered carriers under each wing, giving a total of 32 rockets with 25 lb, 60 lb or flare heads. After AAEE changed the cables to the carriers, single tier firing was satisfactory; further modification to the upper tier prevented its rockets being ignited by the lower tier which went first. SARAH search equipment in WX507 was soon cleared in 1956.

British Aircraft Corporation TSR2

On cancellation of the TSR2 programme in mid-1965, the second machine, XR220 (two Olympus 320) was nearly ready to fly, and remained at Boscombe throughout 1966 on ground trials—nominally attached to B Squadron. A Cullum muffler gave good noise attenuation.

Dassault Mirage IVA

Following the cancellation of the TSR 2, a preview of the Mirage IV 01 (two Atar 9K) was held in France in 1965, and 11 flights made at 70,000 lb after three familiarisation trips in a Mirage IIIB. Although the engines had handling restrictions, cruising at both

50,0000 ft (1.8M) and 200 ft (0.95M) was smooth. The nav/attack system coupled with very good handling throughout the flight envelope soon gave the crew confidence, and the type would, it was considered, have met the RAF's operational requirement.

Hawker Siddeley Nimrod

Prototype. Prior to delivery to Boscombe Down in May 1968, the prototype XV148 (four Spey 250) had been flown by AAEE at Woodford on a preview. Comparisons with the Comet 4 were favourable in both performance and handling. At 160,000 lb the control harmonisation had been improved, and the unrestricted use of coarse elevator gearing at low altitude a significant advantage in a submarine hunter. Simulated attack manoeuvres revealed some weak features, notably the poor view for the pilots in critical directions. Stalling was docile in straight and turning flight, and the anti spin parachute fitted in place of the MAD boom was not deployed. At Boscombe, the effects of individual malfunctions were investigated, including landings without the yaw damper, and then in fine elevator gear; extensive tests of handling and performance under asymmetric power gave no surprises. On return in 1971, XV148 had four AS11 / AS12 air-to ground missiles; 18 of the former and 21 of the latter were fired at targets up to 5 miles distant with acceptable results.

MR Mark 1. Take off techniques varied between the firm and AAEE, and the prototype was joined by XV227 in early 1969 in further tests. Precise measurements and thus a comparison of the benefits of the two handling methods became difficult partly on account of the differing airspeed errors (XV148 had the static vent in the nose and XV227 on the bomb bay skirt), and partly because the effect of power off-takes from the engines was imprecisely known. Nevertheless, investigation was made of the intended operating configuration at low level and modest weight involving flight on two engines; the acceptable weight was determined by the ability to climb on one engine. In 1969 XV228 with the static pressure source on the bomb bay skirt revealed significant instrument errors at high altitude measured against the datum Javelin. Performance measurements at Edwards Air Force Base in California gave the reassuring result that the firm's figures for take off, climb, landing and rejected take off were accurate; the actual weight achieved was extrapolated to 177,500 lb and temperature to 30°C above standard giving a take off run of 2,025 yd, with 50 ft being reached after 2,310 yd. The wheel brakes and electrical generators needed improvement. Contemporary trials on XV226 in Bahrain added cabin conditioning, bomb bay temperatures, auxiliary power unit (APU) starting and engine oil loss to the list of items needing attention. The APU and hydraulic systems also gave problems during cold weather trials at Fort Churchill, Canada, in early 1970, when ground temperatures down to minus 37°C were

153: The second prototype, XV148, and first production Nimrod MR.1 XV226 over the West Country in September 1968. In production the windows of the original Comet were reduced in number, the ASV 21 radar was fitted, the "eyebrow" windows installed for the pilots, and the starboard wing tank fitted with a searchlight. © Crown Copyright

154 above: *Nimrod prototype XV147 taxys past the Weighbridge hangar, probably on firm's trials but with some AAEE aircrew on board. The jet pipes of the Avon engines of the original Comet remain visible.*

155 right: *Nimrod MR.1 XV148 with a pair of AS11 missiles. 13 of the 18 AS 11s fired were aimed; eight hit the target and two were very close. © Crown Copyright*

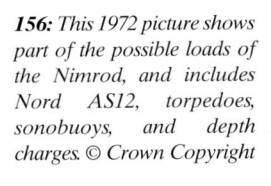

156: *This 1972 picture shows part of the possible loads of the Nimrod, and includes Nord AS12, torpedoes, sonobuoys, and depth charges. © Crown Copyright*

measured. Photographic trials using the F126 (day only) and F135 (day and night) vertical cameras gave good results, as did the hand held F138 camera. The autopilot (SEP6) met with approval, particularly on ILS approaches, but the flight director system (SFS 6) was considered to have poor presentation which limited its value. From mid-1969 XV228 and XV229 made intensive tests of the many integrated systems for hunting and sinking submarines. The magnetic anomaly detector (AN/ASQ10A) with its nine term compensator flew in areas of high magnetic dip with acceptable results, and the main radar (ASV21D) was assessed in the Bahamian underwater test range, both in 1971. Sophisticated test techniques were used to evaluate the efficiency of the navigation/attack system in the primary and back-up modes. XV229 returned later to make performance checks at the increased weight and aft CG of the forthcoming Mark 2 version, plus secure communication equipment involving flights above the Arctic circle.

R Mark 1. Flying by AAEE of this electronic intelligence version took place at Woodford, Boscombe and in Singapore on XW665 and XW666 in 1972. Trials were limited to normal and extended communications and navigation systems; the role equipment was fitted by the RAF later. Representative heaters to simulate the equipment loads were, however, installed in the appropriate areas, and shortcomings in the cabin conditioning became obvious in Singapore; the ASV21D radar reached its maximum safe temperature before being switched off.

157: Canberra B.2 WH876 resplendent in white finish and light blue trim, with starter cartridge smoke clearing the port engine. This long serving machine was one of several, but the intention of painting each of these Ministry owned aircraft in a different colour was only partially realised. The PR.9 from 39 Squadron in the rear was at AAEE between February and November 1965.

FIGHTERS AND SINGLE SEAT STRIKE AIRCRAFT

Hawker Hurricane

The remaining three Hurricanes, LS587 (Mark IIC on gun trials), KZ379 (Mark IV working with Porton) and LB743 (Mark IV on rocketry) had all left by early 1946. PG489 made flame damping its task in the first four months of 1946.

Supermarine Spitfire

After continuous operational use since 1938 the Spitfire remained in front line RAF service, and in production, into the early post-war years. Developments reached AAEE, but the reports, on which details in this book are based, suffered from the rapid disappearance of staff to write them. 38 Spitfires, new and old, featured.

Mark VII. The three aircraft used in wartime for daily temperature measurements (MD114, MD124 and MD190) departed by the end of 1945. A single replacement, MD189, stayed on until early 1947.

158: A pair of nines and a pair of twos in late 1970. Javelin FAW.9 XH897 leads Hunter FGA.9 XE601, with Harrier T.2 XW265 and Phantom FGR.2 XV415. © Crown Copyright

Mark VIII. Interest in the intensive flying of LV674 waned, and it soon departed.

Trainer. G-AIDN, a two seat modification of a Mk VIII, weighed 7,510 lb and handled as the single-seat version with a normal stall (dirty) at 65 kt; the view from the cramped rear seat was poor but adequate. The military test pilots flew the aircraft to 408 kt, but the civil limit was 348 kt.

Mark IX. The purpose of EN314's brief appearance from October 1945 is not now recorded, while the gun tests on RR238 and TA822 appear to have been suspended. The calibrated EN397 continued its work measuring pressure errors in other aeroplanes, and may have done post-war research into diving phenomenon. Research into the aiming of fighters included MH828 (and Vampire and Tempest) from October 1947 in which the damping of induced oscillations was measured using the camera of the gun sight; the results were inconclusive due to the variable conduct of the tests by the excessive number of pilots involved.

Mark XIV. RB146, on cooling, left by early 1946, but trials were made on four other Mk XIVs. NH707 had a Mk 9 RP installation in 1946; the long nose gave a poor view for sighting, but provided rocket attacks were made in a dive, results were acceptable. After TP240's accident in January 1946, armament research was continued on

RM790. Early work on a P14 compass kept MT847 busy for only a few weeks in early 1946.

Mark XVI. A pair of RPs with three tubes and 180 b warheads scarcely affected handling of TB757 in 1946; explosions were gratifying, but accuracy woeful in 23 firings. The GGS 4B gun sight in TE241 had reduced hazards for the pilot in crash landings, but was unacceptable since the aiming view was blocked by the nose. Peacetime handling standards, applied to SL745 (Merlin 266), resulted in the aft limit of CG being moved forward—achieved by flying with the rear fuselage tank empty. The risk of over-stressing the airframe, acceptable in war, was thus reduced in peace.

Mark 18 (the reports change from Roman to Arabic numerals with this mark). Wartime trials of NH872 (Griffon 65) were concluded in August 1945; in spite of strengthened wing structure, the aft-most acceptable CG for combat was achieved only after 50 gallons of fuel had been used from the rear fuselage tank. TP279 arrived in September 1945 with three F24 cameras, adequately heated, giving split vertical and one oblique pictures; several improvements were recommended. A new mounting bracket in TP423 for the GGS 4B sight raised it sufficiently for acceptable firing of the two 20 mm guns and RPs.

Mark 19. SW777 languished awaiting removal for many months after the war, and PM630 spent 18 months until mid-1947 on research into the measurement of pressure errors using radar.

Mark 21. The conclusion of trials of LA187 coincided with the end of hostilities, while intensive flying of LA219 and LA220 (both with Griffon 85 and contra-rotating propellers) continued with very satisfactory results with the exception of oil misting of the windscreen. The misting was cured by a device descriptively called an "anti-oil slinging ring." LA317 came in February 1949, probably for gun sight work, followed by LA326 with a Rotol five-bladed propeller; reports have not been found.

Mark 22. Arriving in November 1945, PK312 weighed 7,006 lb (tare) and 9,864 lb with a 500 lb bomb and 121 gal of fuel. Six 60 lb rockets could be fired successfully up to 433 kt from a Mk 9 RP installation using PK320 in late 1946. Firing of the four 20 mm Mark V star guns from PK547 was suspended following many stoppages attributed to misalignment of the ammunition belt links, but illumination of the GGS Mark IID gun sight proved acceptable after a few improvements. PK408 (called a Mark 24 in the report) carried and dropped three 500 lb bombs in 1947–8. Results of a short handling trial of PK515 in 1946 are not recorded.

Mark 24. The handling report of VN315 (Griffon 61) in late 1946 is missing. VN302 and VN324 made comparative evaluation of the gun sight (GGS 4B) with Mark II star and Mark V star 20 mm guns respectively; the latter, with shorter barrels, gave excessive vibration which contributed to gun stoppages in VN329.

Hawker Typhoon

MN861 returned from Khartoum, and may have started RP trials before being allotted away in late-1945.

North American Mustang

Three wartime Mustangs KH656 (Mark III with a gunsight GGS IID), KH766 (Mark IV) and TK586 (Mark IV) had gone by the end of 1945.

Hawker Tempest

Mark II. MW741 concluded its wartime cooling trials, and MW736 its heating measurements; the four 20 mm guns received little warmth, and a combustion heater was suggested. PR533 suffered an undercarriage collapse in March 1946 on armament work, and PR622 (Centaurus V) had small flaps and a lockable tail wheel in mid-1946 to assist pilots keeping straight on landing; little benefit resulted. MW762, possibly a rogue, spun and made the first recording on the ground of the pilot's voice from the air. PR806 and PR903 bombed and PR599 flew intensively, all in 1946. Armament trials engaged PR550 in 1948–9.

Mark V. Six of this mark remained after the end of the war. EJ891 had an undercarriage door blown off in November 1945 during bombing, while JN740 (Rockets), JN798 (bombs), NV732 (guns) and SN219 (Porton) soon left. JN799 continued research into bullet dispersion and sight harmonisation until 1948. SN354 with P guns (NOT apparently known as pea-shooters!!) weighed 12,655 lb with 160 gal of internal fuel and continued firing trials after a skilful forced landing following engine failure on take off in January 1946. SN352 made check firings of various rockets, including the 305 lb-head triplex variety following rectification of early faults with the RP Mk 8 installation; NV773 investigated gun aiming in 1947–8. After arrival from Beaulieu in 1950, SN329 towed the successful RFD wing target and, in June 1951, the Lewis Bros target which broke up at 170 kt.

Mark VI. NX119 (Sabre V) arrived in December 1945 and weighed 12,984 lb with 184 gal of fuel. It was joined by NX133 for engine cooling the following April, and NX288 spun in 1947 without recorded comments.

159: Spitfire XVI TB757 armed with Triplex rockets weighing 305lb (180lb head) for trials in early 1946. 23 rounds were fired up to 410 kt, but lack of ballistic data spoilt accuracy. © Crown Copyright

160: Spitfire F.24 VN315 ready for handling trials in 1947. The outcome is unknown as the report has not been found. © Crown Copyright

161: Spitfire Trainer Reg G-AIDN on a misty day in March 1947. The rear cockpit was cramped, but deemed acceptable. Two standards of limitations were applied—a Military maximum speed of 408 kt, and civil one of 348 kt. © Crown Copyright

162: Spitfire F.22 PK320 displaying its RP installation Mk IX Srs ii with six 60lb head rockets. Satisfactory firing was achieved up to 433 kt. © Crown Copyright

163: Tempest V SN352 with four Triplex rockets. 46 of these rounds were fired at speeds up to 455 kt, but accuracy was indifferent due to lack of ballistic data. © Crown Copyright

164: Meteor F.8 VZ460 in about May 1953 with a pair of 1,000lb HAH bombs looking very like Hunter 100gal tanks. The bombs produced very adverse handling at high Mach number, and on recovery from dives; speeds were limited to 400 kt/0.7M. © Crown Copyright

165: Meteor PR.10 VS968 in July 1950 with camera nose in evidence. The pilot's step is extended, and the empennage and wings are retained from earlier versions. © Crown Copyright

Republic Thunderbolt

The Mark 1, FL849, left early in 1946, but KJ298, a Mark 2, continued wartime research into turbo charging until mid-1946.

Gloster Meteor

The first Allied jet-propelled aircraft to enter service, in 1944, the Gloster Meteor continued in military use in the UK for half a century. At AAEE, tests of developments continued into the 1960s, while the type provided for the Establishment's support needs until 1972. Over 90 individual aeroplanes are included here in the roles of fighter (day and night), reconnaissance and ground attack, target tug and trainer.

F Mark 1. The sole Meteor in residence at the end of the war was EE212 in two seat configuration; little flying appears to have been done, possibly in view of the claustrophobic rear accommodation. However, at least one Admiral had a ride before the machine was sent away in mid-1946.

F Mark 3. EE230 reappeared in March 1946 with the ammunition capacity of each of the four 20 mm guns increased from 150 to 186 rounds; higher barrel temperatures remained acceptable. A year later the Establishment solved the problem of gun bay explosions by means of a strategically placed gas plug; proving the modification took until early 1949.

Handling with eight RPs (Mark VIII Type 11) was unaffected up to 438 kt on EE394 while the first retractable gun sight (GGS IID Srs (iii)) proved sufficiently robust to maintain accurate harmonisation in EE492. On the handling/performance side, EE336 spent a lengthy detachment from September 1945 at Khartoum flying 300 hours. At 14,500 lb for take off, the maximum rate of climb was 1,900 ft/min and 30,000 ft reached in 31.75 min; 370 kt TAS was achieved at 15,000 ft with a 180 gal ventral tank. Three engine changes were needed, but the airframe withstood the heat and sand well. In the UK spinning claimed the life of the pilot when EE312 failed to recover and the anti-spin parachute broke loose. The programme was successfully completed on EE282, both with and without the 180 gal tank; lateral thrashing of the stick was followed by normal recovery. Clipped wings for the Mark 4 occupied EE455 from June 1946; results are not known. Similarly no reports have been found of performance measurements of EE351 which collided with a lorry at Port Said on its way to Khartoum and was written off, nor of tests lasting six months on an alleged rogue, EE460. Perhaps the most interesting work on this mark concerned EE337 and EE387 which arrived early in 1948 with arrester hooks, strengthened undercarriages (to withstand arrivals of over 11 ft/sec), powered by uprated Derwent 5s and lightened. Take off measurements, corrected for a 40 kt headwind and 12,500 lb all up, gave a take off run of 370 ft; later deck flying showed good correlation. 32 landings on *HMS Implacable* gave rise to comments of "excellent" from the two pilots involved, but also stating that the hood had to be kept closed due to noise and discomfort. EE337 returned in 1952 to give practice for other deck trials.

F Mark 4. With wings clipped by 5 ft 6 in and Derwent 5s, EE520 had a good performance but poor fighting qualities due to a low rate of roll, heavy controls and large trim change with power at the low and medium altitudes, limited by its lack of pressurisation. Guns became very hot after lengthy firing. High altitude handling on RA417 (full span) and RA397 (clipped) revealed further shortcomings due to Mach effects, particularly with the 180 gal ventral tank, when longitudinal stability was marginal with general unsteadiness about all three axes. In 1950, RA397 dropped a wing at 0.82M and rolled uncontrollably above 0.84; it was decided to leave the recommended limit at 0.78 for the RAF. Range at 40,000 ft with 505 gal fuel (take off 16,340 lb) was assessed as 820 nm maximum on RA420. From September 1948 an additional pair of 100 gal under wing tanks on RA484 handled normally, except when one tank only was full—that was bad news. Consumption trials using 100 octane petrol were incomplete when the aircraft crashed in August 1950. Precise pressure error measurements of RA438 for its role as pacer for other aircraft, showed a difference of 4 kt when compared to other Meteors; its first subject was a Vampire in March 1952. EE525 needed full pro-spin control movements to enter a spin, but was otherwise normal. Intensive flying from December 1947, shared by RA486 and VW780, included cockpit heating, misting, hood seal and poor fuel venting among criticisms on flights up to 45,000 ft. VW293 towed winged and other targets in 1951. Other mark 4s appearing in maintenance returns and for which details have not been found were; EE517 (1951), EE598 (1947), and VT232 (1949).

20 mm guns of the Mark II star variety in VT259 were compared in 1950 with the first of the Mark V star type in EE531; the latter became acceptable after AAEE modifications to obviate ground explosions. In 1948 RA382 with a 30 in fuselage extension gave some benefits, but, surprisingly, had heavier rudder under asymmetric power and high stick forces in manoeuvres. This aircraft returned the following year with the addition of the empennage of the Gloster E1/44 giving lighter rudder and elevator but retaining heavy ailerons; the aircraft crashed fatally in unfortunate circumstances. Combined spring- and geared-tab ailerons improved roll performance at high speed on VT241 in 1951, while VW790 had improvements to the pressurisation system, in addition to long wings, extended fuselage and large intakes. In that configuration, VW790 assessed a landing technique without a flare; consistent results were encouraging.

166: Meteor NF.14 WM261 showing its ancestry in unpainted panels to lengthen the nose of the original NF.11 to accommodate the American APS/21 radar. © Crown Copyright

167: Meteor F.8 I-128. A Dutch Meteor in March 1953 with four HSS 804 20mm guns. The chutes for the spent cartridge cases are of the lengthened type, and the rearming panel evident above them. © Crown Copyright

168: Meteor F.3 EE351 in standard pose with the pitot cover flag fluttering in the breeze. Records of the work of this aircraft at AAEE are scant, probably because it had a nasty accident at Port Said in May 1947 on its way to Khartoum. © Crown Copyright

169: *Meteor F.8 WA982 in March 1952 with wingtip mounted dummy Fireflash missiles on a short stay at Boscombe. © Crown Copyright*

170: *Meteor F.4 RA438 with camera windows on the nose for calibration of pressure instruments of formating aircraft. There appears to be another, smaller, window under the canopy, which is, in fact, for rescue. Probably taken in 1951–2. © Crown Copyright*

171: *Meteor TT.20 WD767 with a sleeve target in March 1958. The various fittings under the fuselage roundel and the target tug stripes are of interest. The small bullet attached to the target is a SAAB miss distance microphone which suffered from intermittent electrical connection with the recorder in the Meteor. © Crown Copyright*

115

T Mark 7. After examination in the blower tunnel in mid-1948, EE530 was reassembled and comprehensively spun in 1949, both with and without the 180 gal tank; behaviour was similar to single seat versions and recovery after two turns was recommended. Handling of VW411 revealed increasingly heavy controls above 0.7M (ie rapid increase in manoeuvre margin with speed) giving stick forces per g up to 50 lb; below compressibility effect the figure was 10 lb, and more acceptable. The compass of VW411 gave poor results during navigation and radio assessment, but the cockpit lighting in VW410 met requirements in 1950. An RAE trial in 1949 on VW412 involved AAEE assistance in evaluating the operation of automatic airbrakes to reduce the risk of over speeding. In the following 11 years four aircraft flew with new radio/radar equipment: WS110 (1955) with IFF Mk10, XF274 with ILS and zero reader (1956 and then training until 1968), WL488 with Rebecca 8 (1956), and WL353 with UHF (1960). WA690 started a lengthy stay at Boscombe with a year's flying with dual GGS gun sights; results were generally acceptable apart from snaking above 450 kt. With a new nose job, WA690 investigated the feasibility of using Polycell as synthetic slush on the runway; results were categorised as, "useful"—if only because of the success of using a concrete mixer for the large quantities needed. Further modifications with an ejector seat in the rear led to unsatisfactory handling after firing. 15 years of training and general support duties followed. WA634 proved the Folland Mark 4 ejection seat in 1951 prior to half a century with the rival Martin Baker company. The Establishment's photo-chase, target, instrument rating, conversion and other needs were met by an additional eight Meteor T.7s: VW418 (1957–1964 included oxygen consumption measurements at up to 40,000 ft—unpressurised), VW451 (1949–1950), VW453 (1957–1966), WA709 (1953 towing targets until written off following a landing short of the runway in November 1963), WF822 (1956–1960), WG996 (1957–1967), WL377 (1955–1958) and WL472 (1960).

F Mark 8. VT150, retaining Derwent 5 engines but having a 30in extension of the fuselage and empennage of the E1/44 aircraft, arrived in August 1949. Top speed (raised by 0.02M), better rudder forces, improved elevator and trimmer operation were improvements noted, and confirmed when the F.4 tail was fitted for comparison in 1949. At forward CG, take off run was extended by difficulty in raising the nose. Spinning at all CG, and including entry at 40,000 ft, demonstrated the usual thrashing tendency of the stick; this trial also produced unpleasant snaking, yawing and nose down pitch on recovery. Analysis was aided by the first continuous reading trace recorder giving elevator angle and stick force. Gun firing proved troublesome in VZ467 (four 20 mm Hispano Mk 2*) from March 1950 when guns stopped due to rounds being blown into the breach, and also shells damaged the ventral tank. AAEE suggested elliptical-section ejection tubes which gave good results between 150 kt and 510 kt. A further firing problem affecting Mark 4 and 8 aircraft was cured by considerable strengthening of the nose structure of VZ501 and VZ506. 20 mm guns for Belgian and Dutch Meteors were of the HSS804 variety and needed a few modifications after firing some 38,178 rounds from WK648, I-128 (Dutch) and EG150 (Belgian) in 1952–3. At the same time WA775 tested the latest gun sight (GGS V). Late 1950 saw tests of RPs in double tiers under the wings of VZ473 with mixed results; handing was unaffected but as a launching platform the ailerons were too heavy above 350 kt. Concurrent flying of VZ460 with early spring tab ailerons pointed to a solution, although feel was poor at under 150 kt. Production spring tabs on WH483 gave good results with the rate of roll increased from 65 to 85 degrees per second at 350 kt with no stores. Firing of sixteen 60 lb RP was acceptable up to 480 kt but elevator force reversal occurred on dive recovery, a phenomenon confirmed on WA857 (two Derwent 8) in 1952. The latter also had reduced snaking with airbrakes restricted to 90% travel; both aeroplanes had spring tab elevators to which the reversals were attributed. WH857 also investigated three types of fuel; thrust remained constant—but the volume of fuel required varied inversely with the specific gravity (sg). The lowest sg was 100 Octane petrol[1] at 44°C in bowsers at Khartoum. Early cockpit misting and poor heating led to modifications, successfully tried in VZ500 and VZ442 in 1952. The former also had an RAE-type yaw damper with effective phase advance at high speeds, while the latter had the first clear vision canopy which needed some changes after blower tunnel tests. The only dedicated radio trials on this mark occurred on WF716 in 1953; Rebecca 7 demonstrated accurate ranges of up to 200 nm at 30,000 ft.

External additions took the form of RPs, HVARs, pylon bombs and towed targets. RP Mk VIII Type 8 worked well with a new type of saddle under the wings of VZ473 and WK648 in 1952, while at the same time G-7-1 flew with an additional eight RPs under the fuselage where they suffered slight damage from firing of the guns. WK648 had five in HVAR, limited by their drag to 470 kt; firing may have taken place. A handling limit of 400 kt was placed on VZ460 when carrying two 1,000 lb bombs on wing pylons due to dangerous tightening on recovery from dives. WA904 flew with CATS from 1952, possibly with Firestreak missiles later; WA982 appeared briefly in early 1952 with tip mounted dummy Firestreaks. WH447 investigated target towing in 1955–6.

FR Mark 9. Three Mark 9s reached Boscombe, starting with VW360 in July 1950 when it was soon discovered that, even with cameras adding weight in the

---

1 22,746 Imperial gallons had been arranged for this trial at 31.8d each. (= 2.9 pence per litre)

nose, stick forces were unacceptably light at high altitude (sfg of 1 lb). The F24 camera performed well, although the bay soon became overheated at low altitude. In 1952 this aircraft investigated the effect of AVTAG fuel (sg of 0.79 against the usual 0.755 of AVTUR) in Khartoum; the Derwent 8s ran sweetly. 51,725 rounds of 20 mm ammunition were fired from VW362 during gun trials; structural strengthening prevented breakages. Measurement of the effect of modifications to cockpit cooling occupied WB134 in 1953.

PR Mark 10. VS968, with long span wings, the old type of tailplane and sporting a ventral tank, had three cameras (one nose, two in the tail) and suffered in comparison with the up-to-date handling of the Mark 8 and 9. All controls were heavy, and, with one full under wing tank aileron forces were extremely high (the recommendation to the RAF reads, "ensure the tanks are very securely bolted on"). Servo-tab ailerons on VS969 reduced forces significantly. The F52 camera installation needed modifications; later, WB181 had camera heating improved as suggested by the Establishment. Performance of VS968 at a take off weight of 18,475 lb gave a maximum speed of 479 kt (true), occurring at 5,000 ft, a ceiling of 45,700 ft at maximum power, but only 41,500 ft at continuous power, and initial climb of 5,300 ft/min; 38,000 ft was the most economical height (1.5 anmpg). Thrust boundaries, a recent innovation, indicated a 2g ceiling of 30,000 ft. WB160 tested radios and the original IFF in 1951, and WB164 the new IFF Mark 10 in 1955.

NF Mark 11. Aerodynamically modified to represent a night fighter, VW413 appeared in 1949 and met the specification for stability with a forward CG (21.5% mean chord); however, the ailerons were too heavy and the landing distance excessive. Spring tabs on the ailerons in 1950 proved lighter, and a 40% increase in flap area gave a landing run of 970 yd and, from 50 ft, 1515 yd; both modifications were acceptable. WA546 and WA547 came next in early 1951; the ventral tank gave problems on the former, as the more forward CG gave poor high altitude stability and very low stick forces (1.4 lb sfg). Spinning was normal with little chance of an unintentional spin. During wing tank jettison tests, the tanks hit the wings at speeds above 350 kt. In 1952 gun accuracy was greatly improved by a yaw damper. Inward venting of these tanks was introduced after collapsing on WA547 in rapid descents, and after damage caused by firing the guns on the wings. The engineers commented that access to the inside of the Mark 11 (WD595) had been improved, although more could be done. WD593 demonstrated satisfactory handling with both ventral and wing tanks fitted provided the CG was well forward; a rate of descent averaging 8,400 ft/min could be achieved. The radar (AI 10) and other avionics needed a few modifications after trials on WD589, while WD596 flew with the direct vision panel open; above 200 kt, noise became intolerable. Among shortcomings in 200 hr of intensive flying on WD593 were electrical failures from excessive brush wear, much misting after descent, lack of cooling at low level and an unreliable thermostat to keep the guns warm. Pressurisation was, however, alright. With changes made by the Establishment, gun feed and heating were acceptable in WD797, and a Godfrey cold air unit in WD721 was effective at low level, including at Khartoum in late 1952. While there, AVTAG fuel proved to be acceptable. In 1954 WD587 with AI 17 radar flew at Malta against radio controlled Arsenal 5501[2] target aircraft; the radar aiming spot wandered, producing inaccurate aiming. Tip tanks on WD604 were a novelty, but fed and jettisoned without difficulty, and, later, IFF Mark 10 gave no surprises. WD656 appears in the technical record for an unknown purpose in 1954.

NF Mark 12. WD670, a Mark 11 with extended nose to represent the housing of the American APS21 radar but without a fin extension, displayed alarming and dangerous fin stall at altitude (undiscovered by the firm—Armstrong Whitworth) coupled with rudder overbalance at low speed. A small fin extension on another NF11, WD687, cured both problems in 1953. On return with the radar fitted, WD670 passed its tests including gun firing, with few adverse comments.

NF Mark 13. Intended for Middle East use, trials centred on avionics. Criticism of WM331 in 1953 resulted in changes to WM366 the following year; little improvement was noted. The navigation facilities were, "hardly capable of improvement," says the report; even for 1954 that is a remarkable statement and must have slipped through the normal scrutiny by senior staff. WM366 appeared briefly in 1954, followed by WM367 with Rebecca 7 prior to 16 years of support work at Boscombe.

NF Mark 14. After tests in the blower tunnel, the clear long hood of WM261 was asessed as safe in 1953, and an improvement. The first trial on a production Mark 14 was on WS844 (almost the last Meteor made) in 1955 to assess towing a 30 ft nylon banner target; a snatch take off technique reduced the take off distance by 300 yd compared to the drag method. UHF radios in WS843 occupied only a few weeks, WS805 flew with CATS briefly, and WS832 and WS838 provided photo-chase facilities, the latter until 1969.

U Mark 15. Two flights of VT110 at Tarrant Rushton in November 1957 sufficed to demonstrate normal behaviour of this manned target.

U Mark 16. This drone variant handled as a mark 8 when piloted by AAEE (probably at Llanbedr) using WH284 in 1960. Ten years later WH420 spent three months at Boscombe in connection with the Rapier missile project.

---

[2] Six Arsenal 5501 pilotless targets (looking like wartime V-1s) were assessed by AAEE; damage from rapid parachute descents limited the machines' life.

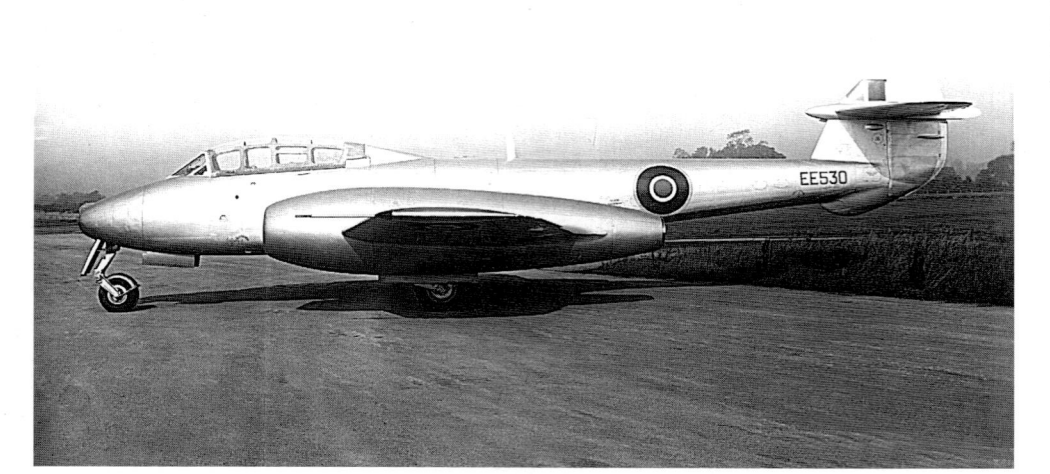

172: Meteor T.7 EE530 in October 1948 at Moreton Valence. Hood jettison tests at AAEE had been completed the previous month, and spinning followed a year later.

173: Meteor TT.20 WD641 with copious dayglo in the fashion current in late 1965. The winch can be seen above the wing tip, and the Rushton target on its mouting under the roundel. Unlike WD767, the stripes have been painted on the drop tanks. © Crown Copyright

174: Meteor F.3 EE394 in June 1948 with eight rockets, seen here at Pendine "on ramp for ground projection" according to the report—ground firing was intended. Air firing was also achieved, and recommended at speeds up to 438 kt. © Crown Copyright

175: Meteor F.8 VZ460 in 1953/4 with a typical wing installation of a 1,000lb HAHS bomb. A pair of bombs caused dangerous loss of lateral control at high speed, and the maximum recommended for Service was 0.7M. © Crown Copyright

176: Meteor NF.11 WD604 with two 100gal wing tip tanks in February 1952. Most unusually, the fins on the tanks are at the front. ie ahead of the centre of gravity. Handling and jettison were unremarkable. © Crown Copyright

177: Meteor T.7 WA 690 with a periscopic sighting mirror for the rear seat. The usefulness of the dual gyro gunsights was limited as no guns were fitted, and snaking occurred above 450 kt. © Crown Copyright

TT Mark 20. After basic radio tests in WM242 in 1959, extended range radios were flown in WM167 in 1962 and entirely new kit in WM151 in 1969. This mark investigated various towed targets over an eight year period from 1957. WD767 had a safe endurance of only 34 minutes at 5,000 ft when towing a 15 ft long sleeve target on a 2,000 yd line in 1957; a partially successful miss distance indicator using a microphone in the target was towed in 1958. Then followed tests on a Dart target (without microphone) which was wastefully dropped after each sortie, and then, in 1961–2, a Mark 3 version having a microphone with poor electrical connections during the launch procedure. To reduce waste, the Delmar target could be retrieved into its wing stowage after use, but many other difficulties resulted in severe operating limitations. WD706 joined in the Delmar flying, while WD641 spent 1965 exploring the usable envelope with a new Rushton target; a surprising outcome was the raising of the take off safety speed from 150 kt to 175 kt—possibly a reflection of changing standards at this late stage in the type's life. WM147 appeared briefly for an unrecorded purpose in 1957.

Westland Welkin NF Mark 2

Between January and June 1949, P17 featured on the engineers' returns, possibly being used for radar investigation.

de Havilland Vampire and Sea Vampire

F Mark 1. Wartime evaluation of TG274 (Goblin 1) continued until it struck the ground during a low overshoot in December 1945. Its top speed of 526 mph (true) had been the highest measured during the war, and subsequent tests showed that it could reach its critical Mach number (0.76) in level flight; maintenance was easy. Gunnery occupied TG284 throughout 1946; serviceability was poor, due partly to repairs to the nose after firing. Snaking during air firing spoilt the aim, and some 15 essential modifications were recommended, but three types of gyro gun sight received approval. Faults with fore-aft movement of the guns were cured in VF306 in 1948. After initial handling of the Goblin 2 in TG330 in early 1946, intensive flying of the new engine on TG381 lasted a month before an engine failure and damage led to replacement by TG447 which also needed two engine changes. Some 87 hr in 134 sorties took six months to complete before TG447 caught fire on the ground. VF314 broadened experience of the Goblin 2 (three engines used in 100 hr of flying) in Khartoum in 1947–8; sand in the controls caused no problems, but the wooden structure shrank at first and the batteries would not hold a charge. Airbrake tests on TG338 were curtailed when the undercarriage failed to extend in time on landing in February 1949 (i.e. the pilot forgot). Mechanical failure of the undercarriage in December 1946 delayed completion of testing of bombs and rockets for Switzerland in J1004; bombs of up to 500 lb could be released safely in dive angles up 80°. Scant details are known about four mark 1s: TG314 spent the latter six months of 1950 at Boscombe, probably with C Squadron, TG386 manoeuvred with wing tanks until the undercarriage extended at high speed and collapsed on landing, TG428 made range measurements, also in 1947, and TG446 apparently left in December 1948.

F Mark 2, or "Vampire—Elephant ears," as this version is frequently referred to in AAEE documents of the period. The Nene RB41 motor of TG276 gave a useful reduction of 14% in take off run and an increase of 20 kt at 5,000 ft. Range was unaltered, but a fire in December 1946 interrupted trials. With the elephant ear intakes replaced in March 1950 by enlarged wing root intakes longitudinal stability was poor, and there was no warning of a sudden pitch up at 0.8M. Maximum level speed at 25,000 ft was 461 kt at 0.765M, virtually the same as the Goblin version; it took 5.68 min to reach 35,000 ft. TG280 made short visits to confirm the effect of the "ears." In late 1947, TX807 had a steel undercarriage, flown prior to leaving for Australia.

F Mark 3. TG275 (Goblin 2) with low tailplane, increased fuel and other changes represented this mark in April 1947. Spinning was very erratic but recovery action always effective after two turns. Other handling was combined with the pressurised VF343; with a pair of 100 gal tanks, longitudinal characteristics were poor, to the extent of stick force reversal in turns preceding a stall. In mid-1948, fitting nose ballast of 66 lb combined with an enlarged inertia weight in the elevator control run gave improved, but still low, stick force per g. VF317 had no trouble with the radio tests, but VV200 (Goblin 2) had freezing guns at 45,000 ft—indicating the need for muzzle covers. VV190 (Goblin 4) confirmed the poor stability when the ideal minimum IAS could not be achieved at the optimum altitude during range tests. An investigation into the effect of mach number on maximum lift served to highlight the limited power available, ie the 2g lift boundary was 48,000 ft, but the thrust was insufficient to sustain a 2g turn above 35,000 ft—a result typical of the period. VV190 probably made the first high altitude calibration with the Meteor in March 1952.

FB Mark 5. Designed for the fighter bomber role, and having wings clipped by one foot each, interest centred on spinning using the prototype VT818 in late 1948; behaviour was similar to the Mark 3. On VV215 loading bombs needed care to prevent the CG from becoming too far aft, and retention of a full load of ammunition (in the nose) recommended. Handling was then acceptable, but misting became an embarrassment, and the machmeter needed to be moved into the pilot's view. On

178: *Meteor F.3 EE387 in April 1948 modified for deck landings with arrester hook and undercarriage strengthened to withstand landings of 11.5 ft/sec (normally 6 ft/sec). Thirty-two landings were made on HMS Implacable in 1948, and a similar number of unassisted take offs at 12,500lb. © Crown Copyright*

179: *Meteor NF.11 WD589 on trials of its AI 10 radar.*

180: *Meteor NF.13 WM331 posing to show all its aerials in July 1953. In addition to those above and below the fuselage and on top of the wings is a further whip aerial on the lower engine nacelle. Characteristic of this mark intended for the heat of the Middle East is a small air intake seen below the pilot's extended foot step. © Crown Copyright*

181: Vampire F.2 TG276. The extra mass flow required by the double-sided compressor of the Nene engine compared with the original Goblin was achieved by the "elephant ear" intakes. Seen here possibly at Hatfield in mid-1949, the aircraft had a better performance than the earlier version. © Crown Copyright

182: Vampire T.11 G-5-7 with 60lb head rockets and 100gal tanks. Some deterioration was apparent in handling, with severe nose up change in trim above 0.79M; performance was considered poor. © Crown Copyright

183: Vampire FB.5 VV216 carrying eight 60lb head rockets. This installation incorporates several AAEE ideas, including shortened struts, to improve the Vampire's rocketing. There is an interesting triangular aircraft in the background. © Crown Copyright

184: Vampire F.3 VF317 with an unrepresentative cockpit cover, and retaining the high tailplane of the Mark 1. Radio/IFF tests kept it at Boscombe for three months from November 1947. © Crown Copyright

185: Vampire F.3 TG275 with the innovations of larger "acorns" where the new lowered tailplane met the fins, but lacking pressurisation. The type remained longitudinally unstable at high airspeeds. © Crown Copyright

186: Vampire NF.10 G-5-2 in early 1950, still bearing the inscription applied for the 1949 SBAC show at Farnborough. Damage on a previous trip led to the entire nose cone detaching at 454 kt, leading to handling difficulties before a safe landing. © Crown Copyright

187: Vampire F.1 J1004 for Switzerland in late 1946. AAEE's role was limited to clearing the various external stores required, as the 500lb bombs here, before similar loads had been assessed for the RAF. © Crown Copyright

188: *Vampire F.2 TX807 with a Nene engine intended for Australia was tested with unknown results at AAEE in late 1947. © Crown Copyright*

189: *Vampire F.1 TG386 in 1947 at about the time of its AAEE trials of handling and performance with the underwing tanks shown. The high tailplane is just visible, as is the wing tip VHF aerial.*

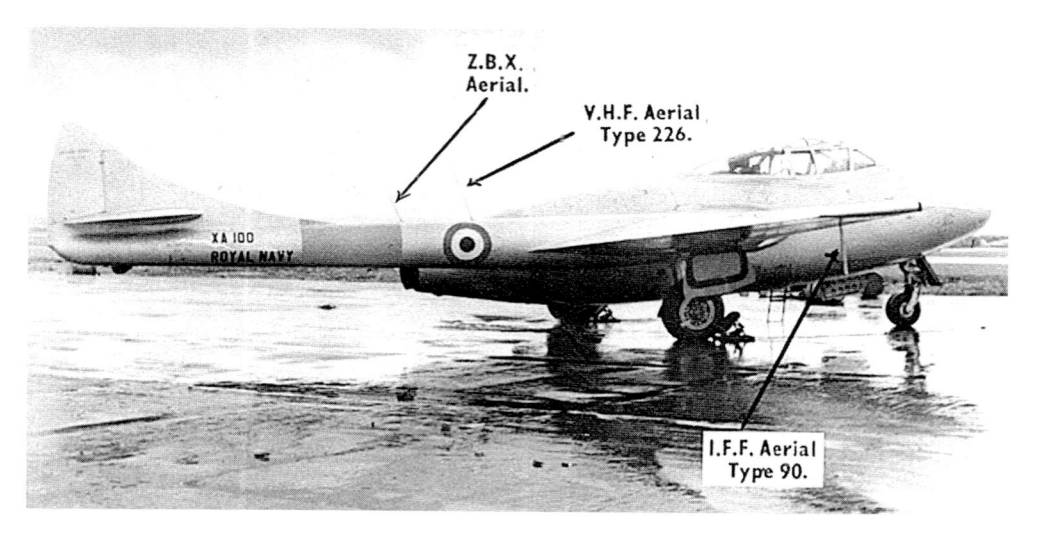

190: *Sea Vampire T.22 XA100, showing aerial positions for tests on a new IFF fit in February 1954. © Crown Copyright*

191: *Sea Vampire F.20 VV136 with the "best airbrakes to date" in mid-1949. They were 40% larger than previous brakes and gave a 70% increase in deceleration. © Crown Copyright*

another trial, the magnesyn compass proved unreliable and in urgent need of replacement. Two 1,000 lb bombs on VV218 reintroduced the reversal of stick forces, this time in dives, while the stall occurred 9 kt faster than in the clean configuration; two bombs (raising gross weight to 11,145 lb at take off) reduced maximum speed to 433 kt, and had an 11% range penalty. The first de Havilland-built aircraft, VZ208, handled as well as the previous Vampires built by English Electric.

Armament tests began with RPs (RP Installation Mark 8) using VV216 and VV220 in mid-1948; modification to cure damage to the tailplane from rocket debris delayed clearance for a year. In the meantime VZ808 joined, and together the three aircraft investigated the range of under wing stores; all could be flown and released at speeds up to 455 kt, apart from 1,000 lb bombs (400 kt) and SCIs (release up to 390 kt). The only handling difficulty involved landing in a crosswind with a single 1,000 pounder; when carrying 100 gal tanks and RPs together, the former had to be jettisoned first if the need arose. In 1951/3, with VZ324 replacing VV216 after damage, additional stores, including 150 gal fuel tanks on, confusingly, VZ216, received attention; the larger tanks gave a sudden nose up change of trim when the airbrakes were extended, and napalm, a very inaccurate weapon, needed to be dropped from under 100 ft. VV475 (1948–9) and VV528 (1950) also made bomb tests, while VZ116 was sent by the RAF as a rogue, but nothing untoward could be found. In 1952, targets, including the 30 ft banner net, revealed the shortcomings of VX985 as a tug; without drop tanks endurance was very short, and with them it took 44 min to reach 20,000 ft. Later, an RFD target gave better results. WA201 appeared briefly in 1951.

FB Mark 9. The cold air unit which distinguished this version from the Mark 5 worked moderately well in VV675, both in the UK and at Khartoum in 1950–1. It was considered that as the cold air unit provided pressurisation, the Marshall blower previously used became redundant.

NF Mark 10. The prototype G-5-2 (Goblin 3) was initially rejected as a night fighter after its second visit in 1950 due to unacceptably low stick forces, poor air and wheel brakes, lack of stall warning in the approach configuration, and a cramped cockpit; in addition the whole nose section tore off at 454 kt. The report omitted any facetious remarks about the desirability of a night fighter having a nose to mount the radar. Level speed had been measured at 470 kt (true) at 15,000 ft, and climb at 3,680 ft/min. After repair and an extension to the span of the tailplane among other changes, handling became satisfactory, and gunnery accurate up to 0.72M. The blast tube assembly also received approval in 1951, together with a Mark 2 reflector gunsight. Radar (AI Mark 10) and the radios performed adequately in G-5-5 in 1951. WP232 had "grossly inadequate escape facilities" and remained cramped, although layout had been improved; at forward CG the restricted aft movement of the stick prevented the nose from being raised on take off at the normal speed. Spinning and flight without the hood gave rise to few comments. In 1953, WP249 developed a

192: Vampire T.11 WZ419. The first Vampire to be fitted with ejection seats and clear view canopy about to undergo the obligatory jettison trials in which some modifications to the hood locking hinges were found to be necessary in May 1953. © Crown Copyright

camera system on the wing tips to record bullet dispersion patterns, and WP243 experimented with a stabilised gun sight. In 1955 WM711, known as an "NF Mark 10 Trainer" was, in the opinion of AAEE, much too Spartan for navigator training; for example, there was nowhere to stow maps, and the Rebecca dial was out of sight.

T Mark 11. The current vogue for side-by-side seating in pilot trainers was followed in this mark. Trials began in July 1951 with spinning on G-5-7 (Goblin 3)—the first Vampire to be systematically spun for four turns; apart from a tendency for the rudder to overbalance, behaviour was normal. Reduced rudder travel later proved to be acceptable. Early experience in the RAF led to tests on WZ448 when a very delayed recovery from right spins was confirmed in 1953; spinning was banned pending fitting of dorsal fin extensions. WZ466 soon appeared with dorsal fins and demonstrated superior spin recoveries with no rudder overbalance; instrument pressure errors remained small. Cockpit assessment of the prototype followed spinning—the main criticism being the difficulty of baling out; canopy-less flight up to 320 kt could be tolerated. Apart from severe pitch up at 0.79M when carrying RPs, external stores gave docile handling, but performance with stores was poor. Unremarkable gun tests continued into 1952. Production handling on WW458 and WZ415 (both Goblin 35) produced no surprises, although RP (Mark 8 installation) firing caused minor damage and needed new rocket saddles. The Mk 5 gunsight gave satisfaction in WZ420. WZ421's cockpit cooling was insufficient for tropical climes, and the engineers found that the wing surface soon deteriorated. Extending the CG aft in WZ417 led to dangerous pitch up at high mach number; with two 100 gal tanks on WZ549 the pitch up was worse with airbrake extension. AAEE considered that ferry flights only were acceptable in the latter configuration. Ejection seats, a single, central instrument panel, and a new canopy characterised WZ419 in late 1952. Stick movement was initially restricted, rear view was poor, and rain obscured the view forward. Introduction of hard hats prevented the firing handle from being pulled until the Establishment reduced the bulk of the seat pack in XD627 in late 1956. Minor snags prevented unrestricted clearance of the new UHF standby radio in XK624 in 1961. WZ414 came for instrument ratings and training in 1954 and XK633 for a similar purpose in 1960.

Sea Vampire F Mark 20. The prototype LZ551 with a hook and an early Goblin 2 motor arrived in February 1946 for an opinion on the deck landing potential of the type. Using a straight in approach and keeping power above idling, the three C Squadron pilots involved considered that deck landings were feasible in the Vampire. Further modifications improved the handling for deck work on *HMS Ocean* in June 1946. Take offs by VV136 (airbrakes of 40% greater area) were measured at 10,250 lb to give a run of 630 ft into a 40 kt wind; other handling up to 410 kt was good. Deck trials using VV138 also followed at 9,840 lb when the entire deck length of 720 ft was required to unstick into a 40 kt wind. There is no comment on the discrepancy in runs between calculation and experience. With a pair of 100 gal tanks the stick forces became extremely light above 350 kt; no great significance was attached to this undesirable characteristic.

Sea Vampire T Mark 22. XA101 was similar to the RAF trainer but had a new canopy on arrival in August 1953; crew escape was thereby made easier. Naval radios in XA100 needed minor changes in early 1954, but UHF in XA169 (1960) and IFF/SSR in XG743 (1968) were satisfactory.

F Mark 51. AAEE had a look at VV568 under this designation in January 1950. The Nene engine had "elephant ears", and handling suffered accordingly at high speed. Airbrakes were noticeable by their absence.

de Havilland Hornet

F Mark 1. In August 1945 hot weather trials occupied PX221 in Khartoum, while PX211 at Boscombe revealed very low stick forces (2 lb per g) to manoeuvre, rudder overbalance and "vicious" behaviour on take off following failure of either of the handed engines. The port engine (Merlin 130) rotated clockwise viewed from the rear and the starboard (Merlin 131), anticlockwise. Intensive flying of PX217 and PX218 lasted until June 1946, and attracted the comment that the compact design made access complicated, and that the cockpit heating at 35,000 ft was unacceptable. PX220 was presented in early 1946 with a larger tailplane, followed by PX247 with a dorsal fin to obviate the rudder overbalancing. A year later PX222 (belonging to the Royal Navy) flew at night without difficulty for the pilot, and with well damped exhausts. After reduction of early vibrations in PX223, the new gun sight (GGS Mk IVA) gave good results, although the artificial horizon as partially obstructed. This aeroplane was used to sharpen the skills of C Squadron pilots for forthcoming deck landings.

F Mark 3. Arriving in October 1946, PX348 joined in the gun sight trials described above. Next, some eight months later, came PX312 for handling with two 100 gal tanks, but lacking the bungee in the elevator circuit; speed was restricted to 290 kt to obviate aileron buffet. Performance was not measured until early in 1950 using PX386; at 17,805 lb maximum speed was 392 kt (true) at 19,000 ft, climb 2,640 ft/min and ceiling 33,000 ft.

Lengthy work on armament using PX393 revealed minor problems with the RP Mark VIII installation, both on its own and when carried with 500 lb bombs; AAEE

193: Hornet F.3 PX383 photographed in mid-1948 to show its new VHF (TR1464) aerial under the wing tip. A communications Dominie is in the background. © Crown Copyright

194: Hornet F.3 PX393 borrowed from No 64 Squadron in mid-1949 for trials of 1,000lb and practice bombs. Results were unremarkable, except when only one large bomb was carried; handling became tricky and pilots were recommended not to attempt a landing. © Crown Copyright

195: Sea Hornet FR.20 (so described in the AAEE report) TT248 in May 1947. This view shows the flaps extended, the hook raised and the camera windows ahead of the roundel. The elevator horn balances needed enlarging as a result of the work on this aeroplane. © Crown Copyright

127

modifications were effective by early 1951, and confirmed on PX395 with 1,000 lb bombs. Landing with a single bomb was not recommended. PX385 extended clearance to the use of 100 gal tanks filled with flame thrower fuel; accuracy was very poor. WF954 made satisfactory releases of ASR Type G in 1952. After radio checks in PX383 in 1948, further tests in 1950 were made on PX347 as equipment had been moved to accommodate an F52 camera with 14 in lens.

The 30 ft banner target by RFD caused the engines to overheat in the climb on PX336 in 1951/2. PX340 featured briefly in 1950

Supermarine Spiteful

F Mark 14. With this anomalous mark number (due to its Spitfire Mk 14 fuselage), NN667 arrived in early 1946 for handling and maintenance appraisal; only the latter, it appears, was completed. The type was below average in that even routine tasks needed a large number of man hours. Carbon monoxide was within acceptable limits, however. RB517 left in July 1946 after a few weeks without recorded results from its performance tests.

Martin Baker MB 5

The only official report on R2496 (Griffon 83) concerns the assessment in March 1946 of its engineering and maintainability; both are described as excellent, and "infinitely better than any other type." One of the few surviving pilots' reports is about the MB5. At 11,145 lb there was no swing on take off, and the spring tabs on all three controls led to a highly favourable rating by all who flew it. The sting is in the final sentence, "It has a relatively poor performance"—a remark made in the light of contemporary jet-propelled achievements.

de Havilland Venom

FB Mark 1. The high Mach behaviour received prompt attention on VV612 (Ghost 1) on arrival in May 1950. At 40,000 ft, 0.85M was reached before the nose and a wing dropped; at 20,000 ft a violent nose up pitch occurred at 0.845, while at 10,000 ft the rudders vibrated above 0.81M. Other handling, at 10,900 lb, revealed that the ailerons and elevator were too heavy at high speed (the maximum rate of roll halved between 230 and 350 kt), the airbrakes were poor, and longitudinal stability needed improving with unacceptably light stick forces when manoeuvring at aft CG. VV613 (Ghost 3) had a heavier inertia weight and other changes to the elevator circuit; some improvement was apparent at low and medium altitudes, but at high level problems remained. In dives from 47,000 ft, a sharp pitch up occurred at 0.85M, then an uncontrollable wing drop at 0.87M, and finally a dive from which recovery was possible only at 23,000 ft when the elevator became effective again; the maximum speed reached was 0.91M (0.94M true). Altogether it was an interesting ride without an ejection seat. Ailerons with cord and larger spring tab were lighter, but did not achieve faster rates of roll. Fitting 80 gal tip tanks aggravated the wing drop at the stall, and reduced the rate of roll. Tip tanks were jettisoned from WE315 in 1953. In production form WE255 had the ailerons rigged up and a fillet at the port wing tip; stalling was a little better, but high Mach behaviour unchanged. Further checks in 1952 on WE257, WE258, WE259 and WE260 showed variation between aircraft and over time with the least desirable behaviour when new. Indeed, WE280, a reported rogue, displayed high mach phenomena at 0.02M below other aircraft. In 1953 WE272 had wing tip slats and other changes which reduced some of the worst aspects of high speed. This machine also had an ejection seat, leading to the recommendation for a straight stick in place of the spade type, as the latter obscured vital instruments at forward CG. The ejection seats in WE468, WE479 and WR288 prevented full aft stick from being obtained; coupled with high stick forces, manoeuvring proved unacceptable. Performance checks on WE269 followed accurate thrust measurement (4,700 lb static), and gave a climb of 6,800 ft/min at sea level, and a ceiling of 49,500 ft; range with 496 gal was 980 nm. The stick shaker of WE260 operated at too low a Mach number to be useful, but powered ailerons in 1953 increased rate of roll and improved high Mach handling. 200 hr of intensive flying on WE259 established the reliability of the type, although the 50 hr life of engine flame tubes was criticised; of 130 recommendations for improvements, the strongest was for an ejection seat. Radios were checked satisfactorily on WE259 with all variations of external stores.

The 20 mm Mark V star guns became too cold at height, and too hot at low altitude, during 117 sorties and the firing of 55,899 rounds from WE258; satisfactory blast tubes and link deflectors were evolved. RP Mark 8 (eight 3 in rockets) underlined the heavy stick forces, but was otherwise satisfactory on WE258 and WE259. The former collided with a Valetta in November 1952; this fatality was the only Venom major accident at AAEE. Modified rocket rails and then a three tier arrangement on WE479 in 1955 gave satisfaction. A short test cleared VP fused bombs on WE267 in 1954–5. Towing a 30 ft net banner, take off distance to 50ft depended on the method used: a straight pull used 1,265 yd, and a snatch (ie, looped rope) 700 yd. WE361 made these measurements in 1954–5 at 12,570 lb.

Tropical trials of WE256 in 1954, bombing by WE288 (Ghost 103) for a year from June 1954, rocketing by WK422 in mid-1954, and gunnery by WR370 in Aden in 1956 added to the sum of Venomous knowledge.

196: Sea Hornet F.20 PX219 prepared for firing of eight 60lb head rockets from RP Installation Mk VIII mounted in the currently fashionable wing tip position. The pilot's view was good, and accuracy well above average in trials in mid-1947.
© *Crown Copyright*

197: Spiteful F.XIV RB517 as tested by AAEE in mid-1946. The classic Supermarine lines remain, while the thin wing is also clearly visible. The undercarriage doors fitted together well once the legs extended after take off.
© *Crown Copyright*

198: Martin Baker MB 5 R2496 in January 1945, a year before it went to Boscombe; it was very favourably received, but while handling was exceptional, the performance fell short of what the current jets were achieving.

199: Venom FB.1 VV612. Although tested entirely at Boscombe, this AAEE photo was taken elsewhere in May 1950. The type exhibited alarming characteristics at high Mach number in its original form as shown. © Crown Copyright

200: Venom FB.1 WE258 in April 1952, armed with 8 three inch rockets which caused damage to the tailplane on firing. High Mach handling suffered and stick forces were heavy. © Crown Copyright

201: Venom FB.1 WE272 in camouflage and showing two of the aerodynamic "fixes"—the wing fences and fin on the tip tank. © Crown Copyright

202: Venom NF.3 WX788 in early 1955 operated at higher all up weight with degraded performance. The empennage is of the final configuration and tip tank fins are absent; ejection seats were not fitted in this interim type. © Crown Copyright

NF Mark 2. The first trial (possibly at Hatfield) on this two seat night fighter concerned its suitability for deck landing; in late 1950 G-5-3 had a good view, innocuous stall and small trim change with flap and undercarriage; poor elevator response at low speed would need improvement. In April 1951, high altitude measurements of instrument pressure in WP227 (Ghost 3) showed small errors in the system, and at low altitude the ASI under read by 4.5 kt at 535 kt. High Mach handling, the controls and poor airbrake were similar to the single seater; severe criticism was made of the lack of ejector seats, and the fouling of the stick in the aft position due to a large survival pack. Later, a stick shaker to warn of imminent loss of control at high Mach lacked sufficient amplitude. The production WL806 (Ghost 103) needed modifications to improve purging of gases during the firing of 25,434 rounds from the four 20 mm guns over a two year period from late 1951. The AI Mark 10 performed well, except at high altitude (where it was designed to work!) when scanner rotation slowed in the low temperatures. The heavy elevator together with rudder overbalance rendered handling unacceptable in early 1953 on WL808 and WL809; dorsal fins on the latter improved the rudder but spoilt the spinning characteristics. Spins were made in WL807 in July 1953, and further modifications to the tail arrangements on WL814 gave a consistent spin in 1953–4; errors from the fin mounted pressure head remained unchanged. WL811 had progressively improved canopy structure, eventually acceptable to pilots and in the blower tunnel. Extensive instrumentation for high level instrument calibration of new aircraft was fitted to WL857 as datum; after two years of installation, fitting a Ghost 103, and calibration of the equipment using five methods,[3] the bright yellow aircraft was fully ready in 1955 only to be replaced by a Javelin in 1958.

NF Mark 3. An improved radar and various other benefits, including powered ailerons, served to make the Mark 3 handling acceptable up to 0.87M. WX786, WX788 were used together with WX790 having anti-skid brakes; WX786 suffered aileron flutter at high speed; the port aileron push rod fractured. However, the increase in weight from 13,387 lb of the Mark 2 to 14,540 lb caused a significant deterioration in performance. Radio and some armament work on WX785 and engineering appraisal of WX787, both in 1954–5, completed Mark 3 work.

FB Mark 4. The single seat fighter bomber WE381 and WR406 with powered ailerons and 77 gal under wing tanks had good roll and improved high speed characteristics when tested in 1954–5, but the elevator remained heavy.

[3] Aneroid, radar, doppler/radar, trailing static and kinetheodolite.

Supermarine Types 510, 535 and Swift

From the innocuous handling of the prototype 510, the extensive changes made in the development of the Swift to improve operational capability failed to overcome the fundamental shortcomings of the wing. The Establishment tested each change as soon as possible after the firm had flown it; great priority was given to obtaining results. See Chapter 1 for political background. Report writing suffered in the urgency of getting the job done—but at least omnibus records were made some time after the event. The Swift was the first RAF aircraft to have reheat, (and a wheel brake booster system), maxaret anti-skid brakes and a G90 combat camera.

Type 510. On its first AAEE trials in October 1949, VV106 (Nene 2) exhibited severe vibrations at low rpm and high airspeed accompanied by intermittent yawing of sufficient amplitude to cause concern about structural integrity. Partially effective changes to the intakes permitted handling trials to be made. It was free from shaking and Dutch roll with light and crisp ailerons up to the maximum usable Mach of 0.93—a significant improvement compared to earlier designs. However, turning performance at altitude appears not to have been fully explored, apart from noting a tendency to tightening. Cross wind landings were "horrid," and the combination of swept wings and a tail wheel condemned. The aeroplane was assessed in March 1950 as suitable for deck landings, in spite of a tendency for either wing to drop at speeds above the stall. One C Squadron pilot joined an RAE deck landing trial making the first swept wing carrier landings on 8 November 1950; the approach at 130 kt (a speed well above those previously used) was straightforward using the new "sinking" approach to land on the long stroke and efficient undercarriage. Take offs were only possible with rocket assistance, even into a 50 kt wind. On one take off, one side failed to fire and a wing tip struck a carrier gun turret; a skilful landing ashore followed.

Type 535. After a short, unreported visit in May 1951, the nose wheel equipped VV119 (Nene) came in March 1952 for assessment of the airbrake. Deceleration was measured at 24 ft/sec^2 at 450 kt, and the airbrake gave steady flight either in or out; selecting out produced a nose down trim change.

Swift Prototype and F Mark 1. WJ965 flew handling trials after arrival in May 1953, and in November crashed fatally when stalling with flaps and undercarriage down. It was suspected that a well developed stall occurred from which recovery was difficult; no anti-spin parachute had been fitted, contrary to instructions. Of the seven production Mark 1s received, three flew only in the Royal Review of July 1953, piloted by A Squadron; they were WK195, WK197 and WK200. WK196 spent four weeks in the blower tunnel; canopy separation was

203: Venom NF.2 WL807 in May 1953 with interim standard empennage; it retains the long Gee navaid aerial and fins on the tip tanks. Under the inboard wing is a small pod. © Crown Copyright

204: Venom NF.2 WP227 in April 1951. This mark had alarming high mach characteristics similar to the Mk. 1 in that control could rapidly be lost due to sudden wing drop. It had the dubious advantage, however, of a second seat to thrill Flight Test Observers. Apart from the radome, aerodynamic features include wing fences, tip tank fins and tailplane extended outboard of the booms. © Crown Copyright

205: Venom NF.2 WL857 in 1957, resplendent in bright yellow finish, and sporting an extra wing tip pitot/pressure head and a temperature sensor under the nose for its calibration role. © Crown Copyright

206: Swift prototype WJ965 on a soggy day in July 1952. Although there are gun ports (two) under the intake, no armament was carried; the tailplane was fixed and a test pressure head supplemented the head on the fin. In November 1953, on another visit, this aircraft crashed fatally. © Crown Copyright

207: Swift F.4 WK273 in a photograph dated January 1959 when AAEE assisted Vickers Supermarine. Features are the yaw and pitch vanes on the nose probe, and temperature sensor above the starboard wing root. © Crown Copyright

satisfactory except for low speeds with sideslip. WK194 tested the pair of 30 mm guns from June 1953; engine surge occurred with firing, both on the ground and in the air, and expended links caused unacceptable damage to the airframe. WK201 and WK202 (Avon 105), both with anti-spin parachutes, revealed several major handling deficiencies at the normal take off weight of 17,200 lb. Above 25,000 ft severe pitch up occurred at very low g, making a turn impossible; the elevator effectiveness fell off above 0.91M, and above 0.93M a wing dropped uncontrollably, and finally, if the airbrakes were used in an attempt to slow down, the aircraft pitched nose down. Under pressure to permit Service flying, clearance was given for maximum speeds of 550 kt/ 0.91M but never above 25,000 ft at any speed.

F Mark 2. With four 30 mm guns, increased weight of 17,640 lb, and increased leading wing sweep inboard, WK214 and WK216 (Avon 105) attracted the following comments from their handling sorties in mid-1954: "... Low thrust, lack of manoeuvrability above 40,000 ft, deficiencies in the longitudinal handling characteristics and liability to engine surge rendered this aircraft [mark] far below the standards required of an operational interceptor fighter." In fact, this mark had a worse pitch up than the Mark 1 and a high sink rate on the approach. Minor modifications were recommended before release to the Service with the same limits as the mark 1. Trials of the four guns in WK219 and WK220 in early 1955 revealed that the stainless steel plate fitted under the fuselage failed to obviate damage, and random engine surging remained bothersome. On a flight to check relighting in March 1955, the engine flamed out in the climb, and WK220 written off in the ensuing forced landing. WK244 came briefly in 1954–5.

F Mark 3. WK248 (Avon 108 with reheat) retained the four guns of the Mark 2, but had extended wing leading edges outboard, Fairey in place of Servodyne elevator power and other changes on arrival in October 1954. Pitch up was decreased, wing drop at high mach reduced and approach handling better; they were still unacceptable. Random reversion to manual control received prompt rectification in WK 253, but very high fuel consumption in reheat added to this mark's deficiencies.

F Mark 4. Weighing 19,470 lb and possessing a "flying" tail for longitudinal manoeuvring, WK272 (Avon 114 with reheat) had adequate pitch control. Unfortunately, lift was not controllable, and an immediate pitch up followed use of the stick, typically giving 3.5g to 8g at 24,000 ft. Climb to 40,000 ft took 6 min, but endurance (fuel capacity had been reduced by 30 gal) woeful with sortie length limited to 25 to 30 min. From August 1957, a lengthy investigation on WK275 determined the elevator/tailplane characteristics in 1957–8 and then languished on the ground for a year. WK279 made two short visits, for brakes in 1955–6 and for radios later in 1956.

208: Swift F.2 WK220 in January 1955. Details of this intriguing trial are missing, but the nose box was probably connected with the armament work of the aircraft. Just inboard of the wing mounted pressure head is a wing fence, fitted in a vain attempt to cure pitch up; also just visible are vortex generators on the tailplane. Engine failure in March 1955 led to the machine's demise. © Crown Copyright

FR Mark 5. WK200 had nose camera bays, but shortly after arrival, the engine turbine disintegrated on the ground, and the aircraft was written off after the ensuing fire in May 1955. WK291's Martin Baker hood passed blower tunnel tests, and later the Rebecca 8 distance measuring equipment needed a blade aerial to give satisfactory ranges. Camera trials for the low level role occupied XD903 from June 1955, and XD904 the following year. Night flying and navigation were the forte of XD917, while WK294 spent June 1954 at Idris, Libya.

F Mark 7. The clearance of this version with yaw damper, extended nose and wings intended solely for trials of Blue Sky (later called Fireflash) involved limited handling of XF113 and XF774 (Avon 116) following aerodynamic tests on WK279 (Avon 114) in early 1955. With a weight of 19,960 lb, and following a few successful firings and jettisonings from XF774 and XF780, clearance was recommended for firing up to 0.34 M between 15,000 and 35,000 ft. XF114 spent six months from March 1957 at Boscombe, and also the month of November 1960.

Dassault 450 Ouragon

A team from AAEE travelled to Bretigny in July 1950 to assess the handling of the second MD 450 Ouragon. It had many excellent features including positive stability throughout the flight envelope, freedom from snaking and Dutch roll, and a well laid out cockpit. On the other hand, the elevator, in particular, was heavy for a fighter, the airbrakes not efficient, and it had a low safe maximum Mach of 0.81 (0.77 for gun firing). This aeroplane later jettisoned its canopy in Boscombe's wind tunnel.

North American F-86 and Sabre

F-86A-5-NA. The pressing need for swept wing fighters in the RAF led to the purchase of American F-86s; two USAF aircraft were received on loan by AAEE in 1951. The handling of 49-1279 and 49-1296 (both J-47-GE-13) was a revelation in superior manoeuvrability and docile behaviour at high speed achieved with powered ailerons and elevator and variable incidence tailplane. Electric aileron and rudder trimmers were novel and well liked, but the ailerons seemed too sensitive, the normal tailplane operation too fast, and the haphazard cockpit confusing. FU-279, as 49-1279 was identified, made extended tests including dives to 1.2M indicated (1.1M true) from over 40,000 ft (reached in 10.42 min), level speeds (580 kt or 0.9M) and manoeuvre boundaries. The 5 g thrust ceiling was 8,000 ft, and the 5 g lift ceiling 22,500 ft. Range on 357 imp gal of fuel was calculated as 790 nm.

209: Swift FR.5 XD903 in July 1956. It should not be assumed that because half the Swift pictures are of aircraft tied down that the Establishment tried to minimise the risk of flying the type! The nose wheel was retracted, and the aircraft situated in the gun butts. The large belly tank and various camera ports can be seen. © Crown Copyright

210: Development Fireflash missiles in early test configuration on Swift F.7 XF774 in 1956. © Crown Copyright

211: F-86A-5-NA Sabre 49-1279. When extensively tested in March to November 1951 it set new standards at AAEE for high speed manoeuvrability and docile behaviour at high usable Mach numbers. The leading edge slats and flaps are down in this view. © Crown Copyright

F Mark 4. XB733 arrived in July 1953 for gunnery, but later harmonisation trials in XB992 demonstrated inherent and inconsistent weaknesses in gun mountings and sighting. The latter spent September 1954 at AAEE, and flew four hours on general handling for comparison with other fighters.

Hawker Hunter

The Hawker Hunter looked right, and it was right—eventually. The early vicissitudes of this design during development were well explored at Boscombe Down, and the original clearance for it to enter service was made because the Super Priority production scheme had resulted in hundreds of defective machines being made, and because of pressure from Fighter Command who needed a modern front line aircraft. The needs of public relations had, no doubt, also to be taken into account. The text here is in two parts—Fighters and Other Roles, both given by mark number.

Fighters

F Mark 1 and Prototype. WB195, the second prototype, arrived in late 1952 for a stay of only two weeks before being returned to Hawker; the heavy vibrations on pulling out from high speed dives at low altitude were found alarming. Otherwise, the performance was good, bur handling spoilt by a low rate of roll above 0.75M, heavy elevator, lack of an airbrake and Dutch roll on the approach. The stall had adequate natural warning before the port wing and nose dropped at 114/110 kt clean and 107 kt with flap and undercarriage down. In the blower tunnel a dummy fuselage proved unrepresentative in 1951; two years later the hood of WT559 required a spring assister to ensure a clean separation.

Production aircraft testing began with WT555 late in 1953; a tailplane/fin bullet-shaped fairing had cured the buffeting (probably first flown by AAEE at Dunsfold in WB188), 40,000 ft reached in 7½ minutes and the fighting altitude assessed as 45,000 ft. On the debit side, the severe pitch-up, a characteristic of early swept wings, became evident, and the need for an airbrake obvious; engine handling was slightly improved during tests by replacing the Avon 104 with a 113 model. WT573 (Avon 107 then 119) and WT576 (Avon 113), both having an airbrake under the fuselage, were generally satisfactory. On the basis of handling these aircraft, CA Release was made—to allow Fighter Command to gain experience of the type while gun firing was improved. Drooped leading edges (saw teeth) on WT568 at the end of 1955 reduced the pitch up and gave satisfactory buffet and manoeuvre boundaries. Meanwhile, no fewer than 65 pilots, including visitors, were involved between May and September 1954 on intensive flying of 63 hours on WT559, plus over 230 hours on WT576 and WT567 (Avon 113 then 115). Engineering and performance were praised—but criticisms included unsatisfactory cabin conditioning and freezing guns, and the early hydro-boosters of the ailerons and elevator failed to re-engage on two occasions of 396 attempts. The most serious and intractable problem of the Hunter was the firing of guns, and included engine surging (compressor stall), pitch down, damage from spent links and cartridges and explosive gas concentrations in the removable gun pack. WT570 (Avon 113) experienced frequent engine surge on firing at altitude; the 8,000 rounds of 30 mm ammunition fired were blamed for a fatigue fracture causing the failure of the nose undercarriage to lower in October 1954. Identical damage, similarly attributed, caused WT558 (twice) and WT576 to land wheels-up in the same year. WT567 and WT559 contributed to remedial action by ground firing to evaluate gas concentration. Aircraft with the later Avon 115 experienced less surging; those with earlier engines were restricted to firing guns below 25,000 ft. In early 1956 some 13,500 rounds were fired (probably from WT556) in an intensive effort to find an effective method of collecting ammunition links. Other gun problems remained to be cured on later marks, but a Mark 1, WT612, with an Avon 121 incorporating fuel dipping and air bleed, fired well up to 48,000 ft and down to 150 kt. A directional auto-stabiliser on WT564 made little difference to accuracy when firing.

100 gal drop tanks gave sufficient range to WT569 for successful hot weather trials in Khormaksar; the fuel-cooled oil cooler and maxaret anti-skid units worked well. A repeat in the heat with the Avon 115 replacing the 113 was complete in April 1955. In the UK WT616 (Avon 116) made tests with a fully powered elevator, while WT557 completed the first trials of the limited radio fitted. Toe operated brakes lacked feel in WT562 when compared to the usual lever on the stick. A British TACAN in WW642 in 1956 received mixed comments. Last of this version at Boscombe was the fuselage WW605 in 1961–2 in the blower tunnel.

F Mark 2. Flying was limited on this version to areas affected by the change to a Sapphire 101 engine; internal fuel capacity of 314 gal was the lowest of any version, although the all up weight of 16,300 lb was 100 lb greater than the similar mark 1. WN888 from early 1954 received praise from the engineers, while WN892 bore the brunt of the flying, mainly concerned with gunnery. The Sapphire proved surge free at all altitudes, but damage was caused by empty cartridge cases striking the leading edge of the airbrake. In 1957 production standard blast deflectors gave improvement in the pitch down previously experienced on firing. WN890 paid an unreported visit in 1954, probably for take off and landing measurements, and then made itself useful from 1960 in the new de-tuner; with a total of only 123 flying hours it was struck off charge in 1963.

212: Hunter F.1 WW642 cockpit to illustrate the extra items for tests of the British TACAN navaid. Possibly the only single seat aircraft to have had Gee. © Crown Copyright

213: Hunter F.1 WT569 in production form with airbrake and, not visible, maxaret anti skid brakes in October 1954. Drop tanks were fitted for trials in Khartoum which revealed only minor shortcomings. The only visible aerial is behind the nosewheel door © Crown Copyright

214: Hunter F.1 WT555—the first of over 2,000 production examples. Seen in October 1953 and differing little in outward appearance from later versions, this Mark lacked range, reliable powered controls, an engine that ran during gun firing and an airbrake among other deficiencies. Production had been ordered well before comprehensive trials revealed so many items in need of improvement. © Crown Copyright

137

215: Hunter FGA.9 XE617 painted for rocket firing in early 1954. The two-inch rocket pods have just been fired, and the various areas daubed with white paint (under tailplane, rear fuselage, ailerons and outboard side of 230gal tanks) show no signs of damage or fire. © Crown Copyright

F Mark 4. The normal all up weight of this mark, 17,100 lb, reflected increased fuel (414 gal); four pylons under the wings could raise this figure when carrying fuel or armament. WT705, the first, arrived in May 1955 and undertook handling and some gunnery while WT703, the next, got on with investigating rocket firing (RP Mark 12 Type 3); modifications to the design cured early damage to the ailerons. WT775 in the blower tunnel cleared the single lever combining hood jettison and seat firing. WT798, WT704, WT736, WT739 and WV276 (the last four with Avon 121) contributed to the advance towards satisfactory gun firing in 1956. One result was the discovery that individual engines gave differing and inconsistent results; very careful adjustment on the ground was recommended. Radio investigation took but a few weeks on WT702, and the IFF10 on WT735 was quickly cleared in 1958; the latter then passed to C Squadron for training. Later the radio compass of WV375 suffered unacceptable interference from Rebecca 7. A brief test of the Radar Ranging Mark 1 in WV330 (Avon 113) in 1956 coincided with tropical trials in Idris on XF970; the report is missing. Worries about the behaviour of full 230 gal fuel tanks in the event of a rejected take off led to an interesting trial in 1962 on a Canberra and continued on WT751. It was considered safer to jettison the tanks well before entering the barrier where a conflagration could be fatal; the only snag was the need to release the brakes as the tanks were jettisoned for the aircraft to run ahead of the fire ball. The trial used tanks with a representative weight of flameproof water. WV325 served A Squadron as a hack for five years after a trial with an air stream direction detector; it left in 1967.

F Mark 5. This version had a basic CG further forward than other marks; handling was disproportionately worse. WN954 (Sapphire 101) from late 1954 demonstrated unacceptable stick force per g, even in power control; only one g could be applied by a single hand with the CG at its forward limit. In manual control even modest manoeuvres were very difficult, and the airbrake, for reasons not elaborated, was inadequate. Its cockpit, representative of early marks, attracted five significant criticisms. The operational shortcomings of the F Mark 5 were no doubt instrumental in the decision to test a 6 x 30 ft banner using, first, a hook under the fuselage with a snatch take off, and then air launched from a container under the wing. The hook was acceptable, but the wing position not, due to the absence of an effective aileron trimmer. WN958 made a short visit in 1956 for wing stores work, presumably cancelled as this version had been rejected for ground attack the previous year. Engine developments in WN955 were flown in 1957–8, and combined with target towing.

F Mark 6. XF833 arrived in February 1954, well ahead of other Mark 6 aircraft, but suffered an early engine failure, landing wheels up in a field five miles from Boscombe Down. After extensive repairs it returned for spinning and armament work. Next came WW592 in August 1955 to complete an intensive handling programme. The more powerful Avon 203 was excellent and the extra fuel welcome. However, pitch-up remained (no saw teeth were fitted), the elevator remained ineffective at high Mach number and gun firing caused pitch down. From March 1956, XF380 confirmed the benefits of leading edge extensions. The follow up electric tailplane, although slow, was very effective when tested on another aircraft; full power jacks to the elevator reduced stick force per g from 16 lb to 2 lb at 525 kt although they stalled at maximum Mach number.

216: Hunter F.1 WT567 tied to the ground for firing trials in April 1954. It has no air brake, but all control surfaces are secured, and the gun pack has yet to be fitted. © Crown Copyright

217: Hunter T.8 WW664 with both old style RP rails under the outer wings, and two inch rocket launcher pods inboard; the single gun of this mark is also shown fitted. August 1959. © Crown Copyright

218: Hunter F.5 WN958 in 1956 with rocket rails, 100 gal tanks and flaps down. The oil breather above the trailing edge of the wing has already caused discolouration to this newish aeroplane. The angle of the pressure head is arranged to point directly into the wind at cruising angles of attack. © Crown Copyright

139

219: Hunter F.4 WT751 jettisoning two 230gal and two 100 gal tanks at 117 kt. This was the scene some 0.84 sec after selection by the pilot and shows the sparks generated by friction of the tanks on the runway. (see Canberra at photo 127). This trial simulated a Mk 9 aircraft rejecting take off and needing the barrier for which external tanks were unwelcome. © Crown Copyright

220: Hunter F.4 WT703 with 24 three inch rockets. Modifications to obviate minor damage to the ailerons produced a satisfactory installation in April 1956. © Crown Copyright

221: Hunter FGA.9 XF442 in late 1964 with three inch rockets/60lb heads and two inch pods together with 230gal tanks. The "Sabrinas" for collecting spent cartridge cases are well shown. (The eponymous Sabrina was also alleged to act, but who cared?) © Crown Copyright

Spinning on XE588 with the leading edge extensions ended in disaster on the first sortie when incorrect recovery action led to a fatal crash in November 1957. With all major modifications incorporated, the F Mark 6 was assessed as fully developed in 1957 with good overall handling, good firepower, and with the ability to carry external fuel or armament. Minor drawbacks included reduced rate of roll from aileron jack stall at high IAS, and the need for a brake parachute. Performance included a take off run of 550 yd (at 17,800 lb), under six minutes to 40,000 ft, and maximum level speeds of 620 kt and 0.95M. Contemporary gun testing involved XE551 in, appropriately, Aden; extra servicing of the radar ranging Mk 1 and GGS Mk 5A was needed in the heat. At Boscombe, no fewer than five aircraft joined in gun firing:- XE558, XE598 (also G 90 camera), XF377, XF381 and XF452. The omnibus report (January 1957) on guns in all marks states that 199,014 rounds were loaded and 159,608 fired in the air over 30 months of trials; the only remaining problem, pitch down, neared solution with trials of blast deflectors. A list of essential modifications needed to the Radar Ranging Mk 1 with the Gyro Gunsight Mk 5A followed trials on XF381. Combinations of fuel tank, bombs and rockets using inboard and outboard stations under the wings probably occupied XE605 in 1957 and XE531 from early 1955 . Some speed and other limitations resulted. Radio and radar clearance up to June 1957 was made on some aircraft already noted, and XE543; cabin conditioning of XE600 completed items in the original F Mark 6 CA Release. AAEE borrowed XF376 from Handling Squadron, apparently for photographs as publicity for Armstrong Whitworth, the maker.

XG290 began a long association with AAEE in tests of navigation equipment in 1957, followed by gun sight/rocket assessment; later it helped establish servicing schedules before flying for Porton. XE601, of even longer association, had, in 1959, a sub-miniature radio compass, affected by the old Rebecca, and, in 1961–2, an underwing banner target which met with approval provided the recommended procedures were followed for streaming. Earlier, XE587 had towed a 6 x 30 ft banner from a belly mounted hook. The purpose of further tropical trials at Idris in 1957 by XJ714 is not known; in the UK an instrumented gun pack in XK140 rapidly proved the efficacy of the earlier modifications. Over 200 full spins completed by XF429 and a T Mark 7 demonstrated their consistent nature, but also emphasised the importance of centralised ailerons for recovery; a white dot was painted centrally on the dash board to help the pilot in his moments of confusion. Pressure errors following installation of ARI 2313 equipment required measuring in XG161 in 1969. The reason for XG210's turning up at AAEE are not known—possibly for training, while XF378 with Firestreak missiles in 1957 is unreported because the requirement was cancelled. Cold (Norway) and hot (Bahrein) tests of XG232 filled (where appropriate) with a new type of hydraulic oil appear to have been successful.

Other Roles

T Mark 7 and 7A. Following blower tunnel tests of a dummy two-seat front fuselage in 1955, XJ615 arrived the following year and attracted several major criticisms of the cockpit. The right hand throttle position for the right seat pilot was rejected, a single central instrument panel recommended, and a horn to warn of canopy operation required. Spinning of XJ615 was consistent with F Mark 6 behaviour, while the single 30 mm gun under the starboard fuselage became acceptable in 1959 once a gas seal was fitted round the blast deflector. XL563 joined XJ627 in trials of the dual GGS Mark 8 combined with the radar ranging; results were satisfactory, although canopy structure restricted the view in some directions of attack. In 1963, WV318 was used to assess bottom diamond sighting, followed by ILS investigation. XL566 visited Bahrain for tropical clearance in 1958, while, in Boscombe's blower tunnel, XL574 tested an unsuccessful rain dispersal system; the following year a windscreen wiper proved more useful on XL564 prior to two years' service with the Establishment in the training role. IFF with SSR on XF310 was flown in 1968; EMC tests on XL596 in 1972 were not. 1966 saw the replacement of Meteors for training by XL612 (T Mark 7), XL611 and XL616 (both T Mark 7A) ; XL611 crashed fatally on 14th May 1968.

T Mark 8. This version required tests for its naval role, and included WW664 with airfield arrester hook from 1958, UHF radios and then two inch rockets from a Launcher Rocket No 3 Mark 1. The latter was cleared for a maximum of only 12 per firing before a routine trip to Bahrain was made. Further armament work occupied WV363 in mid-1963.

FGA Mark 9. Radio trials lasting over a year occupied XF617 from mid-1961, and included yet another hot weather trial, this time in Aden where the radio bay cooling proved adequate. XF442 was dedicated to armament work—mostly rockets; early in 1962 the standard three inch/60 lb head variety were cleared for firing up to 550 kt in dives of up to 60 degrees, and in all parts of the world after a detachment to Bahrain. In 1966 drag and thus range were measured for a variety of stores such as RP, SNEB/MATRA pods, 230 gal tanks and others both individually and in combination. XG207 assisted in armament in 1964.

FR Mark 10. Referred to as a Mark 6 (FR) in one report, XF429 (see above) returned and did much clearance work over four years from March 1959. Three F 95 Mark 2 cameras in the nose (left, right and centre) proved trouble free, but the original electronic bay cooling was poor—improvements tested in 1962 in Idris revealed that only the VHF failed to work adequately. Handling in the reconnaissance role with ailerons of reduced power raised no adverse comment in XE621.

XG168 visited for unreported armament trials from November 1960, possibly to assess the effect of gun firing on photography. Two new F 95 Mark 4 cameras with auto exposure, and then a Mark 7, both on XF426, made good pictures in 1966.

GA and PR Mark 11. Converted from old Mark 4 aircraft, the first of this naval training version arrived in May 1962, and WT810 concentrated on clearance of 25 lb bombs, three inch R Ps and two inch rocket packs; the main restriction imposed was a ban on using the radio during loading. 10 days sufficed for radio trials of XE712, and the TACAN investigation took little longer in WT721—both in 1962. The latter should properly be regarded as a PR.11 when it returned in 1964 with a nose camera. Fuselage and wing tip carriers for practice bombs justified the presence of WT808 in 1966; XE707 had IFF/SSR two years later.

Gloster Javelin

Prototypes and FAW Mark 1. Four AAEE pilots flew WT830 (Sapphire SA6) at Moreton Valence in March 1954,[4] and at Boscombe three months later. With everything working as advertised, handling was docile within the limited flight envelope permitted, ie excluding stalling, spinning and manoeuvre boundaries. Without hydraulic power, the elevator and rudder were manageable, but the ailerons could scarcely be moved; at least one successful landing was, however made following hydraulic failure. Also, the stick was so close to the pilot that pulling it back could inadvertently operate the trim switch. Greater fuel capacity was considered necessary, and transonic buffet became excessive at the low figure of 0.9M. Meanwhile, a dummy fuselage in the blower tunnel consumed a large number of canopies before a design satisfactory for use with ejection seats was achieved. Incorporating improvements, WT830 returned and, with XA547, XA548 and XA561 (all Sapphire 102 and 103), completed initial trials for CA Release between July 1955 and March 1956. Among major deficiencies noted was a strong tendency to spin at the stall with no natural warning. XA561 failed to recover, even when the anti spin parachute was streamed, from a spin which became flat with an unusually rapid rate of rotation; the pilot ejected after making a running commentary of events. As a result of this accident, artificial stall warning, triggered by small vanes on the wing tips, became a standard feature.

Other inadequacies were lateral and longitudinal control at high airspeed, poor directional dynamic stability at high altitude and serious icing and misting. Cockpit lighting was, however, good, as were asymmetric handling and performance, airbrakes, and freedom from engine problems when firing the guns. Assessment of the AI 17 radar involved XA549, XA544 and XA563 in late 1955; some ten recommendations for improvements resulted, but the spacious and well laid out accommodation for the navigator received praise. Gun firing using the new Blind Predicting Gunsight (BPGS Mk1[5] in conjunction with the radar) involved WT827, XA554, XA558 and XA559; some 55 sorties were flown, and 31,565 rounds of 30 mm ammunition fired from minus 1g to plus 4g at speeds up to 560 kt and altitudes up to 48,000 ft. The many modifications to the Javelin resulting from AAEE's engineering evaluation were summed up in the report as follows: "It is unfortunate that the ... work of the firm was not quicker and more comprehensive, because [with earlier elimination of the snags] it would have been an outstanding aircraft." In 1956 analysis of drag started with XA547 (weight 32,335 lb) in the clean configuration as a result of the unexpectedly poor climb of the Mark 4; XA551 with vortex generators and thicker trailing edges on the ailerons also participated. Induced drag accorded with theory, but profile drag was some 30% higher; individual engines were found to have thrust output varying between 8,000 and 8,400 lb. In 1957 the effect of four Blue Jay (later Firestreak) missiles on XA547 had little effect on drag or handling. XA623 made a brief mention in the Servicing returns in 1956.

FAW Mark 2. XD158 without radar, managed 30 hr flying between May 1956 and February 1957. Later trials were concerned with the effects of changing to the American AI 22 radar on XA769 and XA770 which also did radio and navigation tests from early 1957. XA771 joined other versions in Firestreak evaluation from 1958; at least one live firing concluded the comprehensive carriage, slaving and acquisition phases. XA778 arrived in March 1961 for calibration as the datum from 1963 for high level pressure error work; it left in 1969.

T Mark 3. Apart from the front hood landing on top of the instructor's position when jettisoned in still air on the ground, blower tunnel tests were successful. Similarly, while the UHF radio of XK577 was unacceptable, all other radios and navaids passed examination in 1961–2. The rear gunsight (GGS Mk 5) in XH390 may have been a good idea, but the periscopic viewing arrangements rendered sighting almost impossible; the front sight (GGS Mk 7) gave reasonable viewing and acceptable results with radar ranging. XH433's main task was flying fast and low to evaluate a moving map display; frequent failures rendered results inconclusive.

FAW Mark 4. From June 1956 XA631 and XA720 took a year to complete the CA Release trials of this version (AI17) with a flying tailplane (on the Mark 1 the

---

[4] Exactly ten years previously four AAEE pilots had visited Moreton Valence to fly the first Meteors

[5] This sight was also tested with AI 22; two years work could not resolve the fundamental problems.

222: Hunter T.7 WV318 in July 1969 on loan from Handling Squadron for use as a chase. © Crown Copyright

223: Hunter GA.11 WT808 in May 1966 showing the position of six of the eight 25lb practice bombs; the installation was cleared without difficulty. © Crown Copyright

224: Javelin F(AW).9 XH897 resplendent in its new conspicuous paint scheme in September 1968, prior to taking over the task of pressure error measurement. Just inboard and aft of the port aileron can be seen the cone of the trailing static source; it had a small explosive charge for jettisoning if needed, and the warning triangle is near the roundel. Three pressure heads are visible, while on the side of the extreme end of the nose is the camera window for "snapping" the subject aircraft for accurate measurement. © Crown Copyright

225: Javelin F(AW).1 XA547 posed in July 1955 for its "mug-shots." It had the pen nib tail fairing of early machines, and appears to have no radar. It lacked the vortex generators which were fitted following AAEE trials. © Crown Copyright

226: Javelin F(AW).2 XA778 seen at an air display, this faded "dayglo" orange machine was for about five years the pressure error calibrator; it had uprated engines from a Mk 7. The nose pressure head is partly visible.

227: Javelin F(AW).1 with radar in late 1955. It was frequently unserviceable, and made slow progress on assessment of the AI 17 radar. A cord connects the engine intake blank with the bungs in the gun ports. © Crown Copyright

228: Javelin prototype WT827 in Gloster photograph at the time of AAEE flying in late 1955. This aircraft is included with three others in a report on gun firing, but it appears to have no guns! Perhaps it was used on assessment of the gunsight. The blunt rear fuselage and metal canopy for the navigator are features.

tailplane could be used only as a trimmer). It proved completely reliable but gave a disappointing improvement in handling, and lacked power duplication. Vortex generators and thickened trailing edges to the ailerons did not prevent unacceptable wing dropping at 0.95M; it was easy to over stress the aircraft above 0.88M at medium level, as happened on one occasion. The stall warning device failed to warn of impending stalls, also above 0.88M; yaw and pitch dampers were recommended. In 1957 XA720 had drooped leading edges to the wings (known as Stage 5), and, at 31,240 lb, raised the buffet boundaries for later marks. XA721 (Sapphire 102 and 103) and XA723 (weighing 36,700 lb) joined the drag investigation. XA725 suffered extensive damage in July 1958 with an engine explosion and fire on start up; XA760 appears to have arrived just in time to be broken up in 1962.

FAW Mark 5. No separate handling trials were needed as the difference from the Mark 4 lay in the extra 250 gal of internal fuel. XA641 in 1958 and XA711 in 1960/2 became involved in measurements of gun and ammunition temperatures; rounds held in the firing position reached over 100°C at times. Extending the blast tubes ahead of the leading edges provided a cure.

FAW Mark 6. Similar to the Mark 2 but with the extra 250 gal of internal fuel, the only Mark 6 at AAEE, XA821 (Sapphire 107 and 108), towed a 6x30 ft banner and demonstrated the system's reliability in 1959.

FAW Mark 7. No fewer than 14 machines of this extensively developed mark attended AAEE from May 1957 when XH704 arrived for performance measurements with production standard tail fairing and four Blue Jay (Firestreak) missiles. XH706 and XH712 (Sapphire 203 and 204 of increased thrust) with yaw dampers, fully powered rudders and finer, ie longer, fuselages gained 5,000 ft in operating height; 50,000 ft could be reached provided no acceleration or turning were required! Operating from 2,000 yd runways posed no difficulties. The operational reliability trial on XH714 ceased abruptly in February 1958 when the pilot was inadvertently ejected; the entangled pilot was killed and the navigator's seat failed to function correctly with fatal results. Some 96 hr had been flown, and the AI 17 radar shown to be unreliable. A fighter identification system giving a discreet image on the radar screen had mixed results in XH710 and XH713. Clearance was recommended for the Firestreak between 0.7M and 0.97M up to 47,000 ft following live firings at the Aberporth range from XH705. Hot weather trials of XH757 came to an end when over-reading fuel gauges led to a flame out landing and major damage in October 1958, and similar damage the next year to XH722 at Idris after engine failure on take off. The latter trial, of gun heating, indicated the need for extended and vented blast tubes, and that two hours were needed after firing before the guns cooled to a temperature acceptable for re-arming. XH783 (1959) and XH746 (noise making by its Sapphire 210/205 engines in 1962–3) remained on the ground at AAEE. The first Javelin air refuelling was

229: Javelin F(AW).7 XH704 in September 1957 about to assess the effect on handling of the dummy Firestreak missiles. In evidence are the "flying" tailplane, vortex generators on the top of the wing and a pitot intake just ahead of the fin. © Crown Copyright

230: Javelin FAW.7 XH780 with the first refuelling probe on a Javelin just about to make contact with the drogue basket. in the hands of Flt Lt Bernie Noble of A Squadron. This form of probe gave a large and unacceptable increase in drag, and was improved for production. Russell Adams photo

231: English Electric P1 WG760 on AAEE preview at Warton in March 1955 when the outstanding handling and performance came as a great tonic after the disappointments of the current fighters. Extremely short range and imposed flight restrictions left the team impatient for more liberal limitations. © Crown Copyright

made in XH780 flying from Moreton Valence; the first probe produced excessive drag, but the aircraft had good stability and controls as a receiver. Handling with four Firestreak missiles occupied XH753 (Sapphire 205/206) in early 1959, and XH708 flew 22 hours on unknown tests in 1957.

FAW Mark 8. Sporting reheat to its Sapphire 205 and 206 engines, the reliability trial of XH967 stopped when a jet pipe joint failed causing considerable damage in August 1959. XH966 with its AI 17 radar took part in the live Firestreak firings, XH968 had marginally acceptable UHF radios, and XH970 jettisoned its large underwing tanks (230 gal each) on the runway with satisfactory results up to 140 kt. Autopilot tests on XH969 took place in 1960.

FAW Mark 9. The refuelling probe of XH965 necessitated complete and successful repeat trials of existing avionics in early 1960, followed by new Violet Picture homing aid tests in XH759, and then an extra VHF in XH964 for ferrying. Hot weather Firestreak firings from XH711 took place from Akrotiri in Cyprus; some temperature and other limitations became apparent. XH839, also in the heat, obtained no cooling benefit on the ground in the radar and radio bays from a Cooling Trolley Mark 2; the Mark 5 Trolley was worse. XH967 became the last Javelin at AAEE when it flew to Duxford in 1975 after eight years as the datum aircraft. Three aircraft appeared very briefly—XH762 (receiving from the Victor tanker in 1965), XH896 (extra radios in 1963), and XH891 (F95 camera trial curtailed by extensive fire on engine starting in 1967).

Dassault Mystere IVA

Two of these fighters were flown in France in October 1955, 10 had a powered elevator, and 37 a flying tail. The latter had much superior high speed characteristics, since the former became ineffective above 0.9M. However, 37 had "catastrophic" instability at high indicated airspeeds. Both had a poor rate of climb, and a lengthy starting procedure.

English Electric P1 and Lightning

P 1A and P 1B. After unsatisfactory initial tests of the canopy jettison in the blower tunnel, minor changes were made in time for the first flight of the prototype P 1A, WG760, from Boscombe in August 1954. 13 flights by A Squadron from Warton in WG760 (two Sapphire 5) comprised the first preview assessment in March 1955. 40,000 ft could be reached in four minutes, but the imposed limit of 1.15M constituted a severe limitation as acceleration was brisk approaching this speed; handling was easy and docile throughout the flight envelope. Criticisms included the very uncomfortable Mk 3 ejection seat, the lack of an airbrake, and the "sparse" fuel. The need for supersonic drag measurement was identified, and operations from a standard 2,000 yd runway considered feasible with a parachute. Later in the year a second preview assessed the handling at the raised limits of 600 kt/1.3M; the favourable first impressions were confirmed. It was felt that the interception role would be extremely demanding for a single pilot, even with a good ground control. Evidence of reducing directional stability led to a recommendation for an investigation, by the firm, naturally, of inertia cross coupling. The toe brakes of WG763 lacked acceptable feel. XA847, a P 1B (two Avon 24R) arrived in December 1957 when the cockpit was cramped and too small for many pilots; the artificial horizon hid behind the stick, and the attack sight posed an obstruction to safe ejection. In April 1959 the cambered leading edge improved buffet boundaries, but the original fin and split flaps were retained for successful gun firing tests. Evaluation of aerial refuelling in XA847 during 1960 indicated the need for a longer probe, and great care in positioning to achieve contact. Further gun trials took place on XA853 in 1962–3, leading to some firing restrictions at high speed and low level.

Lightning Development Batch. XG308 (two Avon 24R) with a larger fin and increased travel for the tailplane weighed 31,700 lb and had much improved high altitude handling; at 58,000 ft it performed as earlier aircraft 10,000 ft lower. 1.7M, 700 kt and 62,000 ft were

232: P1B XA853 in February 1964—after the end of its flying career making itself useful putting a detuner to the test at full power. © Crown Copyright

233: *Lightning F.6 XR769 in the ferry configuration with two 260gal over wing tanks, runway arrester hook and probe; an intake guard is fitted for ground engine running. 45,000lb all up weight at take off could be increased by flight refuelling.*
© *Crown Copyright*

234: *Lightning DB XG313 revealing its rocket launching tubes. Arrows point to the cameras and external test instrumentation. It was decided that the dispersion of the rockets would render this system ineffective.*

235: *P1B XA847 in the winter 1957/8 at the time of the third preview; a cambered leading edge was fitted. The test probe was fitted to the nose cone, and the belly tank and fin of the original small variety. The Firestreak missiles were dummies.*
© *Crown Copyright*

reached, but reheat malfunctions and poor throttle box spoilt the full benefit of the exceptional performance. Indifferent fuel gauges kept pilots from knowing the fuel remaining. XG308 later spun with Firestreaks fitted. XG310 in original configuration remained low and slow on auto-ILS (Mark 13 auto pilot) development over three years from late 1959, while XG307 with the larger fin investigated the effect of malfunctions of the autostabilisers; the latter's Rosemount pitot static system gave good subsonic results in 1967. By June 1960 five other machines, all with plain flaps and larger fin had contributed to the clearance work for CA Release. XG313 made extensive handling tests of the flaps, stability and control at various CG, including the extended aft position, and, later, trials of the dispersion of two inch rockets; XG325 assessed the flaps on manually flown ILS; XG331 had near production standard controls and stability aids; XG337 demonstrated emergency behaviour and XM134 (production Mark 1) undertook further handling work, including the engines. Overall, control forces throughout the large speed range were good, with innocuous transonic behaviour, although shock effects on instrument readings could cause confusion; between 1.4 and 1.5M longitudinal static stability became slightly negative, but caused no difficulties. Reliability flying of XG331 (Avon 210) was stopped after 89 hr as more development of the 50 points of criticism was needed; 14 pilots flew 100 sorties, but did not fire the rocket armament. Among the most serious criticisms were the shortcomings of the fuel and electrical systems. The engineers commented, "Equipment layout, installation, routing and access have suffered due to (density in the airframe). In particular, defect investigation is likely to be time consuming." Prophetic words. After radio and tropical trials, XG333 joined XG326 in firing using the Pilot Attack Sight (PAS Mk 1). Both initially suffered from gun stoppages when all four fired together; the faults were cured by 1963. XG309 evaluated the Firestreak missile installation in 1960, and XG311 went direct to Aden for tropical trials in 1961. The new belly fuel tank of XG327 was scraped on take off by an enthusiastic pilot in February 1960; it returned after repairs for tests with the rocket doors down. XG329 continued gun development, and later other equipment trials including data link, Decca and TACAN navaids until 1969. The British TACAN navaid in XG335 gave good results once locked on to a ground beacon until failure of the undercarriage to lower led to the pilot ejecting in January 1965 over the Larkhill army range. By 1967, XG336 and XG337 were relegated to providing pilot training after both had completed Red Top missile firing with 13 JSTU. XG330 (OR946 instrument presentation in 1961) and XG310 (further enlarged fin in 1963) contributed to the development of the Mark 3 in, typically, 25 to 35 minute flights.

F Mark 1 and 1A. With the initial clearance of the Lightning completed by the development batch, and XM134 described above, the only production aircraft of the first service version were XM169 (Mark 1A on aerial refuelling in 1961) and XM174 for firing in the butts on the firm's trial.

F Mark 2 and 2A. Initial CA Release trials at Boscombe were made with XN723 in 1962–3 (many of them by the firm); standard weight of the Mark 2 was 34,500 lb. Following complaints from the RAF of failure to transfer fuel when aerial refuelling, XN729 made contacts with a Valiant, and after its demise, a Victor tanker; the faults were not reproduced, although it was found that an outward vent valve could stick shut. From 1963, XN772 acted first as a target, then made braking measurements and, in 1967, assessed the Avon 211 engines. Following the illness of an overheated pilot, the liquid suit trial on XN729 was terminated in 1966. XN728, an F 2A, cleared the IFF/SSR in 1969.

F Mark 3. XN795 in F Mark 3 configuration with 600 gal ventral tank, extra large fin but lacking a cambered leading edge on the outer wing and retaining an Avon 210, weighed 38,539 lb with two missiles, and was subject to preview assessment with XN789, probably at Warton, having in addition a cambered leading edge. The latter gave improved buffet boundaries. XN734 had the Avon 301 of the F Mark 3 for early testing; the Lucas fuel flow controller occasionally limited the maximum thrust obtained. XP693 (finally leaving in 1975 after many trials) and XP694, regarded as pre-production models, arrived in 1963 and 1964 respectively, and XP699 in representative form also in 1964. The temperature limiters of the Avon 301 engines were scarcely adequate, and the use of reheat unnecessarily restricted. Otherwise, the 145% fin and other improvements met with approval. Much time (protracted by unserviceability of XP696) was spent in conjunction with 13 JSTU in optimising a breakaway manoeuvre for use after firing the Red Top missiles in a head-on attack; two missiles were fired on trials. Great care had to be exercised when aerial refuelling to avoid damage to the missiles; the auto pilot functioned up to 2.05M/690 kt, and the aeroplane flown to 63,000 ft.

EMC checks on XP698 in 1963 were repeated on XP699 the following year with Red Tops fitted prior to hot weather work at Wheelus, Libya. XP701 had anti-icing in 1964, but the weather failed to co-operate to prove the system. New IFF was tried in XP757 in 1967–8 and in modified form in XP752 in 1970. XP717 was borrowed for training in 1972.

T Mark 4. After the loss of canopies from single seat aircraft and subsequent extended blower tunnel investigations, the Establishment had ample data to clear the dual seat version in 1959. A preview of XL629 may have been made at Warton, because on arrival of this machine at AAEE in December 1962 trials were limited to an investigation of rapid rolling with ventral tank and two Firestreak missiles and weighing 34,209 lb. Fin

236: *Lightning F.2 XN729 plugged into the port hose of Victor K.1 XA918 in 1965; the Sea Vixen FAW.2 XN685 with a single Red Top missile manoeuvres into position, probably on the starboard drogue.* © Crown Copyright

237: *Hawker P1172 XP980 after the aft main wheel fell off taxiing in May 1968 spoiling the day of the pilot, Gp Capt G C (Geoff) Cairns. The anti spin parachute housing extends to the rear of the tailplane and the ram air turbine is extended.* © Crown Copyright

238: *Harrier GR.1 XV281 with two 100gal drop tanks plus four 28lb practice bombs outboard; just visible behind the nose wheel is the pod developed by Photographic Division for armament trials of fast jets. Test instrumentation included the two cones on a boom on the nose, and seen here swinging in the breeze. The pilot's sideslip sensor is on top of the nose.* © Crown Copyright

strength was the critical factor, and the most testing condition occurred at 0.9M at 30,000 ft where full aileron remained available; rate of roll remained satisfactory at all speeds, but was slowest at 1.2M due to adverse aileron yaw. Handling and engineering assessments of XM966 (Avon 210) took six months from March 1961.

T Mark 5. XM966 (Avon 301) and XS417 made lengthy tests of performance and the radar and radio kit (including cockpit lighting and EMC) respectively in 1964–5. Undercarriage problems were investigated on XS454 from 1968.

F Mark 6. XP693 and XP697 (Avon 301, possibly later Avon 304) did the CA Release flying in 1965 of this variant with a 600 gal ventral tank replacing the earlier 250 gal, and having cambered leading edges to the wings. The report states that any slight criticisms, eg low stick force per g, were far outweighed by the 50% increase in endurance. Concern about the possibility of a heavy, ie damaging, landing led to the recommendations to keep threshold speed at least 175 kt, and for an incidence gauge. Take off distance to 50 ft was 2,275 yd, and rejection of take off at maximum weight simulated at 107 kt without damage to the aircraft. Landings on a wet runway at 34,500 lb, the maximum normal weight, required 2,790 yd with a parachute and 3,330 yd without in still air. These long distances underlined the need for an arrester hook, later tested successfully on XR769. Modifications to the height holding channel of the automatic flight system permitted clearance up to 0.92 M at low level (previously 400 kt had been the limit). Extension of the rocket doors and firing over the Avon 301s was planned for XP697. Flight refuelling posed no undue problems at speeds above 250 kt. In the ferry configuration with two 260 gal overwing tanks, the weight of XR769 increased to 45,000 lb and range by 200 nm. Major shortcomings were the deterioration in performance of the auto pilot which lost its ability to maintain accurate height and heading, and the tiring formation with Victor tankers. In early 1970 XP697 was stalled and spun at Warton and followed the firm's recommended techniques, particularly in the event of uncertainty as to the direction of the spin when the use of rudder was strictly not advisable. One result of the trial was the use of the Jet Provost for routine spinning of Lightning pilots in the RAF. Returning in 1970, XP693 fired 2,732 rounds from its new belly guns; slight damage occurred to the fins of the Red Top missiles. XR717 was available for training between 1972 and 1974.

Hawker 1127, Kestrel and Harrier

Type P.1127. 55 flights producing under 12 flying hours were made in XP980 (Pegasus 3) at Dunsfold between November 1963 and the following April. The consensus was that hovering and the transition to it demanded no unusual degree of piloting skills; longitudinal control needed improvement for approaches to short and vertical landings, and a disconcerting nose-down pitch occurred during vertical landings. 22 detailed recommendations were made, nearly all of which the firm had in hand by the time the report was written. The aircraft came to AAEE for research in early 1966; in sideslips either the fin stalled or half rudder travel occurred before the ailerons had reached one quarter travel. With only 137 airborne hours, XP980 last flew in May 1968 when it shed a mainwheel taxying. XP984 (Pegasus 5) spun readily in late 1965, but the spin was not fully developed after two turns when recovery action was taken; spinning stopped immediately on all occasions. "Lock-in" engine surge frequently occurred, but was easily remedied.

Kestrel FGA Mark 1. XS689, XS690, XS692 and XS693 (Pegasus 5) shared CA Release flying between July 1964 and June 1965, all based at Dunsfold. Vertical take offs and landings were commendably trouble free, but with the nozzles deflected, approaches between 70 and 150 kt became uncomfortable due to destabilising effect of the rotated nozzles. Ground attack manoeuvres posed no difficulties, but achievable lift was noticeably less, up to 2g, than the Hunter. Nose wheel steering was barely adequate. In 1967, XS695 suffered major damage when an outrigger strut sheared on landing at Boscombe, and the aircraft rolled over, but with only slight damage to the pilot, and six months later XS693, on Pegasus 6 tests from Filton with an AAEE pilot, had an engine failure and the pilot baled out beside Boscombe's runway.

Harrier GR Mark 1. In January 1967 a preview assessment of XV277 (Pegasus 6IR) at Dunsfold confirmed the expected improvement in vertical take off and landing compared with the Kestrel, but also revealed disappointing manoeuvre boundaries defined by buffeting and wing rocking. Longitudinal characteristics had scarcely changed and needed improvements, as did the engine surge margins. Vertical take offs were made at 17,000 lb, and conventional flying at 20,600 lb; the operation of engine temperature limiters made vertical work difficult. Later in 1967 XV280 with a new wing (boundary layer fence and vortex generators) and hard points for stores and XV278 with a "self shortening" undercarriage both demonstrated worthwhile improvements in achievable lift and landings respectively. Wing stores, including two 1,000 lb bombs inboard and two MATRA rocket pods outboard made little difference to handling—a feature attracting the comment "remarkable" in the report. The FE541 inertial navigator (IN) in XV281 achieved the desired accuracy after both normal and rapid alignment, but updating accuracy and map synchronisation were poor; weapon aiming release at 450 kt in 30° dives required reduction in the lag of the altimeter information to produce acceptable results. Between mid-1969 and mid-1970 the five Harriers flown by the Establishment accumulated 331 hours in flights lasting between ten minutes and over

239: Harrier T.2 XW275 at Sigonella, Sicily in 1969. It has a large fin and an extension to the rear fuselage housing an anti-spin parachute. The micro-detonating cord (MDC) of the front cockpit cover is well shown. This aircraft remains in use at Boscombe Down as the advanced controls test bed.
© Crown Copyright

seven hours. Reliability was very good; the report comments that the Harrier was, "better than complex fighters." The long flights had been made during flight refuelling of XV741 in preparation for the trans-Atlantic air race, flown by two A Squadron pilots in that aircraft and XV744. Following preparatory work by XV739, two machines, XV281 and XV740 (both Pegasus 101), made 58 sorties on *HMS Eagle* in early 1970 during which short take off techniques were developed; these required very accurate manual rotation of the nozzles (in both time and angle) and a device for pre-setting the angle was an essential recommendation. The existing range of external stores was flown in five combinations. With a pod (gun or camera) on the fuselage station and at weights up to 22,800 lb, measurement of fin loads during rapid rolling resulted, *inter alia*, of a limit of 180° in roll being imposed at 4.5g. In the winter 1969–70, XV741 experienced no engineering malfunctions at Cold Lake in Canada, but the pilot nearly froze prior to engine start and the avionics misbehaved intermittently. The following summer, XV741 underwent hot weather trials at Yuma in the desert, and again remained serviceable up to 50°C; the 25 gal of water for the engine was sufficient for one vertical take off and landing. The main comment concerned the excessive cabin and equipment temperatures experienced. Meanwhile, in the UK, trials over many months and involving XV277, XV281, XV738,

XV739 and XV740 (all Pegasus 101 except XV739 with a Pegasus 102 and XV738 with Pegasus 11) had been used to evolve short take off techniques, including a computer to calculate safe parameters. Accuracy of the FE541 computer in air-to-air and air-to-ground modes was assessed in XV740 during 1971–2. The camera pod with one F135 and a fan of four F95 Mk 7s gave good results, while some work on the radios was needed to eliminate interference. From October 1971 rockets, weapon aiming accuracy, rapid rolling and navigation kept XV279 busy until after 1975. In 1972 XV281 cleared the BL755 cluster bomb when carried on, and released from, wing and centre line carriers, and, in 1973, operation from a 50 ft wide strip of aluminium planking. The firm put XV742 in the environmental hangar to test the Mk 2 auxiliary power unit in mid-1972. In preparation for use on the GR 3, XV278 (Pegasus 6) tried six MATRA 116 rocket pods without nose cones in early 1975; a year earlier, XV279 had generated large sideslips during rapid rolling with the similar MATRA 155 pods.

Harrier T Mark 2. During the second half of 1970, XW264 and XW265 handled in general similarly to the Mark 1, but with a few significant shortcomings, including directional stability at high Mach number, an unsatisfactory interconnection between the tailplane and airbrake and lack of sideslip indication in the rear

240: Harrier GR.1 XV281 in May 1968 with SNEB rocket launchers outboard and multi striped safety flags on the various covers and pins to be removed before flight. Vortex generators are on the top surface of the wings. © Crown Copyright

241: Two Harrier GR.1s XV739 (nearer) with a 500lb bomb and four rocket pods, with XV739 carrying rocket pods, a gun and centre line pod. Probably Spring 1972. © Crown Copyright

242: Harrier GR.1 XV280 refuelling from the port hose of Victor K.1 XA918 in August 1967. The outcome of this trial was influential in the decision to use the Harrier in the London—New York Air Race nearly two years later. © Crown Copyright

243: Harrier GR.1 XV279 in November 1971 with six Type 116MT Matra rocket launchers, and an AAEE made eight camera photo-pod on the centre line pylon.

cockpit. A year later, with a larger fin and other alterations, XW175 (in Sicily) had acceptable handling. XW265 (Pegasus 101) achieved successful aerial refuelling and from both seats, and also operated from grass up to 17,500 lb. In February 1975 the BL755 cluster bomb was added to the armament cleared for use.

Harrier GR Mark 3. XV788 (Pegasus 103) introduced this mark to AAEE in September 1975, and immediately after EMC checks started work with *HMS Ark Royal*.

Harrier T Mark 4. For two months in 1974, XW934 (Pegasus 103) was engaged in "speech procedures," after handling at the new forward CG.

McDonnell Phantom

FG Mark 1. In July 1968 a party from AAEE observed trials by the US Navy of XT597 and XT859 on *USS Coral Sea*; the usual U S Navy technique of launching with the stick fully back initially led to dangerous over rotation on leaving the catapult. Using a less aft stick position on *USS Kentucky* the next month was better. The first AAEE trials involved XT857, XT865 and XV567 on *HMS Eagle* in March 1969; the critical approaches for deck landings were made difficult by poor longitudinal characteristics and poor engine response. However, using the audio device and maintaining 19 units on the airstream detector gave a consistent approach of 138 kt at normal weight. The need for a fatigue meter to replace the unreliable US model was highlit when it was discovered in XT857 that many cases of severe manoeuvring were not being recorded. AAEE joined RAE to form a team for launching trials at Bedford in late 1968 (XT872) and early 1970 (XV587), although the latter involved no flying; XT873 catapulted from Bedford in 1973 prior to radar warning tests. In 1969 XT598 and XV574 helped with pilot conversions for a few months, before the former continued with clearance of various bombs and Sparrow missiles. All the foregoing had Spey 202 engines; XT858 in December 1969 had Spey 203s for investigation of fast light-up of the reheat.

FGR Mark 2. A new aerial for the UHF of XV410 gave a significant improvement; and the British IFF worked well; in 1973 the first radar warning receiver in British Phantoms alerted the crew to all but one threat radars. Clearance for nuclear weapons (HE 550 lb MC and HE 2,100 lb MC) occupied XV442 and later XT912 in 1970; the BRSL safety lock was the navigator's responsibility with the pilot having all of the other selections. No flying was involved in the EMC[6] investigation of XT900 in December 1969. Releases of dummy nuclear "shapes" from XT898 and XT852 were made using the planned visual mode. Good results were achieved from the infrared and radar reconnaissance pod on XV406 provided the inertial navigator (IN) was accurate; five essential modifications were recommended. The alternatives of fans of F 95 Mk 7 or F 126 cameras were also tested, as was the American KB-18A horizon-to-horizon camera in XV415 in 1969–70. Results of the latter were impressive in good weather conditions. The IN was also critical to the accuracy of the SUU-23A gun of XT898 in 1971; the manual mode using a fixed range and continuously computed impact point was used. Although not designed for the firing of 68 mm SNEB rockets, the inertial navigation system (IN) gave acceptable results in XT928 and XV427 in 1971. Singapore hosted XT853 (Spey 201) in late 1973 for trials of rain erosion.

Dassault Mirage IIIA

Two AAEE pilots flew 0-1 (Atar 9C) and 0-8 (Atar 9C and SEPR 841 rocket) in France in January 1960 at the request of the French authorities. Handling was very easy and viceless providing the pitch and yaw stabilisers functioned at high altitude, and with a comfortable, well laid out, cockpit. The airbrakes produced little drag, unlike the brake parachute which did, although streaming in a crosswind could make for an interesting landing. With 4,380 lb of fuel plus Matra rocket pods gross weight was 17,920 lb. Performance with the rocket firing was startling; a climb (*sic*) at Mach 2 ended with a pushover at 59,000 ft. At 5,000 ft reheat used 23,320 lb/hr, so it was not used at low altitude a great deal. It is little wonder that this paragon sold in thousands worldwide

Sepecat Jaguar

Prototypes. Two flights of the prototype F-ZWRC at Istres in France by an AAEE pilot in January 1969 were marked by poor lateral behaviour at low speed, and by an uncomfortable throttle box. Later, with shortened airbrakes and big wing fences there was some improvement, but a very serious shortcoming was revealed on single engine approaches which were marginally feasible using full dry power, or bursts of maximum reheat to maintain speed. An intermediate standard of partial reheat (PTR) was tried in December 1971, and the production Adour 102 from July 1972. Jaguar testing continued with XW563 (two Adour) at Warton in early 1971 when the latest standard of engine was flown for two sorties. Throttle synchronisation and linkage were poor leading to asymmetric thrust, and some thrust pulsing occurred in the climb; overall, there was an improvement on the earlier standard. The aircraft came to Boscombe in September 1973 for nuclear weapon work lasting until early 1975. XW560 arrived in

---

[6] Appendix 5 has a list of equipment and armament cleared for EMC

244: Phantom FG.1 XT897 in its role as pressure error measurer, posing with Hawk T.1 XX154 in March 1975. The Phantom also had a commitment for navigation trials, and later had a striking paint job. Here it has a more modest "A & A E E" on the fuselage, while the Hawk has a black inner wing. © Crown Copyright

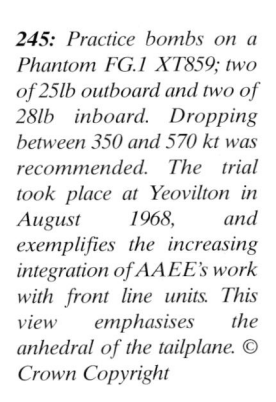

245: Practice bombs on a Phantom FG.1 XT859; two of 25lb outboard and two of 28lb inboard. Dropping between 350 and 570 kt was recommended. The trial took place at Yeovilton in August 1968, and exemplifies the increasing integration of AAEE's work with front line units. This view emphasises the anhedral of the tailplane. © Crown Copyright

246: Phantom FG.1 XT596 poses with an orange target towing pod by Flight Refuelling. © Crown Copyright

247: Mirage IIIA A.01 in 1960. The AAEE preview of this French aircraft included a configuration similar to that shown, but with the addition of a second centreline bomb.

248: Jaguar T 2 XX136 shortly before its demise in November 1974 on wind up turns in a configuration similar to that shown—ie large centreline store plus wing bombs.

249: Boscombe Down's efficient Fire and Rescue Service extinguishes the fire in the rearend of Jaguar XW560 in August 1972 after the pilot Mr Paul Millet of BAC had made a sharp exit.

250: Preview of the USAF TF-15A 71-291 at Edwards AFB, USA, in October 1975. Sqn Ldr R H Beazley of A Squadron in the front cockpit is not asleep.

September 1971 and caught fire on take off in August 1972 with a firm's pilot; it was written off. High incidence handling and spinning (in which engine flame out or surging always occurred) of the French-built M 05 in 1974 led to the recommendation for an audio stall warning device. XW566 (Adour 102) spent time in the "hot" hangar from mid-1973 before trials of external weapons from late 1975.

GR Mark 1. XX108, XX109 and XX110 arrived over a one year period from May 1973, and concentrated on weapon accuracy, handling and gunnery respectively for the CA Release of the type; XX109 included an assessment of the rudder compensation device to counter fuselage twisting. XX112 and XX113 also arrived in 1973, but were flown exclusively on Weapon System Accuracy Measurements (WSAM). XX720 spent six months in North America from July 1974, first in the heat of desert air bases where the most serious complaint was extreme misting of the canopy after descents into humid air. Then followed ground temperatures down to minus 26°C at Cold Lake in Canada where engine starting became difficult and the shock absorbers collapsed. Several alarming uncommanded roll manoeuvres in service led to a brief EMC test on XX731, immediately followed by a comprehensive check on XX744 in which all Test Divisions of AAEE participated; interference of the aircraft's avionics by powerful ground radars was the culprit.

T Mark 2. XX136 arrived in May 1973 and departed (in the aerodynamic sense) in November 1974 when investigating the effect of miss set rudder trim during high g turns. A sudden and extremely disorientating series of tumbling manoeuvres led to both pilots ejecting successfully. The presence of centre line stores had produced significantly degraded handling.

North American TF-15A

The AAEE was denied, by the Ministry of Defence, the opportunity of flying this advanced fighter at the SBAC show at Farnborough. However, a team went to the USA in October 1975 and flew TF-15A 71-291. the pilot was favourably impressed overall, but unfavourably surprised by the performance.

Panavia Tornado

The first preview by AAEE of this tri-national swing wing aircraft took place from Manching, Germany in 1975; only four sorties were possible in a period of several weeks. These delays coupled with the early standard of the engines limited the value of the flying of D9591, but which nevertheless demonstrated promising handling characteristics.

251: Meteor NF.13 WM367 in August 1972 on its last flight after a lengthy spell on Navigation and Radio Division trials. In the background the roads for a new housing estate have been laid, and the extensive mobile home park can be seen behind. © Crown Copyright

252: Wessex HU.5 XT484 in March 1967 on RFA Lyness for checks of handling and blade "sailing" of which none was observed. Floatation gear in stowed in the wheel hubs. © Crown Copyright

HELICOPTERS

Sikorsky Hoverfly

Mark I. KN985 (Scarab R-550-3) came from Beaulieu in September 1950 and was shortly joined by KL108 on research into the effect of engine failure in the hover at 15 ft; at 2,480 lb the maximum acceleration on landing was 3.25g. KK990 included measurement of engine power on the ground prior to departure in July 1952. KK989 spent January 1951 at Boscombe.

Mark II. KN841, KN846 and KN862 were sold for scrap after receipt from Beaulieu in September 1950; only KN841 made a few flights.

Bristol Type 171 and Sycamore

Type 171 Mark 1. The first British helicopter at AAEE was VL958 (Wasp Junior) in May 1949. Handling at 4,850 lb was described as easy with control characteristics better than current helicopters except at high speed (maximum 100 kt). In still air, 340 yd were needed to clear a 100 ft obstacle, rate of climb 750 ft/min and ceiling 10,400 ft; minimum rate of descent in auto rotation was 1,570 ft/min.

Type 171 Mark 2. Partial failure of the Leonides LE 21HM engine led to a hurried and damaging landing of VW905 in September 1952 but after most trials had been completed; comments on handling largely repeated those of the Mark 1, but reflected the effects of a weight of 5,200 lb.

Type 171 Mark 3. Incorporating the experience of the earlier marks, including driving the accessories from the rotor rather than the engine gear box, WA577 (Leonides LE 23HM) weighed 5,200 lb in early 1951; vertical take offs were possible in still air, climbing at 210 ft/min, with range measured as 222 nm at 75 kt, and 188 nm at 93 kt. The left pilot had to change hands to adjust the trimmer and the rotor brake was inadequate. The new stiffer trim spring was liked and handling generally pleasant. The similar WT933 repeated performance tests at 5,200 lb at Khartoum; a wind of 13 kt was needed to achieve a vertical take off, and maximum rate of climb 570 ft/min with a ceiling of 12,600 ft. Handling at maximum weight required great concentration by the pilot From May 1951, WT939 included a major research trial relating handling qualities, control forces and positions as required by the "bible" (AvP970) with qualitative measurements and opinions of pilots. Among findings was that most frequently pilots found the position and force used on the cyclic and collective levers to be acceptable, although not meeting the AvP970 desiderata. WT939 suffered three accidents in its five years at Boscombe; the first, in 1953 involved a rotor blade sailing (drooping) into the tailplane, two years later similar damage resulted from down wash from a nearby Bristol 173 (family squabble?), and in 1958 control was lost in a demonstration of rearward flight and the aircraft destroyed. WA576 stayed for a year from February 1958 for general research work.

Sycamore HC Mark 10. The military application of rotary wing aircraft involved WA578 (Leonides LE 23HM) having large fuselage blisters intended for carrying two stretchers. At 5,200 lb performance was only slightly affected, but longitudinal stability deteriorated and buffet and vibration levels became unacceptable at high speed. In 1952 various tensions in the control trimmer springs and other control changes were made. Later trials in the heat and humidity of Malaya included flying at 5,400 lb into clearings; vertical take offs could just be made at 5,000 lb. Other results noted were the restricted view over the nose, rotor blades close to the ground and blade deterioration. The aircraft was destroyed following engine failure in July 1956.

Sycamore HC Mark 11. Investigation of the Decca navigation aid occupied WT924 for a lengthy period from 1951.

Sycamore HR Mark 12. WV783 (Leonides 173), intended for work over water and having a winch, performed and handled as previous versions at 5,400 lb. Gee Mk 3 and Rebecca Mk 4 navigation equipment had many poor features, and reliability of the radio altimeter bad due to extremes of aircraft attitude. WV784 could hover at 10 ft above the water, simulating the dipping of sonar microphones, but only in winds above 10 kt at representative weights. Height and drift meters were fitted. The pilot, sitting on the left, had an almost impossible task because of the need to change hands to trim, and of the great concentration required; the pressing need for electric trimmers on the cyclic control was amply demonstrated in this 1953 trial.

Sycamore HR Mark 14. With the incorporation of many improvements (including the pilot sitting on the right) resulting from the earlier development aircraft, XE306 (Leonides 173) achieved vertical climb of 460 ft/min in still air at 5,400 lb, and benefitted from the more natural positioning of secondary controls on the collective lever. In 1955, XE307 extended the cleared weight to 5,600 lb, but vertical take offs became marginal in less than 14 kt of wind. The trials of XE308, spread over 12 years from 1953, included radios, navigation,

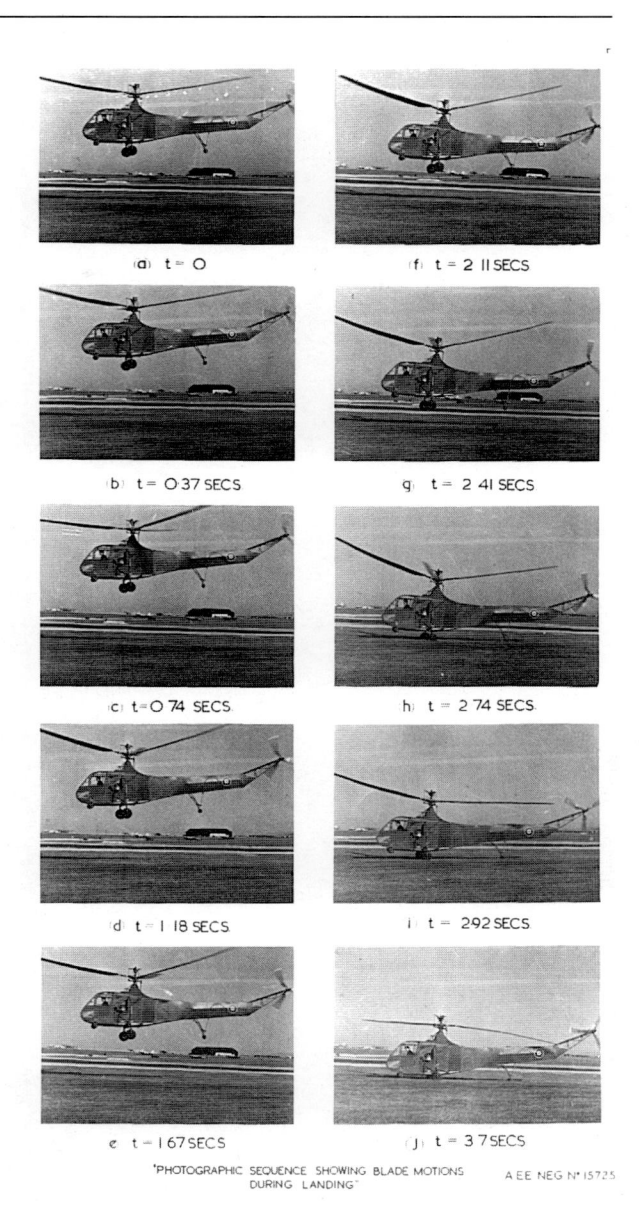

253: Hoverfly I KK985 in October 1950, just after arrival of AFEE from Beaulieu. Frames from a cine film separated by 2.52 seconds taken during an investigation of engine failure in the hover. Reactions had to be quick. "1.18 secs" shows the pilot pulling the collective up producing an acute disc angle; "2.74 secs" shows touchdown, and "3.7 secs" the blades are already drooping in the 3.25g impact. © Crown Copyright

external loads up to 1,000 lb, updated UHF radio and, in 1964, cold weather flying in Canada to investigate the efficacy of anti-icing fluid in the icing rig at Uplands. Its days ended in November 1965 when it rolled over on take off. The change between ground attitude and that in the hover required very well co-ordinated control inputs when taking off and landing. New rotor blades of sealed wooden construction carried XJ918 for over 100 hr of flying in Malaya in 1959 without signs of deterioration. XG502 had IFF/SSR in 1967, and XJ380 ensured range safety at Lyme Bay for a brief period in 1960–1.

Sycamore HR Mark 50. XA219 (Leonides 173) of the Royal Australian Navy (RAN) had a lengthened

254: Sycamore HC.14 XE307 in 1956, beautifully poised for performance and handling at 5,600lb, when a wind of 13 kt was recommended for a safe take off. © Crown Copyright

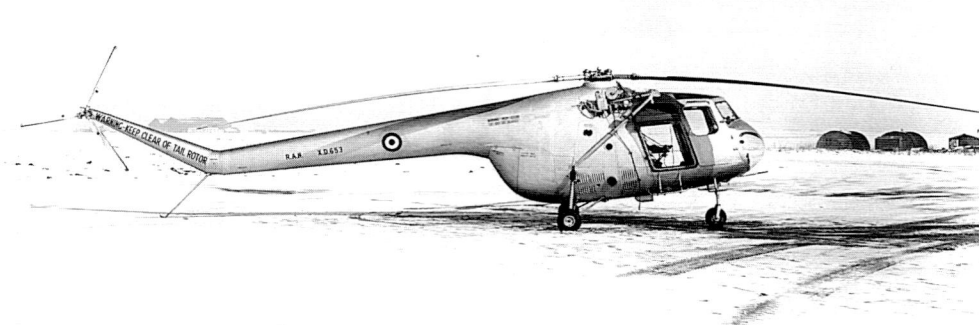

255: Sycamore HR.51 XD653 for the Royal Australian Navy, showing the winch arrangement on the starboard side. Huts used by the runway costructors are evident in the background in 1954. With an 800lb load on the winch, the aircraft hovered with 10° starboard list; pilots found this angle acceptable in the Northern hemisphere! © Crown Copyright

256: Sycamore HC.10 WA578 in early 1952 equipped with blisters for stretchers. Longitudinal instability became most marked at high speed and was accompanied by severe tail vibrations. © Crown Copyright

257: Sycamore HC.14 XE308 in camouflage (adding significant weight). Flt Lt G (Gordon) Smith about to lift 1,000lb with difficulty in October 1956. © Crown Copyright

258 above: Sycamore HR.12 WV784 in August 1953. It was the hovering trial in this aircraft, more than any other, that confirmed to pilots and boffins that the pilot needed to be on the starboard side. The pilot here is clearly seen on the port, and use of the trimmers, out of sight in the centre of the cockpit, necessitated a change of hands; the exercise of hovering required great concentration and was extremely tiring. © Crown Copyright

259 above right: Sycamore Mk 3 WA577 in mid-1951 with a wooden main rotor. Lowering the collective lever fully (by releasing a catch) applied the rotor brake. © Crown Copyright

260: Bell 47B-3 G-AKFB has a bubble canopy from a later version, and is seen here under test by AAEE at, probably, Blackbushe in August 1950. Handling was liked, but the type lacked power. © Crown Copyright

161

undercarriage and a winch in 1952. Handling and performance were unchanged, apart from a slight shortfall in range (now 171 nm); the strong criticism was repeated of the need for the pilot (sitting in the left seat) continuously to change hands for trimming.

Sycamore HR Mark 51. This version for the RAN was a considerable improvement with the pilot seated on the right, and a winch. XD653 and XD654 made the trials including lifting an 800 lb load on the winch; hovering involved a 10°list to starboard (carefully avoiding the inappropriate term "right wing down").

Bell 47 and Sioux

Some 14 years separated the test of an early Bell 47 and the arrival of the developed version known as the Sioux.

Bell 47B-3. In August 1950, G-AKFB (Franklin 6V4-178-B32) started flying at Boscombe at 2,177 lb, achieving a climb of 520 ft/min and top speed of 73 kt (80 kt indicated); at least 10 kt of wind were needed for vertical climbs. Handling was normal, and could be flown hands and feet off the controls for short periods with the friction damper locked.

Sioux AH Mark 1. Based on the Model 47G-3, the first Mark 1 to arrive, some 14 years after the B-3 model, was XV132 (made by Augusta); its visit was short. Trials on XT127 began in March 1965 and results have not been found. XT155 (made by Westland) spent over two years from early 1966 at Boscombe, and trials included an unacceptable Leigh crash location beacon. Intended to be ejected only when the aircraft crashed, the trial beacon, with a mind of its own, made an unscheduled departure in February 1968. XT506 spent the first two months of 1967 in Canada, where engine starting without external heat could be achieved only at minus 5°C; with heating, starting and operating were satisfactory down to minus 30°C. Flares proved acceptable on XT250 (Lycoming O-135-B1) in mid-1967.

Sioux HT Mark 2. New radios for RAF training soon passed muster in XV310 in 1967–8, and followed flare clearance work on XV312. EMC of the flares had to wait until 1971 (XV320).

Westland WS-51, Widgeon and Dragonfly

WS-51 Mark 1. The first of Sikorsky's helicopter designs to be adapted by Westland, the prototype WS-51,

261: Sioux AH 1 XT250 modified with flares on the port front skid. The uncomplicated rotor head can be seen to advantage. Note the horizontal white band around the canopy to give the pilot a reference. © Crown Copyright

262: Sioux AH.1 XT155 in November 1967 with the pilot firmly tied in to the starboard seat. The Pye crash locator beacon under test ejected of its own volition in flight and was rejected pending modification. Note the screens inside the lower canopy—possibly fitted as a reference. © Crown Copyright

263: Sioux AH 1 XT506 at Fort Churchill, Canada in January 1967. Once the engine was running, cold weather was tolerated well by this machine. © Crown Copyright

264: Widgeon G-ALIK probably just prior to AAEE tests in early 1951. Powered controls and metal main rotor blades greatly improved handling. © Crown Copyright

163

265: Dragonfly HR.3 WG662 at the time of its first visit in May 1952 at the start of its use for development of power controls. It had metal rotor blades. © Crown Copyright

266: Dragonfly HR.3 WG662 again in August 1953 with some external changes. The lower window forward of the door has been deleted, and there is equipment under the fuselage. © Crown Copyright

267: Dragonfly HR.3 WN493 with a winch on the port side, and a protective rail for the tail rotor. Probably taken prior to tropical trials in Aden in 1953. © Crown Copyright

G-AKTW, appears in the technical returns, but was, apparently not subjected to the normal, formal reporting procedure in 1949 or 1950. VW209 appeared in 1950 and suffered major damage in November 1951 when the tail cone collapsed during engine off landings. WB810 had a long association with AAEE from June 1949, probably much used for engine development and, later, Porton where Westland records suggest a large external load was carried. In 1952 with a more powerful engine (Leonides 50), an assessment for Malaysian operations at 5,750 lb indicated that a vertical climb would be unobtainable until weight was reduced to 5,200 lb At forward CG, control forces remained too high in the hover. Its gear box failed in February 1956 resulting in significant damage. In February 1951, G-ALIK had powered azimuth and pitch controls and metal rotor blades (thus known as a Mark 1A) giving a remarkable improvement in handling. The need remained for a form of feel and a balance between axes.

Widgeon. G-ATKW (Leonides 50) returned in December 1956 for 7½ hr flying as a Widgeon.

Dragonfly HR Mark 1. Preceding G-ALIK (above) in 1949, VX595 (Leonides 24) could just manage a vertical lift off in still air at 5,870 lb, climbed at 685 ft/min and reached 12,600 ft; maximum speed was 81 kt (true) or 72 kt (indicated). The poor downward view made autorotative landings (at 1,210 ft/min) difficult to judge. The unpowered controls made handling tiring, and made the constant large movements needed for winching almost impossible. Heavy vibrations and uncomfortable thumps added to the pilot's woes at high speed and in the transition to the hover. It fell over in a gust of wind in October 1950 and hurt itself badly.

Dragonfly HR Mark 3. WG661 had rigging faults and was replaced by WG663 for full handling and performance trials in early 1952. The servo-assisted controls gave acceptable cyclic lever forces, including during winching; weight remained restricted to 5,870 lb and maximum speed reduced to 80.5 kt (true), measured, no doubt, with a very keen pencil. Vertical climb outside the ground cushion was 180 ft/min in still air. WG666 completed the radio tests in 1952–3, and WG661 (flying properly in 1958) checked the Green Salad homer. WN493 in Aden in 1953 needed a 10 kt wind for a vertical climb at 5,870 lb; in addition loading required care to avoid an unacceptable CG. Reducing fuel by 50% alleviated both problems. WG662 (Leonides 50) made four visits between 1952 and 1955 and had power controls after the first. WG714 arrived late in 1950 and made AAEE's first helicopter night landing, at Imber, in March 1951; it was destroyed in October 1953 following malfunction of the artificial horizon in cloud leading to loss of control; remarkably, no injuries were sustained in the ensuing crash landing under partial control. Subsequently, three artificial horizons were required in the unstable helicopters. Two years of navigation of WG725 at AAEE are not recorded in discovered documents.

Dragonfly HC Mark 4. XB251 (Leonides 50) made vertical take offs at 5,450 lb in Malaya in 1953. Careful piloting techniques were needed, both to avoid over pitching the rotor blades, and to control the lack of directional control at speeds under 30 kt, particularly important in operations in jungle clearings.

Dragonfly HR Mark 5. WG667 with repositioned aerials for the Violet Picture homing aid successfully overcame shortcomings found earlier in the same aircraft when a Mark 3.

Westland WS-55 and Whirlwind

Prototype. WW339 (R-1340-57) came to Boscombe in March 1952 and demonstrated its exceptionally good handling qualities with servo assisted controls; stability was satisfactory by contemporary standards. In manual, ie servos off, control forces became very heavy. At 6,800 lb, a vertical climb of 100 ft/min in still air and standard conditions could be made; other data included a rate of climb of 805 ft/min, ceiling of 12,600 ft and maximum cruise of 89 kt. At 7,300 lb handling became tricky and a wind of 10 kt was needed for a vertical climb.

HAR Mark 1. Handling of XA863 in 1954 remained similar to the prototype, but it was considered that for service use the control forces in manual were too high, and that an emergency servo system was needed. Vertical climb in still air could be made at 7,200 lb, with acceptable but degraded performance up to 7,500 lb. The compass and airspeed indicator were hidden by the hand on the cyclic control. Radio tests came to a halt when XA865 suffered major damage as the main rotor blades sailed into the rear fuselage on the ground in a gusty wind in October 1954. The Newmark Mk 14 autopilot of XA864 in 1957–8 was an advance, but remained unacceptable for all weather operations on account of unprotected potential runaways and other shortcomings.

HAR Mark 2. XJ429 (R-1340-40) had emergency servo controls and repositioned toe brakes assessed as suitable for UK and Malaysian operations. It weighed 7,800 lb with an external load of up to 1,200 lb and produced performance figures which were just adequate, but careful planning in the prevailing conditions was needed to ensure that a vertical climb of 180 ft/min[1] could be made. Gee-3 navaid and SARAH homing aid worked well. Supplies dropped from XJ759 in 1960 led to clearance for service use, together with UHF radios.

HAR Mark 3. Performance of this mark with increased power was disappointing, due largely to increased basic weight for ship-borne work, and, in the

---

[1] The need to achieve a vertical climb of 180 ft/min had recently been introduced into requirements.

268: *Dragonfly G-AKTW on a brief visit in 1949/50. There appears to have been no formal report written on this visit.*

269: *Whirlwind HAR.10 XP300 in July 1962 in the mountains of France following a hot weather trial; This turbine powered version had a high standard of engine and rotor speed control once the required careful adjustment on the ground had been made.*
© *Crown Copyright*

270: *Whirlwind HAR.1 XA863 during a winching demonstration in August 1954. Provided the power controls were functioning, the exercise posed no undue demands on the pilot.*
© *Crown Copyright*

case of XJ395 (R-1340-3) at least, the need for 210 lb of ballast to maintain an acceptable CG position. Payload became a mere 500 lb if a vertical climb capability was to be achieved in still air in even modest temperatures. Following climbs to 11,300 ft, XJ395 suffered control failure and crashed; three Flight Test Observers were killed. At Idris in 1956, XJ401 achieved the coveted vertical flight at 7,300 lb, some 300 lb less than the UK all up weight. Handling trials of XJ397 in 1955 had identified no fewer than nine essential modifications, including two to the primary flying controls, before service release could be recommended. XJ401 returned in 1957 for a full investigation of performance; modifications successfully increased permitted weight to 7,800 lb in standard conditions. Major changes to XG586 by 1957 included the ability to carry an 18 in Mk 30 torpedo; dropping conditions included a speed of under 25 kt, and height under 35 ft. In 1959 XJ394 had a new FH5C artificial horizon suitable for helicopters, and then took over range safety duties until 1969.

HAR Mark 4. Preceding the Marks 2 and 3 at AAEE, XD164 (R-1340-57) arrived in July 1954 retaining the earlier very heavy manual reversionary controls and poor brake pedal position. Maximum weight flown was 7,200 lb, reduced to 6,740 lb for vertical climb in still air in the UK, but 6,500 lb on trials at Idris where oil cooling became inadequate. A small number of unsuspecting troops were persuaded to leave the aircraft in the hover. XJ411 had the AN/ARC5 radio compass—a novelty giving satisfaction once the aerial had been moved.

HAS Mark 7. The Leonides Major 155 engine of greater power than the R-1340 again proved disappointing. Following measurements in XG590 (later written off in June 1958 after transmission failure), it was concluded that in a 30 kt wind the radius of action would be 33 nm with a 30 min hover at the rescue site. In the strike role the radius reduced to 19.5 nm! Duplicated hydraulic supplies made manual control a remote possibility—just as well since manual flying was considered impossible in XK906. Ground resonance could be avoided by prompt action. Operational reliability at AAEE was good (240 hr in 70 days) in spite of the need for frequent replacement of defective items; noise and exhaust gas made the cabin uncomfortable. Unserviceability limited cold trials at Fort Churchill in Canada to six flights of XG597 in 1958, but included some assessment of the accuracy of the gyro compass in an area with a dip angle of 76°. the radios of XG593 at Boscombe gave no problems. XK941 went to Idris in August 1958 where the severe overheating, some handling and above all performance limitations of the type became manifest. Great care was needed to avoid resonance on landing, and maximum permitted speed reduced by 10 kt with a limit of 8,000 ft altitude. Later, and despite the need for additional handling limitations, the maximum gross weight was increased to 8,000 lb. Improvements in XN258 gave satisfactory engine cooling in Kano in 1959, but the effect was spoilt by sudden losses of power among other, less alarming, phenomena. UHF radio (XG591) and Violet Picture homing aid (XM687) were cleared in 1959, and IFF/SSR (XG594) in 1968. XK596 returned in 1960 with a modified main rotor clutch, tested over 120 hr after carriage, release and jettison trials of torpedoes on both inboard and outboard stations, including jettison during auto rotation. Following limited success with a Mk 14 autopilot in 1960, XG593 fired a pair of machine guns from the port fuselage and rockets from a Matra tube. XG589 flew for Porton for nine years until 1973.

HCC Mark 8. XN126 (Leonides 160 with an electric starter) had extra radios for the Queen's Flight; range was just acceptable in 1959.

HAR Mark 9. This turbine-powered Naval version did not appear at AAEE until XN310 (Gnome 101) came in 1965 for evaluation of the avionics, cleared for ambient temperatures up to +30°C only. Two years later, XL899 fired 4$^{1/2}$ in reconnaissance flares over Lyme Bay, and XM666 fired SS11 missiles over Luce Bay in Scotland in 1969.

HAR Mark 10. No fewer than 16 of this version appeared on the books of AAEE between 1960 and 1975, starting with XJ398 and XP299 (both Gnome101) for handling and performance; cockpit layout was criticised and a rudder trimmer needed. However, the high standard of engine control and rotor governing had "at last" been achieved, but doubts remained about the pilot's ability to contain a computer runaway. Over 50 hr of hovering within 30 ft of the sea gave confidence that the rescue role would not contaminate the engine compressor. XP333 showed that very careful rigging was necessary to achieve the best engine/rotor performance. Later, a torque meter replaced the fuel flow meter as the primary power indicator in XJ398, following a recommendation made in 1962 as a result of trials in Idris on XP300. Other results from Idris included poor performance of the VHF and standby UHF radios due to heat. XD163 made water landings with floatation gear intended for the Mark 12. Aerial systems in XN126 (HF radio) and XJ764 (UHF radio) needed brief trials in 1965. Clearance followed carriage and firing of Nord SS11 missiles from XP301 in 1962. XJ409 replaced the Mark 7 with Porton from 1972. XP351 and XP356 spent the winter of 1971–2 on icing research. Brief trials included XJ396 (autopilot in 1965), XJ729 (engine computer checks in 1963), XP303 (Violet Picture homer in 1961–2), XP329 (gun in 1962) and XP399 (IFF/SSR in 1972).

HCC Mark 12. The flotation gear stowed on the wheels of XR486 of the Queen's Flight had little effect on handling or performance in 1964.

271: Sikorsky S-55 WW339 in April 1952 when it demonstrated good stability by contemporary standards. Just ahead of the rotor head is a direction finding loop, and the static vent appears to be just ahead of the roundel. © Crown Copyright

272: Whirlwind HCC.8 XN126 of the Royal Flight in September 1959. Three improvements on the normal machine are apparent: the double step and hand rail to assist entry, and the duct for the engine intake; there was also an electric starter to replace the cartridge type. © Crown Copyright

273: Whirlwind HAS.7 XG593 in June 1962 with a MATRA rocket launcher, and beneath it, a gun. The tube is tilted up relative to the gun to allow for the drop of the slower rockets. There is a box on the nose of unknown purpose. © Crown Copyright

274: Whirlwind HAR.2 XJ759, a long serving support helicopter about to delight some children by bringing Father Christmas clattering from the air at the festive season of 1958. © Crown Copyright

275: Whirlwind HAS 7 XK941 in August 1958 at Idris in Libya. Severe cooling problems of the Leonides engine were manifest, and the adverse effect of high ambient temperatures on handling were significantly greater than anticipated. © Crown Copyright

276: Whirlwind HAS.7 XG589 in January 1966 showing its long term affiliation with AAEE by the inscription above the roundel. © Crown Copyright

277: Whirlwind HAR.9 XM666 in September 1969 with a pair of Nord SS11 missiles for use against targets between 1,000 and 2,000m distant. The "Rescue" notice has been liberally interpreted. © Crown Copyright

278: Whirlwind HAR.10 XP301 in early 1962 armed with Nord SS11 Type A1 missiles. The aircraft handled well, and firing was possible up to 80 kt; the missiles were protected from hot engine exhaust by the heat shield. © Crown Copyright

Saunders Roe Skeeter

The first Skeeters flown by AAEE were machines built for civil purposes, but assessed for the Army's needs, and tested to military standards. The Westland company took over Saunders Roe during development.

Skeeter Mark 3B. WF113 (Bombardier 702) flew at Eastleigh for the AAEE in early 1953 when the overriding fault was violent ground resonance, resulting in some damage during trials. At 2,000 lb and in still air, vertical climb was 60 ft/min, but with 11 kt of wind 100 ft/min could be achieved at 2,070 lb. Other performance data included climb of 720 ft/min, ceiling of 9,300 ft and top speed of 80 kt at 335 rotor rpm; control forces were light with good response.

Skeeter Mark 4. The company's records indicate that the sole machine of this mark spent a short time at Boscombe on resonance tests.

Skeeter Mark 5. Modifications to the undercarriage of XG303 (Bombardier 702) in mid-1954 successfully eliminated violent resonance, but the climb remained poor. The need to maintain the non-governed rotor rpm above 300 was essential as controllability below this figure became marginal.

Skeeter Mark 6. In early 1955 XJ355 (Gipsy Major 30 Mk 2) demonstrated superior performance including a vertical, still air, climb of 150 ft/min at 2,150 lb and a ceiling of 12,200 ft. It was pleasant to fly, and coped adequately in a wind "fairly severe for a light helicopter." The Establishment found it suitable for Army work. XK773 was categorised as a write off after a landing accident in June 1956; it nevertheless reappeared with a Gipsy Major 130 four months later modified with army radios and two collective levers for the pilots' left hands. Vertical climb could not be achieved, and the engineers found much in need of improvement.

Skeeter AOP Mark 12. In 1958 XK482 made extensive repeat handling and performance tests judged to be acceptable for the Army's use; night flying was cleared only in visual contact with the ground. The following advice was included, "Care must be taken in rearward flight ... as the cyclic [control] fouls the harness." The light fast rotor (330 rpm) with low momentum suffered rapid decay of rpm if the engine failed, and needed prompt action by the pilot to avoid catastrophe. A further quirk was the poor performance at high tip speeds, finally explained by the tip sections expanding due to the radial movement of air inside the blade under the action of centrifugal force; this thickened the blade section and gave greater drag! XL739 (Gipsy Major 140) flew 400 hr from September 1958 before cold weather trials in Ottawa in the winter 1959–60; the increase in vibrations were attributed to wear during the intensive flying, and to thermal effects on the main drag hinge friction damper. One result was the need for frequent replacement of the radios. Parallel trials of XL807 in Norway in early 1959 showed the need for more heating, demisting and oil dilution. An exhaust driven supercharger in XM528 caused the engine to run far too hot in Aden; the benefits were thus marginal and of no use to the Army. Further cooling trials of normally aspirated engines in XL734 and XL739 in 1960–1 showed that the oil remained too cool to permit boil off after dilution. In 1966, XL764 had new radios, replacing those approved in XL813 five years previously.

Bristol Type 173 and Belvedere

Type 173. With two main rotors and two engines (Leonides LE25HM), XF785 could not be assessed for civil operations largely on account of excessively heavy, manual, controls; trimming, vibrations, the balance of power output and the absence of a warning of engine failure received criticism in January 1954. Little improvement was found later after modifications, but investigations continued into 1955. For one experiment on this aircraft the yaw and roll controls were almost completely crossed. The pilot needed to give his undivided attention to keeping the machine upright. A pilot's assessment of 10 (the very worst) was accorded on the Cooper Harper scale.[2]

Belvedere HC Mark 1. AAEE classified XG451 and XG452 thus, although both were regarded by the firm as prototypes on arrival in April 1960. While the former concentrated on armament and radio work at Boscombe, the latter was prepared for flying to Idris with a long range tank. Completion of the transit flights in record time from London to Malta was rewarding for those involved, and the hot weather trials (up to over 40°C) achieved the desired results up to 18,500 lb. The turbine engines (two Gazelle 101-NGa2) performed well; approval for normal flying of the slightly high jpt and oil temperatures experienced was formalised later. The type absorbed a high number of maintenance man-hours per hour flown. Back at Boscombe sloping ground up to 6° could be managed, but handling an external load reduced performance significantly; without an external load a ceiling of 7,000 ft and a limit of 95 kt were recommended. The 11th Belvedere built, XG457, was the first to have all the current modifications of the production standard in March 1961, including duplicated power to the flying controls, throttle stops at flight idle and other changes to the rotor and engines. Although many minor improvements remained to be rectified, clearance was recommended for temperate operations at 19,000 lb with a maximum load (internal or external) of 6,000 lb; fuel capacity was 588 gal. Assessment of XG460 for

---

[2] Cooper Harper scale was used to quantify handling characteristics, from 1—excellent all round, to 10—unflyable.

279: *Skeeter AOP.12 XM 528 on skids for tests of an exhaust driven supercharger, of which there are no clues in this view. After flying in Aden and the UK, the supercharger was found to be unsuitable. © Crown Copyright*

280: *Skeeter AOP.12 XL807 in March 1959 on wheels, having spent two months in Norway where the need for several essential items to combat the cold had been identified. © Crown Copyright*

281: *Skeeter 6 XJ355 on extensive performance and handling tests in April 1955 from which its suitability for army communications and reconnaissance was confirmed. © Crown Copyright*

282: *Bristol Type 173 XF785 in August 1958. It is in the second configuration tested at AAEE with four-bladed rotor and "H" type tailplane. The long nose probe sampled airflow ahead of the downwash. Wartime Nissen huts remain in view. © Crown Copyright*

283: *Bristol Type 173 XF785 in 1954 demonstrating the very nose high attitude in the flare after a steep approach. A pilot at Farnborough managed to tip over backwards in a similar manoeuvre in 1961. The original three bladed rotor and "V" tailplane are fitted. © Crown Copyright*

284: *Belvedere HC.1 XG452 in the French Alps after its record breaking flight from London to Malta in June 1960. The tail configuration differs from that of the prototype. © Crown Copyright*

173

instrument and night flying resulted in a limited clearance, with recommendations for a standby artificial horizon, auto stabilisation and rotor governing. XG452 continued on various tasks, including stability research in 1961, paratroop dropping in 1962 and radios in 1963. The RAF's XG475 was flown in Singapore, and cleared for ferrying only at a weight of 19,500 lb. Cold weather and icing trials of XG468 in Canada in the winter 1962–3 were followed by assessment of the Decca 8 navaid in 1964.

Hiller HT Mark 1

Known also by its US Navy designation (HTE-2), XB513 (Franklin O-335-6) received a brief assessment at 2,300 lb from late 1953. Handling differed from other helicopters and was considered suitable only for *ab initio* training; the cyclic control became unusually sensitive near the maximum speed of 68 kt (indicated). Vertical take off in still air could be achieved only by the unacceptable expedient of reducing rotor rpm.

Westland Wessex

Prototype. Fourth Sikorsky design to be tested at AAEE, and the third to be made and developed by Westland, the WS-58 Wessex remains in RAF service at the time of writing, some 44 years after the prototype reached Boscombe Down. G-17-1 (R-1820-58) unmodified from American standard, underwent a brief handling evaluation in September 1956. It was found pleasant to fly, but ground resonance, cabin noise and the high cyclic break out forces received adverse comment; the potential payload and cruising speeds, both well above contemporary service helicopters, received favourable comment.

HAS Mark 1. Regarded as representative Mark 1s, XL729, XM301 and XM326 (all Gazelle NGa13) shared initial type tests, primarily in the ship-borne antisubmarine role, for a year from June 1959; XM326 had an Iso Propyl Nitrate (IPN) starter and the others electrical. At 12,600 lb performance and handling were basically acceptable, but vibrations, tendency to ground resonance and poor engine response were shortcomings; indeed, the altitude limitation of 7,000 ft was imposed because of heavy vibrations. Vertical climb in still air was 650 ft/min and the absolute range calculated as 267 nm. The crew of XM301 received static electrical shocks during successful winching trials of suspended loads. A major exercise involved a Beverley, XM330 and much pushing and shoving to get the helicopter inside the freighter for transport to Idris, where jpt and oil temperatures exceeded some limits leading to doubts about the feasibility of operating at the full weight of 12,600 lb in tropical areas. Criticisms included cabin ventilation, the rotor brake and breakage of the tail rotor. The peripatetic XM330 (Gazelle 160), with long range tanks only partially feeding, reached the French Alps in June 1961 for trials up to 10,000 ft; success was attributed in part to a very satisfactory rotor speed governor by Napier. Sea level tests at Hal Far followed and many "dunks" into water made; the Flight Control System Mk 3 considerably assisted hovering. Indeed, the report on handling tests of XM328 in states, "with auto stability ... [the Wessex] is superior to many fixed wing aircraft for instrument flying." In 1961 simultaneous tests of the same control system at Boscombe on XM327 included coupling to a Mk 19 autopilot with encouraging results after partial success the previous year on XM300. The long series of Wessex de-icing investigations in Canada started in February 1961 with XM837 in the spray rig at Uplands in Ottawa; when colder than minus 10°C, the electrical de-icing system of both main and tail rotors failed to prevent large lumps of ice from forming and flying off. The next winter saw XM331 with a fluid system at Uplands; failure was aggravated by excessive consumption of fluid. In the UK XM328, XM329 and later XM838 made the usual checks of the radios and navigation kit, including the novel hovering doppler, and the ASDIC (AN/AQS-4). The Collins 618T HF radio of XM874 interfered with the avionics controlling auto-hover in 1963. An unknown aircraft coped well with wind and ship's movements on *HMS Devonshire*, the first ship to have a helicopter designed as part of its armament, in late 1962.

Most of the armament trials lasting two years from April 1962 involved XM330 and possibly XS121 (Gazelle 161) from mid-1964, whose repertoire included Depth Charges MK 15, Nord SS11 missiles, Torpedoes Mk NC43 with parachute, fixed twin 0.303 in guns with heat shield, cabin mounted 7.62 mm gun, and 2 in rocket pods over the wheels. XS863 lingered on until after 1975 with Porton.

HC Mark 2. Extra power for troop carrying by the RAF led to coupled Gnome engines, first tried at AAEE in XL728 and XM299 in 1962. Engine handling was considered adequate given the early standard of the engines and their governors. Initial handling of XR588 (coupled Gnome 101) at 12,600 lb, also adequate, led to CA Release recommendation in December 1963; provisos included the need for protection of the rotor against overspeeding in the event of an upward runaway of the fuel computer. Meanwhile, XR498 flew in stages to Idris where sand filters were fitted for performance, handling and engineering tests at up to 13,500 lb. Ground resonance caused the aircraft to fall over and suffer damage in August 1963. Flying already completed showed that the engine bay overheated and that the exhaust circulated into the cabin, but more significantly that performance was drastically down on expectations due to the inability of the rotor to utilise the extra engine power. Of the 14 modifications considered essential were an indicator on the pilot's coaming for collective pitch angle, and reduction of vibrations at even modest bank

285: Belvedere HC.1 XG449 at Boscombe in September 1964 with what appear to be a pod containing a machine gun, a hoist over the door and a pannier under the forward fuselage. No report of its relevant work has been found. © Crown Copyright

286: Hiller HT.1 XB513 under limited assessment as a primary trainer for which a maximum permitted speed of 68 kt, inability to climb vertically in still air and an unduly sensitive cyclic control made it unsuitable for any other purpose. © Crown Copyright

287: Wessex HAS.1 XM301 demonstrating its ability in October 1959 to lift a Land Rover while the Army observes; the pilot's emergency jettison was foot operated. Several ground crew received nasty shocks from static electricity. © Crown Copyright

288: Wessex HAS.1 XM326 in August 1961, having previously participated in performance and handling trials with iso-propyl-nitrate (IPN) mono fuel starter replacing the electrical type; both were satisfactory. Here, it was ready to make tests of rotor speed governing. It had a long boom to sample air outside the rotor downwash and a device under the fuselage—possibly for tethered hovering. © Crown Copyright

289: Wessex HAS 1 XM330 in Malta in August 1961 as part of tropical trials. It had a Flight Control System Mk 3 and a Mark 19 autopilot, and together these aids permitted "hands off" hovering over water. On the starboard door is a cylindrical device, probably containing the extra fuel. © Crown Copyright

290: Wessex HC 2 XR503 at Idris, Libya in August 1966—the fourth year that this Mark had ventured thither. 1966's highlight was assessment of the momentum particle sand separator door seen attached to the nose. Two engines failed within 14 flying hours of arrival. © Crown Copyright

291: Wessex HC.2 XR588 in July 1964 with a wide track undercarriage, sand filters and some protection on the leading edges of the blades. Blades and engines had a short life in the sand. © Crown Copyright

292: Wessex HU.5 XT774 with two inch rocket pods. The wheel had a protective cover, and there was a plate over the installation— possibly to avoid dazzling the pilot. 21 firing flights were made © Crown Copyright

293: Wessex HAS.1 XM331 at Ottawa on the second winter's trials. Fluid de-icing on the blades did not prove effective, even when used in excessive quantities. © Crown Copyright

angles. The next year XR588 continued hot weather tests with engine intake filters and the main rotor blades protected against sand erosion. Engine life remained short in spite of the filters, the engines ran too hot and the unprotected tail rotor rapidly wore away; the wide track undercarriage proved successful. Returning via the French Alps, it was found that capability became limited by directional control, ie stall of the tail rotor, rather than engine power. At Boscombe, XR494 completed engine handling and confirmed the need for rotor overspeed protection. In 1964, XR505 towed vehicles up to 4,000 lb on the ground by wires up to 80 ft long; handling remained satisfactory provided that auto stability was operating. 23% more power was needed when towing. XR588 repeated the trial in 1965, but with various improvements to the pilot's information including tension on the wire and wire angle. On level smooth land a Centurion tank moved on the power of the helicopter. New radios worked well in XR497 before departure for Uplands in January 1964 where starting and operating gave few problems down to minus 17°C. 1966 saw XS679 with improved avionics and a projected map display of great benefit to tactical freedom. Further desert flying in 1966 with "momentum particle sand separator door", and also including anti icing on XR503 gave disappointing results as one engine failed after 1.6 hr in the sandy air, and a second a little later; the tail rotor again suffered severe erosion. XV727 with electrically heated windscreen crashed in the mountains of Norway in January 1969 on winter trials; the cause was partly attributed to mismanagement, and the crew suffered major injuries. XV729 handled at the increased all up weight of 13,600 lb.

HAS Mark 3. With advanced, duplicated, autopilot controls and a new radar for hunting submarines, XT255 (Gazelle 22) evaluated the handling in mid-1965; the flight control system was good, but doubts remained about the adequacy of the pitch control for automatic transition into the hover. The engine and rotor were well matched with good governing characteristics. Later, production standard governors suffered from hysteresis. Performance at 13,500 lb met the specification with the exception of a low endurance when fully equipped for the antisubmarine role. XT257, joined by converted Mark 1s XM834 and XM836, made a year long assessment from March 1966 of the antisubmarine capabilities; although the need for several improvements became apparent, the overall results were acceptable. Included in this work was the Blue Orchid doppler and GM7 compass of XM331; some interference occurred between the HF radio and the flight control system, and between the sonar and radar. Electrical reliability checks took XT256 five months in Malta in 1966. In the UK, meanwhile, 600 lb bomb and machine gun trials on XM871 lasted one year from mid-1966. XM919 flew 124 hr at El Centro in USA from July 1967 and later moved on to Fort Churchill in Canada. At temperatures between +32°C to +43°C blowers in the cabin and radio bay

294: Wessex HAS.3 XM871 in February 1967 armed with a 7.62mm general purpose machine gun mounted at the window. The operational case for an anti submarine helicopter to carry a machine gun has not been elucidated. © Crown Copyright

circulated very hot air without affording any cooling benefit; the crew, radios, radar and engine governor continued to function. With metal main and tail rotors performance was adequate, but in sideways flight to the right, yaw control became marginal as the 30 kt requirement was approached. XM923 joined the team in Canada in 1968–9 and hovered in the icing rig and possibly returned to Uplands, Ottawa in early 1970 where little natural icing limited the results of the trial; enough evidence was gathered to recommend a ban on flying in freezing rain, and the fitting of an accurate thermometer to allow pilots to avoid these conditions. In 1969 vibrations and then sonar equipment occupied XS127 and XP137 spent the winter months of 1970 at Lossiemouth seeking icing conditions.

HCC Mark 4. Both XV732 and XV733 (the latter at Yeovil), extensively equipped with additional radio and navigation aids for the Queen's Flight, were given priority treatment in 1969; the VOR navaid and emergency intercom needed improvement.

HU Mark 5. XS241 arrived in 1963 and much clearance of handling and performance was "read across" from the similar Mark 2; gun and rocket armament was similar to the Mark 1. Three avionic items needed improvement, viz, IFF 10, radio altimeter 7 and telebrief, but the five blade tail rotor gave good yaw control at high altitude. XS485 cleared the IFF in 1967 and XS484 had a radio altimeter 7B with marginally better accuracy in 1968. XT484 (*sic*) made day and night operations from *RFA Lyness* at weights up to 13,000 lb; the report notes that there was no blade sailing. The numerous cold weather trials on Wessex HU5s reflected the need for successful operations in Norway by this version. 87 hours flying from Fort Churchill in Canada occupied XS506 (Gnome 112/113) in 1965–6; temperatures down to minus 35°C soon revealed the need for better lubricants, among other shortcomings. In 1970, XS482 went to Uplands with a new nose door (known as modification 1051); engine damage occurred less frequently, and a modified type by AAEE gave scarcely better results. The following winter the "1051" nose door was rejected, but natural icing in temperatures down to minus 10°C could, it was found, be tolerated by the main rotor without de-icing. In 1971–2, in Norway and Scotland, a new nose shape by AAEE, known as the "Cold Running Nose Door"(hardly surprising in those temperatures!) gave good results in most conditions, the criterion being a build up of ice on the detector of less that 1 mm/min. For the winters 1973–4 and 1974–5, XT762 joined XS482; the "1051" door was tried again, but with anti icing fluid; re-circulation of snow in the hover led to damaged engines, as did ice shedding from the door in forward flight. Further work indicated that ice did not entirely shed from the main rotor with resulting unacceptable loss of performance. This investigation was aided by an AAEE designed camera on XT762 turning with the rotor to provide a continuous record of accretion. EMC checks of XT457 were made on the ground in 1965, and in the air on XT458; armament work was quickly completed on XT667 in 1971, but two inch rockets needed over a year to clear using XT774 in 1967–8. XT486 (intercomm) and XT460 (intake) appeared briefly.

Westland Scout

Conceived by Saunders Roe, the Scout was developed by Westland as a five seat army liaison type.

Scout AH Mark 1. XP165 (Nimbus 101) was sent in December 1960 directly to Aden where the maximum weight of 5,000 lb was imposed because of restricted engine power. Vibrations, particularly at the top speed of 120 kt, caused concern, as did the erosion of both rotors and the engine in the sandy conditions; the manual controls were considered acceptable only for emergencies. With powered controls and a Nimbus 102 of greater power, XP189 went to Chakari in India in 1961; in the temperatures experienced (up to 44°C) the potential output of the engine remained unrestricted by the airframe limitation on torque transmission. Engine unserviceability reduced flying to under 10 hr. 1962's hot and high tests involved XP165 in Idris, Khartoum and Nairobi. Handling received restrained approval for an interim clearance, pending an increase in tail rotor diameter and many other improvements to both engine and airframe. Hovering at 14,000 ft over Nairobi for 37 min raised the gearbox oil temperature to within 1°C of its limit; in view of this achievement it is surprising that the vertical climb performance was below that required. Other specified parameters were achieved with the exception of the range of 115 nm (150 nm required) with a 1,000 lb load. Cold weather trials in Canada stopped when XP849 arrived too heavily on the hard snow in January 1963. At Boscombe, XP192 investigated the flight envelope within which the risk from an engine failure was minimised, a particularly important aspect of Scout flying in view of the rapid decay of rotor rpm without the benefit of engine power. This risk was amply demonstrated when the aircraft was written off in one engine-off test in November 1962, without injury to the pilot. Gentle manoeuvres only were recommended following trials with the CG moved aft by a mere half an inch in XP846 (Nimbus 101). Changes to the cyclic gearing overcame the difficulties at aft CG, but the firm worried that handling was then too sensitive; the AAEE pilots found the new controls delightful, and the Scout became the standard against which other helicopters were judged. In 1965 the Mk 28 autopilot from the Wasp gave some help to the pilot of XR637, but its value as a stabiliser was limited; it was a single channel device.

Load carrying evaluation started on XP848 in 1962 with external stores of up to 1,500 lb, for all of which the strop length was critical to the handling of the aircraft; the three methods of release were: a button on the cyclic

295: Wessex HAS.3 XT257 equipped with nose probe and camera aiming circle for tests of the automatic flight control in the hover. 110 flying hours were flown on radio evaluation. © Crown Copyright

296: Wessex HU.5 with a pair of 7.62mm Machine guns on special mountings. A hoist can be seen over the door on the starboard side. © Crown Copyright

297: Scout AH.1 XP889 seen with a stretcher on the day of arrival in October 1963; 80 kt was considered to be the maximum acceptable speed. The large wipers and spray bar for the windscreen are also featured. © Crown Copyright

control, another for the pilot's foot, and automatically on touch down of the load. Supply dropping from the door could be made with light (350 lb) packages. Drawbacks to the Lucas hoist on XP851 limited use; later, an improved hoist on XP908 lifted weights up to 400 lb. The maximum speed of 80 kt was recommended with external stretchers following tests on XP889 in 1963; machine guns of 7.62 mm calibre fired successfully from XP903 in the 12 flights of the trial. Deicing fluid failed to cover a sufficient area of XP847's windscreen, but replacing the P12 compass with the G4F type was an advance. XP190 and XP846 made the initial radio and navaid appraisal in 1962, followed by a compact VHF/FM set and crash locator beacon in XT624 in 1967–8, and IFF/SSR in XT634 in 1971; XT639 flew with a pressure sensor installation in 1975, probably for use in Northern Ireland. XP189 made comprehensive checks of the characteristics of the standard articulated rotor in 1970; the following year the hingeless rotor for the Lynx flew with less vibration, particularly in turns. Brief autopilot trials on XP166 (Nimbus 101) finished at the same time that 200 hr of endurance flying were achieved on XP850. Three days at Boscombe sufficed for "roping" from XP857 (Nimbus 105) in August 1964, while 13 months from mid-1972 were needed for icing and autorotating trials in XT626. Other trials were, XR640 (rotor rigging and performance 1965–6), XW280 (EMC in mid-1970) and XR635 (radios in 1975).

Sud Alouette

AH Mark 2. XR378 (painted as XJ378) made two short visits to AAEE in 1961, flying a total of 87 hours, and XR232 completed 54 hours from September 1964. Details of their trials are lacking.

Westland Wasp

HAS Mark 1. Naval sibling to the Scout, the Wasp went immediately to the deck for its first AAEE trial. XS463 (Nimbus 101) flew on and off *HMS Nubian* in February 1963 with the ship in motion, both by day and night; the aircraft had no auto-pilot or -stabilisers, nor a radio altimeter. These aids to safe flying, plus greater illumination of the ship, became priorities. Interestingly, the trials of the emergency floatation gear did not take place until late 1964. In late 1963, XS533 flew from *HMS Leander*, which also needed better lighting; the innovation of an ultra fine collective blade setting allowed the pilot to achieve positive contact with the deck by pushing down on the lever. Better but not ideal lighting was seen in early 1964, and in 1967 day and night flying from *HMS Undaunted* led to no serious complaints. Tropical trials at Idris employed XS528 (Nimbus 104) in 1963; although flown at 5,500 lb, the recommended maximum for the Navy was 5,200 lb. In 40°C

298: Wasp HAS 1 XS527 in August 1964 on board HMS Mohawk in water off Aden. Although having increased power, this aircraft still needed a wind over the deck to take off in the heat at maximum all up weight. The pilot's sandals are non-standard! © Crown Copyright

299: Scout AH.1 XP847 in late 1967 with a hoist, and UHF communications. The static vent is just ahead of the serial number, and the wheels helped with ground handling. © Crown Copyright

300: Alouette AH 2 XR378 (cunningly painted XJ378) in August 1961 with a stretcher on the starboard side. © Crown Copyright

301: Saro P.531 XN332 in April 1959 at the manufacturer's airfield, Eastleigh, possibly at the time of the first AAEE preview flying. © Crown Copyright

302: Wasp HAS 1 XS528 in August 1963 located at Idris, Libya. Two Mk 43 torpedoes were fitted, raising the all up weight to the maximum. Performance met that specified by the MOD at all points. © Crown Copyright

303: Wasp HAS.1 XT417 with four Nord AS 11 missiles for handling trials in early 1967. Top speed reduced by 4 kt, otherwise no differences were apparent in handling. © Crown Copyright

304: Hughes 269A XS684 was preferred to the Brantly, but range and take off deficiencies led to rejection. © Crown Copyright

183

and still air vertical climb was 200 ft/min; the ceiling was not measured, but at 12,000 ft the climb remained at 600 ft/min. Among items identified for improvement, a canopy for ground use received the strongest plea. Combined tropical and deck tests of XS527 (Nimbus 103) took place on *HMS Mohawk* in 1964. A weight of 5,500 lb was cleared provided the wind speed was adequate, and five further changes to the governor were proposed to overcome large torque fluctuations. During the *Mohawk* trials, a continuing observation of the Mk 28 autopilot supplemented information from XS532 and XT414 at Boscombe; investigation of "worst case" single failures, ie, runaways, led to the imposition of a minimum altitude of 200 ft within a speed range of 40 to 95 kt. 1966 tests of a device to protect against runaways revealed unacceptable shortcomings. The implications of failure of power to the flying controls in cloud received attention in XS476 and XS527 (Nimbus 101) in 1964; manual flying was considered just acceptable for a safe landing.

Two trials, possibly connected, involved XS528 in measurement of vibrations at high altitude where harsh vertical thumps occurred every revolution of the main rotor (colourfully known as "wumpers"), and XS530, which examined the reported experience of fatigue and nausea. Changing the drive couplings to the tail rotor, replacing Westland main blades with a set by Parsons and fitting a wooden tail rotor gave slight improvement. Expensive maintenance in service of the friction-type of blade hinge damper led to a successful trial of hydraulic dampers on XS528 in 1967. With a strop length between 5 and 80 ft, and at speeds below 86 kt and bank angles up to 20°, external loads of 1,500 lb were cleared by XS532; using a Lucas air operated hoist, weights up to only 500 lb could be lifted. The ship's electro magnetic environment of *HMS Naiad* was used to clear the IFF/SSR of XT414 in 1965. Handling of XT417 in 1967 remained unaffected by four Nod AS12 missiles, although top speed was reduced by 4 kt; firing of the missiles took place in June 1968 from XT569. Following inconclusive trials behind the Pembroke fitted with a spray rig, XT423 flew in the cold and icy air of Ottawa in the winters of 1968–9 and 1969–70; as a result operations in stratoform cloud down to minus 5°C were found to be acceptable. EMC checks on XT435 in 1965 and XT778 the following year were followed by pressure error measurements in XT793 in 1975.

Hughes 269A and 300

Competing with the Brantlys, the Hughes, XS684 and XS685 (both Lycoming O-360-C2D), were preferred, but did not meet the range requirement. Take offs in warm weather could be made only up to 3,000 ft, handling was pleasant at 1,600 lb with good stability but hard seating caused a certain numbness. The engine ran too hot in tropical temperatures. The developed version (Hughes 300-269B) N9302F visited in early 1964, and flew 21 sorties interrupted by severe rotor vibrations and a hint of control limitations; it was not considered robust.

Brantly B 2A and B 2B

In the summer of 1963, XS681 (B2A) and XS683 (B2B) (both Lycoming O-360-B1A) competed against the Hughes 269 for a potential Army order. The rotor was too low for entry with blades turning, high speed handling was barely acceptable, and take off could not be made at airfield elevations above 1,600 ft. Engine temperatures remained acceptable in tropical conditions at Idris.

Hughes 500

During a European sales tour, five flights of N9000F (T 63-5) were made in December 1966. The very poor weather made meaningful assessment difficult, although comments included the plea for flying without the firm's pilot on board.

Lockheed 286

A short assessment of this five seat helicopter took place at Van Nuys in USA in December 1968. Its non-articulated rotor blades conferred excellent handling in the calm conditions prevailing, with low vibration and outstanding control response. Stability was good, and it could be flown for short periods with the hands off the controls; however, vibration and instability at high speed spoilt the overall impression.

Agusta-Bell 204B and 205

The civil 204B, I-AGUG (Gnome 1200) was flown at Boscombe in June 1965, and the heavier military 205 MM80474 (T-53-L-11) in Italy the following month. Both had very good handling with commendably smooth reversion to manual control at all weights and positions of the CG; at 9,500 lb (205) some limitation in yaw control became apparent at high altitude.

Bolkow 105

The opportunity was taken in May 1970 to fly this German helicopter with a semi rigid hingeless rotor powered by two T63-C18s. Control response was assessed as good-to-excellent with good stability except at aft CG where it rapidly became poor.

305: Tri-Service togetherness in Hughes 300-269B N9302F in March 1964 during a short preview. Maj J P R Jackson has the stick on the left of the machine and next to him is Flt Lt R F Munday, with a Naval Lieutenant colleague on his right. © Crown Copyright

306: Brantly B-2A XS681 competed with the Hughes 269 in 1963 for an Army order; marginal performance and low rotating blades led to rejection. © Crown Copyright

307: This Hughes 500 N9000F flew at Boscombe in poor weather in December 1966 during a tour of Europe.

308: Agusta Bell 204B I-AGUG could not be flown at Boscombe in June 1965, where this photograph was taken, due to unserviceability. A team went to Italy later to assess this civil type. The 48ft main two bladed rotor is restrained by a rope, and the engines gases exhaust to starboard. © Crown Copyright

309: Agusta Bell 205 MM80474, flown at Boscombe in June 1965. The AAEE team was favourably impressed with both handling and performance of the type at high weight and high altitude. © Crown Copyright

310: Jet Ranger N8590F given a preview assessment in 1967. Its steadiness was liked, but performance was too low for consideration as a military machine. © Crown Copyright

Bell Jet Ranger

The second pre-production aircraft N8590F with Allison 250-C18 turbine engines had a low performance during preview handling in 1967. The absence of vibrations was noteworthy.

Sud Aviation 330 and Puma

SA330. The second prototype, F-ZWWO (two Turmo IIIC4) was flown in France at Bretigny and Istres in April 1966 at 14,112 lb. While performance appeared adequate, handling deficiencies included high control forces, vibrations and a limited view; a torque meter, a second alternator and more cooling for the main gearbox were required. Later, handling on sloping ground met with approval, but reservations on rotor governing remained, and more evaluation was needed of the autopilot/stabilisation system. In 1970 the SFIM/Newmark Flight Control System gave good stability in straight flight, but was unsatisfactory in manoeuvres.

Puma HC Mark 1. XW241, a French built machine, tested early in 1970 had satisfactory British avionics, apart from the compasses which did not meet the UK requirements for accuracy, and the radio altimeter which locked on to under-slung loads. The loads carried weighed up to 4,410 lb on a strop between 20 and 100 ft in length, handling remained acceptable with and without the ASE stability aid. In 1972 comparison of the French and British techniques for engine off landings showed that the former involved a lower nose up attitude and longer ground run than the latter. Production avionics in XW198 were cleared in 1971, but updated radios in XW241 later that year required extensive improvements. XW233 (two Turmo III C4) flew in the cold air of Canada early in 1974, continuing in Norway the following winter with *Bouclier* icing protection enabling a clearance to be given for temperatures down to minus 5°C, provided snow was not falling. XW230 had already made some icing tests from late 1973, and probably went to Canada; it subsequently spent eight months on the ground at Boscombe. Short visits for trials are recorded for the following: XW213 in mid-1972, XW216 for "roping" troops in 1972, XW231 for engineering assessment of role changes in late-1972, XW237—winching and other investigations in 1974–5, new radios in XW227 in mid-1974 and abseiling (roping) and Night Sun illumination kit on XW202 in 1975.

Bell AH-1G Huey Cobra

A visiting AH-1G (T-53-11), quoted as 64-7015, was flown at 7,700 lb and reported in glowing terms, particularly regarding the high top speed. The only criticism was of the poor governing of the rotor.

Sikorsky S-61 and Westland Sea King

S-61. Three of the four aircraft supplied by Sikorsky flew at AAEE where they were known as Sea Kings. XV370 (two T-58-G-100) arrived in July 1968 and flew 71 hr in 46 days, a very creditable total; no report has been found. XV371 and XV373 (Gnome 1400—ie, license-built T-58) were subjected to the engineers' scrutiny at Boscombe from early 1969, and flew in ambient temperatures between minus 10°C and plus 30°C without serious criticism, although high speed flying led to excessive transmission oil temperatures. They then evaluated the effect of failures and runaways of components of the automatic flight system with the pilots deliberately delaying recovery action to simulate service conditions. Results contributed to the initial CA release recommendations. Bridge laying was added to XV373's repertoire in 1970; the effect of rotor down wash on the suspended bridge was measured.

Sea King HAS Mark 1. After making the first Sea King deck landings in the hands of two D Squadron pilots, XV642 (two Gnome 1400) went to Canada in 1960/70 for cold weather and then icing trials, the latter at Ottawa; a boundary layer fence under the windscreen and "mushroom" engine air intake guards helped to make limited flying in icing acceptable. Ice accumulations on the HF radio aerial led to the decision to remove it; other items suffering in the cold and included undercarriage oleos, emergency floatation system and fuel drain. The following winter, with many improvements including heated "mushrooms", continuous operation in ice and snow was considered acceptable. Further clearance for flying in snow followed trials in Norway in early 1972. Less success attended icing trials in 1973–4 when a Sikorsky shield for deflecting solids was found liable to shed lumps of ice into the engines. XV643 had submarine hunting gear similar to the latest Wessex standard, but with a doppler height sensor and a better radio altimeter; apart from the excess size of the scanner radome, clearance was soon recommended. The team taking XV651 to California managed to extend the hot weather trial to six months over the British winter 1970–1; all systems functioned satisfactorily up to 35°C when the scanner overheated. Adequate performance in sideways flight to left and to right in hot and high (9,500 ft) conditions enabled a previous flight limitation to be removed. Combining the results of the four aircraft mentioned led to the conclusion that performance up to 20,500 lb was not significantly different from the American version, although airspeed indications were susceptible to yaw. In-flight refuelling, ie, hovering, from a "Helicopter Refuelling System Mk 3" was successfully completed, but the hose needed improvements. It took six months from July 1973 to clear the Mk 44 and Mk 46 torpedoes and their simulators on XV656, but only a few weeks were needed for trials with XV671 on *RFA Olmeda* in mid-1975. Assistance to RAE in 1975 was given for a LORAK equipment trial on XV647.

TRANSPORTS

Avro Anson

The first Anson arrived at AAEE in 1935, the last departed in 1967. Post war use included tests of new versions, and old versions on support duties.

Mark I. Communications flying continued with LT764 until early 1946.

Mark X. NK500 arrived in May 1947 for communications use by CATS.

Mark XI. NL141 met its end in 1953 as ashes during fire practice after seven years with CATS. NL200, another communicator, suffered damage following brake failure in May 1950, one year after arrival.

Mark XII. Wartime trials continued until December 1945 on NL171 with a modified elevator circuit giving a small improvement in longitudinal handling. Further benefit was found with the metal wings and tailplane (adding 220 lb to the weight) of NL172 from April 1946, although handling remained below current standards. The report makes the uncharacteristic statement, "NL172 is recommended as acceptable for service in view of the history of the type."

PH775 chugged down to Lyme Bay daily for six months in 1950–1 to check for ships prior to armament trials by other aircraft.

C Mark 19 and Civil Avro 19. G-AGUD with fixed pitch propellers performed briefly in 1949 prior to RAF use at Cairo, and followed G-AKUD with variable pitch a little earlier. Carburettors in RAF Cheetah 15 engines became worn, and VM360 had a revised version (AV 70MH) with a single lever, approved in 1947–8 at the start of many years service at AAEE. VL301 made dive attacks releasing 250 lb depth charges in 1953, followed by clearance of IFF Mk 10. UHF radios occupied VM371 for ten weeks in 1962. Insecticide spray gear, first tried under VM373 in 1948, gave the Anson a new role in

314: Beverley C.1 WZ889 on the weighbridge in April 1954 when both horizontal and vertical CG were measured, in addition to the weight. Although cropped, the nose probe is nearly as long as the Venom in the foreground. On the Venom, the mass balances under, and the anti spin parachute on top of the tailplane can clearly be seen. © Crown Copyright

Africa. VP509, a Series II with a metal frame, spent most of 1951 at Boscombe.

T Mark 20. This all-purpose trainer met with limited approval in VM305 and VM411 from December 1947; bomb aiming and radio training were satisfactory, but poor layout and lack of space rendered navigation training unsatisfactory. VM305 stayed on for range safety purposes until relieved by VS505.

T Mark 21. Four Mark 21 aircraft are recorded in servicing returns between 1950 and 1967: VS562 was assessed for stability, VV884 and VV973 (two Cheetah 17s) communicated, while the long serving WD402 was available for odd jobs, including evaluation of the radio altimeter Mk 5 which proved accurate in the Anson above 100 ft; WD402 left in August 1967 after use for communicating.

T Mark 22. Rebecca 4 and Gee 2 caused some interference to extra radios fitted to this version for training radio operators; tests were on VM306 in 1948. In August 1959 the machine was destroyed approaching to land.

De Havilland Dominie (biplane)

The wartime R9545 (two Gipsy Queen VI srs I) contiued communicating until a bowser savaged it in December 1947. Other Dominies (all two Gipsy Queen III) replaced American aircraft for communications in late 1945: R2487 until1950, X7353 until at least 1949, X7381 and X7411; the latter tipped on its nose in a gusty wind in February 1949.

Avro York

C Mark 1. Post war, the York provided supporting services at AAEE, although there is some evidence that MW139 was used in 1947 for handling at 70,000 lb with a new or modified central fin in response to complaints by BOAC. LV639 arrived in such poor condition in mid-1947 that it was hastily sent away. Ferrying to and from the hot weather site at Khartoum was provided by MW139 (1948) and MW234 (1954–6), and possibly MW313 in between. Parachuting from MW132 and MW179 took place in mid-1953. Longer term use for research included tests of the Mark 9 autopilot in MW304 (1948–50) and bubble sextants by Kollsman and by Hughes among much other navigation equipment in MW112 (1949–54).

Douglas Dakota

Mark III. FZ564 joined a Fortress in September 1945 for investigation of criteria for the certification of civil aircraft. A twin engined machine was needed, and a mark III chosen in preference to the supercharged mark IV with the latter's complication in performance reduction.

315: Communications Anson C.21 WD402 posing beautifully in the snow in January 1963. © Crown Copyright

191

316: Anson T.20 VM305 seen here at Woodford in 1947, prior to AAEE's acceptance testing the following year. As a navigation trainer, it was roundly condemned for lack of space and poor layout. © Crown Copyright

317: Communications Anson C.21 VS562, bearing the prototype markings from its original configuration as the first T.21.

318: Avro 19 (called an Anson by AAEE) G-AGUD. The Civil Aircraft Test Section made performance measurements in a brief trial in 1949.

319: *York C.1 LV639 in March 1946. A year later it went to AAEE, but was in such poor condition that the Establishment could not accept it.*

320: *Dakota (Dart) KJ829 in April 1950 for a short stay to obtain some performance data to meet civil C of A requirements. © Crown Copyright*

321: *Viking C.2 G-AIJE used for several years on icing research; among special equipment was a naval ASH radar pod under the fuselage (not fitted here). The Civil Aircraft Testing Section logo is on the nose.*

Mark IV. KN407 may also have been involved in work for civil aviation for two years from October 1945. Five static vents were placed on the starboard rear fuselage, and the most accurate position chosen—zero pressure error at 130 mph was achieved. Overseas flights were made in 1947 to Nairobi and Asmara. Next, in April 1950, came KJ829 with Dart turboprops for three weeks of civil certification (CofA). At a modest 26,000 lb take off run was 680yd, and landing run shorter; climb on two engines was 1,250 ft/min, 120 ft/min on one engine reducing to a descent of 55 ft/min if the undercarriage alone was down. Rudder control was ample, and the safety speed of 85 kt determined by the recently introduced criterion of 1.2 times the stalling speed. KK127 transferred from Beaulieu and dropped some dummy paratroops before leaving in January 1952. KJ881 stayed only three months in 1952, and KJ945's task was to support trials at Khartoum. In 1967 there was no shortage of volunteer pilots for KN645 fitted with modern avionics to meet the needs of the RAF CinC in Norway; an F49 Mk 4 survey camera was also tested. Despite frequent hastening action from the CinC's staff, there is no existing evidence to suggest its popularity delayed departure from Boscombe.

Vickers Viking

A Wellington pilot would have found himself at home in the Viking, the first British post-war airline, and the fabric covered wings would also have been familiar. AAEE's interest was twofold: handling and performance by CATS to meet the evolving civil standards, and some engineering assessment. Later use by the RAF involved Boscombe only in the small changes made.

The first prototype, G-AGOK (Hercules 130), arrived in January 1946 some seven months after its first flight, for weighing. The aircraft was also subjected to tests for exhaust contamination (nil), and after return to the makers at Wisley, joined the next two machines in ground tests of all the systems; the oil cooler alone met with disapproval. G-AGOL was probably flown by CATS at Woodbridge. VW214 (ex-G-AGON) made hot weather trials in Khartoum from September 1946 before returning for "rough weather" tests; after receiving metal-skinned wings, flying continued until 1951. Three RAF aircraft designated C Mark 2, VL229, VL232 and VL233, each spent two months in late 1947 on trials of take off performance. In early 1949 VL228 (Hercules 134) with modified tailplane and elevator for the Valetta was compared with the original configuration; there was some improvement, but adequate stability was lacking and elevator response poor at low speed. Following icing problems by airlines, VL226 appeared in late 1948 for instrumentation prior to icing research lasting several years, and including flights to Southern Europe. Results of tests of the fluid de-icing system were spoilt by an unusually mild winter, and it did not prove possible to determine the flow considered necessary to combat all icing conditions. Two minor trials in 1955–6 occupied VL232 (Queen's Flight—IFF Mark X) and VL233 (unsatisfactory PTR 61M radio). With a pair of Nene engines in late 1949, CATS used VX856 to explore the effect of jet propulsion on take off performance; in 1953 an early artificial stall warning device had fundamental problems, and could not be recommended.

Vickers Valetta

C Mark 1. With a large freight door and floor strengthening, VL249 (Hercules 230) required no handling tests at first, but had short checks of CO contamination and flame damping in August 1947. A year later handling was easy and generally pleasant, but the rudder was heavy and the stall with power on produced a sharp wing drop; large trim changes with power and speed changes attracted little criticism. In Khartoum, the lack of almost any ventilation attracted unprintable expletives from the overheated crew and passengers. Serck oil coolers were insufficient, but those by Gallay efficient in the Sudan where two engine performance was measured. At 36,500 lb and 5,000 ft above sea level, take off run was 1,025 yd, climb 1,080 ft/min and ceiling 18,300 ft; specific air range was 2.01 anmpg. Back in the UK, VL264 had a very poor single engine climb, but improved handling from a weaker spring in the modified rudder and 30in of cord removed from the trailing edge of the elevator. Two pressure vents on the leading edge of the wing of VL270 gave satisfactory stall warning, and permitted approaches at 85 kt at maximum weight to give landing runs of 750 yd, compared to 775 yd in VW824.

VL263 from April 1948 revealed much mutual interference between the radios and a large quandrantal error on the D/F; the navigation facilities were far below the standards required. This aircraft returned later for parachute work, including ASR apparatus in 1951 and was fitted with cable laying equipment; results of trials are not known. Fully modified with large tailplane, metal elevators, lightened rudder and other changes VW140 was also described as easy and pleasant, presumably better than VL249 of a year earlier; the type remained tiring in even slight turbulence. An accident to VL262 on arrival at Khartoum in May 1948 was followed four years later by trials of dropping steel drums and dummy men from the front escape hatch; all just missed the port propeller. The firm and then AAEE flew several sorties attempting to snatch a Horsa glider from the ground; the exercise was abandoned after one success in March 1951 because of persistent snapping of the weak link in the cable. Unremarkable radio tests were on VW802 (IFF Mk10 and STR18B HF radio—1951–2), VW838 (ILS/Zero reader—1956), VW198 (UHF radio—1961),

322 and 323: Top—The enlarged elevator of Viking VL228 with inset hinges and metal covering. Lower—the original fabric covered elevator of Valetta VL249 with horn balances. The metal was the better, but adequate stability was still lacking. © Crown Copyright

324: The Establishment's tame pig in March 1972—Valetta C.1 WJ491 which served faithfully but without distinction for over ten years, seen her in its favourite resting place outside the old control tower, relaxing with its minute outboard flaps drooping and three curly static dischargers like tails on the fin. © Crown Copyright

325: Viking (Nene) VX856 in February 1950 during exploration of the effects of jet propulsion on take off performance under civil regulations. The low nacelles contain the twin wheel landing gears. © Crown Copyright

326: Valetta C.1 VL249 at Khartoum in 1949 showing the carrying position for external stores, fitted here to provide drag and weight during oil cooling trals. © Crown Copyright

327: Valetta T.3 VX564 in January 1951 with a line of astrodomes denoting its navigation training role; handling characteristics were indistinguishable from the Mark 1. © Crown Copyright

WJ499 (TACAN navaid—1961) and general update of radios in WD157 (1965). VW203 had scarcely begun its trials with paratroopers in November 1952 when it collided with a Venom in the circuit; the rear facing seats saved most passengers from serious injury. WD171 carried freight briefly in 1955, and WJ491 spent 11 years from 1961 on similar work.

C Mark 2. With fewer and marginally less uncomfortable seats, this mark was represented by VX580 on trials of the Decca 8 navigation system in 1962.

T Mark 3. The navigation training facilities and radios needed a few improvements when flown in VX564 in 1951; handling was similar to the Mark 1. Modernised navigation equipment in WG256 (1961–2) and radios in WG266 (1964) left no traceable records.

T Mark 4. With AI17 interception radar and other aids to be found in night fighters, WJ465 was assessed in 1956.

Avro Tudor

Tudor 1. Maker's tests of G-AGPF (four Merlin 102) started at Boscombe on 25 April 1946, and by the end of May weights up to 78,000lb had been flown. AAEE (CATS) testing then revealed rudder buffet, shortly followed by modifications to increase the size of the tailplane, fit a larger elevator tab and lengthen the engine nacelles. After further flying to 80,000lb and more modifications, another series of tests at Boscombe from December 1946 was interrupted the following May by a major change in the proposed use of the type. The latter half of 1947 was spent in CATS intensive flying including a trip to Khartoum prior to leaving Boscombe in April 1948. The main AAEE trials on G-AGRD concerned de-icing in the winter 1947–8, after brief visits starting in March 1947. During the same month G-AGRI appeared fleetingly before leaving for Khartoum and Nairobi the following February. With new propellers fitted in an attempt to improve performance, an engine caught fire in June 1948. A further modification to give faster feathering of the propeller involved the so-called "hot pot" oil system for use in flight; the requirement for complete stoppage within 10sec was met. AAEE analysed the results of cabin heating in G-AGRK in early 1948; the aircraft may have been at Boscombe.

Tudor 2. Over 105ft long, the Tudor 2 G-AGSU (four Merlin 600) arrived in July 1946 and completed tests at 80,000 lb. Various modifications included new wing fillets and a seal on the wing leading edge hinge; CO gas was absent from the cabin. VX202 (four Merlin 621), a freighter, spent three months from May 1948 on handling in UK, at Nairobi and at Khartoum. Handling was good at all CG with three or four engines operating; the stall was gentle. The report apparently contradicts the earlier statement when it says that it was unpleasant with directional shaking in bumps, and thus tiring to fly. At 80,000 lb take off to 50 ft took 1,750 yd, and the range 1,840 miles, under half that specified; maintenance was difficult. The report comments that the climb was adequate for the British Certificate of Air worthiness (CofA), although there was no requirement in the Ministry specification against which these early Ministry Tudors could be measured.

Tudor 4. A development of the Tudor 1, three of this version reached Boscombe. G-AHNJ spent a month there prior to issue of its CofA in July 1947, G-AHNK (four Merlin 623) appears to have arrived in October 1948, and G-AHNN (four Merlin 621) included a trip to Khartoum checking fuel consumption in mid-1948 immediately after gaining its CofA.

Tudor 7. A "one-off" development of the Tudor 2 with four Hercules 120 engines, G-AGRX is reported as being at Boscombe in May 1947. It returned, as VX199, in December 1948 for brief checks to clear its use by the TRE at Defford.

Tudor 8. An early Tudor 1 with four Nene 2 engines, VX195 first came for four weeks at the end of 1948 before six months of handling and performance in 1949–50. The take off run at 80,000 lb took 1,050 yd, the climb 2,500 ft/min and, at 12,400 ft, maximum speed was 382 kt (true); the stall was a gentle nose drop preceded by moderate buffeting. Handling at extremes of CG position was limited by inadequate trimmer range—but considered acceptable for Ministry use at RRE.

Miles Marathon

Marathon 1. Just three months after the type's first flight, G-AGPD (four Gipsy Queen 71) arrived in August 1946 for what were described as limited CofA trials. Despite some longitudinal instability at aft CG, handling was easy and pleasant with a gentle stall at 53 kt (flaps and undercarriage down); the rudder was heavy in comparison to the other two controls. There was no CO gas in the cabin—nor heating or ventilation! Shortly after return, the aircraft crashed fatally in May 1948 following over stress caused by miss-set fin incidence; this device had been fitted to help control after an outboard engine failure, but fin angle needed to be reset for cruising. G-AILH measured take off and other parameters in Nairobi and Khartoum in 1949–50. The woeful climb following an engine failure in UK temperatures became a descent in the hotter climes; at 18,000 lb the climb on three engines was 95 ft/min in UK, a descent of 60ft/min at Khartoum and a descent of 205 ft/min at Nairobi (5,000ft above sea level). During investigation on G-ALVW of the best flap angle for grass take offs (26

328: *Tudor Mk I TT176/ G-AGPF seen at Radlett in 1946 for the first post war SBAC show, having been diverted from its work at AAEE to appear.*

329: *Tudor Mk II G-AGSU, probably at Woodford in September 1946 at the time of AAEE flying.*

330: *Marathon prototype U-10 looking very shiny in July 1946, a month before going to AAEE. Apart from minor handling criticisms, the performance in the event of engine failure left much to be desired, thus with four engines there was four times the risk. The propellers could not be feathered. © Crown Copyright*

331: *Marathon T.11 XA260 used for approval of locking the elevator gearing tab which gave satisfactory stick-force-per-g. Further performance checks were also made following engine failure—a very slow climb was possible once the undercarriage was raised.*

degrees) and the effect of braking propellers on landing, an engine fire terminated activity; the trial had already shown little benefit from the slow acting reverse. Performance guaranteed by the firm was demonstrated on G-AMDH (Gipsy Queen 70/3) in 1950–1; range remained critical and relied on very careful filling to capacity of the fuel tanks. 10,000 ft was reached in 16.3 min, and ceiling 17,000 ft; the recently introduced "accelerate-stop" test needed 1,150 yd; handling remained pleasant.

T Mark 11. Following the production of unsold Marathons, the RAF took the type as a navigation trainer, and VX229 (four Gipsy Queen 71) made tests in 1952 at the aft CG resulting from the role equipment. The ten major criticisms included lack of stall warning, low stick forces for manoeuvring and lack of a tail bumper; in addition the variable pressure errors and wandering in heading needed attention. Asymmetric power tests in XA260 revealed the need to raise the undercarriage to achieve even a minute rate of climb at safety speed of 95 kt; pressure errors were small and acceptable, but the crew parachute escape facilities were unacceptable. On return in 1954, XA260 had the elevator gear tab locked giving increased and acceptable stick forces. Radio and navigation equipment passed muster in XA250; the results of the investigation into the vibrations of XA270 are not known.

Bristol Freighter/Wayfarer

The first prototype, as VR380 in late 1946, had high concentrations of CO gas in the cabin; holes in the fuselage at the wing roots were held to blame. After rectification and an increase in wing span, flight at 37,000 lb with one propeller feathered gave a climb of 280 ft/min; specific air range was 1.7 anmpg, but the achievable range is not quoted in the report. VR382 (a Mark 2A) dropped survival (SEAC) packs successfully once the toilet had been removed -presumably prior to take off. In 1951 a Mark 31, WJ320 may have flown to Winnipeg and Singapore; in 1953 paratroops could jump from either side door, but not simultaneously due to the risk of collisions.

XJ470, another Mark 31, spent 13 years from 1955 supporting the Establishment's work throughout Europe.

Handley Page Hastings

Prototypes, C and Met Mark 1. With the arrival of TE580 in June 1946, the Hastings started over quarter of a century of association with Bobcombe Down; this first prototype stayed in the hands of the firm—with AAEE taking interest in the findings, including various tailplane angles of dihedral. Returning in late 1948, the optimum flap setting for take off was investigated. With 40° of flap at 75,000 lb, the distance to 50 ft could be reduced to 1,440 yd using a steep initial climb at 100 kt; a safer method involved holding the aircraft near the runway until safety speed (119 kt) had been reached, but the distance increased to 2,100 yd. Attempts were made to increase engine power by modifying the air intakes to reduce heating by the engine; slight improvement resulted. After repairs following undercarriage failure in February 1949, TE580 made extensive pressure measurements in which only small errors occurred. TE583 (four Hercules 101) came in January 1947 with an enlarged tailplane without dihedral; several handling deficiencies were manifest. Changing the elevator balance tab gearing and introducing a bungee gave only a marginal improvement to the very heavy elevator and large trim change with flap operation; the changes, in fact, made the elevator too sensitive in the cruise. Rudder tramping aggravated handling under asymmetric power. Further modifications, including interconnection between the flaps and elevator trim tab, improved one aspect of handling on the production aircraft, TG501 from late 1947, but extremely poor stability in the climb and large trim changes with power on the approach continued in evidence, as did the rudder tramping. In May 1948, TG502 had its tailplane set 16in lower with a 2° increase in incidence; although better on the climb, trim changes on the approach were unacceptable. At forward CG extreme care was needed on landing to prevent tipping over, and the brake lever continued to crush pilots' fingers. A stall warning light operated by pressure differential between the wing leading edge and a datum proved partially effective provided there was no icing present. On the credit side, the firm was praised for the attention given to maintenance, and the satisfactory operation of the navigation equipment. TG503 went to Australia and New Zealand as part of its intensive flying; the main comment concerned the poor ventilation on the ground in hot areas. Tropical trials at Khartoum by TG509 from October 1948 invloved much flying at maximum power to the detriment of the engines and their cooling arragements. In connection with the Berlin airlift, a technique was evolved for take off with one engine inoperative; the run was 1,100 yd, and 50 ft reached after 1,740 yd. Returning in 1950 for assessment in the meteorological role, TG503 could not reach 30,000 ft until weight had been reduced; by shortening the range requirement the lower fuel load (2,650 gal) enabled the altitude to be achieved, but with overheating engine oil. At the maximum weight of 78,000 lb, top speed of 273 kt could be achieved, and the ceiling 25,000 ft. At Khartoum, the cylinder temperatures rose beyond their limits at maximum continuous power settings. No advantage was apparent in TG622, a meteorological aeroplane, having reduced cable tension to the controls; in 1956 the SARAH rescue receiver was satisfactory.

332: Bristol 170 VR380 flew at AAEE between late 1946 and August 1947. The fixed undercarriage and simple plank wing together with the large door in the nose gave Boscombe and many other users a simple workhorse with fair range but little speed.

333: Hastings C.2 WD476 instrumented for take off tests at increased weight with uprated engines in May 1951. This aeroplane demonstrated the difference in take off distance to 50ft between the two current techniques—"hauling off" and climbing at 100 kt took 1,250yd while "holding it down" to achieve a safe speed of 125 kt needed 2,120yd. © Crown Copyright

334: Hastings C.4 WD500 at Radlett at the time of AAEE's trials, limited to passenger comfort and new radio aids to navigation. Both left something to be desired—most noticeably the cooling on the ground at Khartoum in Sudan in October 1951. © Crown Copyright

335: Hastings prototype TE583 on the new weighbridge in August 1954 with the back end being raised to level the fuselage datum. No report has been found, but the purpose of the visit to Boscombe of this Sapphire test bed was flight testing of the Victor's escape door. © Crown Copyright

Just after arrival with a large "Paratechnicon" under the fuselage, TG499 crashed fatally in September 1949 when air loads caused breakage of the device, which then hit the tailplane. More success attended the series of stores parachuted from TG500 from mid-1949. Six men were needed to despatch 28 panniers (each about 300 lb), then later drops of two 600 lb cans plus other items; the diverse nature of the items dropped included parachutists, jeeps, 75 mm guns and fuel in steel containers. Rescue equipment was initially (1951) released from external racks, but the Lindholme gear was pushed out of the side door. Overseas support kept TG500 at AAEE until 1972 after trials dropping Lindholme gear in 1951. TG524 and TG568 made short dropping trials, and TG620 needed one modification after launches from the Chute Mark 5 during 1950. Two meteorological aircraft, TG527 and TG623 completed trials of doppler equipment and UHF and VHF radios, while another, TG565 examined the EKCO weather radar in mid-1963. TG509 supported an overseas trial, thanks to a loan from Handling Squadron in 1965. TE583 (two Sapphire and two Hercules) spent six months in 1954 on flight tests of the Victor escape door.

C Mark 2. With further changes, including a 10% increase in tailplane area and a spring tab to the elevator, TG502 (four Hercules 101) returned as a Mark 2 with satisfactory results. However, the ailerons were considered heavy at first and there were lateral oscillations; by mid-1949 all was well. Landings at 71,000 lb were measured at 1,170 yd from 50 ft to rest. Production standard handling in WD475 introduced mild rudder overbalance, not considered serious; more concern centred on the inaccurate standby compass.

Carrying two external tanks, WD476 (four Hercules 106) carried 3,020 gal for tropical trials and weighed 80,000 lb all up. At +45°C, it took 3,550 yd to reach 50 ft(2,120 in UK) using the existing safe technique (safety speed 125 kt); by "hauling it off", the distance could be reduced to 1,980 yd. Radius with full fuel was 1,060 nm in standard conditions, reducing to 800 nm in the tropics, due largely to hot fuel. Noise in the cabin remained excessive, while raising the permitted engine temperatures cured overheating; a more accurate pyrometer was, however, suggested. An unidentified aircraft with Hercules 216 engines raised the cleared take off weight to 83,000 lb.

WD476 achieved good results with static line jumping, with dropping 350 lb panniers provided the airspeed was low, and with two jeeps. The first live parachuting from TG502 with the lowered tailplane indicated the need to remove the life threatening radio

201

336: Hastings C.2 WD496 in April 1968, near the end of a long life at AAEE as a "hack" for many pieces of kit for Navigation and Radio Division. At that date it had a nose probe and a small pannier for radar trials, in addition to the extra aerials along the fuselage.
© *Crown Copyright*

337: Hastings C.1 TG500, a long serving support aircraft seen in many parts of the world for almost 20 years until 1972.

338: Hermes Mk II G-AGUB in September 1947, a few months before AAEE were asked to check stability at maximum weight and limits of CG.

202

altimeter aerial under the fuselage; after years of support flying it was the last Hastings to leave AAEE in December 1972. Following problems in service with dropping half-ton trailers, effective modifications by AAEE were tested in WD496 in 1953; thereafter this aircraft became a flying laboratory for many radio and radar equipments until 1972. WD493 dropped containers full of rifles in 1959. Aerial shielding rendered the TACAN unacceptable in WD498 in 1961, while the Blue Silk doppler in WD477 gave satisfaction. WJ336 (radios in 1963) and WJ337 (three engined performance at 84,500n lb in 1959) each spent less than a month at Boscombe.

C Mark 4. WD500 (four Hercules 106) needed more effective heating for the comfort of its VIP passengers, among other faults found on a trip to Khartoum in 1951. Five years later WJ325 checked the operation of the IFF and ILS. In 1962, WJ328 spent a month at Boscombe testing the TACAN navaid.

T Mark 5. The large radome for the NBS Mk1 radar scanner did not greatly affect handling of TG505 in 1959, and the navigation/bombing system functioned well in this training version. Updated avionics took two months to clear in TG503 in 1969.

Handley Page Hermes

Hermes II. To complete tests for a Cetificate of Airworthiness (Cof A), AAEE was, according to Handley Page records, asked to check stability at maximum weight (75,000 lb) and at forward and aft CG; the tests were completed on G-AGUB (four Hercules 120) between July and September 1948. CATS confirmed that the lengthened fuselage and lowered tailplane gave acceptable but not ideal handling, suitable for the modified Hastings.

Hermes IV. G-AKFP (Hercules 763) completed firm's tests at 86,000 lb at Boscombe from July 1950 and then AAEE measurements of performance at 82,000 lb. At the latter weight take off run was 1,200 yd, and distance to 50 ft, 1,430 yd; landings at 75,000 lb required slightly less distance. The initial climb of 805 ft/min became, with the starboard outer propeller feathered and flap at take off, a descent of 75 ft/min; with full flap the descent was 490 ft/min. Repeating the measurements at Khartoum and Nairobi, the performance was worse, in spite of new engines of greater power which, however, ran hot. Asymmetric power (three engines at maximum power and one feathered) could be controlled down to 100 kt.

Hermes V. G-ALEU went to Boscombe, probably in December 1950, for Ministry acceptance after some flying by the firm there, and then again in the Spring of 1951 for research into reduction methods for performance of turbopropeller aeroplanes. Double slotted flaps featured on G-ALEV (four Theseus 3 Series 502) in three months of trials from February 1951.

Airspeed Ambassador

G-AGUA (two Centaurus 631S) alone represented this type at AAEE in a two phase test to assess its acceptability starting in February 1949. The first phase included stalling and concentrated on single engine performance. Stalls were gentle and minimum control speed (Vmca) determined as 105 kt clean and 110 kt with 15° of flap; single engine climb was poor even with the flaps raised. The Establishment remarked that flapless landing distance remained to be measured. The trial was abandoned because of severe lateral oscillations in the rear fuselage. On return the oscillations had been improved by a friction damper in the rudder circuit; however, rudder friction was 70 lb, making control unpleasant. A new wing was suggested! With the starboard engine wind milling, the rate of climb was a mere 95 ft/min (well below the BCAR airworthiness requirement), and trim change on overshoot could only just be contained by large force on the stick. The Navigation Section participated in trials of Decca's own Ambassador G-ALZP.

Scottish Aviation Pioneer

Prototype. On arrival in January 1949, G-31-1 (Gipsy Queen 32) went to CATS and in March was numbered VL515 on purchase by the Ministry. Flying resumed with a revised rudder with reduced balance, and later increased. Tests included pressure error measurement (ASI under-read by 11 kt at an indicated 30 kt), and handling tests to civil requirement (BCAR). The latter were generally met, with two exceptions—instability with flaps down and power on, and a tendency to increase bank angle of 30° at 1.2 times level stalling speed. Take off distance to 50 ft was 665 yd, some 65yd further than with flaps up, and at 4,250 lb the rate of climb was a mere 400ft/min. The engine suffered from running too hot, by being inaccessible and by lacking power to the extent that the aircraft failed to leave the ground in July 1949—the pilot should have selected a longer run. Returning one year later as G-AKBF powered by a Leonides 501/4M, it was assessed for the Australian desert where, it was calculated, take off run would be 190 yd, and 50 ft reached after 330 yd. Violent pitching at low speed, rudder overbalance in sideslips and difficult taxying in strong winds spoilt handling. Moving the wheels forward assisted taxying, but a deHavilland propeller did not help engine cooling, while modifications to the rudder were of slight benefit to

339: Hermes Mk 4 G-AKFP in 1949, just before AAEE's measurements of performance which included tests in Nairobi, Kenya. This photograph includes as a period piece the little shelter for the fire extinguishers in the foreground. © Crown Copyright

340: Hermes Mk 5 G-ALEV at the 1950 SBAC show at Farnborough prior to trials at AAEE for which a report has not been found.

341: Ambassador Mk 2 G-ALZP in a photograph dated December 1965; Navigation and Radio Division joined in Decca's trial of their navigation system. © Crown Copyright

342: Pioneer Mark 2 G-AKBF under assessment with the Leonides engine for Australian desert service in March 1951 after minor improvements to the fin, rudder, aileron circuit and movement forward of the main undercarriage. After 2 years of work at AAEE, no order was forthcoming for the type from the antipodes.
© *Crown Copyright*

343: Pioneer CC.1 XL664 with four Nord SS11 missiles. Aiming in Aden's bumpy air destroyed accuracy, and a lucky hit produced disappointing results. © *Crown Copyright*

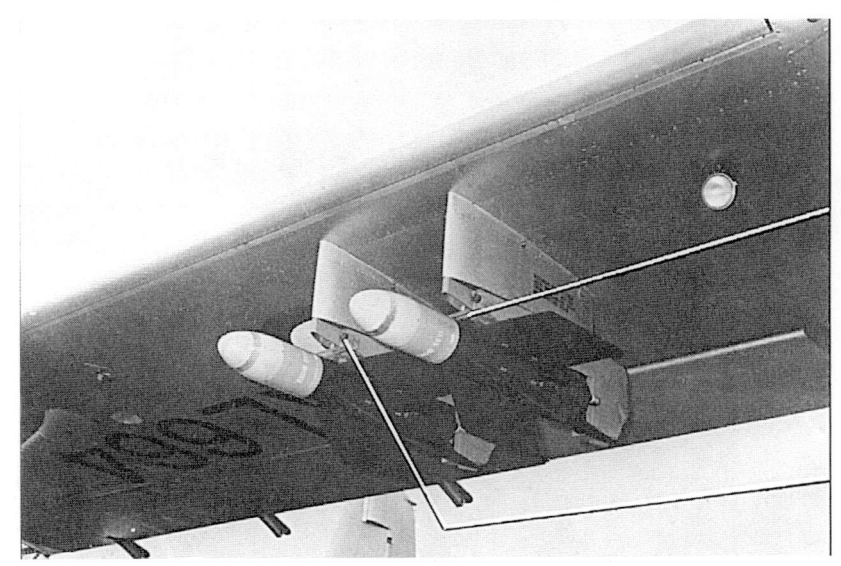

344: Pioneer prototype VL515 in summer of 1949. The Gypsy Queen engine was insufficiently powerful to realise the type's potential, and there was criticism of the ailerons at low speed.
© *Crown Copyright*

205

345: Apollo Mk 1 VX220 on a wet day at Boscombe; probably after six months of dedicated development testing of the Decca Navigation system. The photograph is dated 25 March 1953, about the time that the undercarriage collapsed terminating further flying.

346: Sea Prince T.1 WF119 in late 1951. A smoke float appears under the wing, an oil cooler under the engine and an arrow type trailing static under the fuselage, while the lengthy nose probe has a test vane. With its large rudder and generous trim tab asymmetric power presented no handling difficulty; performance, particularly in hot conditions, was, however marginal at high weight. © Crown Copyright

347: Dove prototype G-AGPJ in 1949 on radio trials, seen here at a location with mountains in the distance. The small cockpit became cramped with the amount of kit installed; over the years, the situation became worse. © Crown Copyright

overbalancing. Servicing was straightforward. Known as a Pioneer Mark 2 in February 1953, the aircraft needed a run of 115 yd using flap at 5,400 lb, but the shorter distance to 50 ft could be acheived without flap; the landing run took 125 yd from an approach at 30 kt. Crosswinds up to 10 kt were tolerable, but the ailerons remained the limiting control at low speed, and became heavy at high speeds up to 175 kt. A too-vigorous landing collapsed the undercarriage after a few days.

CC Mark 1 aircraft were: XE515 (radio in 1954), XL666 (modified standby radio in 1959), XL700 (dropping loads up to 600lb in 1956) and XL702 in 1963. XL664 fired SS11 missiles; it was found possible for the pilot to fly and aim in calm air in the UK but in the turbulence of Aden aiming became haphazard—and the random hits on targets produced little effect. Further trials were abandoned after a crash following mis-slection of fuel tanks causing the engine to stop. Civilian radio tests kept G-ANAZ at Boscombe for only a few days.

Armstrong Whitworth Apollo

The unhappy story of the Apollo reached a conclusion at AAEE in the case of the first prototype, VX220 (four Mamba 104). For six months from September 1952 until an undercarriage oleo cracked, it flew on developmant of the Decca navigation system. VX224, with a modified undercarriage, was probably assessed in 1953 for test pilot training before going to ETPS at Farnborough.

Canadair C 4

An early aircraft, G-ALHD, for BOAC underwent a brief handling assessment at AAEE in May 1949. In the late 1960s, another aircraft,G-ALHY, spent some weeks in the Weighbridge hangar surrounded by bowsers as the Accident Branch of the CAA investigated the nuances of the fuel system following fatal crashes of the type. An E Squadron pilot then joined the flying team. Cable stretch of the fuel feed selector allowing fuel migration unknown to the crew was established as the cause.

Vickers Viscount

A single example, the prototype, of this singularly successful airliner found its way to Boscombe in 1950 for a quick assessment. G-AHRF (four Dart RDa4) flew pleasantly, stalled benignly unless the pilot persisted in heaving on the stick when the wing drop became violent, and the only poor feature was the seating position. Instrument pressure errors were large at higher speeds, and the Establishment discovered that at lower altitude, cruising was more economical on two of the four engines; no comment is made of the possible effect on fare paying passengers on seeing two idle propellers. Its undercarriage collapsed at Khartoum before trials were complete.

Percival Sea Prince

C and T Mark 1. AAEE interest in the Prince began in March 1950 after purchase of the type by the Navy for communications and observer training. WF136 (two Leonides 24), a communicator, handled well up to 11,000 lb, but rapid trim change on raising the flaps required a slower operation. Deck landings were considered to be feasible once the ASI was in the pilot's view and the throttles eased; a normal land undercarriage prevented actual arrivals on a carrier. Internal noise measurements were made in WF137.

Cabin layout, including the sonobuoy installation, for the training role appeared in G-ALCM in February 1951, and the handling described as "inappreciably" different from the other aircraft. WF118 (two Leonides 25) had a self centring nose wheel, rudder bar nearer the pilot by 5in and internal stowage for sonobuoys; satisfactory radios (VHF—1951 and UHF—1960) completed its tasks. WF119 (two Leonides 125) had excessive static friction in the elevator control, but otherwise handled well on two engines at 11,850 lb. However, when the instructor and thus CG moved aft the elevator became "twitchy," in the uncharacteristically descriptive word of the report. Wth one engine stopped and its propeller fully coarsened, rate of climb was poor at 160ft/min in standard conditions; a reduction in weight in hot environments was recommended. Enhanced engine cooling proved acceptable at Khartoum in 1953. ASV19a radar replaced the ASH type in WP310 in 1953. WM735 had modification N198 in 1955, and WF128 appeared for an unknown test in 1974.

C Mark 2. WM756 (two Leonides 125)had a very badly designed and uncomfortable position for an observer in the right seat, although the kit worked as advertised. In 1968 modernised radios equipped WJ350.

de Havilland Dove, Devon and Sea Devon

Dove. The sole Dove to reach AAEE was G-AGPJ (Gipsy Queen70/2) in October 1949 for test of the radio and navigation equipment. VHF (STR 9) and HF (AD97/10) for communications, ADF for navigation and beam approach for landing functioned well, but cockpit layout was poor with susceptibility to switches being knocked inadvertently, and difficulty in operating the morse key.

207

348: Devon C.1 WB531 in April 1962 on a rapid trial of the UHF radio. © Crown Copyright

349: Known as the Blackburn Freighter, the prototype Beverley WF320 received only a limited assessment in July 1952, but was found to be very slow in roll and uncomfortable in any turbulence. © Crown Copyright

350: Heron C.3 XH375 undergoing extensive inspection. Photographs of this activity were not normally taken; the reason for this one is unknown. © Crown Copyright

Devon C Mark 1. Clearance for Service use was made on the basis of civil C of A, and initial trials were limited to military radios and IFF in XA880 in May 1954. The door of VP952 jettisoned without hitting the airframe in 1955. VP979 (two Gipsy Queen 71) worked for Porton and completed some Decca calibration work between September 1959 and 1966. WB531 had UHF radio in 1962 which overheated in the tropics, and the following year also with Gipsy Queen 71s, completed tests to civil standards (BCAR), probably at Idris. The single engine climb criterion could be met only at 7,500 lb (normal maximum 8,500 lb), and only then if the undercarriage was up, and the propeller of the failed engine feathered.

Devon C Mark 2. VP971 performed with two Gipsy Queen 175 engines of slighlty increased power, VP961 confirmed the effect of other modifications on performance while VP972 (1966) and WB530 were shared with Handling Squadron. VP973 helped out with the Air Transport Flight in 1972.

Sea Devon C Mark 20. Checking of naval communicating and navigating equipment justified the presence of XJ321 for four months in 1955. IFF/SSR fitted to XJ350 received the attentions of AAEE in 1968.

Blackburn Beverley

Prototype. Known at AAEE by its original name of Blackburn Freighter, WF320 (four Hercules 261) made a short visit in mid-1952 for a handling assessment, limited in scope by the absence of the rear ramp and doors. Power assisted controls were well received, but it appears that manual reversion was not tried. Rate of roll needed improvement, and there was no natural stall warning, the trim lacked sufficient range at aft CG, and the aeroplane was laterally unstable; handling in calm air was satisfactory. The change in vertical CG could become significant as fuel decreased; the ASI over-read by up to 14 kt.

C Mark 1. The duplicated hydraulic power to the controls removed the need for manual reversion in WZ889 (four Centaurus 165), and produced handling qualities appropriate for the role of freighting. At 129,930 lb and full flap the stall at 74 kt was marked by the nose and right wing dropping. With an outer engine failed and the propeller feathered, full power on the remaining engines could be contained down to a satisfactory 100 kt. Although 295 kt was the design speed, structural strength limited flying to 210 kt—and that achieved only in a steep dive. There remained no stall warning, with heavy elevator (very bad at forward CG on take off and landing) and asymmetric reversal of propeller pitch on landing made control difficult. From August 1955, XB259 (four Centaurus 173) at 134,975 lb met requirements, but heavy controls again spoilt handling by reducing manoeuvrability; torquemeters were needed, and the large number of turns of the trimmers excessive. XB263 had a good navigation layout but vibration and noise were severly criticised; astro shots were inaccurate without use of the autopilot. XB266 made good celestial navigation using the autopilot for steadiness, after making six rocket assisted take offs. XL150 had UHF radio in 1959, XB284 twin radio compasses in 1960, XM111 subminiature radio compass in 1961, and XB285 tested updated avionics in 1963–5. XB262 (four Centaurus 173) had two months in 1955 in Idris, Libya, and, nine years later, XB269 (four Centaurus 175) had the "All American" ground proximity device as a prelude to low level airdrops. XB261 spent most of the 15 years between 1956 and 1971 at AAEE on dropping trials of great variety, starting with various numbers of paratroops from the rear boom (up to 24 with full kit) and 35 from each side door. Up to 40 panniers in five sticks went over the rear ramp; flaps were raised to produce a nose up attitude; other trials included the Lindholme Rescue gear, army vehicles of many types and development of ultra low level dropping techniques.

Percival Pembroke

C and C (PR) Mark 1. A light communicator, WV698 (two Leonides 125) arrived in March 1953 for handling; the elevator lacked sufficient power initially to raise the nose on take off at forward CG; rapid modification, included balance tab ratios, cured the fault, but the elevator trimmer needed a greater range. Three designs of propeller were tried in attempts to improve the single engine climb; it remained critical to the extent that weight needed to be reduced in hot climates; auto feathering was recommended. Awkward entry to the right seat of WV699 precluded access by a large man, and some navigation instruments needed moving. Flight at the extended aft CG with the door removed was acceptable up to 150 kt, and 185 kt with it in place. WV700 (probably tested at Luton) had a modified taxy lamp and DC electrical system. Crew escape through a narrow cockpit was the only serious comment on the crew station of WV701. Two 250 lb bombs on WV739 gave concern because of the long take off in tropical conditions, and following a dive attack stick forces became very light. A team of two despatchers did their bit in throwing out ASR Type A rescue kit, and wicker panniers; the large shift in CG needed careful handling. In 1962 a developed ASR type A kit was cleared by WV706, and WV735 had IFF Mark 10. XK885 spent three years from April 1972 on Establishment communications, and XL956 had a spray rig in mid-1968 for Porton to simulate chemical attacks for training; an attempt was made to use the rig for helicopter icing. Minor work took place on: WV733 (two Leonides 127)—(radios in 1962), WV740 (VOR navaid in 1965) and XK884 (distance measuring equipment in 1974).

351: *Comet I XB XM829 in July 1963 nearing the end of its productive time at AAEE after many trials on navigation equipment. © Crown Copyright*

352: *Comet C.2 XK671 at the time of its CA Release trials at AAEE. in August 1956. The Establishment's role for the Comet was limited to assessing its RAF equipment, and a brief look at handling. © Crown Copyright*

353: *Comet 4 XS235. This photograph dates from after 1975, but epitomises the role of the aircraft in advancing navigation accuracy and safety, just as the lighthouse in the background did in former times. A further analogy is apparent in this maritime setting—much of the equipment tested was intended for the Nimrod. © Crown Copyright*

354 and 355: An interesting modification of Pembroke C.1 XL956 originally intended to provide training by aerial spraying to simulate gas. Right—the spray boom under the fuselage, below—the 56gal pressurised tank inside. Later use as an icing tanker for the Wasp helicopter proved of limited use. © Crown Copyright

de Havilland Heron and Sea Heron

Heron C Mark 3. XH375 for the Queen's Flight had additional avionics, tested at AAEE in four weeks in April 1955; modernised equipment was probably the reason that XM296 appeared in mid-1962.

Sea Heron C Mark 20 (called a C Mark 1 in AAEE report). Naval signalling apparatus, ie radios, caused the presence of XR444 (four Gipsy Queen 30 Mk 2) in 1962, and IFF/SSR that of XR445 in 1968.

Fairchild C-119G Boxcar

Great difficulty was experienced by the Establishment in obtaining 53-3182 and another Boxcar for periods sufficiently long enough to develop drills for up to 40 British paratroops to jump from this American workhorse; by mid-1955 the job was done.

De Havilland Comet

Mark 1. XM829 (Mark 1A—four Ghost 50) arrived in September 1958 from Air France, and left for fire training at Stansted in February 1964 having flown over 1,100hr on a wide range of equipment trials. These included Decca 7, 8 and 10, Blue Parrot doppler for the Buccaneer, an astro set, and a moving map with TV projection—all navaids, a Mk22A altimeter and a prototype flight data recorder.

Mark 2 and C Mark 2. G-AMXD (a Mark 2E—two Avon RA29/1 outboard and two Avon 117 inboard) spent four months with CATS at Boscombe and in Canada from December 1958 before going to Farnborough as XN453. The Establishment was asked to comment on the handling, although CA Release had already been given on the basis of the civil C of A. Criticisms included the spring feel for the elevators making the control too light at high speed, and the advice that pilots should remove the feet from the rudder pedals during turbulence in gusts was felt to be unnecessary. XK671 (four Avon 117), a C Mark 2, soon went to the RAF in 1956 after clearance of the handling, new navigation aids and radios; three years later XK697 flew 32 hours to assess the new "q-feel" to the elevators. XK655 came from Watton in April 1959, for tests of its IFF Mk 10, and XK699, a normal C Mark 2, had TACAN and VOR navaids in late 1961.

Mark 4 and C Mark 4. The RAF's XR395 (four Avon 350), a C Mark 4, made a short visit to test its avionics in 1962 prior to entering service with No 216 Squadron. Two long serving laboratory aircraft were XS235, a civil 4C, for over 15 years from 1963, and XW626, also a civil 4C, for four years from 1972; they continued the work of flying radio and navigation equipment

356: *Comet C.2 XK655 on the approach to land showing its many aerials and radomes for its intelligence gathering role. Its brief stay at Boscombe was limited to assessment of the newly installed IFFMk 10.*

357: *Twin Pioneer CC.1 XM940 posing in almost the identical spot that the single Pioneer used when similarly armed with four Nord SS11 missiles. No unusual results were observed in March 1960.* © *Crown Copyright*

358: *Britannia 312F XX367, the Establishment's last long range support aircraft—seen here near the end of its days after 1975.* © *Crown Copyright*

359: *Argosy C.1 XN 815 in October 1962 in soft ground at Martlesham Heath, AAEE's home between 1917 and 1939. The nose wheel doors have been removed.* © *Crown Copyright*

360: Twin Pioneer CC.1 XL966 in July 1958 with door removed for parachuting, or store despatch. The tail wheel has been protected to avoid snagging of rigging lines. © Crown Copyright

Scottish Aviation Twin Pioneer

CC Mark 1. AAEE trials of this certified ten seat civil aeroplane were limited to its military applications. Four aircraft arrived in the Spring of 1958: XL966, XL967, XL968 and XL969; they shared the initial work until the last, XL966, left in 1960. The engineering, radio and navigation assessments were soon completed; casualty evacuation could not be approved without significant modifications. The main door provided the means of despatching ASR Mk 2 and Mk 3 rescue kit, supplies by free drop or by parachute flying at 75 to 85 kt, up to four 500lb CLE Mk 3 store containers, and a stick of up to 11 paratroops flying at 85 to 105 kt with the flaps up. Two machine guns on the undercarriage stub wings, or two 1,000 lb bombs, were cleared and both aimed by methods not entirely scientific—accuracy being aided by diving the aircraft in the general direction of the target. Four 200 w loud speakers broadcast at adequate volume but dubious clarity. In 1960 XM940 carried and fired up to four Nord SS11 missiles.

CC Mark 2. Armament and radios kept XP294 busy in 1961 and 1963 respectively. XP295 had more efficient speech broadcast equipment in 1965–6 and XM957 made brief checks of single engine performance in March 1966.

Bristol Britannia

C Mark 1. XL635 had its RAF navigation fit checked, possibly at Lyneham in 1959; the layout and range of aids, "left little to be desired," in the words or the report; it was, however, not a stable aircraft for celestial navigation. Twin VOR navaid in XM518 needed but a few weeks to test in 1964.

From May 1972 XX367, a Srs 312F, supported the AAEE trials a long way from home until after 1975.

Armstrong Whitworth Argosy

Selected for RAF service after the civil version had its Certificate of Airworthiness, AAEE's work centred on its military equipment and role.

C Mark 1 and E Mark 1. The third of the military version built, XN816 (four Dart 101) made extensive tests of its navigation, radio and flight instrument systems from September 1961. Apart from gross errors in the standby compass, later reduced to 12° (still very large), the kit worked as advertised; the four crew were, however, cramped and ill-ventilated on the upper deck which had poor lighting. After extensive preparation of the autoland avionics, including the Mk 10C autopilot and radio altimeter Mk 7, XN816 made 233 landings under automatic control (most at Bedford as Boscombe's undulating runway was less than ideal); the system required manual closure of the throttles from 70ft (radio). XN815 demonstrated its abilities on dirt and other unpaved runways (including Martlesham Heath, AAEE's old home). With the nose wheel doors removed

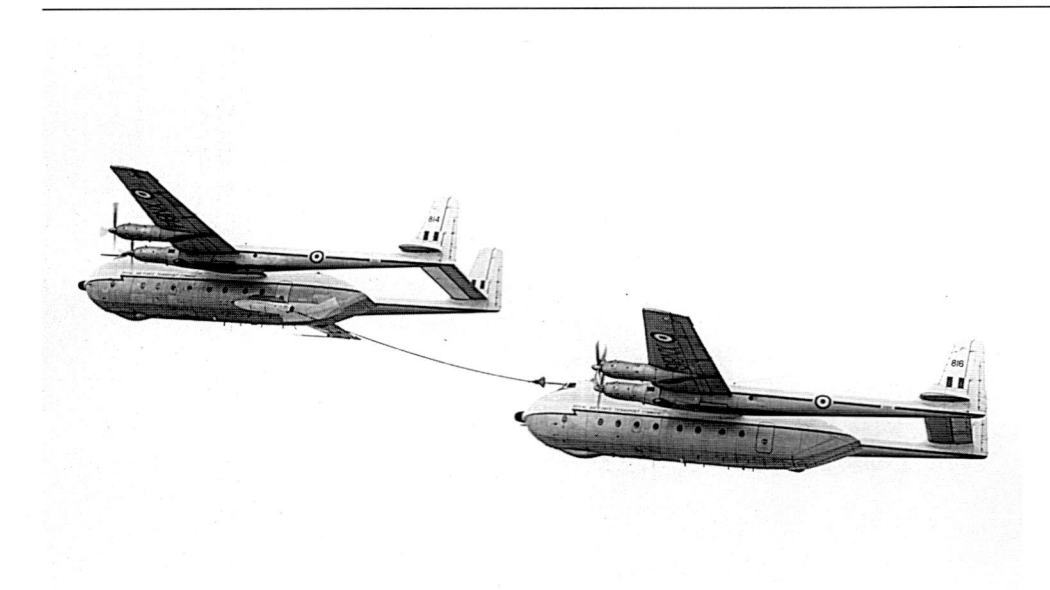

361: A rare sight—Argosy C.1 XN814 refuelling XN816 in January 1966. The tanker has a Mk 20B refuelling pod, and has an area of the lower fuselage painted white to record any strikes by the hose and basket on trailing and winding in. © Crown Copyright

362: Andover prototype G-ARRV arrives in the snow of February 1965. There were some hazards for paratroops and other minor snags found in a trial lasting only two weeks. © Crown Copyright

363: Andover C.1 XS595 does its party trick of squatting by folding the main undercarriage. In the background relaying of the concrete outside C Squadron is visible. © Crown Copyright

364: The installation of an F96 Mk 1 camera in a push-out cupola on Argosy C.1 XR105 in September 1963. The trial also assessed a handheld F117 camera; both gave acceptable results. © Crown Copyright

and tyre pressures reduced, one limiting condition on undulating surfaces was a wavelength of 150 ft with ridges over six inches high. XR105 made 32 sorties in 1963 carrying and dropping bombs up to 1,000 lb, flares of the 4.5 in variety and 20 lb fragmentation bombs; the Establishment had to fix a large number of electrical faults. Very accurate bombing was made from 11,000 ft using the T3 sight, and the hand held F117B camera and F96 Mk 1 in a push out cupola made good pictures. Use of the side doors for dropping stores up of to 700 lb from XP446 posed no problems. Static line jumping by up to 54 fully equipped paratroops needed modifications by AAEE to reach a satisfactory standard, using XN818 in 1961–2. Dropping stores over the opened rear clam shell doors of XN817 started with gravity extraction of nine one ton containers in sticks of increasing length; a cunning system of extraction was evolved, and later using a 2° climb technique. Results of tests of freezing controls on XN856 in 1962–3 are not known. XN819 flew to Aden and back in 1961, before being fitted with lightweight ILS/VOR navaids, tested in 1963. Aerial tanking with a Mk 20 refuelling pod was the purpose of XN814's visit in 1965–6; several types took fuel. Mutual interference checks of the E Mark 1, XN855, in 1971 showed that there were several minor instances of "crosstalk", not considered significant.

Hawker Siddeley 748 and Andover

HS748. A team travelled to Agra in 1972 to clear paratrooping and bundled supplies from Indian Air Force HS748s. H-1176 was successfully used for 30 troops to jump under the control of three despatchers; 22.5° flap at at 105 to 115 kt proved best.

C Mark 1. 20 flights of G-ARRV, a civil aircraft modified to represent the military Andover in early 1965, sufficed to confirm its easy and safe handling. There were some hazards for paratroops, and the rear door took too long to close. Arriving for the first of five visits in December 1965, XS594 completed handling, performance and paratrooping investigations before overload/STOL performance and then despatch of unusual loads. Navigation trials at Boscombe on XS595 (two Dart 201) preceded operations in 1966 from dirt strips in Aden at 45,000lb; an AAEE designed debris guard on the nosewheel reduced damage from stones. By the end of 1966, the Establishment had flown 579 hr on Andovers of which 156 hr were on XS595, some accumulated during cooling trials of the Decca Mk 1(Air) navaid, and other flying during rough strip trials in November 1966. Further unprepared strips were measured by a "profilemeter" and a "penetrometer" prior to landings by XS596; the meters were of marginal use as suitability depended on unmeasured bearing strength. In 1968–9, XS647 tried a membrane landing strip; a forward CG caused most problems. The fuselage strakes of XS597 posed an obstruction to paratroops jumping from the side door, and airpeed consequently reduced to an uncomfortable 105 kt to permit a safe clearance; trials took place from Idris. After much work, a total of six one ton (actually weighing 1,800 lb) containers in a single stick were dropped. Much pushing on the control column by the pilots accompanied the movement of each store as it slid over the tailgate, threatening to raise the nose skywards; a system of auto separation prevented the possibilty of a recalcitrant store from jamming at the *moment critique* and adding to the pilots' woes. Later, a technique using a 2° climb was evolved for use at low level with 6 ft parachutes. 1968 saw XS640 in the public address mode with loud speakers and normal handling at low speed with take off flap selected; broadcasting trials were, by popular demand, made during hours of normal working. Other tests were: Supply dropping (XS611 and XS606 in 1973–4) and fuel icing (XS613 in March 1971).

C Mark 2. Rapid trials of the version of the civil HS748 involved XS789 (90hr flying in one month), XS791 and XS794 (two Dart 150) in 1964 to clear the type for a forthcoming Royal tour of the Caribbean. Equally rapid modifications were made to the compasses after trials had shown excessive errors; no doubt it was felt the delivering Her Majesty to the wrong island posed an unacceptable risk. Actual tropical trials took place in August 1965 on XS794.

365: Andover C.1 XS597 in 1966 showing its test flying status for despatching troops and stores with nose probe, and black and white chequered rear fuselage. © Crown Copyright

Short Belfast

Airworthiness trials to civil standards were in the process of completion when AAEE started work on military operating aspects of the type in which evidence lingered of the firm's nautical traditions.

C Mark 1. Navigation and radio evaluation started in June 1964 on XR364 before its delivery to Boscombe where it joined XR365 and XR366 to complete the work on these systems; XR366 included flights to Singapore and Idris in 1966. Comments were numerous but minor, apart from the noise level in the crew deck where 117dB were measured against a requirement for no more than 97dB. 258 hours of flying on XR366 (four Tyne 101)in 1965–6 established *inter alia* that scheduled servicing required 4.6 man/hr per flying hour, and unscheduled another 2.5 man/hr—both low figures. Cold weather trials in Canada in the winter of 1967 made lots of use of the efficient APU, but other parts of the aeroplane showed a need for improvement. The numerous control runs and their routing through pressure bulkheads suffered icing build up, the undercarriage shock absorbers collapsed, and to the great surprise of those on board, the entrance door disappeared in flight. XR365 returned in 1972 to establish techniques for operating at a take off weight of 250,000 lb (previously 231,000 lb); the performance did not meet civil criteria, and military standards applied. Take off using 15° of flap needed a run of 2,195 yd with 35 ft being reached after 2,565 yd; in the landing configuration the gentle stall occurred at 110 kt. To the same standards, the three engine take off was cleared at 175,000 lb, with very low rate of initial climb and restrictions on acceptable cross wind components. Failure of the second engine on one side with the opposite engines at maximum power could be handled down to 110 kt using 5° of bank into the live engines, or 125 kt with wings level; this was an unusually large benefit from using a small bank angle. XR363 received a lightning strike during performance tests in 1966 and the following year XR371 made a 20 hr flight with the help of aerial refuelling, and returned to No 53 Squadron just 48 hr after leaving. 51 successful automatic landings in XR264 in 1967–8 showed the lateral displacement on touch down to be excessive and in need of improvement. However, a study in 1969 concluded that operation to civil Category IIIA (zero feet cloud base and 200 m visual range) could be achieved.

Beagle Basset and 206

CC Mark 1. XS742 (two GIO-470-A with two blade propellers) went to Idris in July 1964 and suffered an uncommanded undercarriage retraction on the ground. From July 1965, joined shortly by XS743, flying concentrated on single engine performance at 7,500 lb; in

366: Belfast C.1 XR366. This aircraft carried out most of the type trials including overseas at Singapore and Idris, Libya in 1966 immediately followed by the cold of Fort Churchill in Canada. At 250,000lb all up weight, the Belfast was the heaviest RAF propeller-driven aircraft. © Crown Copyright

standard conditions climb was 30 ft/min below specification, but in warmer conditions at Idris, a "climb" using one engine at maximum power resulted in a loss of 1,000 ft in the process! Hot air to the carburettors further reduced climb by 70ft/min, although cropping the propeller blades made no measurable difference. Both these aircraft remained at Boscombe until after 1975. Production aircraft XS765 and XS769 demonstrated no improvement in climb, and these four aeroplanes also jointly made take off and landing measurements, taking an average 1,000 yd to reach 50 ft from either tarmac or grass sufaces. Taxying appears to have been fraught until the propellers were cropped. Landings gave inconsistent results due, it was thought, to variable brake effectiveness. Consumption tests led to the remarkably short range of 215 nm being calculated with a 1,500 lb payload—ie a five-man V-bomber crew with full kit. 344 hr flying on XS743 gave confidence in its reliability. Heated engine sumps in XS774 during flight in icing conditions were examined in 1966–7, more accurate fuel gauges observed in XS781 in 1970 and IFF/SSR assessed in XS772 (two Continental 101) in 1971–2. XS770 joined the Comunications Flight in early 1975.

Beagle 206S. G-ATYE (two GTSIO-520C with three bladed propellers) made a brief performance trial in November 1966 in which the extra power of the supercharged engines gave a more satisfactory single engine climb, among other benefits.

Vickers VC-10

C Mark 1. XR806 and XR807 (both four Conway RCo43 Mk 550) spent part of 1966 under scrutiny by AAEE of those military parts not reached by the ARB/CAA for the civil version. Avionic trials in UK and Bahrein in XR807 resulted in a few minor improvements being suggested, and at 323,000lb all specification performance points were met or exceeded. With an engine cut well below rotation speed, the 50 ft point was reached 2,035 yd after brake release. The trials ended with an overnight 15 hr flight involving two aerial refuellings by XR806—the easiest type to fly in the receiving position in the opinion of the pilot.

de Havilland Buffalo

Several successful sorties dropping troops using the PX Mk 3 parachute were made in a four day visit by 9456 of the Canadian Forces in Setember 1969.

Lockheed C-130 and Hercules

C-130A and B. Trials of theses early model C-130s are reported as the first part of the AAEE Hercules series,

217

367: Andover CC.2 XS789 for the Queen's Flight on its radio trial in June 1964, which included a flight to Bahrain. On a trial some years later, unusual handling was found to be due to stowage of much gold-plated china ware in the rear compartments. © Crown Copyright

368: Argosy C.1 XR105 in aggressive fit with offensive weapons. The original caption read, "Light Series Carriers fitted, Aircraft loaded, -24 x bombs, aircraft 'F' 20lb, fitted with No 108 Mk 1 tail units, and fuzed (sic) with Fuzes No 873" ... precisely! © Crown Copyright

369: Basset CC.1 XS743 in March 1966 undergoing a little manhandling; 35 years later the aircraft was flying from Boscombe Down with ETPS © Crown Copyright

370: *VC-10 C.1 XV806 getting the full electromagnetic pulse (EMP) treatment in the radio environment simulator (REG)—but never referred to as "empreg-nated." © Crown Copyright*

371: *Hercules C.1 XV177 in March 1967 displaying its original paint scheme and chequerboard markings to aid analysis of air drops. The port rear door is open and the baffle ahead of it extended, ready to drop paratroops. © Crown Copyright*

372: *Skyvan 3 G-AWWS in May 1969 when measured performance exceeded published figures, but the stall required a tricky technique to achieve. © Crown Copyright*

but the location and conduct of the trials is unclear. AAEE reported that gravity extraction of up to eight one ton containers, and parachute extraction of double medium stressed platforms had been made.

C Mark 1. The British avionics of XV177 received attention in the UK and in Bahrain between February 1967 and late 1969; the main criticism concerned the inability of the cooling systems to cool the aircraft—the avionics apparently continued to operate while their human operators felt the heat. The two Sperry C12 compasses demanded a new procedure for swinging. In 1971, XV207 had Rebecca 12, and techniques were developed by 1973 for using it as a homing and positioning aid for the dropping zone. The UHF homing aid in XV218 in 1972 had an indicator blocking the pilots' view and thus condemned. XV178 spent over eight years on clearance and development work associated with the delivery of personnel and stores to their intended point on the ground, and also with the establishing of a free fall height record for parachutists from 40,000 ft. In 1968–9 one ton containers were increased up to a total of 16, including sticks of various lengths, up to a maximum payload of 40,000 lb, and down to 400ft above the ground. Stores mounted on a medium stressed platform could be dropped from 600 ft with the main parachute extraction technique; previously, using a separate extractor, the minimum height had been 1,200 ft. Perhaps the most interesting trial involved the ultra low level airdrop (ULLA) manoeuvre developed initially at Farnborough with a Beverley, and continuing on the AAEE Hercules intermittently for five years from early 1967. Success depended critically on accurate height keeping during extraction, and the STR40 radio altimeter proved ideal in maintaining 15 ft above the ground once suitable presentation of the information to the pilot had been developed. Some 30 sec before the drop the drogue deployed, the release slip operated at the *moment critique* deploying the main parachute which pulled out the load. By 1972, three platforms of a combined weightof 42,000 lb were successfully dropped. Low level trials included assessment of methods of marking the dropping zone by day and night. The RAF used Lockheed figures for their operating data manuals (ODM), but the Establishment had long suspected that critical figures were optimistic. In 1974 a performance trial on XV178 (four T56-A-15) was mounted following discrepancies found on the W Mark 2. Results showed that the actual rate of climb on three engines immediately after take off was 200ft/min worse than the ODM figure, with a 320ft/min reduction in the later, *en route,* climb achieved. XV191 (early 1974) and XV196 (late 1975) helped with dropping tests when XV178 was indisposed; Italian parachutes dropped from XV206 were soon cleared in February1971.

W Mark 2. The unique conversion of XV208 for meteorological research led in 1973 to the first AAEE performance trials of the Hercules, revealing the shortfall against previously accepted figures. Handling was generally similar to the Mark 1, but the minimum control speed was found to be slightly higher with concomitant increase in the take off speeds and thus distances. The autopilot was unaffected. Trials were made of the forward facing 16mm cine camera, two video cameras pointing over the probe and the vertical F95 Mk 4 camera.

Short Skyvan

Since the Short Skyvan had received Government funding, G-AWWS (two Garret 331-2-201A) spent 30 hours flying under scrutiny by AAEE in 1969. At 13,500 lb it was straightforward and pleasant to fly and considered suitable for freight and passengers; the stall was safe with adequate warning and performance exceeded the published figures.

Britten-Norman Islander

Take off and landing measurements of two aircraft, G-AYCU (two O-540-E) in 1970 and G-51-243 in1971, were made at the request of the Department of Trade and Industry. Although simple and safe to fly, the take off distance to 59 ft at 6,000 lb from a paved runway at 387 yd exceeded the firm's figure of 340 yd by 14%, while the comparable landing numbers were 436 yd against 400yd by the firm. The Establishment commented, nevertheless, that the measured distances were creditable. Seven parachutists in G-AYRU of Netheravon and a despatcher were very cosy in the cabin—but considered acceptable in 1970 for adventurous training.

Government Aircraft Factories Nomad

This aeroplane (VH-SUR with two Allison 250-B17) created a favourable impression in 1972 during a very brief assessment. The efficient lateral control was by ailerons (flaps up) and by spoiler (flaps down), while longitudinal control was by the all-moving tailplane.

Pilatus Porter

Assessment of the Turbo-Porter, HB-FDP, for the Army was curtailed by poor weather, but enough flying was done to demonstrate the outstanding capabilities of the type. 10 take offs and full stop landings were made in the length of Boscombe's 10,500 ft runway in October 1968.

MISCELLANEOUS TYPES

Percival Proctor

Brief performance measurements of G-AGLN *(sic)* were made in March 1949; the report is wanting.

Bristol Beaufighter

The wartime X7574 was joined by V8319 (both Mk 1F) for use as targets and for target towing; both had left by mid-1946, the former after a landing accident in April. Gun trials on JL955 (Mark VI) were not completed after the war. RD834 (Mark X) came in July 1946 for use on general purpose bombing, and RD854 was photographed in 1959 outside the new hangar awaiting its compass swing.

Lockheed Hudson

The last remaining Hudson, AM553 with passenger seats received major damage on take off in September 1945 when the mainwheels hit soft ground leading to a ground loop.

Stinson Reliant

FK818 and FK894 were removed promptly in 1945 on the outbreak of peace.

Miles Martinet

Mark I. Spinning trials in the winter 1945–6 of HP413 with raised rear cockpit were not permanently recorded.

Supermarine Sea Otter

ASR Mark 1. Flame damping measurements finished in August 1945 on JM913. In 1951, the ASR Type G gave no problems on release from JM909.

ASR Mark 2. Equipped as an amphibian for air/sea rescue, the Mark 2 required only to be tested at AAEE for the new radios fitted, including ASV II which caused some interference on other equipment in RD875 and RD869 in 1945–6. Handling of RD876 was considered to be satisfactory for deck landing with modified elevator and rudder to accommodate a sting-type of arrester hook under the tail.

Beechcraft Traveller

Mark 1. Two Model 17 six seat (at a pinch) biplane communicators, FT461 and FT466, departed in December 1945; the former, at least, returned to U S Navy service.

373: Auster AOP.9 WZ663 in March 1955 in what looks suspiciously like a posed shot to illustrate propeller swinging. The aircraft is chocked, into wind, the elevator is raised, the ground is firm and free of detritus and there is a fire extinguisher with operator immediately available. However, the interesting bits of this Auster are shown below (in photograph 384). © Crown Copyright

374: Martinet TT.1 HP413 seen in December 1945 has an anti spin parachute band around the fuselage, together with a frame for keeping the rigging line free of the rudder. © Crown Copyright

375: Sea Otter ASR II RD876 in May 1946 with a hook for deck landings. It proved adequate. © Crown Copyright

376: Desford G-AGOS in early 1946 during trials; its performance was unremarkable. Its handling qualities are now unavailable. © Crown Copyright

Fieseler Storch

The captured Storch VG919 continued in general use for a few months in 1945. Runway performance was outstanding—take off in 150 yd and landing in 42 yd -the latter made possible by the CG remaining well behind the main wheels and thus permitting hard braking on touch down.

Airspeed Horsa

TK994 was sent from Beaulieu, and was the glider which a Valetta attempted, with but a single success, to snatch off the ground in 1951.

Miles Monitor

TT Mark 2. After two fatal accidents, the second to NP409 in August 1945, the Establishment found little enthusiasm for the target towing Monitor. Intensive flying continued on NP410, but progress was hindered by unserviceability attributed to lack of robustness; poor detail design hampered routine servicing. A cowling came loose and damaged a wing of NP406 in October 1945 so NP411 completed the handling tests in late 1946. By then the type had been cancelled, although NP408 appeared in early 1947 for radio trials.

Piper Cub

VM286 received modifications for hooking on to a 500 ft long cable suspended between two poles. Having unloaded 54 crates, erected the cable, postponed the trial until the wind was favourable and briefed the intrepid aviator, all was ready on 12th February 1946. A slow well judged approach led to a hook-up half way along the cable with a safe deceleration. The attempt at take off was less auspicious; about half way along the run the aircraft tipped on its nose and brought the experiment to a halt. Film records showed the elevator to have been moved down immediately before tipping; the pilot, who was undamaged, expressed astonishment at the evidence of his actions. His pride, but not his career, was affected. It was concluded that work on the Brodie Suspension System, as the device was known, should be suspended, on the argument that where it was possible to erect the system, it would also be possible to make a short landing strip with saving in equipment, transport and time.

Junkers 88 and 188

These two machines, having been used post-war by Porton, appeared in May 1946 engineering returns, and languished unserviceable until broken up by AST Hamble in December 1947.

Reid and Sigrist Desford

Existing reports of this two seater, G-AGOS, during its brief stay at Boscombe in 1946 indicate that with two Gipsy Queen 1 engines its tare weight was 2,410 lb, and loaded 3,300 lb. The pressure instrument errors were small and maximum cruising speed at sea level was 137 kt (true).

Heston A2/45

VL529 (Gipsy Queen 33) preceded its competitor by a year, but the report on 38 hr of handling in the Wiltshire air in mid-1948 has not been found The engineers found 17 items in need of improvement.

Supermarine Seagull

AAEE's responsibility for testing the intended successor to the Sea Otter was restricted to carbon monoxide (nil from the Griffon 29) and deck landing of PA147. *HMS Illustrious* steaming in the Channel in December 1949 received the trials party including two AAEE pilots who had had but little practice on type. Interest centred on the benefits of the variable incidence wing adjustable between zero and plus eight degrees. The highest acceptable setting was five degrees; eight degrees produced an attitude too nose down for a carrier landing. At any setting, poor lateral control made approaches difficult in any but favourable conditions.

Avro Ashton

In late 1951, brief handling tests were made on WB490 (four Nenes) to assess suitability for trials work. Controls were described as "not excessively heavy," and once panels on the engine nacelles had been sealed the critical Mach rose from 0.67 to 0.69, although 0.65 was recommended as the maximum for normal use. Poor cockpit layout would be acceptable for test pilots, the report says. CATS used the aircraft into 1957 without recorded difficulty; a wide variety of research trials were flown. The following year WE670 with two wing nacelles capable of carrying and dropping bombs up to 1,000 lb was cleared at 82,000 lb all up weight. Critical Mach was reduced to 0.64 when a strong nose down pitch needed a strong pull to overcome. Opening the bomb doors created an unpleasant buffeting above 200 kt.

377: Heston A.2/45 VL529 in November 1947, just before its AAEE trial. This fragile looking air observation post reveals many novel features, including the pusher, twin boom layout, a high, bulged canopy for both pilot and observer and what appears to be a swivelling pitot head on the nose. The handling report as not been found.

378: Seagull prototype PA147 in November 1949. AAEE's interest centred on deck landing of this variable incidence design; the benefit of optimising incidence was reduced by the poor roll control on the approach. © Crown Copyright

379: Beaufighter TT.10 RD854 makes a pleasant picture in April 1959 as it passes through Boscombe Down en route to the Far East. © Crown Copyright

Auster

This manufacturer produced a range of designs, treated together here, since all, whatever their type, were known as "Austers" and nearly all were characterised by a high wing, and had a single engine.

AOP Mark V. Two wartime Porton aircraft based at AAEE met their ends in similar fashion within a month of each other at the end of 1945. NJ631 was run over by a landing Firebrand at Farnborough (piloted by the Superintendent, RAE). The circumstances of NJ630's demise are more bizarre. Having been picketted in a field due to bad weather just before Christmas, a redundant pilot training nearby as a clerk saw his chance for a nice seasonal present and went for flight which ended fatally when he crashed. Replacements, TW513 and TW519 soon arrived, but the former crashed in July 1946 after running out of fuel and was replaced in turn by TW384. TJ645 spent 1951 at Boscombe.

Auster "S". Incorporating the firm's own ideas, WJ316 suffered by comparison to the re-engined Mark 6 in 1951 tests; handling was better than the Mark 6 with the exception of heavy ailerons.

AOP Mark VI/6. Weighing 2,123 lb with 23 gal of fuel, TJ707 (Gipsy Major VII) was found in early 1946 to be more robust than earlier marks with reasonably harmonised controls. It was easy to overspeed the engine, the elevator trimmer rotated in the wrong sense, and there was some CO gas inside, and the "Set, Wireless, Army Type 62" worked. VF518 crashed in May 1948 just after arrival. The Bombardier 702 powered VX125 from October 1950, but the handling of the aeroplane had deteriorated slightly; the airspeed indicator over read by 9.5 kt at 125 kt. Compared to the contemporary Auster "S", VX125 had a marginally shorter take off (295 ft vs 345 ft to unstick) and a longer landing run (665 vs 630 ft); it was some 220 lb heavier at 2,245 lb, but identically powered. Best climb was 1,010 ft/min. Carriage and dropping of loads was limited by their effect on CG, but some success attended the laying of cables from a spool at low speeds.

T Mark 7. Pilots at AAEE disliked carrying out spinning tests of this trainer version without parachutes; behaviour of VF665 was benign and it always recovered. Handling improved in WE566 in 1951 with a modified elevator and tailplane, but the ailerons remained heavy. WE555 appeared briefly in 1959.

AOP Mark 9. This was the last fixed wing Air Observation Post of the Army before helicopters took over. WZ662 (Bombardier 203) handled well in 1954, and attracted the adjective "pleasant" in the report, but still lacked warning of the stall—a shortcoming made unacceptable by the propensity to spin even without rudder input. Engine cooling just met requirements. WZ663 soon followed; magnetic items spoilt the accuracy of the compass, jettisoning the door damaged the tailplane, and Army set 62 continued in use. The F95 Mk 5 camera on a wing pod became acceptable on the third visit of WZ672 in 1963, but sighting arrangements remained too complicated, and the radio (PTR170) performance was degraded by fuselage shielding. Picking up 2-to-3 lb message bags into WZ702 required the door to be removed, thus inducing exhaust gasses. WZ677 and XP254 also served, and XK376 continued earlier cable laying—achieving success at 250 ft and 60 kt.

Autocrat. G-AJIZ made comparative tests between a normal and a Goodyear swivelling undercarriage in 1948–9. The latter permitted satisfactory landings in crosswind components up to 18 kt, but it was not considered possible to predict any benefit for large aircraft from this novel arrangement.

Auster B4. Designed as a light air ambulance, XA177 (Bombardier 702) appeared in April 1952 and soon revealed its limitations. The castoring tail wheel and low rudder power made taxying difficult in any crosswind, there was no stall warning and the elevator trim range inadequate. At 2,700 lb take off run was 240 yd, and distance to 50 ft 465 yd. Revisions to the fin and rudder gave a partial improvement to cross wind handling in 1953.

Auster Autocar J/5G. On arrival in March 1951 civil G-ANVN became military XJ941 when it was discovered that no engineer had a civil "A" license to sign the documents for flight. It spent two years on spray development for Rhodesia.

Auster A2/45. Identified by the specification number for which it was built, VL522 (Gipsy Queen 34) arrived in May 1949. The two crew sat back to back, each having a good view. However, the CG when loaded was well aft, thus spoiling handling which required the pilot's full attention; in particular, landings were frequently made tail wheel-first, and with the stick near its front stop at touchdown.

Hawker E.38/46 – P1052

This experimental swept wing aeroplane came to AAEE in July 1949 for evaluation as a fighter, from both aerodromes and ships. At 9,100 lb, handling of VX279 (Nene 2) was pleasant with good acceleration at high altitude; 515 kt level speed was achieved at 25,000 ft, and 0.87M above that altitude. CL_{max} in turning flight was maintained to 0.84M, and 0.9M attained before handling became difficult; the elevator was much too heavy. Dummy deck approaches suffered from Dutch rolling at 110 kt (12 kt above the stall), but otherwise ship landings were considered entirely feasible.

380: Ashton WB490 in early 1954 with wing pods, nose probe and an inscription on the cleaned panel of the fuselage. It reads, "Civil Aircraft Test Section Boscombe Down." The pods were fitted by CATS to the outer engine position of the Lincoln wing used. © Crown Copyright

381: Ashton WE670 in November 1952 with nacelles on the wing, each capable of carrying a 1,000lb bomb. Limited in use to 0.64M, and with other features unacceptable to the RAF, this type fulfilled its role satisfactorily as a laboratory. © Crown Copyright

382: Auster Type S WJ316 secured adequately to Mother earth. AAEE found the S Type better than the Mark 6 with a Bombardier, but very prone to ground loop

383: *The prototype Auster T.7 VF665 shows its classic Auster lines. Spinning trials without parachutes made test pilots nervous.*

384: *Auster AOP.9 WZ663, probably in 1964, with loud speaker on top of the fin, capable of broadcasting recordings of gun fire and other likely jungle noises for use in Malaya.* © *Crown Copyright*

385: *Auster AOP.9 WZ672 in 1963 with wing mounted camera pod, and what appear to be flares under the fuselage. The pilot's sighting arrangements were found to be too complicated.* © *Crown Copyright*

386: Auster B.4 XA177 in May 1952 in its original configuration which gave unsatisfactory handling, including very low stick force per g at aft CG, ie with a patient in the Ambulance compartment. © *Crown Copyright*

387: Auster A.2/45 VL522. Known at Boscombe by its specification number, this aeroplane competed with the Heston. This machine with its back-to-back seating could easily be loaded to give an extremely aft CG—leading to awkward handling, including cases where the stick had to be held near its foremost position on the approach. © *Crown Copyright*

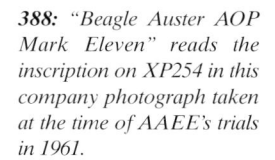

388: "Beagle Auster AOP Mark Eleven" reads the inscription on XP254 in this company photograph taken at the time of AAEE's trials in 1961.

389: Hawker E.38/46 VX279 in July 1949 displays a typical Hawker profile of the era. With swept wing and straight tailplane, it could just be controlled up to 0.9M, and maintained a reasonable maximum lift coefficient up to 0.84M, although the thrust was inadequate to sustain turns at this speed. © Crown Copyright

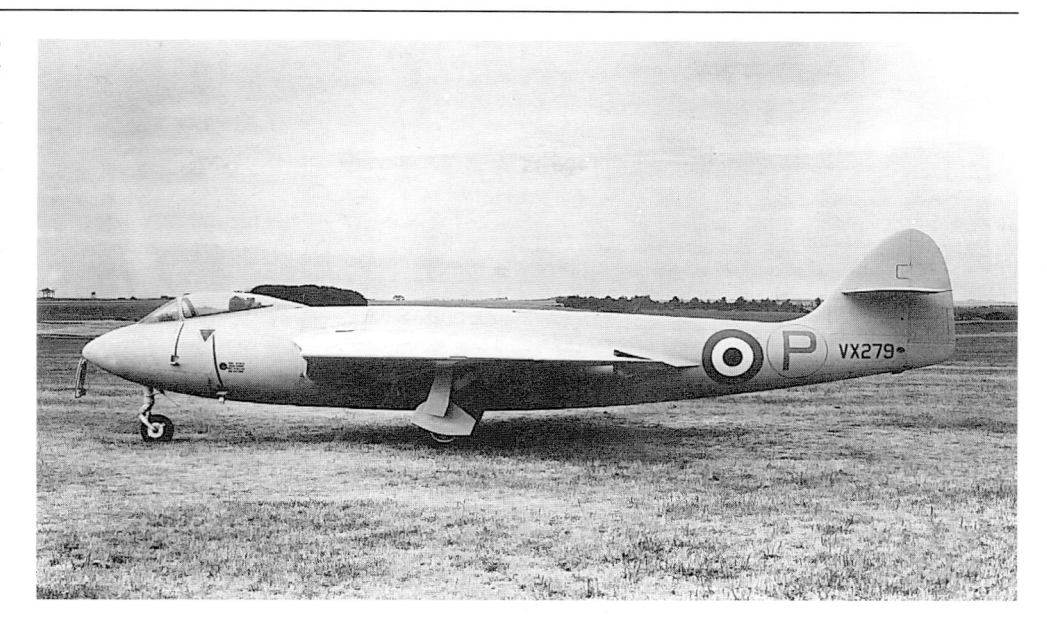

390: Avro 707C WZ744 in an Avro photo. Operated by Civil Aircraft Test Section, it gave experience to pilots and boffins of delta stability and control characteristics.

391: Beaver AL.1 XP769 on a trial of a hand held F 95 Mk 5 camera, operated from the rear seats. The hatch is open just ahead of the roundel. Satisfactory photographs could be taken only below 1,000ft. © Crown Copyright

392: ML Inflatable XK781 with the "Gadfly" wing, probably in 1958. Conceived as a bizarre manifestation of cold war necessity, the inflated wing did not produce acceptable handling, and, as far as is known, only one passenger was carried, Mr Eric Backhaus, whose flight took him barely across the runway before pilot, Lt M Hedges and machine gave up the unequal struggle. © Crown Copyright

Armstrong Whitworth 52G

Among the heterogeneous collection of flying machines transferred from Beaulieu was the AW 52 glider RG324; it was immediately sold to its maker.

Avro 707C

The two seat tail-less delta wing WZ744 with very low stick force per g gave pilots relevant handling experience at Boscombe in 1953 prior to the main period of Vulcan testing.

U-120D

One (XE725) of the 20 pilotless targets bought for duties at Aberporth was assessed there in 1955 by an AAEE team. Within sight of the controller the autopilot performed adequately; out of sight it was unreliable.

de Havilland Beaver

Extensive tests of G-AMVU (Wasp Junior) over six months in 1953 gave a convincing demonstration of performance and ruggedness. Take off and landing on all surfaces, in varying winds and all loads were uneventful; measured on smooth surface and reduced to standard conditions, take off run was 185 yd, reaching 50 ft after 325 yd, while landing distance was slightly longer using the absolute slowest approach of 40 kt. Good stability and stall behavior were spoilt only by a lack of sufficient trim range at forward CG. XP769 (Wasp Junior-39) tested operational equipment from 1961, including hand held F95 Mk 5 camera, various radios and a crash locator beacon. In Aden the engine oil overheated. The VHF radio of XP775 attracted little comment. In 1967 XP822 had the F95 camera in an acceptable pod. Modifications to the VOR navaid of XV270 produced good results in 1968, while IFF/SSR and a Decca 19 navigator were fitted in XV271 three years later.

ML Aviation Inflatable Wing

Likened by some to the products of the Durex company, all three aircraft made lingered at Boscombe long after their "use by" date, having arrived in 1957–8. Internal wing pressure was maintained by the motor of a domestic vacuum cleaner fixed in the rear seat. Existing flying reports feature only XK776 (Mikron III), the first, which could be flown only in calm conditions due to very poor lateral control provided by the sole movable surfaces—inflated trailing edge elevons. The take off run of over 300 yd was reduced marginally after the trailing

393: ML Inflatable XK776 lacking its rubber covering, and showing signs of distress after Flt Lt G R K (Geoff) Fletcher's experience of structural failure on take off in October 1957. The two broken struts which impinged on the propeller can be seen. © Crown Copyright

394: ML Inflatable showing details of wing construction and fins. The Establishment flew many odd designs over the years—this was one of the most eccentric. © Crown Copyright

395: Edgar Percival's Number 9 (E.P.9) XM819 in March 1959. The Establishment found little good to say about this design, from an excessive under-reading of 15 kt at an indicated airspeed of 40 kt, to poor aileron response and a badly laid out cockpit. © Crown Copyright

edge had been given a reflex section. Structural integrity failed on one take off when the two rear fuselage struts broke causing the wing to move back damaging the engine struts and the propeller. To the dismay of the pilots, repairs followed. Such flights as were flown had limited duration as the engine quickly overheated. XK781 and XK784 also featured in engineering returns of the period.; the latter, the trainer version, attempted one minute one minute (sic) flight with two souls on board in January 1958.

Edgar Percival EP9

The classic series of tests in 1958–9 on the two machines of this light army type revealed an almost uniform (good description for an army aeroplane!) list of unacceptably bad features. XM797 and XM819 (Lycoming GO/480/B) were flimsy, draughty, leaky and had poor brakes; the main compass had very large errors and the standby could not be seen by ordinary pilots who managed to find the cockpit and thought the layout poor. Handling was docile but low aileron response and inadequate drag from the flaps were criticised; an attempted take off with a single wing store proved foolhardy when the wing tip struck the ground as the wing dropped at 30 kt (indicated—the ASI under read by more than 15 kt). At 3,700 lb the take off run was 305 yd, distance to 50 ft 446 yd and the landing figures slightly less; the best climb was 500 ft/min, and ceiling 10,800 ft. In tropical temperatures at Idris the climb became minimal, although the engine rpm and temperature remained just within limits. The radio, in a separate test, gave no problems.

Blue Steel

Treated for reporting purposes as an aircraft, this air-to ground missile made some demands on the scientific staff, both in UK and in Australia between 1958 and 1964.

British Hovercraft Corporation SRN 6

XV616, a Mark 2, ventured to sea with an AAEE team on board; noise measurements indicated that damage to undefended ears would occur after 30 minutes.

396: One of a number of towed targets tried in the mid-1950s. Features include the canting of the nosewheel after touchdown following release to clear the runway for the tug landing behind. © Crown Copyright

TRAINERS

Miles Magister

The wartime L8253 and N3782 were replaced in 1946 by BB667 and then in turn by BB666 for the civilian training scheme. The latter pair had been civil aircraft early in the war, and were more properly Hawk Trainers.

De Havilland Tiger Moth

Mark 2. T6859 arrived in December 1946 for training. T5895 and DE249 arrived later, but became casualties of an errant Ambassador with brake failure in March 1949; DE249 had just been repaired after landing damage. The Gipsy Major 1 of T7340 remained cool while towing a Sedburgh glider in 1953–4. On take off 50 ft was reached after 625 yd, 320 ft/min climb and ceiling of 4,250 ft achieved.

Airspeed Oxford and Consul

Postwar trials on Oxfords centred on two aircraft—both concerned with rockets. A Burmese contract machine (UB339 called a Consul) spent three days at AAEE in October 1949 from which it was concluded that eight missiles (25 lb heads) on an RP VIII installation could be fired satisfactorily. There may have been problems, as two years later RR345 turned up for further RP work for the Burmese, but this time with 60 lb heads; release was acceptable. Communications justified the presence of V4026 from March 1946, probably NM331 (1948–9) and NM692 until it suffered an accident in March 1952. Instrument flying practice kept the pilots sharp using AS504 (1954–5), HN379 (1947–9), NM528 (1952–4) and PH412 (1953–5). PH509 and EB811 were broken up on arrival from Beaulieu in 1950 and did not fly.

North American Harvard

Mark IIB. In January 1953, responding to the needs of the RAF in Kenya, KF183 arrived fitted for dropping eight 4 in flares and eight 20 lb fragmentation bombs; trials were successful and the aircraft remained in use as a photographic chase until 1975 when it was put into storage. FX373 paid but a short visit in 1949, probably connected with its subsequent use in Rhodesia. Other Harvards were FX402 (1948–9) FX216 (1950), KF562 (1949), probably for training civil servants; FT375 (1954 until after 1975) and KF314 (1949 until after 1975) stayed to chase dropping aircraft, a job for which the type remains most suitable. Two machines came from Beaulieu in 1950—FX278 which apparently had to be written off in 1953, and FX371 which crashed fatally in June 1952.

397: Jet Provost T.3 XM346 equipped with tip tanks and ejection seats. The pitot head is under the port wing and the static source just behind the fuselage roundel.

398: Rails for 60lb-head rockets under the wings of Oxford RR345 in 1951; firing was acceptable.

399: Prentice T.3 HV903 for India. With Gipsy Queen 70/3, a three bladed propeller and lighter ailerons than the RAF version, handling was slightly improved in December 1950.

400: Prentice T.1 TV163 in April 1947 with anti spin parachute and rudder protection, characteristic turned up wing tips and heavily strutted canopy. It was under powered and had heavy controls. © Crown Copyright

Percival Prentice

Prototypes and T Mark 1. To the criticisms of TV163 (Gipsy Queen 32), viz, heavy controls, insufficient rudder, low power and too much flap, were added rudder overbalance and increase in aileron friction on exposure to the sun in TV172; both trials took place in 1947. TV166 had good engine and oil cooling, and at 3,860 lb could fly 395 nm on its a tank of fuel. At 4,000 lb climb was 800 ft/min and ceiling 14,123 ft using the propeller control to hold rpm at 2,400. Spinning of VN684 in 1948 produced no rudder locking, and no difficulty in recovery within the first four turns; thereafter, the spin became flatter and slower taking more time to recover. Further spinning in 1949 of TV172 with fuselage lengthened by three feet was little better. VR190 and VR191 completed 300 hours flying each with few major observations; engine changes had to be made after every 75 hr flying. Deliberate heavy landings caused no damage—a fact highlit in the report. VR211 (Gipsy Queen 32) flew over 1,000 hr in the hands of A Squadron between January 1951 and September 1960, and VR197 gave CATS training in early 1949, while TV168 spent two sessions in the blower tunnel.

T Mark 3. HV903 (Gipsy Queen 70/3) had a three-bladed propeller when flown in 1950 for the Indian Air Force, and the ailerons were lighter than previous machines for the RAF.

Bristol Buckmaster

T Mark 1. Having completed its handling trial as the war ended, RP137 remained for three months to be assessed for maintainability; the liberal provision of panels made servicing straightforward. TJ717 was flown by AAEE in February 1946 at Filton where the lockable tail wheel received praise.

Boulton Paul Balliol and Sea Balliol

Prototype. The Mercury 30 power plant of VL892 was an expedient, and AAEE's assessment limited to a preview from December 1948. The term, "easy and pleasant," to describe handling in the report is contradicted by a list of unsatisfactory features: rudder overbalance, high stick force per g and heavy ailerons. The former comment may have referred to flying using the original spectacle control, and the latter to flying by conventional stick control. Some aerobatic manoeuvres proved difficult, and spinning was not attempted.

T Mark 1. VL935 with a Mamba engine spent the first three months of 1950 at AAEE; no report has been found of this turboprop aircraft. Reference to the favourable deck handling of the Mamba version is however, made in a later report of the Merlin variety. In 1952 VL892 returned when its Mamba engine was quiet and free of vibrations and considered suitable for tyro test pilots at ETPS.

T Mark 2. With a Merlin 35, the production standard VW898 was whisked off to Khartoum on arrival in early 1949 for reasons not immediately apparent for a trainer. A pair of 45 gal drop tanks made transit flying possible by extending range from 635 nm to 1,025 nm; apart from useless windscreen wipers, the 52 hr in transit passed with little drama. Engine temperatures tended to exceed limits in the heat. At 8,350 lb, 50 ft was reached 610 yd after starting the take off run, but landing took 810 yd to come to rest. Other performance, at standard conditions, included maximum speed of 252 kt (true), climb of 1,780 ft/min and ceiling of 22,600 ft. Engineering features were praised, although some items such as the fuselage fuel tank proved time consuming to change. Meanwhile, back at Boscombe, the crisp handling and feel of VW900 pleased pilots, but haphazard cockpit layout and directional trim changes with speed did not do so. The

401: Sea Balliol T.21 WP333, the pride of C Squadron in 1965; it had been saved by re-purchase from the scrap merchant. It shows little sign of its many deck landings over many years, and was cherished by Navy men and civilians alike. © Crown Copyright

402: Prentice T.1 VN684 showing the revised rudder and elevators in a successful attempt to improve spinning; recovery after four turns was consistent and easy. © Crown Copyright

403: Balliol prototype VL892 before transfer to AAEE in December 1947. Flat turns remained in vogue, but were not the type's strong point as the rudder overbalanced; the other controls were considered to be too heavy.

404: Balliol T.2 VR599 in late 1949 armed with four 60lb rockets and eight practice bombs. Handling was acceptable up to 320 kt, but minor modifications were needed for satisfactory firing of the rockets. © Crown Copyright

405: Balliol T.2 VW898 at Khartoum in June 1949 with the under wing tanks needed to reach this destination. Apart from inadequate cooling in the Sudan, one of the few criticisms concerned the poor windscreen wipers making the transit difficult in rain.

406: Sea Balliol T.21 VR599 in April 1953, converted from Mark 2, showing the smaller diameter propeller, hook, reinforced undercarriage and lack of fin flash. © Crown Copyright

407: Athena T.1 VM125 in March 1948, eight months before delivery to Boscombe. © Crown Copyright

237

408: *Athena T.2 VW890 en route from Boscombe to Khartoum in mid-1949 with a pair of under wing tanks to make the journey feasible. Although an engine needed replacing prior to departure, the Merlin 35 fitted for the trip ran well throughout the transit and trial.*

409 left: *Athena T.2 VW891 in August 1949 equipped for test flying. Externally, the yaw vane on the starboard wing tip and the protective frame around the fin are in evidence. © Crown Copyright*

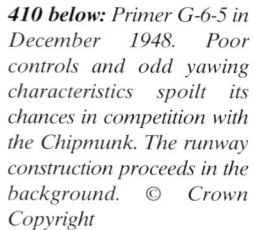

410 below: *Primer G-6-5 in December 1948. Poor controls and odd yawing characteristics spoilt its chances in competition with the Chipmunk. The runway construction proceeds in the background. © Crown Copyright*

aircraft lacked dive brakes; these were fitted to VR595 and produced no buffet or longitudinal trim change but induced a roll. Modified airbrakes on VR599 cured the roll but smaller flaps introduced an increase in stalling speed. Docile spinning of VR592 and VR593 with leading edge spoilers became oscillatory after two turns and vicious to the left; characteristics improved on VR591 with reduction of tailplane incidence. Manoeuvring stick forces had been improved by early 1950, but an airfield assessment of deck approaches showed poor engine control and lack of elevator effect on cutting the power. In November 1950 more dummy approaches in VR597 were followed by landings on *HMS Illustrious* by VR598 (with a hook) and possibly VR596. Previous shortcomings were confirmed, with additional criticism of the ailerons and rudder, and of the view from the right seat. VR591 returned with a spring tab and a stiffer elevator which partially restored satisfactory handling at aft CG. VR597 with a spring in the elevator circuit overcame the problem at all stages of flight, confirmed on the production WF989 in 1952. CO contamination, long a problem, was substantially improved, but not eliminated, on VW899 in 1951–2 by the AAEE modification of fitting shields along the fuselage; similarly, a windscreen wiper was only a modest improvement, but sleeve and banner targets were towed acceptably. Blackburn-built WN526 spent six weeks under examination in 1957.

Radios took two weeks to clear in VR590, but armament took a little longer, starting with the single machine gun in VR599 in June 1950. Bombs, rockets and the camera gun followed, until a fuel feed failure led to a forced landing and major damage. Armament clearance was extended to flares (Reconnaissance 4 in No 3 Mk 1) in 1952.

Sea Balliol T Mark 21. VR599 had a hook, folding wings, a throttle switch for the airbrakes and other changes for nautical work on arrival in early 1953. Handling was similar to the land based mark 2 with all the improvements; deck landings, again onto *HMS Illustrious*, took place in June 1953. A faulty filler cap led to syphoning fuel and major damage in the ensuing forced landing in May 1957. The only remaining design fault was the restricted view from the right seat; WL716, was similar. WP333 had a poorly placed compass master unit in 1954; five years later the new UHF radio sounded noisy. WP328 shuttled to *HMS Ark Royal* in 1957 during a six month attachment. WL732 served C Squadron until its disbandment.

Avro Athena

T Mark 1. The first prototype, VM125 (Mamba 1), a Mark 1, arrived in November 1948, but no report has been found.

T Mark 2. VW891 (Merlin 35) with three seats flew initially in August 1949 with an aft CG and displayed docile and comfortable handling characteristics, although the ailerons and stall warning needed improvement, and speed changes were accompanied by large longitudinal and directional trim changes. Forward CG was similar. At both CG positions, the spin developed violent oscillations after a few turns; recovery was normal in all cases and use of ailerons had little effect. Stability measurements gave slightly high stick forces for a trainer, while the forces in out-of-trim dives were definitely too high. A failure of the Merlin 35 engine delayed departure of VW890 (with a smaller fin) for Khartoum until May 1949; the round trip took 51.5 hours of transit flying using two 45 gal external tanks which extended range to 1,180 nm from 720. At 35°C and 9,500 lb the take off distance to 50 ft was 780 yd; landing from 50 ft at 8,300 lb took 1,015 yd. Back at Boscombe, the smaller fin produced lighter pedal forces and thus more pleasant aerobatics, while VW890 had a climb of 1,610 ft/min and top speed of 257 kt; ceiling was 24,200 ft. In both aircraft the instructor lacked a blind flying panel, and shared flap and trim controls with the pupil; it was concluded that the type met the specification. VW892 pleased the engineers for its ease of maintenance, but embarrassed its pilot who forgot to dangle the Dunlops, leading to a wheels-up write off in April 1952. VR567 on loan from Manby completed uneventful tests of bombing and the G45 camera gun in 1950–1. VR568 spent three months at AAEE in mid-1950.

Fairey Primer

Constructed pre-war in Belgium by Avions Fairey and secretly shipped to England "for the duration", OO-POM came to Boscombe in March 1948 powered by a Gipsy Major 1. The only report found highlights several engineering shortcomings. No such criticism was made of the production version G-6-5 (Cirrus Major III) later in 1948, when it was submitted as a private contender for an official requirement for which the Chipmunk gained the order. The tandem seating was good, but extremely heavy ailerons spoilt control harmonisation, yawing caused nose down pitch, and the permitted speed (156 kt) was too low and easy to exceed. At 2,220 lb take off run was 210 yd, climb 760 ft/min and top speed 122 kt (true).

Fairey Junior

A brief assessment in November 1949 of this simple trainer intended for student private pilots was probably made at the request of its maker; minor damage due to undercarriage failure was soon repaired. Viceless and extremely easy to fly, OO-TIT (Micron 2) received the accolade "excellent", obviously well abreast of developments; OO-ULA also flew.

411: *Chipmunk G-AKDN in July 1948 in a photograph to illustrate the proximity of the aerial to the fin causing loss of reception. The flying controls were well harmonised, and only minor comments made. © Crown Copyright*

412: *Chipmunk T.10 WB549 in December 1949, the first production aircraft of many hundreds to serve the three Services for over four decades. The aerial is under the starboard wing, and other earlier comments had been rectified. © Crown Copyright*

413: *Ercoupe 415CD VX147 Evaluated for private pilot instruction, this machine remained at Boscombe for a few years for local instruction. Its novel interconnected ailerons and rudder made most manoeuvres easy, but made others impossible or dangerous. © Crown Copyright*

414: Two AAEE Sea Vixens FAW.1 XJ480 launching and possibly XJ484, folded on board HMS Victorious in 1959.

415: The view looking aft on HMS Victorious in 1959, and including Gannet T.5 XG873, probably on its deck suitability trial, plus a Royal Naval Dragonfly in "midnite" blue finish.

416: Buccaneer prototype XK523 after landing on HMS Ark Royal off Malta in 1960.

417: Sea Fury T.20 VZ345 being flown by the Commandant, Air Cdre Geoff Cairns, from Cologne/Wahn to Boscombe in October 1974. The aircraft had been in use in Germany for several years, and was given to AAEE as a goodwill gesture resulting from the MRCA/Tornado programme. © Crown Copyright

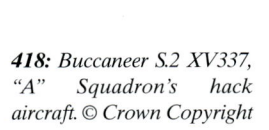

418: Buccaneer S.2 XV337, "A" Squadron's hack aircraft. © Crown Copyright

419: Shackleton MR.2 WR960 over the South coast in September 1967 illustrates two test items—the two yellow camera pods under the wings and the bomb bay doors marked every foot alternate black and white. This aircraft made the very extensive and time consuming clearances for all the bomb bay loads possible with the Phase 3 modifications. © Crown Copyright

420: Meteor T.7 XF274 resplendent in grey/dayglo finish in May 1967. A long serving communicator, trainer, instrument tester (as here with the amber panels for the rear seat) and general hack, it retained the zero reader and ILS from earlier trials. © Crown Copyright

421: Meteor T.7 WA690 under tow in the snow of March 1966. It was intended to be the ejection seat test vehicle, thus the two warning triangles under the canopy. © Crown Copyright

422: Hunter FGA.9 XE601 diving, spraying and pulling for Porton. This illustrates the training role of this machine using water. © Crown Copyright

423: Phantom FGR.2 XV406 showing its reconnaissance pod and long range GAL tanks in July 1971. © Crown Copyright

424: Jaguar T.2 with the stores cleared by AAEE up to June 1972, laid out in the Weighbridge hangar for the benefit of senior visitors. © Crown Copyright

425: Harrier GR.1 posing at the same time as the Jaguar. Most stores are similar, but there are additional items. © Crown Copyright

243

426: Lightning T.4 XL629 in original form with small ventral tank and the "130%" fin. Now mounted on a plinth as a "Gate Guardian" at Boscombe Down.

427: Kestrel FGA.1 XS695 outside the Weighbridge hangar in 1967 shortly before shearing an outrigger on landing, turning over and trapping Flt Lt Derek Parry. He was unharmed. © Crown Copyright

428: Lightning F.6 XS929 in REG about to undergo electromagnetic bombardment from the radars in the background, and other sources. © Crown Copyright

429: Jaguar GR.1 XX109 with a large centreline tank which reduced already poor directional stability even further. The old hill fort of Chiselbury is just ahead of the tip of the fin. © Crown Copyright

430: Four Hunter T.7s and T.7As ready for business, T.7A XL616 nearest; date probably early 1970s. They were used for chase, photography, ratings, training and communications © Crown Copyright

431: Harrier GR.1 XV741 awaiting its AAEE pilot, Sqn Ldr T Lecky-Thompson, in April 1969 for the flight from "RAF St Pancras", London to New York. No doubt the gentleman in the bowler hat was persuaded to remove it before take off. The aircraft has a probe, wing tips and long range tanks for the trip—the fastest East to West. © Crown Copyright

432: The long serving Argosy C.1 XN817 in working configuration with rear ramp open ready to dispense a load. The chequer marking assisted measurement of clearances and separations, while the nose probe was for test pilot training when used by ETPS. The exhaust of the auxiliary power unit is to the rear of the wing trailing edge on the boom. © Crown Copyright

433: Beverley C.1 XB261—a long-time resident on heavy dropping trials. © Crown Copyright

245

434: *Gazelle AH.1 XW846 in the spray rig at Uplands, Ottawa in the winter 1975/6. The photograph appears to have been taken to illustrate the volume of snow and ice that the rig could produce; the Gazelle is unoccupied. © Crown Copyright*

435: *Wasp HAS.1 XS569 in June 1968 sporting a pair of Nord AS12 missiles. The sighting head can be seen above the port seat, together with a shield under the rotor © Crown Copyright*

436: *Wessex HCC.4 XV733 resplendent in bright red and Royal badge struts its stuff at Boscombe. Special windows, entry steps and floatation bags in the wheels are features. © Crown Copyright*

437: *Scout AH.1 XT625 at the Icing Rig at Uplands, Ottawa. © Crown Copyright*

438: *Canberra B.2 WJ638 on 20 February 1967 demonstrating a runway ejection of a dummy man. The telescopic gun remains in the aircraft and there are 44 triangles painted on the nose, indicating the number of ejections since the practice of painting triangles began.* © Crown Copyright

439: *Alouette AH.2 XR232, tested in 1964, seen here over Stonehenge at a later date.* © Crown Copyright

440: *Lightning F.6 XP693 with cambered leading edge, large ventral tank with two 30mm guns, a pair of Red Top missiles and flight refuelling probe. The proximity of the missiles and probe made flight refuelling interesting.* © Crown Copyright

247

441: Hercules C.1 XV178 in classic formation with two Harvards (KF314 at rear and KF183 in foreground) with the weighbridge hangar behind. XV178 was for several years the Airborne Forces' trials aircraft at Boscombe. © Crown Copyright

442: Basset CC.1 XS742 in January 1972 in use for communications and training test pilots; the nose probe has yaw and pitch vanes. © Crown Copyright

443: "B" Squadron Canberras in October 1968—a sharp formation on a gloomy day. Leading vic (bottom to top)—WJ638 (B.2—ejection trials with open rear cockpit), VX181 (PR.3 prototype—over 17 years old), WV787 (B.8 icing tanker), WT205 (B.15 armament hack) and WH854 (T.4—last without ejection seats for pilots). Rear vic, WJ632 (TT.18 on CA clearance), WH876 (B.2 flight refuelling training —dry contacts only) and WK121 (B.2 hack). One other Canberra (WF922 or WK164) failed to start and missed this Balbo. © Crown Copyright

1/72 SCALE

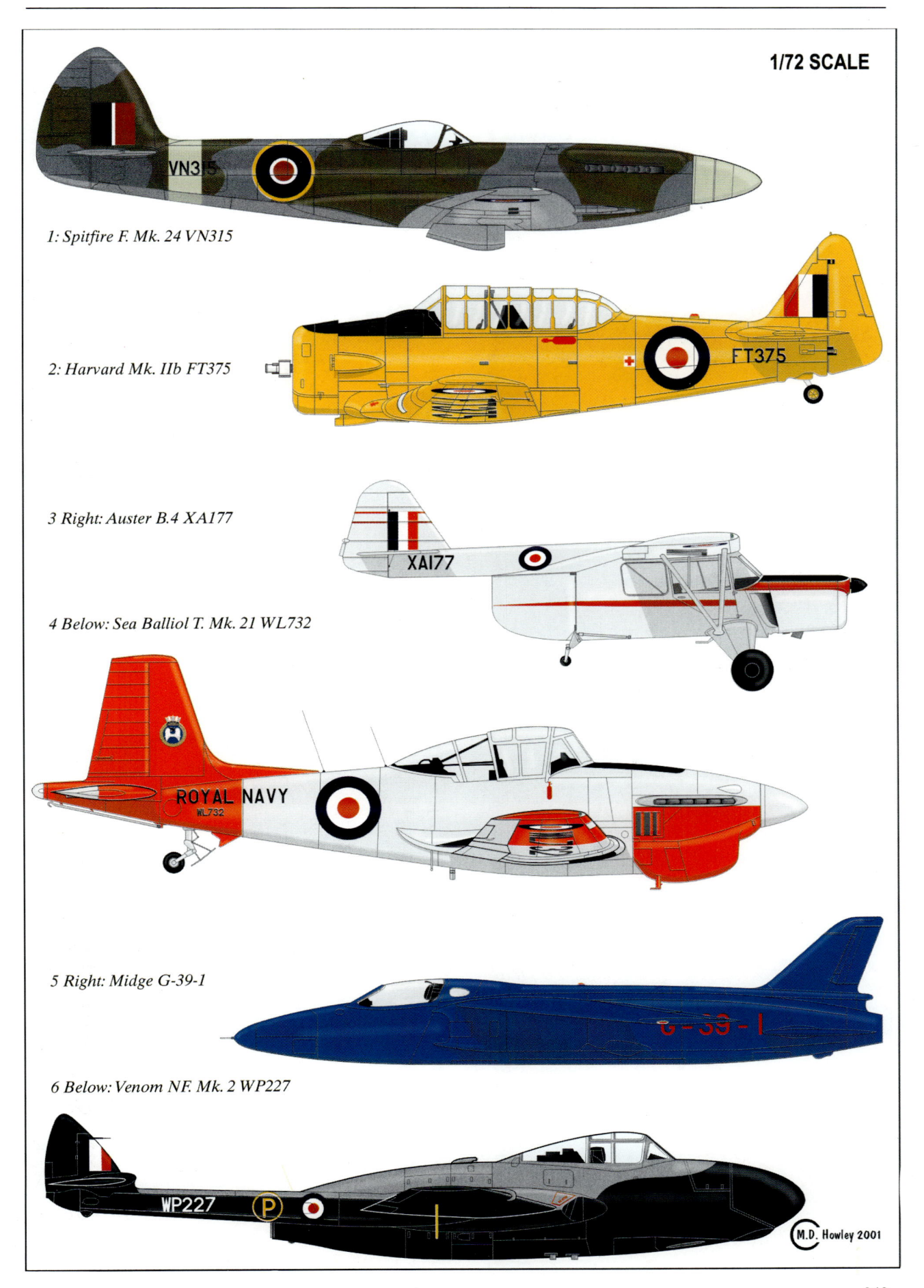

1: Spitfire F. Mk. 24 VN315

2: Harvard Mk. IIb FT375

3 Right: Auster B.4 XA177

4 Below: Sea Balliol T. Mk. 21 WL732

5 Right: Midge G-39-1

6 Below: Venom NF. Mk. 2 WP227

249

1/96 SCALE

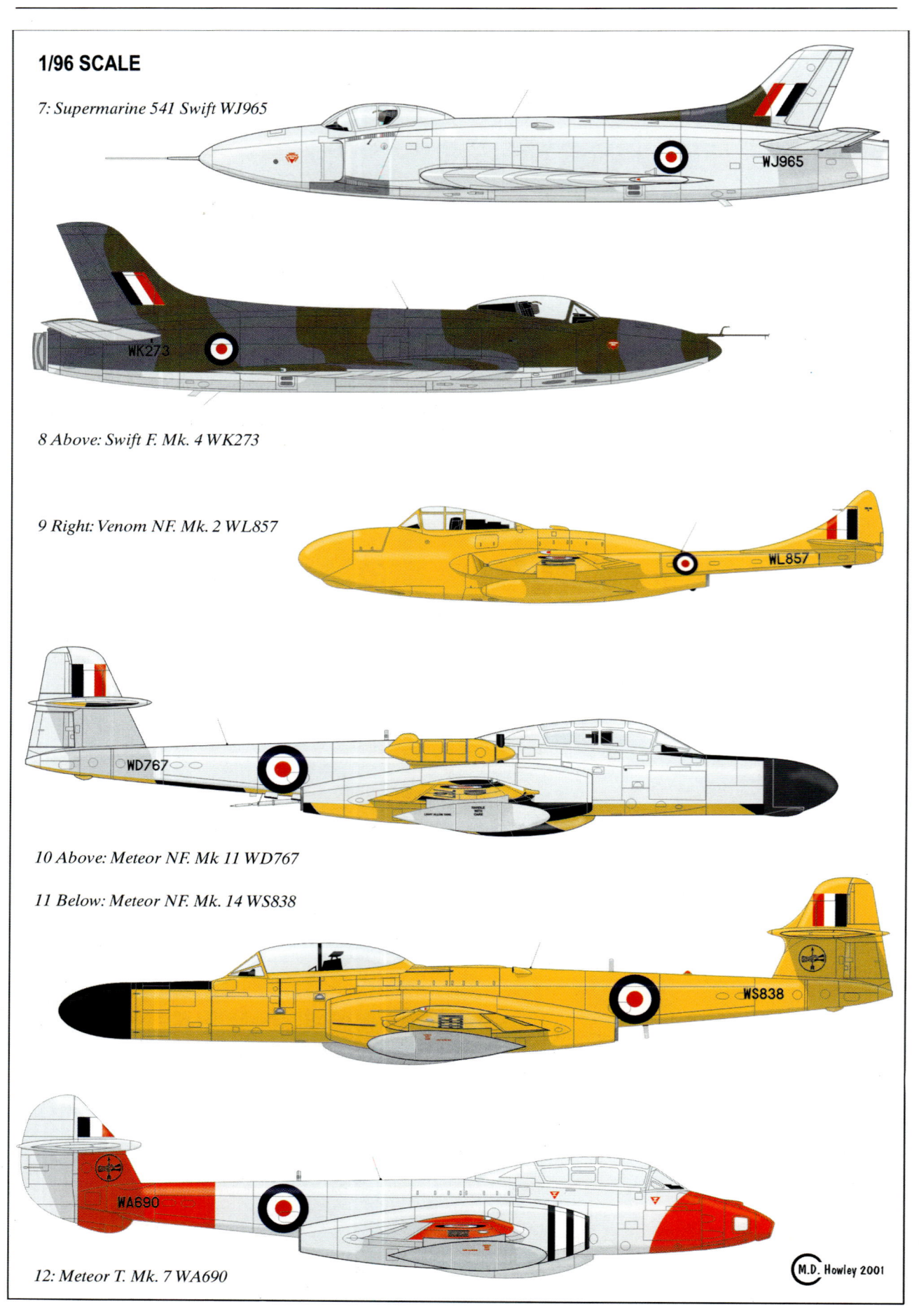

7: Supermarine 541 Swift WJ965

8 Above: Swift F. Mk. 4 WK273

9 Right: Venom NF. Mk. 2 WL857

10 Above: Meteor NF. Mk 11 WD767

11 Below: Meteor NF. Mk. 14 WS838

12: Meteor T. Mk. 7 WA690

1/111 SCALE

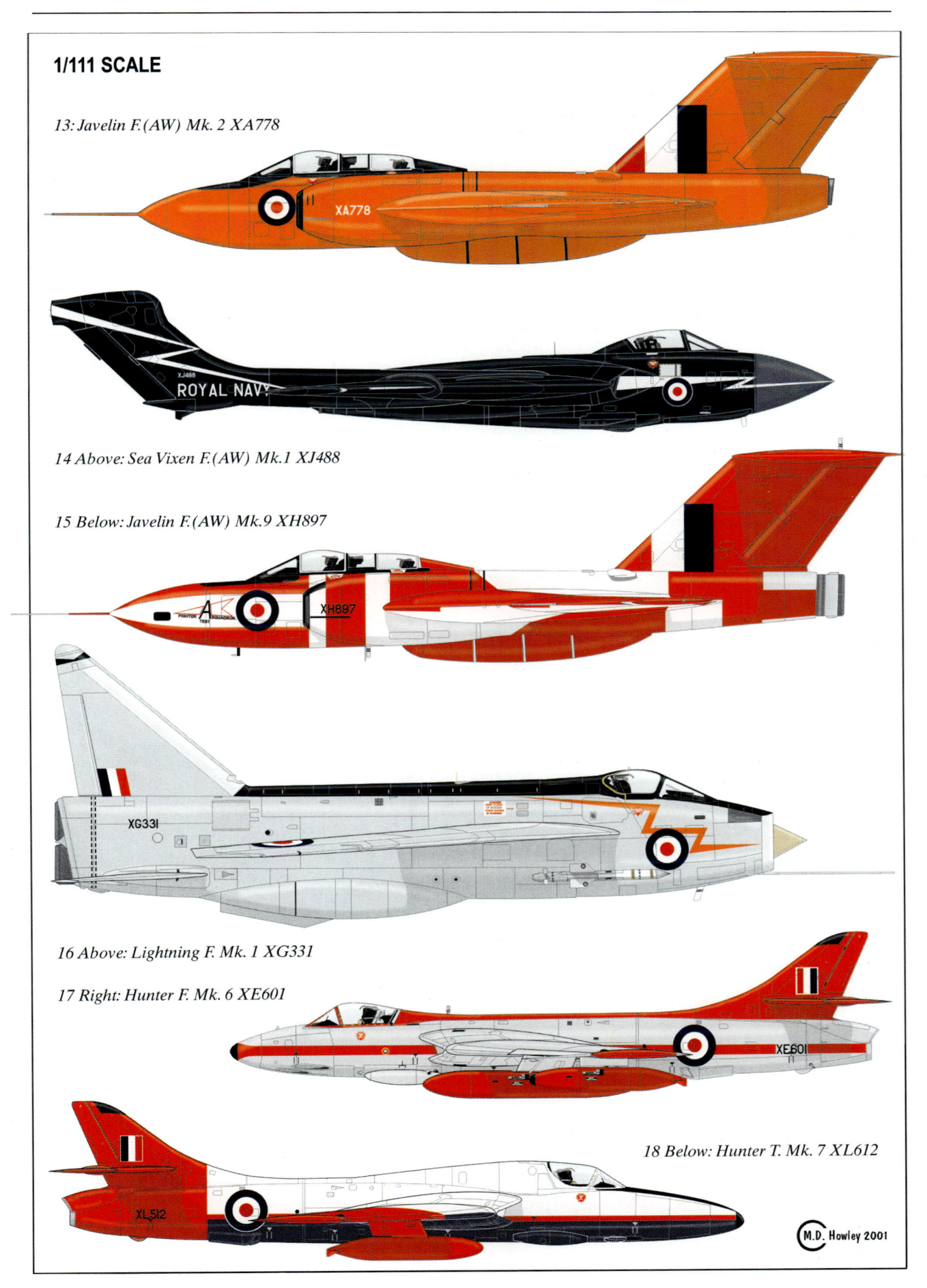

13: Javelin F.(AW) Mk. 2 XA778

14 Above: Sea Vixen F.(AW) Mk.1 XJ488

15 Below: Javelin F.(AW) Mk.9 XH897

16 Above: Lightning F. Mk. 1 XG331

17 Right: Hunter F. Mk. 6 XE601

18 Below: Hunter T. Mk. 7 XL612

M.D. Howley 2001

251

1/120 SCALE

19 Above: Belvedere HC. Mk. 1 XG449

20 Right: Whirlwind HAS. Mk. 7

21 Below: Whirlwind HAS. Mk. 7

22 Right: Wasp HAS. Mk.1

23 Below: Wessex HAS. Mk. 3

24: Wessex HCC. Mk. 4 XV732

M.D. Howley 2001

252

1/160 SCALE

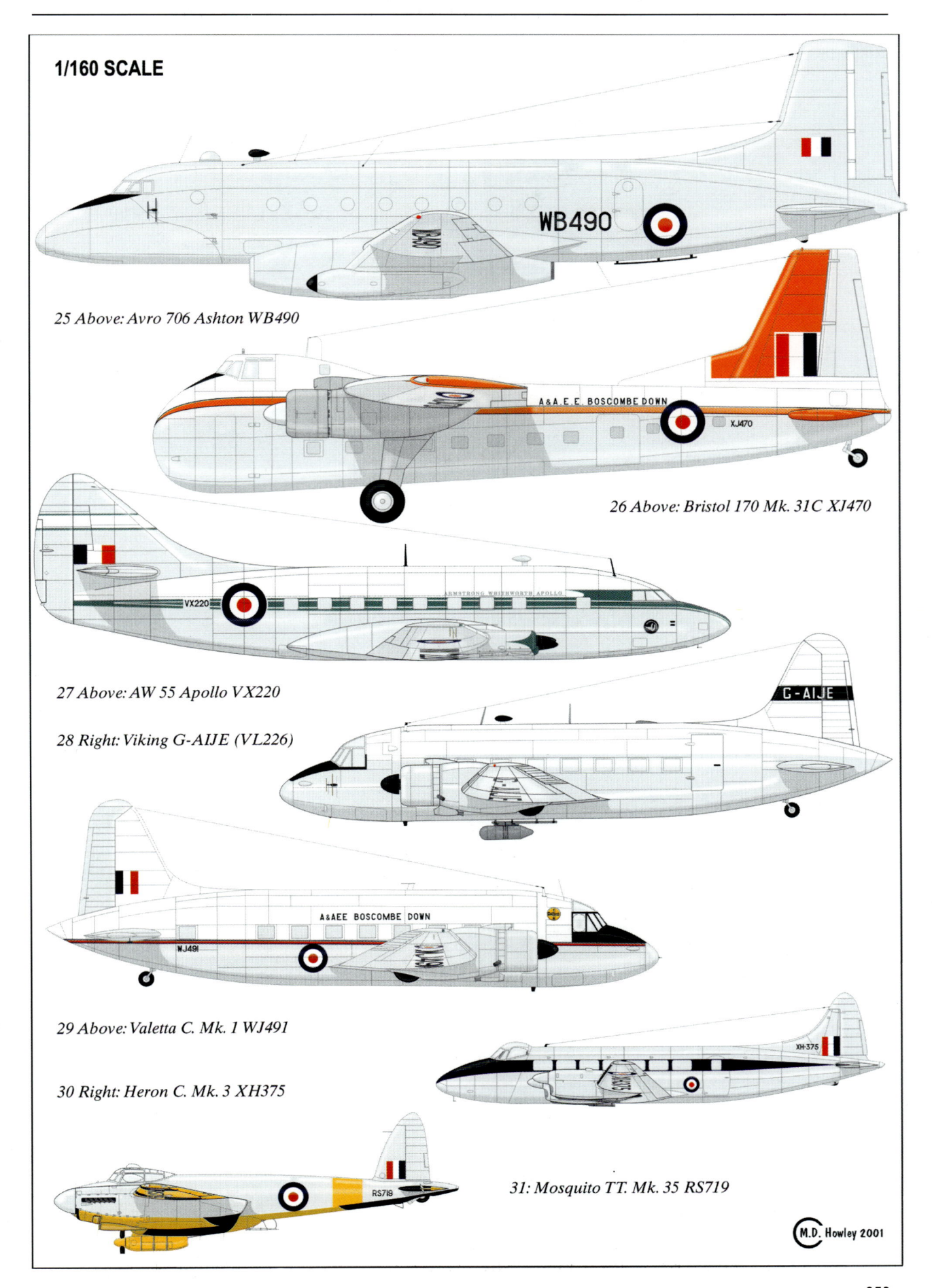

25 Above: Avro 706 Ashton WB490

26 Above: Bristol 170 Mk. 31C XJ470

27 Above: AW 55 Apollo VX220

28 Right: Viking G-AIJE (VL226)

29 Above: Valetta C. Mk. 1 WJ491

30 Right: Heron C. Mk. 3 XH375

31: Mosquito TT. Mk. 35 RS719

M.D. Howley 2001

NOT TO SCALE

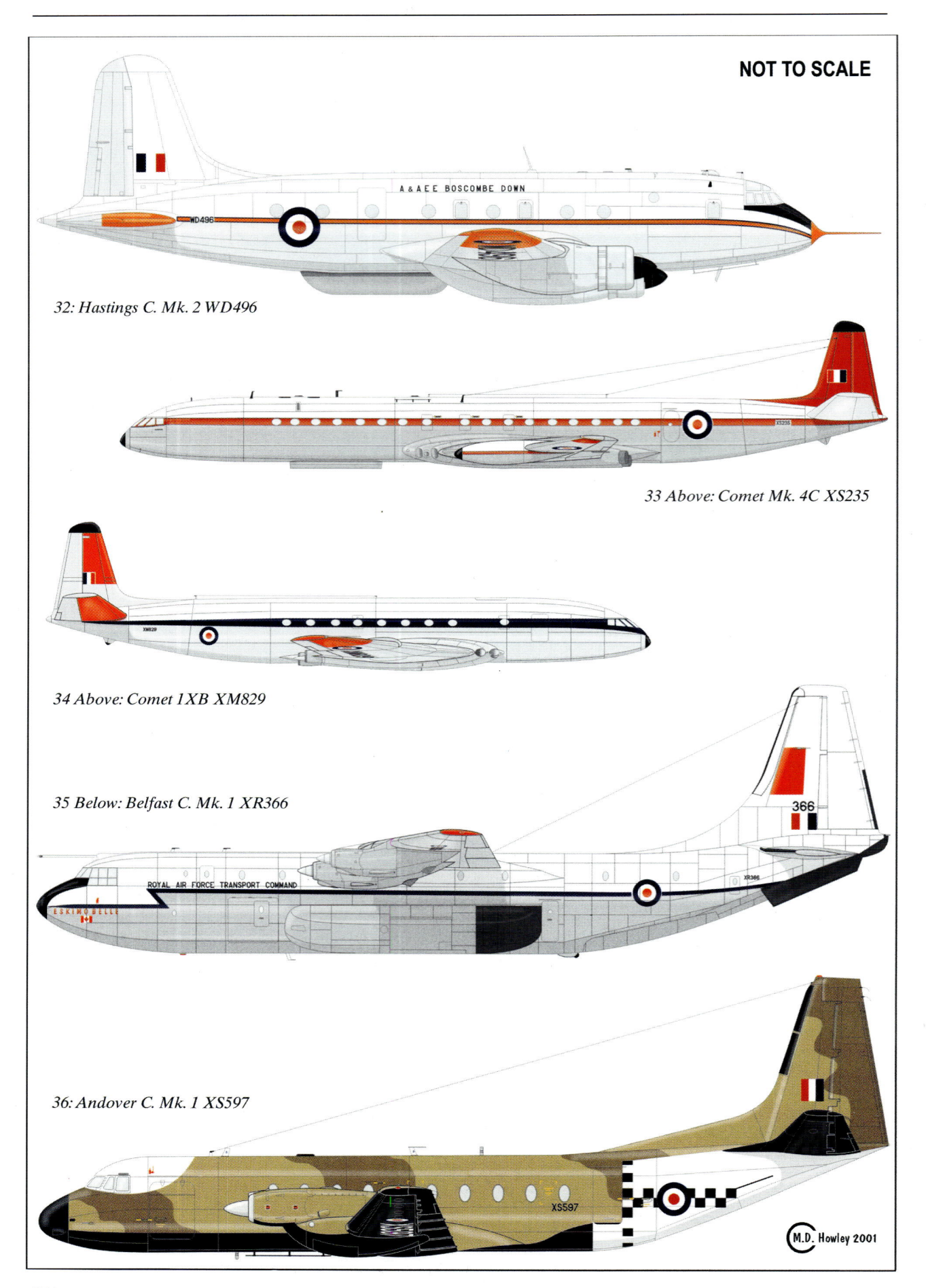

32: Hastings C. Mk. 2 WD496

33 Above: Comet Mk. 4C XS235

34 Above: Comet 1XB XM829

35 Below: Belfast C. Mk. 1 XR366

36: Andover C. Mk. 1 XS597

1/130 SCALE

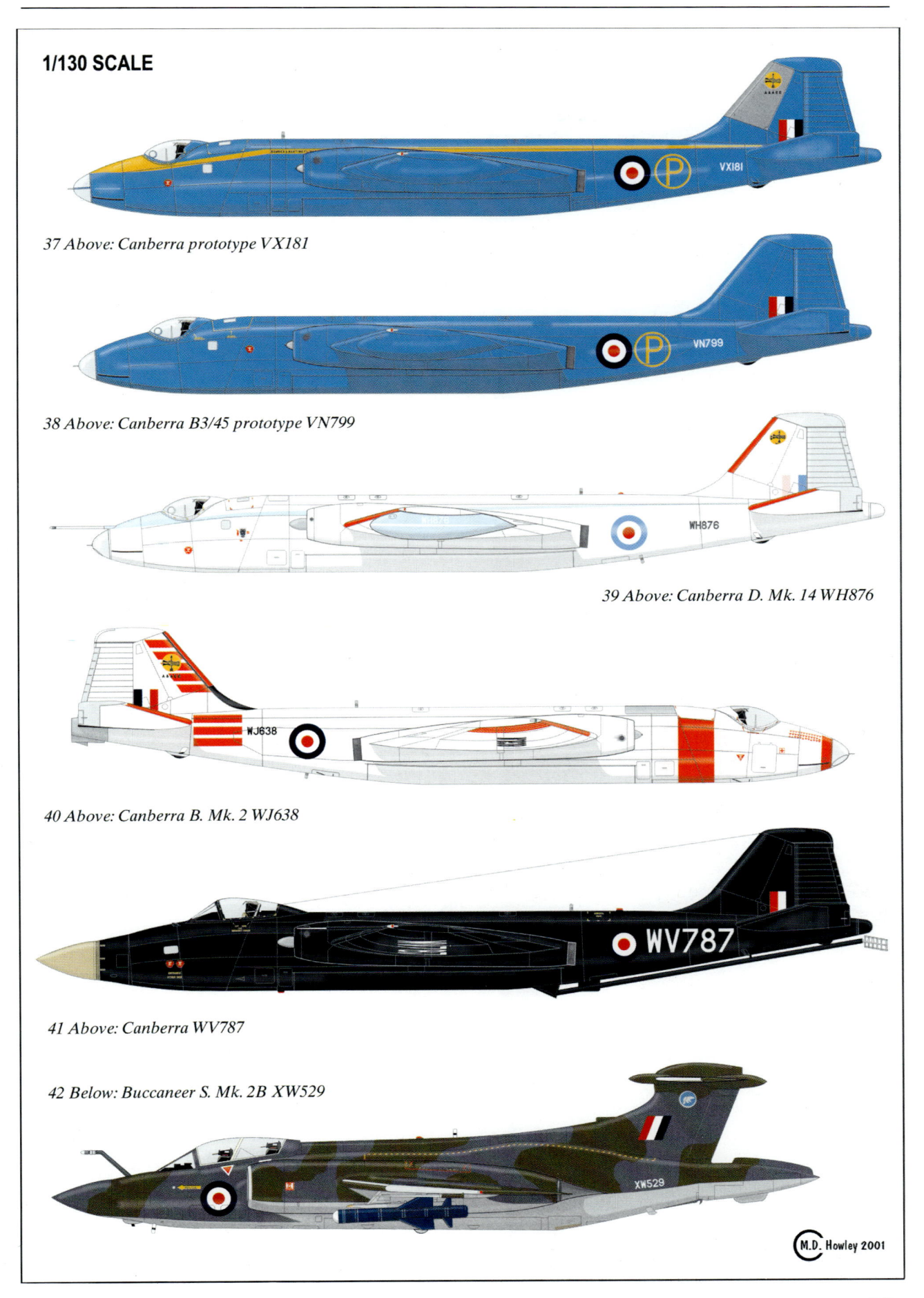

37 Above: Canberra prototype VX181

38 Above: Canberra B3/45 prototype VN799

39 Above: Canberra D. Mk. 14 WH876

40 Above: Canberra B. Mk. 2 WJ638

41 Above: Canberra WV787

42 Below: Buccaneer S. Mk. 2B XW529

M.D. Howley 2001

255

1/144 SCALE

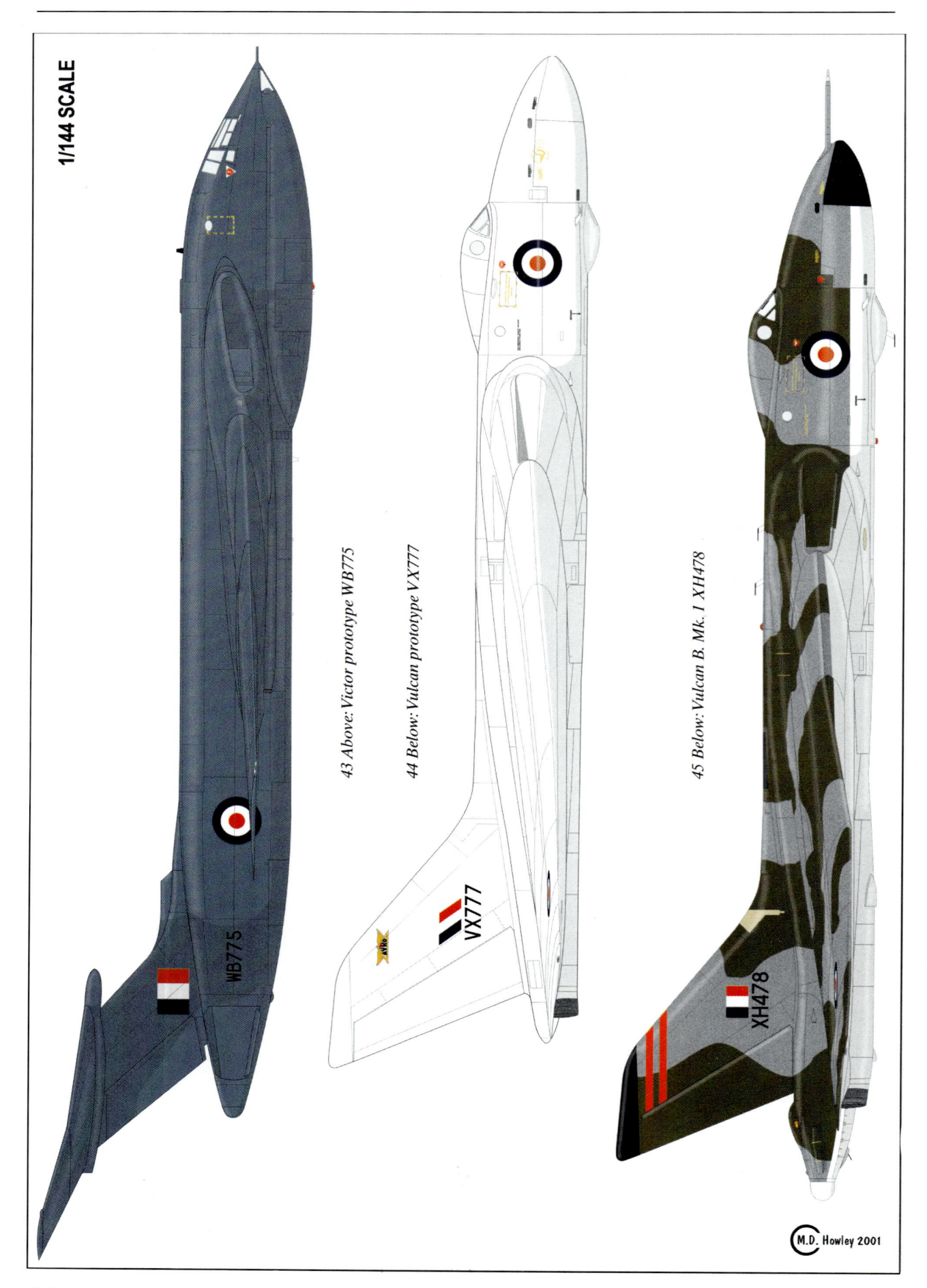

43 Above: Victor prototype WB775

44 Below: Vulcan prototype VX777

45 Below: Vulcan B. Mk. 1 XH478

M.D. Howley 2001

de Havilland Chipmunk

Two Canadian-built Chipmunks, G-AJVD and G-AKDN (Gipsy Major 10) passed handling tests with flying colours at AAEE in late 1948 after radio reception difficulty in 'DN earlier. Adjectives like "excellent" appear in the formal report, a rare accolade; desirable improvements were increases in rudder power and range of nose up trim. Take off run was 170 yd, climb 920 ft/min and ceiling 16,200 ft; top speed was 121 kt. The three items in need of changes, ie, radio, rudder and elevator trim, proved acceptable in WB549, the first production machine from the parent company in England. Intensive flying of WB550 in early 1949 gave no cause for concern, and the slightly enlarged rudder was a further improvement In mid-1958 WP804 (with a tail parachute reluctant to deploy) spun unremarkably both with and without fuselage strakes; similarly a glider hook had no effect on the spin of WP903 in 1961. WP903 with a one-piece canopy had previously been rejected for Royal use. In 1954, WG466 towed a Sedbergh glider, climbing initially at 360 ft/min after taking 600 yd to reach 50 ft on take off; the oil remained cool. Changes to the radio coupled with baggage in the rear compartment placed the CG aft of the previously cleared limit so WP930 made a brief visit in February 1953 for stalling and spinning. All stalls were defined by the starboard wing drop making entry into left spins difficult. Radios were soon approved in WG307 in 1969, and in WK634 in 1974; the PTR170 radio was cleared in WG407. No report has appeared of the outcome of trials by WG419 on aluminium planks and a membrane runway.

Ercoupe 415CD

The interconnected ailerons and rudder (and nose wheel steering) were designed to simplify the pilot's task, particularly during training, on G-AKFC (Continental C75-12) tested from May 1947. It was very easy and generally pleasant to fly, and it was considered that tyro pilots would need less time than with conventional controls to fly solo. Criticisms included the inability to land across the wind and wallowing in even slight turbulence. Many pilots, including newly qualified PPL holders, flew the aeroplane at Boscombe after purchase by the Ministry as VX147, but it suffered frequent unserviceability.

Vickers Varsity

Prototypes. Developed from the Valetta, *ab initio* training of all aircrew trades (later including advanced pilots) was the job of the Varsity. VX828 and VX835 arrived in August and June 1950 respectively, each powered by two Hercules 265. Handling of the latter at aft and forward CG met Service requirements, although the automatic retraction of flaps from full to the take off position occurred at too low a throttle setting on application of power. With flaps fully down and power off, the stall was at 70 kt (37,500 lb) and accompanied by a wing dropping. At the same weight, take off distance to 50 ft varied between 870 yd using a steep initial climb and 1,040 yd for maximum acceleration to the safety speed of 105 kt; distance to stop from 50 ft required 965 yd and careful use of the brakes. Rate of climb reached 1,640 ft/min, ceiling was 26,800 ft and economical cruising speed determined as 232 kt (true), achieving 2.1 nm per gallon of fuel. The novel latching propellers designed to reduce the drag from a failed engine were considered to offer little benefit. Apart from the H2S Mark 4A bombing radar, all the other radio, radar and bombing equipment of VX828 was assessed as satisfactory, and the layout for two pupil navigators considered excellent. All the small bombs and flares for which the pannier under the fuselage was designed could be carried and dropped without difficulty, although loading was awkward.

T Mark 1. WF326 arrived in mid-1951 and left almost immediately for Khartoum where the loading of bombs whose cases reached well over 50°C caused burnt hands. Either Serck or Gallay oil coolers gave satisfaction, but cabin temperatures were excessive, while in cooler climes the heating failed to meet requirements. In 1955 ASR Type A Mk 2 rescue kit achieved clean separation when launched from the entrance door. Contemporary early tests on WF327 included the twin cell launch chute, and landing distance measurements; with 47° flap setting (the optimum) 630 yd were needed from 50 ft. WF417 dropped flares in 1952, and thereafter a stream of Varsities over 20 years cleared avionic equipment as advances were made as follows: WF897 (STR18B HF radio in 1958), WJ939 (sub-miniature radio compass in 1960), WF328 (radio in 1960) WJ887 (testing apparatus for leader cable auto land ground installations in 1963), WJ908 and WJ939 (GPI 4 doppler plus UHF radio and VOR/ILS landing aid in 1965), WF374 (Decca 8A navigator in 1968), WJ918 and WJ944 (TACAN navigation kit in 1969), WJ940 (radio in 1963), WJ947 (TACAN navaid in1962). WL641 (radios in 11962) and WL684 (autolandings in 1964–5).

Handley Page (Reading) HPR2

Prototypes. WE505 (Cheetah 18) arrived some two months after its rival P56 from Percival. The reports are repetitive in the use of the word, "unacceptable." Intended spins became a steep spiral dives with the ailerons locked over, the rudder became ineffective on landing, trimming on the approach was impossible, and the weathercock stability excessive which emphasised the poor rudder power. The ailerons received praise, as did the cockpit layout. Modifications to WE505 included

444: *Varsity T.1 VX835 during its initial assessment in July 1950 when handling and performance were acceptable with minor improvements.* © *Crown Copyright*

445 and 446: *HPR.2 WE496 in the winter of 1950/1 with two attempts to improve handling. The lower picture shows an even taller fin and a mass balance. Although handling was considerably improved by these modifications, the aircraft's spinning behaviour remained unacceptable, and elevator behaviour remained unconventional.* © *Crown Copyright*

a new fin and rudder, interconnected flaps and elevator tab, and shorter undercarriage legs. Handling was slightly improved, but spins remained unconventional, elevator forces became tiring, and there was a marked tendency to nose over with use of wheel brakes. With so many faults unresolved, the HPR2 was not selected, although WE496 returned later with further aerodynamic changes.

Percival Provost

Prototypes. Percival's P56 competed with Handley Page's second design from Reading for selection as the RAF's standard pilot trainer; the P56 won. WE522 (Cheetah 18) arrived in May 1950 and impressed immediately with its handling described as "most satisfactory ... no vices whatsoever." Minor criticisms concerned the invisibility of some instruments behind the left stick, lack of obvious warning before the stall, a suspicion of aileron overbalance at low speed and the need for better sealing to keep out exhaust fumes. The engineers found only insignificant points needing improvement. The Cheetah engine tended to overheat while escorting the Leonides-engined Provost to Khartoum in mid-1951. WE530 suffered a split propeller in March 1951, had a Leonides 25 in October 1951, and handled similarly to WE522 (which had a Leonides125 by mid-1952), with a tendency to enter a left spin on recovery from the right if the control centralisation was at all delayed. Stability remained good; a desirable increase in manoeuvring stick forces needed an increase in tailplane incidence and an increase in inertia weight in the elevator circuit to achieve the desired 4.5 lb/g at aft CG. WG503 (Leonides 25) needed increased cylinder and oil cooling in Khartoum in mid-1951, and some fuel vapour locking occurred. Bulky survival kit and a hot pit with insufficient airflow made life uncomfortable for the pilots, particularly during the 71 hr transit flying. At 4,300 lb and 5,000 ft and 30°C, the take off distance to 50 ft was 480 yd; landings took further.

Mark 1. WV418 (Leonides 126) arrived in February 1953, jettisoned canopies satisfactorily in the blower tunnel, pleased the engineers for its ease of maintenance and handled as well as the prototypes, with the addition of several bursts of 15 sec inverted flight. Inverted spinning on WV421 and WV422 resulted in unacceptable negative g on recovery, and was thus not recommended. 200 hr of intensive flying revealed only one snag—the windscreen wiper was useless and some cockpit lighting was considered superfluous. WV508 aerobatted and navigated, presumably on separate flights in 1953–4, and WV510 had UHF radios in 1961. The two machine guns, RP Mark 8 rockets and 20lb bombs of WV614 in 1954 had no adverse effect on handling, and "were suitable against a primitive enemy;" Burma had ordered the type. Demisting and deicing featured on WV577 in 1955, and a short test kept WV686 at AAEE for nine days in 1960.

T Marks 52 and 53. WV425 (Mark 52) tested the F24 camera in two weeks in November 1960 . In the same year, WW452 (Mark 53) had the F24 vertical camera intended for Muscat.

Hunting Percival Jet Provost and Strikemaster

Existing reports, apparently complete, curiously make no mention of any handling trials on the Marks 1 and 2, although XD674, XD675, XD676 (Mark 1) and XD694 (Mark 2) are all recorded in the servicing records made at AAEE in 1954–5. Indeed, the Jet Provost is the least well documented of any type in the period under review.

T Mark 1. A test fuselage in the blower tunnel in late 1954 gave confidence of safe canopy separation at speeds between 80 and 280 kt. XD674 arrived in November 1954 for stay of six months, possibly involving flying by both AAEE and the firm, while in 1955 XD676 (Viper 101) was handled and reported only by ephemeral letter/postagram, now lost, and XD675 had an engineering appraisal Switching on the fuel booster pump caused deviation of the compass, and resonance in the blind approach aerial system rendered tuning unreliable. This rivetting intelligence is all that has been found on the early trials of the RAF's first *ab initio* jet trainer.

T Mark 2. The short undercarriage was probably assessed during brief visits of XD694 from December 1955.

T Mark 3. Identified as a Mark 3 in the report G-23-1 (Viper 102) weighed 6,278 lb and had no ejection seats in April 1958. Another "easy and pleasant" aeroplane should, it was concluded from the preview handling trial, make a good trainer. Lack of natural stall warning and malfunctioning of the ice detector spoilt the overall impression. Purchased by the Ministry as XN117 (Viper 9), it flew at 7,720 lb up to 325 kt with four RPs in preparation for a trial in Aden. XM356 made five short visits from August 1958 totalling some 70 hr flying. Single fleeting trials on XM354 and XM365 in 1959 were made while XM347 spent a little longer on its performance tests—all three without surviving documentation. Following a high level sortie, XN463 flamed out on a GCA approach and crashed in October 1960 after four weeks investigating overheating of the battery. The trial continued, possibly on XN467 until mid 1961. A six month engineering trial on XN468 involved 120 hr flying from June 1961, while only 15 hr were needed for an unrecorded handling trial of XM383. XM349 and XM350 underwent operational reliability tests, completing 193 and 190 flying hours respectively in under four months; serviceability was good and the minor points raised included water contamination of the hydraulic system on occasion. Spinning with the original tip tanks was unacceptable on XM346 early in 1959, but satisfactory after modifications in mid-1959. Fuel in the new tip tanks

447: HPR.2 WE505 in November 1950 demonstrated several unacceptable handling characteristics, including inability to spin, inadequate rudder power, and excessive out-of-trim stick forces. It compared unfavourably with the Provost. © Crown Copyright

448: Provost T.1 WV614 in mid-1954 with two 0.303in guns and six rockets. Handling remained excellent up to 215 kt and it was a good platform for firing. © Crown Copyright

449: Jet Provost T.5 XS231; the nose probe is well supported. © Crown Copyright

450: Jet Provost T.2 XD694, probably in December 1955. The undercarriage of this version was shorter than the preceding Mark 1, and can be seen retracted here. © Crown Copyright

451: Strikemaster Mk 80 G27-9 or 902 of the Royal Saudi Air Force. Seen in this poor photograph in the environmental hangar (there was no AAEE flying) positioned for engine running into the attenuator. Aircraft systems were tested at elevated temperatures and humidity.
© *Crown Copyright*

452: Fokker S-14 K-1 when tested by AAEE for the second time at Schiphol Holland in January 1954. It was a straightforward looking aeroplane with uncomplicated handling, but remaining under powered, even with the Nene having replaced the Derwent.
© *Crown Copyright*

453 below: French Magister 308 bringing a senior visitor to Boscombe in April 1966. Activity in the background looks typical—a Meteor, Anson and Vulcan on the hangar side, and a Hastings, Beverley, Victor, Vulcan Canberra, two Shackletons and an Argosy opposite.
© *Crown Copyright*

454: Caproni F-5 MM553. Delightful handling was offset by a weak undercarriage, lack of natural stall warning and lack of thrust. © Crown Copyright

455: SIPA 200-02 F-BGVB in June 1954 probably at Villacoublay, Paris. Its viceless handling was offset by woeful performance, but it was considered suitable for ab initio instruction. © Crown Copyright

456: Midge prototype G-39-1 in September 1954, ie only five weeks after the first flight. Limited to 450 kt/0.95M, it made an immediate and favourable impression, but badly needed an airbrake and exhibited lateral rocking on the approach. The proximity to the runway gave the pilot a thrilling sense of speed on take off. © Crown Copyright

457: Gnat Fighter XK741 on a warm day in April 1958 with a pair of 500lb bombs, and two temperarure sensors under the nose. © Crown Copyright

262

during spinning tests was considered to have been responsible for the reluctance of XM456 to recover, leading the two pilots to eject in August 1962. Radios and the Rebecca navaid of XN503 functioned as advertised, as did its IFF/SSR in 1969. XM352 became part of the scenery from early in 1965, and made trials of ejection seats, oxygen equipment (including man mounted regulators), and, in 1970, the Mk 6 PB rocket seat.

T Mark 4. Two of this version feature in the servicing returns, but neither is reported in a surviving document. XP547 (Viper 202) spent five weeks in late 1961 on engineering assessment, and XR701 featured later.

T Mark 5. In April 1967 XS230 completed a preview in which the stalling, lateral and directional characteristics and oscillations at high mach needed improvement. By July, these features had been remedied, and it spent the next seven years on training and support work. From early 1969, XS231 with a pressurised cockpit revised nose and integral fuel tanks handled like the Mark 4, but manoeuvring stick forces were far too high, and turbulence in the approach configuration caused unpleasant yawing. Some interference on UHF was traced to the IFF SSR. XW314 tried the new ultrasonic undercarriage position indicator in conjunction with PTR175 radio; the device worked, and wheels-up landings likely to be reduced as a result.

A **Strikemaster Mark 80** for Saudi Arabia, G27-9, was heated in the Environmental hangar for the firm's trials in 1968.

Fokker S14

An AAEE team travelled to Schipol in May 1952 for a short evaluation of this Dutch side-by-side intermediate trainer. K-1 (Derwent 5) the prototype, proved straightforward, but with heavy controls. It was steady about all axes, and spinning and high Mach behaviour made it an ideal trainer; vibrations with extension of the airbrakes were not thought to be serious. Its usefulness would be limited because the performance fell well short of current fighters and the view for formation was restricted. A second visit found K-1 with a Nene 2; any benefits were not discovered because of structural limitations (12,639 lb) and poor weather. The engineers said it was a "sound design." L-1, a later aircraft, came for jettison trials in the blower tunnel in 1955; the jettison handle needed two hands to pull.

Fouga CM170 Magister

Nr 03 (two Marbore II) at Bretigny had a visit in mid-1953 from AAEE as part of the search for a standard NATO trainer. While being straightforward to fly, the ailerons were very heavy and the rudder far too light, the Mach limit too low and the view from the rear seat inadequate. Workmanship received the engineers' praise. In 1956 aircraft Nr 02 and Nr 12 were flown and found unsuitable for advanced training in view of the previous comments of which only the rudder had been remedied.

Morane Saulnier M-S 755

Nr 01, alias F-ZWRS, (two Marbore II) had unusual engineering but good workmanship when examined at Bretigny in mid-1953. Handling gave no cause for concern, apart from snaking with airbrakes extended and over-sensitive longitudinal trim. However, the speed limits imposed (330 kt and 0.76M) were considered too low.

Caproni F-5

At Ciampino, Rome, MM553 was briefly flown in late 1953 as a potential NATO trainer. The AAEE team was briefed that because the undercarriage had collapsed taxying, no spinning would be permitted. The logic of this apparent *non sequitur* has not been established. However, aerobatics could be "executed with delightful precision." Other comments included the need for changes to instrument layout, more performance, stall warning and more comfortable seats.

SIPA S200

Flown at Villacoublay in June 1954, F-BGVB (Palas) had excellent handling with no vices or adverse features, and thus suitable for *ab initio* training. Nevertheless, considerably more thrust was needed as overshooting was marginal, and cockpit layout seemed haphazard.

Slingsby Cadet

T X Mark 1. The wartime prototype of the single-seat Cadet, TS291, a glider for cadets, stayed on the strength for 20 months from April 1953 for assessment behind a Chipmunk and Tiger Moth. It probably never flew since a parachute could not be fitted as required by current regulations.

458: Dominie T.1 XS709 in 1965/6 when this adaptation of an executive jet was considered suitable for navigation training. Cross wind landings required care as weathercock stability on the ground was poor. © Crown Copyright

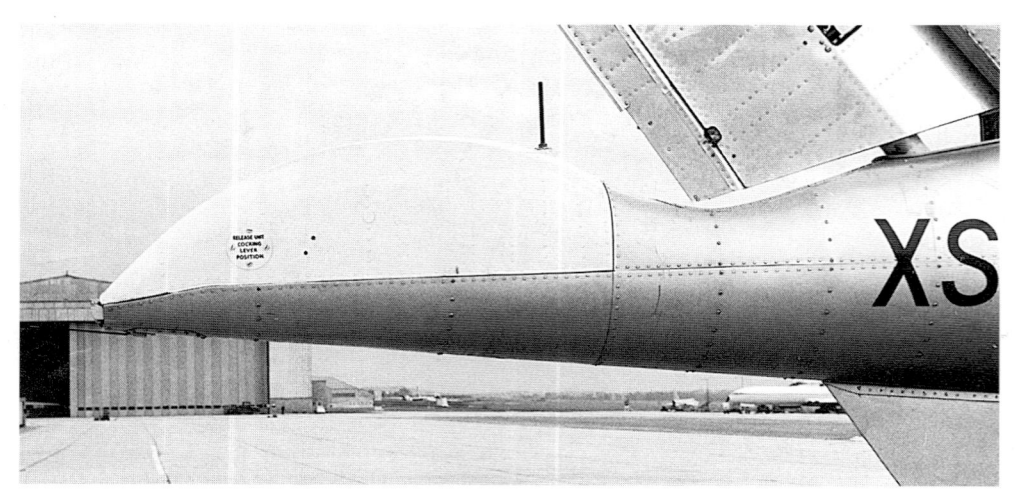

459: The tail parachute installation on Dominie T.1 XS709, fitted for stalling trials in early 1967. © Crown Copyright

460: Pup-150 Reg G-AVLN over Old Sarum in November 1968 for a second "look" by AAEE. Extreme CGs, night and instrument flying confirmed the favourable impression created on the first preview. © Crown Copyright

461: Bulldog T.1 XX514 over the airfield in April 1973. The aircraft appears to be standard. © Crown Copyright

Slingsby Sedburgh

T X Mark 1. WB933, a two seat glider, flew behind the Tiger Moth for trials in 1953, and for training until 1955.

Folland Midge and Gnat

Conceived as a lightweight fighter, the majority of Gnats at AAEE were trainers, but preserved documentation is scant. The firm used Boscombe's runway for much of their own flying as Chilbolton's was a little short.

Midge. Tests in the blower tunnel on a dummy fuselage coincided with preview flying of G-39-1 (Viper 5) in September 1954, only five weeks after the type's first flight. Within the flight envelope of 450 kt/0.95 M cleared by the firm, the overall impression was very favourable for this small lightweight fighter; lateral rocking and lack of drag on the approach received mild rebuke. The Establishment had no hesitation in recommending further development of the fighter Gnat.

Gnat Fighter. In January 1957 A Squadron flew XK739 (Orpheus 1) at Chilbolton making several very short flights (fuel capacity of 165 gal only) as part of preview handling. Restrictions on stalling, spinning and high altitude manoeuvring nevertheless permitted sufficient scope for an encouraging report which noted that further improvement to handling was expected from the fitting of a flying tail and an uprated engine. The 22° droop of the ailerons with extension of the undercarriage gave a more satisfactory approach than that of the Midge. XK767 had among other modifications a flying tailplane with an electric trimmer as part of a complicated longitudinal control system. The aircraft crashed fatally in October 1958 during investigation of the effect of failure of the electric motor; the hydraulically-powered tailplane suffered a seizure of a relay valve making control with the simulated trim runaway impossible. XK741, the replacement, made the take off and landing assessment followed by dropping 500lb bombs. Gun firing trials stopped after some 4,800 rounds had been fired due to the busting of the blast supressor.

Two fighter versions for India, IE1060, tested in the blower tunnel where the automatic jettisoning of the canopy prior to firing of the ejection seat proved effective with consistent delay between the two events and IE1071 in March 1962 for measurement as a calibration aircraft. Radios for Finland received approval in G-39-6 in 1958 concurrently with restricted clearance of XN122 for the RAF's own trials in Aden.

Gnat T Mark 1. The few reports written and preserved include an investigation into the effect of radio transmissions on the compass of XR540 in 1965 and the tests of IFF/SSR of XP505 in 1969. In October 1962, XM696 was written off by A Squadron during a firm's investigation into landing speeds. Cabin conditioning tests were made on XR543 at Idris in late 1963 when the gold film (Sierracote) experimentally applied to the canopy effectively reduced glare but did not keep the cockpit cool on the ground. Other aircraft flown on trials were: XM691 on four occasions (all pressure error measurements) between 1961 and 1967, XM692 for a few handling flights, XM693 for spinning in 1961, XM697 for electrical system evaluation, XM698 (Orpheus 100) for evaluation of the ILS landing aid with the OR946 instrument panel, XM704 for 159 hr flying on operational reliability until September 1962, XM705 for the TACAN navaid and reliability, XP500 (Orpheus 101) for checks of production standard in 1962 and RHAG arrester gear trampling in 1964, and XS110 for trampling the new RHAG in 1974.

FIAT G-82

As part of the search for standardisation in NATO, AAEE flew the prototype G-82 operational trainer with a Nene RN2/21 motor in November 1954. Handling was very easy despite heavy ailerons and rudder overbalance, but no spinning or night flying could be carried out. The rear seat view was poor, and the instrument layout most odd. The engineers found the design and maintainability generally satisfactory. With modifications, the first and second prototypes were tested in April 1955. The powered ailerons gave a disappointing rate of roll, and the airbrakes could not be used at high speed, while the spin was violent and oscillatory with tip tanks empty, although satisfactory with them full.

De Havilland Dominie (monoplane)

T Mark 1. Cleared under civil rules (BCAR), AAEE's role reduced to examining the differences for navigator training; changes of CG involved stalling and the fitting of an anti-spin parachute. XS709 (two Viper 301) was assessed in 1965 as well suited for its role, although the stall lost its natural warning at high altitude and artificial warning became necessary, while cross wind landings could be tricky as, unusually, the aircraft tended to swing out of wind. Equally unusual was the rudder bias to counter asymmetric thrust, a device meeting with approval, and the effective yaw damper. XS710 with XS711 completed 211 hr flying including tests of the navigation equipment—surprisingly unreliable in view of the antiquity if much of it. XS714, primarily engaged on HF radio tests in 1967, also checked the cross wind landing limits. XS726 had the IFF/SSR in 1971.

462: Fournier RF-5 Reg G-AYZX in mid-1971 with two intrepid A Squadron aviators; the type was insuitable for air cadets. © Crown Copyright

463: The two contenders for the RAF's Multi Engine Pilot Trainer (MEPT). The Jetstream 200 G-AXFV (foreground) was well liked—but later production aircraft failed initially to reproduce the favourable handling of this prototype. The Commander N9203N (rear) revealed several shortcomings for the training role. The Jetstream was flown by Capt B J (Jake) Wormworth (Canadian exchange officer) and the Commander by Flt Lt W G (Bill) Gevaux. © Crown Copyright

464: Jetstream T.1 XX475 with an instrumentation nose probe, but lacking the pitch and yaw vanes. © Crown Copyright

Miles Student

This small jet trainer (XS941) spent eight days at Boscombe in August 1958, and probably fired its underwing, podded guns.

Beagle/Scottish Aviation Pup and Bulldog

Pup Srs 2. G-AVLN (O-320-A2B), flown at the firm's airfield in March 1968 at 1,900 lb produced favourable comments, summarised in the report: "... very good handling—well suited for training. Control characteristics ... such that while [the aircraft] was docile to fly, there was sufficient scope for good piloting standards to be achieved by a student." Seven months later, at Boscombe, the comments were reinforced after spinning, night and instrument flying at extreme CGs.

Bulldog. The civil prototypes G-AXEH (IO-360-A1C) at Prestwick, whither Bulldog production had been transferred, and G-AXIG (IO-360-A1B6) at Boscombe were tested under similar arrangements, with the handling being described as better than the Pup. The spin was fast but with consistent recoveries; some cockpit improvements were suggested, including the need for a trim wheel for the left hand.

T Mark 1. XX513 undertook the CA Release flying from March 1973 with only one major fault—the engine stopped during several spins, but always restarted. The PTR170 radio needed an extra aerial. XX514 helped with handling in 1973, XX522 had a new Bendix radio in 1974 and the maximum wind for parking was evaluated in the blower tunnel in 1975.

Fournier RF-5

G-AYZX (Umbach SL 1700E) came to Boscombe in June 1971, immediately on importation from France for assessment as a trainer for air cadets. In addition to sensitivity to even light crosswinds, the low performance, especially the climb, was unacceptable. The flight manual figures for take off and landing were found to be up to 40% optimistic, and the many manufacturing faults attributed to poor quality control.

Scottish Aviation Jetstream

This Handley Page design had become Scottish Aviation's responsibility by the time that G-AXFV (two Astazou XVIC) went to AAEE in mid-1971 for assessment in competition with the North American Rockwell 690 for selection as an RAF trainer. At weights up to 12,500 lb, it had pleasant and straightforward handling with a performance better than the firm's brochure claimed. The favourable impression was reinforced by a successful test landing at forward CG with the elevator control disconnected and using engine power and trim for pitch control. At low speed with high power, as in an overshoot, a divergent phugoid developed, becoming pronounced at an aft CG. However, with a period of 85 sec it was easily controlled, even by tyro pilots. At 130 kt longitudinal stability was neutral. The Establishment recommended several aspects for improvement.

T Mark 1. From July 1973, when XX475 and XX476 appeared, it soon became clear that handling had deteriorated markedly since tests on the civil machine. Longitudinal control, particularly on the approach, became unacceptable on account of the oscillations induced by any control input, whether throttle, flap selection or pitch adjustment; high break out force of the elevator exacerbated the situation. In April 1974, with the reluctant agreement of AAEE, CA Release for instructors' flying only was given. Later stalling of XX475 with an anti spin parachute revealed characteristics which varied from a 90° wing drop to very mild depending crucially on the propeller pitch and configuration; the artificial warning and a stick pusher gave adequate protection for the Service. In the meantime XX479 tried metal strips on the elevator to relieve oscillations with slight benefit in calm conditions; only with the addition of reduced friction in the control runs and other changes was an acceptable standard achieved. Even then, turbulence and crosswind conditions made accurate flying of the short coupled aircraft difficult. Radio in XX489 and further handling continued after 1975.

North American Rockwell 690

Competing with the Jetstream in mid-1971, N9203N (two TPE 331-5-251) had a lively performance, with good stability and controls in 75 hr flying. The aft-most CG tested required to be moved forward, the cockpit required changes and the fuel capacity needed to be increased for acceptability. Weight was 9,850 lb for trials. The engineering assessment found unacceptable safety features.

Slingsby T53B

Assessed as a glider for air cadets at 1,285 lb, 1721 arrived in January 1971, and XV951 was flown at the firm (Kirbymoorside) the following April. Low control forces for manoeuvring and an unacceptable wing drop at the stall meant that the type could not be recommended in its current form; 39 on order were cancelled.

Slingsby Venture

T Mark 1. XW983 (Stamo-MS 1,000 car engine) spent two months from May 1971 flying 32 hours at AAEE prior to joining the Air Cadets. At 1,220 lb the climb was poor, but otherwise handling of this licence-built Falke SF25B was acceptable with minor changes.

Hawker Siddeley Hawk

The preview involving 10½ hr flying at Dunsfold in April 1975 on XX154 (Adour 151) started with the original wing fence and 10 vortex generators on each wing; sorties with and without the MATRA rocket pods were flown. A generally favourable impression was spoilt by lateral unsteadiness and wing rocking on the approach coupled with excessive noise above 480 kt. In addition, with flap and undercarriage down, natural stall warning disappeared. Manoeuvring stick forces met requirements, but the very small stick movements involved gave concern about possible inadvertent overstressing of the airframe. Later, with reductions in the number of vortex generators and the size of the wing fence, unsteadiness and stall warning received approval. XX159 started trials at Boscombe in July 1975.

465: Venture T.1 XW983 in July 1971 under evaluation for the Air Cadets. The pilot is Sqn Ldr I (Ian) Strachan whose extensive gliding experience was put to good use in this motorised glider. © Crown Copyright

466: Hawk T.1 XX154 on early trials of the MATRA rocket pods. The familiar nose probe with vanes was fitted. © Crown Copyright

CARRIER AEROPLANES

467: Sea Venom FAW.20 WM507 in late 1954 with eight rockets; the Sea Venom was the 27th type to use the RP Mk VIII installation. Up to 500 kt firing was satisfactory. © Crown Copyright

Fairey Swordfish

General purpose bombing by LS364 ceased in August 1945.

Grumman Wildcat

JV875, a Mark VI, departed in late-1945 after RP trials.

Grumman Hellcat

Mark IIs, JX901, which persevered with successful American RP Mark 5 trials until November 1945, and JX998 had gone by late-1945.

Fairey Barracuda

Mark II. Successful endurance tests were completed in September 1945 of mineral oil and synthetic seals in LS837 (Merlin 32).

Mark III. With the reintroduction of the wartime Barracuda MkIII into front line service, RJ924 confirmed handling as acceptable for deck landings in 1947. Two years later, RJ769 (Merlin 32) carried 16 sonobuoys, aerial leading, under the wings with 10 more in the rear cockpit; release speed was restricted to 200 kt. In 1951, on RJ916, 28 sonobuoys (Type T1945) could be carried and released up to 170 kt. Anti-submarine and other flares (on RJ919), and ASR gear Type G joined the Fleet's armoury after AAEE's tests (on RJ781 in 1952).

Mark V. Many of the Barracuda's early handling vicissitudes reappeared in the Griffon powered Mk V. At the end of the war improvements on PM940 (Griffon VIII) included spring tabs on the ailerons and rudder, but the elevator remained too sensitive. Refinement to the tabs on RK535 in 1946 further improved handling, but without benefit to the longitudinal characteristics. Consumption was low (2.98 anmpg), giving a range of 840 nm on the 300 gal carried; maximum speed of 211 kt occurred at 10,500 ft. PM941 was weighed on arrival in September 1945; with 2,000 lb of stores and full fuel the total was 16,516 lb. Handling with two 250 lb bombs under each wing revealed a left wing down tendency considered to be just acceptable. In production standard, maximum weight was restricted to 15,250 lb, thus preventing carriage of a 2,000 lb bomb on RK531 in 1947. RK533 tested the radio in mid-1946.

468: *Barracuda V RK535 in January 1947 when the type was forced to continue flying in front line service, and Fairey was still trying to get the aerodynamics right! The spring tab on the rudder was at last acceptable, but the aileron circuit remained stiff.* © *Crown Copyright*

469: *Barracuda III RJ916 in August 1951 showing the load of 24 Type 1945 non-directional sonobuoys. Carriage was satisfactory upto 250 kt, and release up to 200 kt.* © *Crown Copyright*

470: *Firefly T.1 MB750 in late 1947 probably. It was considered suitable for converting pilots to type, but jettisoning the hoods was a danger to both pilots.*

Fairey Firefly

One of a trio of wartime designs needing much development to "get right", the Firefly continued in production until 1956 in many versions which have been difficult to identify with confidence.

Mark I. Z1909 had finished RP work, and DT985 its bombing by mid-1945, while MB465 continued taking air/air photographs until an icy runway claimed its undercarriage in December 1946. MB647 continued research into gun development until October 1947. Z2033 made a fleeting visit in September 1947 for spinning—possibly a reported rogue. AAEE modifications rendered the RP Mark VIII installation (16x60 lb head rockets) acceptable on PP427 in 1946, but the addition of a pair of 90 gal drop tanks caused excessive acceleration (g) on releasing the stick in dives. The four 20 mm guns of PP468 fired well, but wing twisting spoilt accuracy; serious damage to MB621 in October 1947 curtailed trials of window and flares. Several stages of improvements to the gun feed mechanism failed to overcome the unsatisfactory gun bounce in 1948 in PP605; a pilot failed to control a lurch on take off in 1949, and clipped the superstructure of *HMS Illustrious*. PP639 came twice to sharpen up pilots prior to deck trials but the engine failed too far from the airfield in March 1954. PP562 and possibly MB735 may have done something at AAEE.

Lack of Naval interest at first in a Firefly trainer led to the appearance of the civil G-AHYA in August 1946, retaining its Griffon XII, but fitted with dual controls. The two pilots had good views, and handling replicated that of the fighter; rudder overbalance was noted in the climb. The same aircraft reappeared as MB750 in late 1947 for official tests in the blower tunnel; both occupants were in danger from jettisoned hoods. Another trainer, DK550, is shown in the maintenance return for September 1952.

T Mark 2. Also a trainer (and duplicating the mark number of the earlier version) converted from the Mark I, MB520 was assessed for bombing and gunnery instruction in 1949 and 1951 respectively. Twin GGS V gunsights had electric ranging considered much superior to the manual version.

T Mark 3. Designed for observer training (and also converted from the Mark I), the only trials showed some danger to the rear occupant when PP391 was put into the blower tunnel.

FR and TT Mark 4. The speed of Z2118 (Griffon 72S) was limited to 322 kt due to the temporary dorsal fin, fitted in a successful attempt to cure handling problems found in wartime. From mid-1946, the Griffon 74 of Z1835 had adequate cooling when carrying full external ordnance, provided that the pilot gave judicious attention to the position of the radiator flap. The principle post-war trials of this fighter-reconnaissance version were of production machines, four of which arrived in 1947, all suffering major accidents within just over a year. TW694 suffered an engine failure, landing wheels up, in April 1947 shortly after arrival; the following December the pilot became lost in TW693, ran out of fuel and force-landed; RP trials had been partially completed. TW689 had completed jettison tests of the nacelle tank when the tail oleo failed. The damage was repaired and, for the first time on any aircraft, rough ground trials made; the Firefly was considered good on the evidence of this trial. In August 1948, the month after the previous trial, TW690 was severely damaged after its tailwheel collapsed following a year's general performance work, including pressure error checks. With modifications to avoid interference between rockets and guns, PP482 cleared the RP installation, but in the cockpit, the airspeed indicator had to be moved to avoid being hidden by the gunsight. After radio tests, TW722 continued as a photographic platform until 1949. The new single piece hood of MB649 jettisoned cleanly in early 1950, as did the ASH nacelles of TW735 whether the undercarriage was up or down. Fleeting visits were paid by TW718 (1948), and VG964 (1951).

Target towing modifications and trials of VH143 preceded transfer to the Royal Canadian Navy.

AS and TT Mark 5. Intended for the reconnaissance, night fighting or antisubmarine roles, TW746 had, in fact, radios for all three on tests in 1948; not, perhaps, surprisingly, interference occurred between them. 12 sonobuoys (four each wing and four under the fuselage) were released cleanly up to 200 kt. VT393 made six visits between July 1948 and September 1952; the first included acceptance of the great improvement afforded by power folding of the wings, although unlocking remained a manual action. Thereafter, RPs, bombs, sonobuoys and mines were cleared singly and in combination with varying degrees of effort and modification. Among the last flame damping tests were made on VT477 in 1949; shrouds gave the better results. VT428 from January 1951 extended the range of stores to include ASR Type G rescue gear, American high velocity rockets, and guide chutes to carry spent cartridges clear of various stores. WB381 (1950) and WB402 (1951) also served at AAEE.

Banner targets could be towed without difficulty by WB406 using a Type G winch under the fuselage, but the 32 ft span target was damaged or disintegrated at speeds above 150 kt.

AS Mark 6. Returning for its sixth visit in the guise of an antisubmarine Mark 6, VT393 re-cleared the RP and bombing installations. WD845 had a large sonobuoy container requiring several improvements, including a fairing, to make it compatible with rocket firing. Modifications were also needed to the radios of WB343.

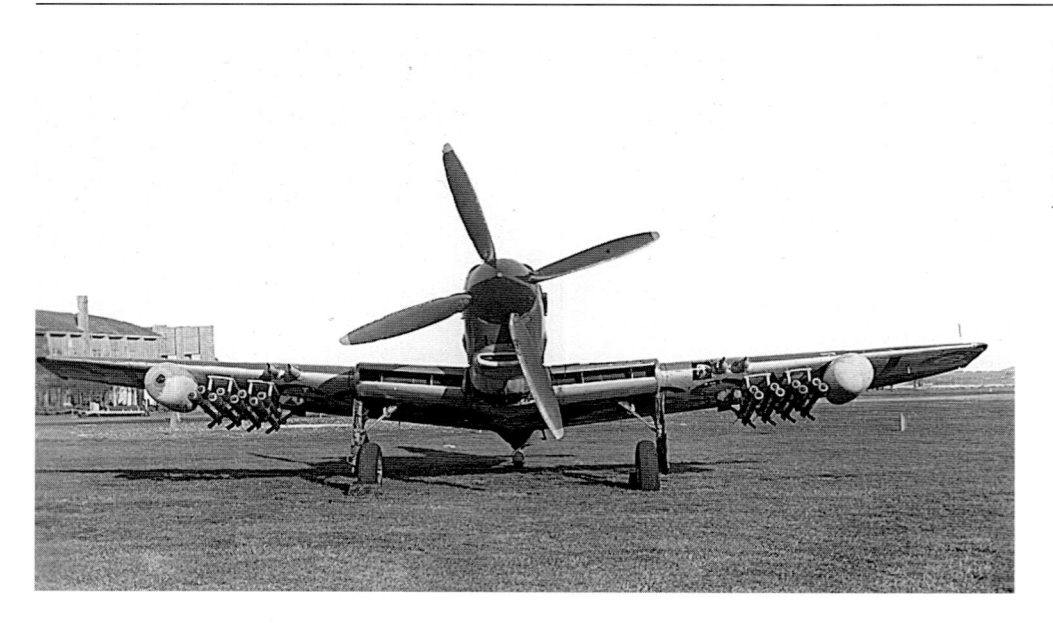

471: *Firefly FR.4 TW693 in mid-1947 with sixteen 60lb head rockets on the standard Mk VIII installation. Minor modifications were needed to avoid interference on firing.* © *Crown Copyright*

472: *Firefly TT.5 WB406 in 1951. The winch (a Type G) beween the undercarriage legs and various devices to protect the control surfaces can be seen.*

473: *Firefly FR.4 TW693 with sonobuoy containers outboard of the undercarriage doors. The opening in the front of the starboard underwing tank is interesting.*

474: Firefly A.S.6 WD918 seen in Naval markings, arrived at AAEE in May 1954.

475: Firefly AS.7 MB757 in November 1949. Actually a Mk 1 with only the aerodynamic attributes of the Mk 7, it had three handling shortcomings which, as it was an interim type, the Navy was expected to accept.
© Crown Copyright

476: Firefly A.S.7 with crude flame dampers and sonobuoy containers in July 1951 for deck work and handling. Some deterioration in handling was apparent, particularly at low speed.
© Crown Copyright

477: *Firefly AS.7 WJ215 in April 1952 with high aspect ratio fin and rudder which cured overbalance, but the aeroplane remained unpleasant to fly. © Crown Copyright*

478: *Seafire F.47 VP463 in April 1949. The 90gal belly tank made little difference to handling which was considered poor longitudinally until a larger inertia weight was fitted in the control run. © Crown Copyright*

479: *Seafire F.45 LA443 in about August 1945 shortly before departure. It had an interesting rudder with wide chord, a fixed tab, a trim tab which appears to be split into two, and an unpleasant looking hook. © Crown Copyright*

480: *Seafire F.46 LA541 in early 1946 with bubble canopy and contra-rotating propeller—the fin therefore lacks the large tabs of the Mk 45.*

The torpedo system of WD918 took two months work in 1954; meanwhile very quick appearances were put in by WD848 (photography in 1954), WD882 (trials for Royal Australian Navy in 1952), WD886 (1952) and WH629.

AS and T Mark 7. With a third seat in mock up and other changes, MB757 retained the Griffon 37, and also exhibited the lack of stall warning, excessive rudder forces and tightening in turns so much a feature of earlier Fireflies; the Establishment felt that the Navy would not require improvements at this stage. In July 1951, the first proper Mark 7, WJ215 (Griffon 59), needed improved brakes, and, in particular, better low speed handling for deck work. A slightly enlarged fin and rudder helped at low speed, but the high aspect ratio tail organs tested in mid-1952 cured the directional problems; the aircraft remained unpleasant to fly. WJ216 had improved brakes and cockpit layout, but the view for deck landing at night was restricted; this conclusion probably followed collapse of the undercarriage in February 1952 during night landings on the dummy deck. WJ148 had extensive radio and radar equipment for finding the bad guys underwater; it all worked well except for the poor range of IFF. After checking the bombing facilities, WJ146 examined the handling at forward and aft CGs; the comment is illuminating, "No new adverse features were found."

Two trainer versions, WJ194 spent at least three years to July 1961 on an miscellany of tasks and WK367 may have tried jettisoning of wing bombs.

Supermarine Seafire

Mark IIC. Some unrecorded propeller checks involved NM938 in mid-1947.

Mark III. Wartime trials, mostly of external stores, continued on PR314 until early 1946; no significant carbon monoxide entered the cockpit with the hood open. The firing of 188 rockets in salvoes of eight or four cleared the RP Mark VIII installation of PX921 in late 1945, while the metal elevator of RX338 proved superior to the earlier fabric variety, but with variations between aircraft. Prior to joining the French Navy, SP182 flew at AAEE with an elongated fuel tank under the fuselage.

F Mark 15. The metal elevator of SR490 was equally advantageous on this mark, while the American AN/APX-1 radio worked well in SW793. Handling of SW813 with a fuselage bomb was uneventful in 1946.

F Mark 17. A slight swing on take off resulted in the destruction of SX121 in April 1946 as it hit the Brodie apparatus, and its radio trials were completed by SX272 after repositioning the IFF aerial. A metal elevator, tear drop canopy and a 3 lb inertia weight in the elevator circuit characterised SX153 with satisfactory handling, including a 50 gal drop tank. Spinning SX157 with no external stores was normal in 1946. A 30 ft banner target on an 800 ft long rope was within the capability of SP324 whose engine remaining adequately cool in 1951. In 1946-7, four Mark 17s completed armament clearance. SX297 and SX361 did the RPs, although firing from under 50 ft was difficult as the nose obstructed the sighting, SX389 needed the gun sight to be raised for acceptable aiming, and SX360 did the bombs and external fuel tank.

F Mark 45. The Griffon 85 powered the contra-rotating propellers of LA446, with pleasant and easy handling with no directional trim change with alterations to speed and power, of particular benefit on the approach. LA443, retaining the Griffon 61, carried and dropped bombs of up to 500 lb at speeds up to 450 kt; LA498 tested the radios.

F Mark 46. Spinning of TM383 (Griffon 67) at the fore and aft limits of CG was normal with the new empennage of this mark. No report has been found of the handling trial of LA541, nor of the RP with 50 gal drop tank on LA564. LA552, which caught fire after the undercarriage collapsed following an energetic turn off the runway on landing in July 1946, had just completed clearance of the RP Mark VIII installation.

F Mark 47. PS944, the first to arrive in November 1946, concentrated on deck landing technique; 70 kt proved the best indicated airspeed for the approach from which a three point landing was easy giving a rate of descent at touch down of 7.2 ft/sec. Handling, described as satisfactory by wartime standards, included neutral stability in the climb, low stick force per g, and non-linear increase in rudder force with displacement; the Establishment recommended compliance with current standards. In 1949 PS944 returned with strips on the elevator trailing edge, thus raising usable mach number from 0.78 to 0.82—an academic point for the pilot who had no mach meter. Previously, in 1948, PS952 (Griffon 88) demonstrated up-to-date handling with a 13 lb inertia weight and a spring tab for the elevator. However, the following year, VP463 with a 90 gal drop tank had longitudinal behaviour worse than before, until it was realised that the previous small inertia weight was fitted in error; in 1949 the heavier device gave satisfaction, although rudder overbalance could be induced.

Guns sometimes stopped firing under negative g in PS946, but results were otherwise approved, as was the gunsight GGS Mk 4B in VP449 in 1948. Intensive flying occupied PS954 from November 1947, deck landing trials justified the presence of PS949 in 1947 and PS948 until damaged following engine failure in October 1948. The final trials took three months in 1950 on VP437 clearing wing bombs.

481: Seafire F.47 PS946 in mid-1947 in a delightful cloudscape. Some stoppages occurred during firing of the guns under negative g.

482: Firebrand T.F.4 EK692 in June 1946 with airbrakes extended. They gave very light stick forces, and much buffeting. The Navy accepted these failings, but the Establishment had misgivings. © Crown Copyright

Blackburn Firebrand

Mark III. Wartime trials continued on DK408 (cure for wing flexing on gun firing), DK393 (dive brakes with unacceptable buffet- tests ended with an engine failure in September 1945), and DK392 (modifications to prevent CO gases entering cockpit). DK394 came later with a satisfactory remote sensing compass.

Mark IV. With the Centaurus IX, EK602 weighed 16,639 lb carrying a 1,900 lb torpedo and 239 gal of fuel, had a new radio (TR5043) and had poor static longitudinal stability at low speeds; the rudder was an improvement. In December 1945 EK616 dived at up to 302 kt carrying a Mark XV torpedo with a modified air tail. Sixteen 60 lb head RPs under EK605 proved too many for lateral trim; eight were just right, although longitudinal problems remained. Other armament included bombs up to 1,000 lb, a torpedo or mine under the fuselage. EK692 arrived in January 1946 with horn balances on the elevator and with tailplane incidence increased by three degrees. These major changes proved effective up to 380 kt, but dive brakes induced buffeting, and stick forces for manoeuvring were very light. The Navy accepted these shortcomings in the face of the Establishment's misgivings. EK736 benefitted from mark III experience and remained free of CO gas. The engine failed in mid-trial on EK630, but sufficient work had been done to show that some cylinders ran hot. EK691 came for eight weeks in early 1950.

Mark 5. While EK743 flew intensively, handling of EK742 focused on the proposed interconnection giving five degrees of flap on selection of dive brakes in a successful attempt to reduce buffet; for the trial, selection was made manually. An engine failure in November 1951 ended its career. Automatic interconnection on EK844 proved reliable in late-1949 after earlier disappointments. "Good" was the comment on powered ailerons in EK732 in 1948, but deck landings were not recommended in the event of hydraulic failure when roll control became marginal. Taking off at 14,845 lb without stores gave a maximum rate of climb of 2,720 ft/min with 2,700 rpm and plus 8$^{1}/_{2}$ psi boost; flying at 140 kt gave very economical cruising (over three miles per gallon), but this consumption is not translated into range in the report. Gun firing from EK848 in 1948 required deflectors to prevent damage, but a pair of ASR Type G rescue gears needed no modifications to EK655 in 1951. The reason for EK778's visit is unknown.

Grumman Avenger

Urgently required before the Gannet could be ready, the Avenger re-entered naval service in 1954; it was the 22nd type to be fitted with the RP Mark VIII installation.

Mark II. A ground trial on JZ625 lasted two months to January 1946 assessing the loading and handling of 1,000 lb (Uncle Tom) rockets.

Mark III. The trial of American RP Mark 5 on JZ635 was terminated in December 1945; several shortcomings had been found. In the same month, cockpit contamination was confirmed in the observer's position of JZ689 (R 2600-20). Some 20 Uncle Tom rockets, fired from ten inch tubes, completed the air firing tests in KE439 in 1947.

AS Mark 4 and TBM-3. The loan of a TBM-3 (No 53358) in 1953 gave early handling experience of the type about to be re-introduced into the Navy. In September 1953, XB355, joined later by XB358, arrived for handling and firing trials of the RP Mark 8 installation; speeds between 150 and 230 kt were suitable for firing. Fitting the ASV 19a radar in place of the American AN/APS-4 in XB358 attracted only minor comments; 1955 trials of the Mark 30 torpedo dropped from the bomb bay also went smoothly.

Chance Vought Corsair

Of the three Corsairs remaining at the end of hostilities, JT406, a Mark II soon left, but the Mark IVs, KD835 and KD903, were retained until 1946 and may have completed their RP and bombing trials respectively.

Grumman Tigercat

TT349 lingered unflown at Boscombe until early 1946.

Fairey Spearfish

A single Spearfish, RA356, was flown at AAEE on handling trials between 14 and 17 December 1946; no report of this large (22,000 lb) carrier borne attack aircraft appears to have been written. The type had been cancelled at the end of the war.

de Havilland Sea Hornet

F Mark 20. In mid-1947 PX219 (Merlin 130/1) had folding wings, but nevertheless gave good results firing rockets. The radios of TT191 (Merlin 134/5) received a qualified acceptance; the airspeed indicator under-read by 7 kt at 310 kt, an unusually large discrepancy. This aircraft then investigated the drag effect of various stores

483: Firebrand TF.4 EK605 in March 1947, the month that the trial of the rocket installation was terminated. The arrangement of rockets is unusual, and the clamps on the wing tips may be related to the setting up procedure. The torpedo carrier is under the fuselage. © Crown Copyright

484: Avenger II JZ622 in late 1945 with a fearsome looking quadruple tube rocket weighing 1,000lb under each wing. the loading hand-winch can be seen. © Crown Copyright

485: A 1,000 lb rocket on its trolley about to leave the bomb dump for fitting to the Avenger. © Crown Copyright

over a wide range of operating conditions joining three others for clearance flying—TT186, TT188 and TT189. The variety of bombs, rockets, photoflashes, mines and depth charges belied the "Fighter" designation. The type of store carried had a pronounced effect on behaviour at aft CG; for example, with rockets alone, handling was pleasant and similar to the clean aircraft, whereas with 1,000 lb bombs, with the same CG, increasing speed above 350 kt required a pull force. Intensive flying of TT195 stopped in December 1948 when it was destroyed by fire on the ground as the oxygen cylinders exploded. TT205 (Aug 47) & TT190 (Feb 49) appeared briefly.

Described by the Establishment as an F R Mk 20, TT248 appeared in October 1947 with excessive stick forces due to the elevator bungee having been removed. Returning with a 10% increase in elevator horn area, good handling was obtained after trying various inertia weights—8 lb was the best. The aileron trimmer needed extra authority.

NF Mark 21. The first of the night fighter variant to be flown at Boscombe, PX230 (Merlin 130/1) met with disaster in May 1947 three weeks after arrival when diving at 480 mph(sic) the port engine detached from the airframe; the pilot left by parachute. Trials continued with PX239 both with and without 100 gal tanks; the rudder became too light and the ailerons buffeted at high speeds. Radios and radar in VV430 (Merlin 134/5) functioned adequately, but the observer's cockpit left much to be desired both in layout and space. Performance data at 17,160 lb included a maximum speed of 363 kt, climb of 2,515 ft/min and ceiling 32,400 ft; 1,000 lb bombs could be carried up to 350 kt—useful in a night fighter! In 1951 ASR gear passed its tests in VV959.

PR Mark 22. Handling of TT187 duplicated that of the Mark 20, although the safe limiting speed when carrying tanks was reduced to 290 kt. Modified tank connectors were cleared by AAEE on the evidence of jettison trials by the firm in VW930.

Hawker Sea Fury

F Mark 10. The first prototype, SR661, arrived in November 1945 for handling checks with a Centaurus XII motor driving the four-bladed propeller fitted to early production aircraft; the only surviving report is about the satisfactory spinning in late 1947. SR666 had four 20 mm Mk V star guns in the wing stubs while the ammunition for the outer pair was housed in the wings; nevertheless, the arrangement worked well, although the rate of fire remained slow at 630 rounds per minute. The first production Sea Fury, TF895, came to Boscombe in late 1946 but left no permanent record of its activities. TF896 (Centaurus XVIII) weighed-in, and promptly crashed after the engine disintegrated in May 1947. After repair, this aircraft returned for extensive handling and release tests of bombs (for the FB.11), rockets, and, in 1949, ASR Type G; the major deficiency was the absence of an aileron trimmer. TF898 established a forced landing technique for the type which was considered to be very difficult; its undercarriage collapsed after a particularly heavy landing on the trial in April 1948. Service pilots were recommended to make overshoots from practice forced landings. Previously handling had been praised after full tests on TF900, and possibly TF950, in the latter half of 1947, with an aileron trimmer the only omission. The following year, TF897 handled without noticeable change when fitted with a larger tailplane and elevator intended for the trainer version. By that time, TF902 (109 hr) and TF908 (119 hr) had flown intensively, including deck landings, without major defect, and TF962 had tested the radios. Carriage, feeding and jettison of 45 and 90 gal drop tanks gave rise to few comments after trials, possibly on TF922.

FB Mark 11. TF958, the first of that ilk, jettisoned the various stores, and investigated the handling at the aft CG which could be achieved with them; the existing limit was retained since a position any further aft caused a rapid deterioration in behaviour. Its days ended after a wheels-up landing in February 1949. A larger inertia weight in VW588 in 1950 restored acceptable handling at the new aft position of CG; however, it was recommended that the smaller weight should be used if CG was not at the extended aft position. The records of flights at high mach number have proved ephemeral. The continuing absence of an aileron trimmer in TF986 remained a problem during trials of asymmetric loads in 1949, but 16 RPs with high explosive or armour piercing heads could be fired, the new standard gunsight was satisfactory, and deflectors stopped empty cases from

486: Sea Fury F.10 SX666 in February 1946 with wings folded. Engineering of the folding mechanism was complicated by the need for the ammunition for the outer gun to be in the folding section. © *Crown Copyright*

487: Avenger AS.4 XB355 in January 1954 with various underwing stores including six rockets which were sucessfully fired between 150 and 230 kt. © Crown Copyright

488: Spearfish prototype RA356 at about the time of its visit to AAEE in December 1946. A report of any trials has yet to be found.

489: Sea Hornet F.20 PX219 with RP rail attachments under the wing, and aerial on the fin fillet. Wartime blister hangars are seen in the background. © Crown Copyright

490: Sea Hornet NF.21 PX239 in early 1948 showing off its thimble-like nose for the radar and bomb carriers under the wings, an odd combination for a night fighting aeroplane. © Crown Copyright

491: Sea Fury FB.11 VW226 in 1951/2 with a pair of window (later "chaff") launchers not seen on another type. They needed minor improvements. © Crown Copyright

492: Sea Fury T.20 VX818 in May 1949 with a pair of 1,000 lb bombs which had little effect on handling. The instructor's periscope characterises the Mark. © Crown Copyright

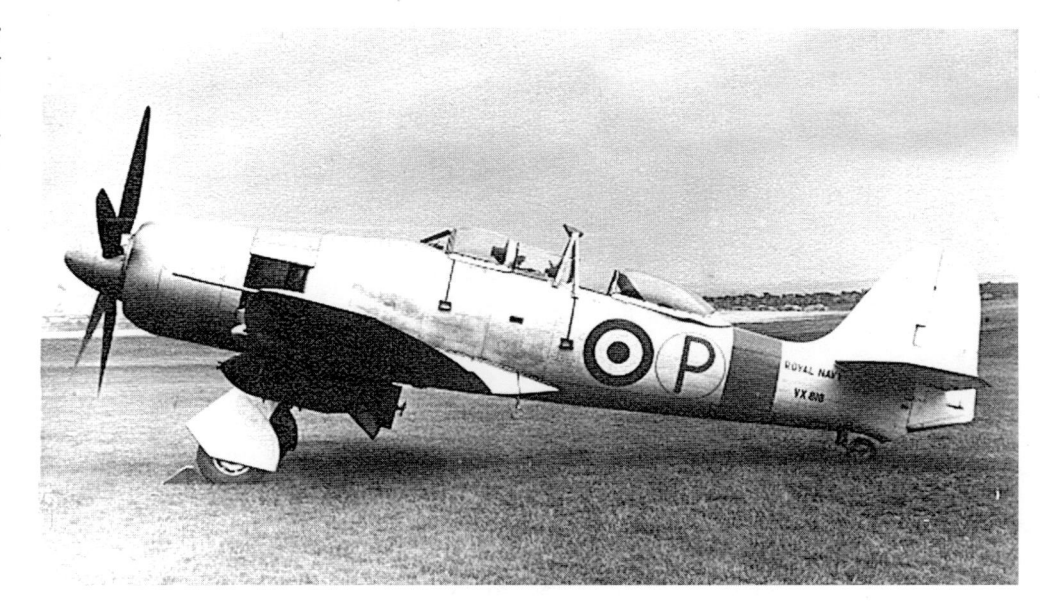

493: Sturgeon TT.2 VR363, probably in March 1950 after the radiator flaps had been modified to reduce excessive trim change with their operation. It was easy and pleasant to fly. © Crown Copyright

494: Attacker prototype TS413 in mid-1948 when brief trials did not produce sufficient data for a decision to be made on the suitability of the type for deck operations. © Crown Copyright

495: Attacker prototype TS409 in late 1949, marked with the sign of the ejection seat. The long stroke undercarriage was an advantage, but the spoilers were not. © Crown Copyright

496: Originally taken to illustrate the G 45 camera gun, this photograph is used here to illustrate the large lump of lead needed to keep the CG respectable on Attacker F.1 WA469. © Crown Copyright

striking other stores. Later, mines and sonobuoys extended the variety of weapons. The radios of TF962 were soon approved, permitting the aircraft to complete deck landings with equally favourable results, after an unusually large number of airfield practices. An interesting divergence of opinion between the firm and the Establishment occurred over the extended range of the rudder trim in VR920; Hawker reported overbalance, AAEE found none. Minor trials of Type B RP installation and other changes followed. American five inch rockets could be fired up to 425 kt, but jettison speed was limited to 380 kt if 90 gal tanks were fitted; VW226 was the aeroplane used. Rocket assisted take offs (RATO) in VW588 were straightforward, and, in 1952, VW228 towed a 30 ft banner target; engine cooling was forecast to be inadequate in tropical areas.

T Mark 20. The two seat VX818 made standard tests, plus assessment of dual gunsights, made acceptable by the harmonisation of the rear seat's mirrors. It handled like a mark 11, but escape needed the rear canopy to be jettisoned at a speed greater than 210 kt, together with the front being slightly open. VX298 spent nearly two years from February 1950 on clearance work, including radio, window launcher, heating (poor at high altitude), RATO, experimental work on early electro-magnetic release units, and five inch rockets. In 1952, procedures were evolved on WG656 to overcome difficulties reported by the RN when firing tiered RPs with drop tanks on. Two Sea Furies were involved in events pointing to the future: spinning clearance for the T Mark 20 was recommended on the evidence of trials by the firm (Hawker), and VZ345 arrived from Cologne, Germany in October 1974 for use by the apprentices.

Short Sturgeon

Lack of suitable peacetime opponents to whom to be offensive led the Navy to select the Sturgeon for inoffensive target towing; although as late as 1947 AAEE tested the four nose-mounted 0.5 in guns in the ground rig.

Mark 1. A party from Boscombe took RK787 for carrier work immediately following arrival in May 1947.

TT Mark 2. VR363 (Merlin 140) was examined from March 1949 by the maintainers who liked the straightforward servicing, but considered that it was possible to cross connect the flying controls. Easy and pleasant handling in the air was spoilt by a large trim change with operation of the radiator flaps; rapid modification by Short effected a cure. Deck trials in May 1949 and January 1950 revealed marginal aileron control on the approach, while single engine landings on the deck were feasible provided a "wave off" (overshoot) did not become necessary; the undercarriage could not be raised if the port engine had failed. Normal climb reached 34,800 ft, at a maximum rate of 2,030 ft/min at 9,800 ft; the highest cruising speed was 282 kt at 23,200 ft. The radios in TS475 worked in 1950, and external stores (flame and smoke floats) separated cleanly in 1951–2. An H-type of winch in VR371 towed sleeve and banner targets in 1950; overheating was considered likely in tropical regions. In 1955 the IFF MkX, also in VR371, needed a few improvements

Supermarine Attacker

Prototypes. This tailwheel jet fighter first flew at Boscombe in July 1946 (and thus made the first maiden flight from the runway), and TS409 (Nene 28) reappeared the following June (the first of seven visits—with a Vickers ejection seat, changed for a Martin Baker Mk 1A for the remaining six) for further flying by the firm prior to AAEE's own work starting in early 1948. The first engineering appraisal highlit the weakness of the mainplane structure and tailplane assembly. Top speed of 508 mph (true) was at sea level, and maximum climb 6,359 ft/min. Meanwhile TS413 with stronger oleos, a hook and spoilers joined for handling; speeds of 515 kt/0.825M were achieved but the elevator became extremely heavy, and the cockpit was cramped and poorly laid out. The low mach number achieved gave concern over the turning performance at altitude. Deck landing trials required a considerable time to establish a suitable approach technique, and no conclusions on suitability could be made on the small number of landings achieved, with the exception of the spoilers which were not needed. TS413 crashed fatally in June 1948, due possibly, it was postulated years later, to a loose spanner. Early in 1950 further deck work on TS416 with the wings 18 in further aft and a longer stroke undercarriage confirmed the heaviness of the elevator, but other features were improvements. After repairs following a wheels up landing, TS409 tried a new 250 gal belly tank; the severe nose down pitch at high Mach was most undesirable, the heavy elevator being of little help, and a new phenomenon—rudder locking could be induced. Following successful spinning, rudder travel was reduced to 75%, but, in 1951, it was considered to be dangerous; a dorsal fin cured the rudder locking. Removing 220 lb of nose ballast to give an aft CG coupled with flat-sided elevators led to acceptable deck landings in mid-1951; demisting and salt clearance then became the worries. TS409 suffered a further wheels up landing in August 1951. Finally TS416 (Nene 1) had steerable tailwheel.

F Mark 1. WA469 (Nene 3) arrived in August 1950 with an improved cockpit (Martin Baker Mk 2A ejection seat), a ventral tank and the old elevator. Trim changes with operation of the airbrakes were reduced by minor modification, and high speed dives caused uncontrollable

497: Attacker FB.2 WK319 in November 1952 armed with twelve 60lb head (concrete) rockets which were successfully fired up to 475 kt. © Crown Copyright

498: The adaptable Attacker FB.2 WK319 with three 5in HVAR rockets under the staboard wing; firings were successful. © Crown Copyright

499: Wyvern T.F.1 TS378 fitted with a double four bladed propeller for carrier trials in mid-1948. The wide radiators under the wings each cool one bank of the Eagle engine. © Crown Copyright

yawing; the Establishment insisted on a limit of 0.78 Mach in service. Gunnery trials lasted until 1953, during which the Establishment was unable to reproduce the loss of control during firing at high Mach reported by the Navy. Deck landings were unaffected by a reduction in flap angle to accommodate RPs. Radios took four months to test in WA471 in 1951, and followed unrecorded tests in WA472. The production standard flat elevator was under test in WA485 at Chilbolton in February 1952 when the aircraft dived into the ground, killing the C Squadron pilot. The new elevator was tested on another aircraft two months later; both the report and the engineering returns identify it as WA535. Non-AAEE records suggest that this identity is in error.

FB Mark 2. In a year of intensive flying, WK319 in the fighter bomber configuration, cleared RPs (Mk8 Type 21), pylon bombs (with WA525), and 5 in HVAR rockets. The armament installations were generally satisfactory, but handling with stores showed that the aileron trimmer was poor, and the airbrake lever awkward to use. These items, plus fitting the new elevator, were remedied for further tests in mid-1953.

Westland Wyvern

The Wyvern typified the tribulations of designers of modern combat aircraft in the immediate post war years. Conceived as a carrier fighter to a 1944 requirement but having the capability to carry a wide range of offensive weapons, the difficulties of harnessing the engine power expected to be available, together with overcoming the control hinge moments at specified speeds and the need for a slow approach for deck landing, all in an aeroplane small enough for stowage on board proved a lengthy process, costing the lives of several test pilots.

Protoypes and TF Mark 1. The firm flew the Wyvern first at Boscombe in December 1946, but it was to be 18 months before AAEE trials began on the third aircraft, TS378 (Eagle 22) with a pair of contra-rotating three-bladed propellers. At 18,000 lb and using 3,500 rpm with +20 psi boost and 20° flap, it was determined from an airfield trial that a take off run would take 600 ft into a 40 kt wind. With four bladed propellers, TS378 was joined in mid-1948 for carrier assessment on *HMS Implacable* by TS380; the very good view was praised, but poor performance and instability on the approach caused anxiety. One year later, with the port elevator balance tab replaced by a spring balance tab, and changes to the outboard wing leading edge, TS378 made 100 landings, many on *HMS Illustrious*; the improvement was marked, but the cockpit layout poor. A curved windscreen, a Malcolm ejection seat and airbrakes on TS375 received generally favourable comment, although ailerons were even heavier with airbrakes out. Handling tests included TS387; recovery from spins was difficult, the rudder locked in flat turns and upfloat of the spring tab ailerons caused premature stall. Rockets made scant difference, a single 1,000 lb bomb gave excessive stick forces (on VR132) and an 18 in torpedo (on VR134) with an air tail caused continuous buffeting up to 385 kt, the maximum flown. AAEE introduced Mark 3 feeds to the 20 mm guns in a successful modification in 1950 to cure stoppages of an earlier version in TS387. The comparative successes of the piston engine version were largely academic, as prop-jet was the vogue.

TF Mark 2. In August 1949 VP109 (Python 1) had delayed power response to throttle movement, and inferior low speed characteristics, led to the conclusion, "Even experimental deck landings under very favourable conditions would be unduly hazardous." At 19,355 lb the poor handling, limited to 20,000 ft on account of possible flame out, was further proved unpleasant when, on opening up for take off, the aircraft nosed over on one occasion. In spite of the pilot pulling smartly back on the stick, "combustion ceased" (ie, "flamed out" in later parlance). Engine response after closing the throttle was timed at three seconds, simulating the "Cut" of a carrier landing; the ensuing delay in touching down would make catching a wire doubtful. The take off run of 620 yd into a 30 kt wind also gave cause for concern. The Python 2 of VW867 was "an enormous improvement" in mid-1950; coupled with the low speed benefits of a larger tailplane with dihedral, this aircraft was suitable for deck trials. The most serious problem remained the large change in directional trim with speed, exacerbated by bumps; this phenomenon was significant for weapon aiming, but did not spoil the pleasant handling. VW869 had a dorsal fin which effectively cured the problem; in comparative tests the fin extension was removed and the aircraft damaged when the rudder overbalanced. After repair it crashed the following month when the cockpit canopy detached leading to a sequence of destruction. This fatal accident led to grounding of the Wyvern pending safety improvements to the seat. VW873 had a Python 3 which lasted 43hr on a reliability trial before the turbine burned out while taxying; an improved hood restraint passed examination in 1951. VW886 had a satisfactory temperature limiter in 1952.

S Mark 4. Retaining the Python 3 in 1952, VW885 and VZ745 each completed 100 hr; a form of warning of high jpt, or preferably an automatic limiting device, was considered vital. The spacious, well laid out cockpit and good view received praise. VW884 received modifications tested over 18 months from July 1952, starting with a fixed detent on the throttle quadrant to mark the position of flight idle, and followed by favourable comments on the lockable tail wheel. A strong rate spring in the rudder circuit gave foot forces sufficiently high to prevent rudder reaching the overbalancing angle previously found; handling remained pleasant, but a stall warning device was considered necessary and ventilation left much to be

500: Wyvern S.4 WL885 in mid-1956 with the RP Mk VIII installation satisfactorily adapted to the carriage of MATRA T10 rockets. © Crown Copyright

501: Wyvern T.F.1 VR134 in November 1949 with an 18in torpedo and MATS tail which together gave continuous light buffet throughout the speed range. Contra rotation of the propellers caused the exhaust stain to trail straight rearwards. © Crown Copyright

502: Wyvern T.F.2 VP109 in August 1949 when the engine and low speed handling characteristics were considered dangerous for deck landings. "Combustion ceased" (flame out) on one attempted take off when the aircraft nosed over being run-up against the brakes. © Crown Copyright

503: Wyvern T.F.2 VW867 in March 1950 with improved longitudinal handling from a larger tailplane with a dihedral. © Crown Copyright

504: Wyvern T.F.2 VW869 with a dorsal fin making "the best Wyvern so far" in March 1951. Vibrations were continuous, and on an air test following a propeller change, the aircraft broke up within sight of the ground. The pilot was killed, in spite of using an ejection seat. © Crown Copyright

505: Failure of the Python 3 motor while on tests of jettisoning mines (Type A Mk 6) gave Lt D J (Block) Whitehead a fright in 1955 in Wyvern S.4 VZ775 © Crown Copyright

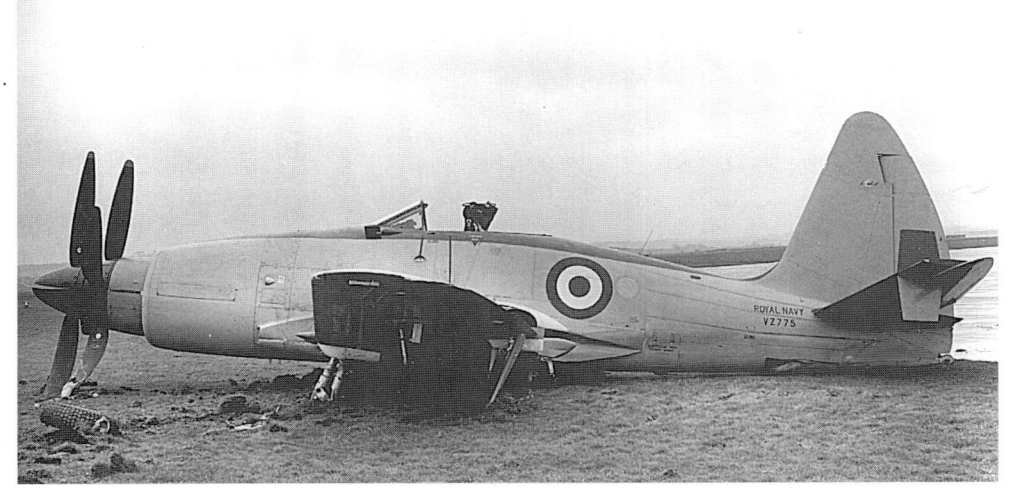

506: Wyvern S.4 VZ790, wings folded in July 1954 to show the 1,000lb rockets hidden underneath. The hook has a particularly neat stowage; also visible are the "finlets" which cured rudder overbalance. © Crown Copyright

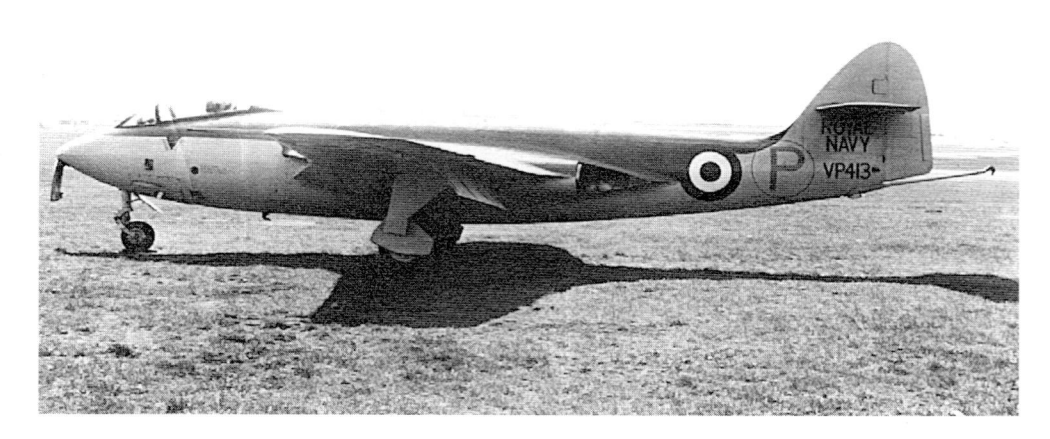

507: Seahawk prototype VP413, probably in 1949, showing the very long hook which suffered bouncing on the carrier deck. Unassisted deck take offs were made without difficulty ... provided the wind over the deck was at least 40 kt. © Crown Copyright

508: Another use for the tail hook—as mounting for the pole to make snatch pick-ups of Dart targets; shown here on Seahawk FGA.4 XE445 © Crown Copyright

desired. The final improvement of small "sub-fins" on the tailplane cured rudder and directional problems, and changing the tailplane incidence cured the longitudinal. VW873, now in Mark 4 form, completed oil cooling trials at Khartoum, and the revised pitot/static system eliminated the previous large errors. Variations between engines were responsible for increasing the maximum speed from 334 to 337 kt and reducing the time to reach 20,000 ft from 12.2 to 11.1 min. Using the new mirror landing aid in late 1952, four aircraft (VZ746, VZ750, VZ774 and VZ777) completed satisfactory deck landings. Production airbrakes on VW870 gave good results up to 435 kt, as did a redesigned hood on VZ748 with a flat windscreen with a wiper. Radio and radar tests of VW885 and VZ774 included the inaccurate ASV 16N radar limited to a maximum height of 9,000 ft in 1953–4, IFF and Green Salad homer (VW883 in 1955). In final production standard, WL885 weighed 15,591 lb (tare), and a maximum, with torpedo, of 24,583 lb.

VW881 and WL885 fired 47,047 rounds of 20 mm ammunition in the course of improving the four gun installation; the Wyvern was a very steady gun platform. Minor changes were made to the RP Mark 8 Type 16 installation in 1953, and high velocity French T10 rockets on new rails were added in 1956. Over a period of nearly three years from July 1953, four aircraft (VZ764, VZ774, VZ775—damaged in October 1952 after engine failure—and WL885) cleared the wide range of external stores, including bombs up to 2,000 lb, ASR Gear, mines, markers and sonobuoys. VZ790 made slow progress with the Red Angel rocket in 1954 when VZ779 was also on armament work

Supermarine Seafang

Nominally a Mark 31, VG474 made two visits, the first in mid-1946 when it had slotted tab ailerons, and the second in 1948 when it had servo-assisted ailerons; no record has been found. VB895, a Mark 32, also made two visits in 1948–9 in connection with explosions in the gun bays of an Attacker. The second was a successful test of AAEE modifications to the feed mechanism (Mk 3 FBM) following investigation on the first. Ten AAEE pilots took the opportunity to try the servodyne assisted spring tabs on the ailerons; the consensus was very favourable. VB895 suffered a minor accident in May 1949.

Hawker 1040 and Sea Hawk

Type P1040. VP401 (Nene number 36) was sent to AAEE in June 1948 for assessment as a potential carrier fighter. Handling in general, the view and tricycle undercarriage received praise, but the stick forces were too low at low speed and too high faster, and the lack of an airbrake and aileron trimmer serious shortcomings. Take off run, the only performance parameter measured, indicated that at 11,000 lb a deck of 780 ft would be needed, assuming a 40 kt headwind; their Lordships may, or may not, have been advised to build longer boats.

Prototypes. Another deck assessment followed in May 1949 using VP413 (Nene 2) with a hook and folding wings; the run to unstick was calculated at 760 ft, and the elevator response at low speed gave some cause for concern. Nevertheless, deck trials went ahead in the following October on *HMS Illustrious* and, as predicted, take offs, with no catapult or rocket assistance, proved interesting. At minimum weight and a wind over the deck of 40–45 kt, the full length was always used. Apart from hook bounce, the deck landing behaviour was very good. Back on dry land more extensive investigations revealed the airbrake to be inadequate, and a sharp nose drop occurred at high Mach (up to 0.86) accompanied by very heavy controls, particularly the ailerons. Overall, the handling received praise at all CG, and the cockpit's only drawback was the unsatisfactory position of the wing folding lever. The engineers found 32 points in need of improvement. The final test on this aeroplane at Boscombe demonstrated the 2g lift ceiling to be 45,000 ft, and the 3g to be 37,00 ft, but the thrust was inadequate to maintain the turns at these rates in level flight. VP422 made five short visits for unrecorded purposes from early 1950.

F Mark 1. Production standard aircraft, WF144 and WF145 (Nene 4 then Nene 101) started trials with deck work on *HMS Eagle* in May 1952; the extra thrust gave adequate take off performance with good handling, but the ASI (single needle) and the hook were criticised for approaches and landings. Shore-based tests showed the improved airbrakes to need stronger jacks as they failed to extend fully above about 275 kt; other remarks concerned the poor visibility in rain, the lack of natural stall warning in the approach configuration, and continuos low amplitude snaking. Night flying of WF151 gave no cause for concern, but the engineers, basing assessment on these first three aircraft, commented on the poor serviceability of the type, bad accessibility and detail defects. The maintenance criticisms also applied during intensive flying of five aircraft at the Naval trials unit at Ford, held jointly with an AAEE team there. Among changes tested satisfactorily were shortening the stick by two inches (WM901), increased mass of elevator balance and carriage of 88 gal drop tanks (WF144). Spinning (WF143 in 1954), and the radio fit (WF180 in 1953) were unremarkable. Gun trials in WF149 ended in tragedy when an unlocked wing folded on take off, killing the pilot and injuring a steward in the officers mess. Firing of the four 20 mm guns caused severe vibration. Tropical trials occupied WF218 in 1954–5, and WF196 made unknown trials in 1957.

509: Sea Hawk FGA.4 WV840 in April 1957 with thirty 25lb head rockets on only the third application of the Rocket Installation Mk 12. © Crown Copyright

510: Seahawk FGA.6 WV909 in March 1955 with banner towing equipment under the starboard wing; the reels of wire can be seen just inboard of the tube. © Crown Copyright

511: Seahawk FB.3 WM983 with 1,000lb rockets under the wings in May 1955, representing the greatest weight that could be carried by this mark. © Crown Copyright

F Mark 2. The powered ailerons of this mark were lighter and increased the rate of roll on WF147 in late 1953. Handling of WF251 the following year confirmed the benefits, particularly for deck work, but also found cruising at altitude tiring on account of snaking and lack of aileron trim. Undercarriage collapse necessitated replacement by WF241 for the obligatory deck landings in 1954, and WF240 arrived in April 1956 for a lengthy stay.

FB Mark 3. The ability to carry external ordnance defined this mark. WF157 handled well with one or two wing mounted 1,000 lb bombs and the limits recommended as the result of trials were: maximum speed—520 kt/0.82M up to 35,000 ft. It is not clear whether this aircraft had powered ailerons for the trial. WF280 in production form spent several months from March 1955 on bombing tests, including release of up to four 500 lb bombs, while WM983 went to the deck and WM992 developed the powered ailerons. The pilot of WF295 derived some cooling benefit from his ventilated suit while operating from Idris in Libya in 1955. WF302 appeared in 1956.

FGA Mark 4. Adding rockets to the Sea Hawk's repertoire created the mark 4, and external load combinations kept WF284 and WV828 busy in 1954–5 with RP Mark 12 Type 2 (twenty 60 lb head rockets in two tiers), and WV840 in 1957 with the Type 3 version (thirty 25 lb head rockets). Four bomb pylons on XE327 were cleared for all 16 loads possible, and, in 1958, variable timing fuses on 500 lb bombs were acceptable on WV904 and XE328.

FGA Mark 6. Tests of the slightly more powerful Nene 103 were soon completed in mid-1955 on XE369, as were the UHF radio trials in 1959 and violet picture homing aid in 1960, both on WV922. XE445 towed 30 ft banner targets successfully in 1955. and the Dart target in 1957; maximum take off weight recommended for the aircraft was 14,800 lb, and minor modifications needed.

Blackburn GR17/45

All three prototypes built reached Boscombe. On arrival in December 1949, WB781 (two Griffon 57) was immediately prepared for deck landing assessment. After very short acquaintance the pilots found the type to have good characteristics with an approach speed of 85 kt; power assisted ailerons were liked. The hook tended to hit the round down of the deck, and the nose was reluctant to rise for take off. With similar power plants plus water injection, WB788 had several aerodynamic changes including sweep back of the wing leading edges giving a rearward CG; this had the effect of reducing the speed at which the nose could be raised on take off thus reducing the deck run. *HMS Illustrious* played host for deck trials in June 1950, and 23 landings were made by AAEE pilots; the long hook necessitated a high approach.

Full handling followed four months later, and serious shortcomings soon became apparent. There was no stall warning, the rudder tramped continuously, the elevator hunted in bumps, the ailerons became extremely heavy without boost, and the noise in the cockpit excessive, compounded by a poor intercommunicating system. By the following January the rudder had been improved. The third aircraft, WB797, had double Mamba turboprop motors, and, like its siblings, went straight to *HMS Illustrious* for trials where the favourable deck behaviour was repeated, but using a 90 kt approach speed. Later, dummy deck approaches using a single engine were rendered tricky by the difficulty in keeping an accurate speed. However, also like the earlier aircraft, the real problems became obvious only when the full envelope was explored. Most of the previous comments remained valid with, in addition, heavy rudder forces on one engine and instability (ie self stall) at low speed with no warning. After rejection of this type in favour of the Fairey Gannet, a limited review of handling up to 20,000 lb cleared WB797 for development flying by Armstrong Siddeley.

De Havilland Sea Venom and Aquilon

FAW Mark 20. After the assessment of the land based night fighter, carrier trials were the priority of WK376 (Ghost 3) in July 1951; lacking folding wings but having a hook, the shortcomings included the need for increased aft stick movement and an aileron trimmer. Six months later, wing fences improved aileron control, but several minor changes to the elevator control and raising the tailplane by four inches were ineffective. Deck trials in this configuration were considered too dangerous. More modifications, including fixed slats and a rubber bungee to balance the weight of the elevator made great improvements, and the type became an excellent deck aircraft. High Mach handling was still difficult, but stick forces had been reduced to such an extent that at aft CG instability needed rectification. WK379 had wing folding and a hook damper and made further deck landings by day; comments included the high stick forces and the need for cockpit changes and for a windscreen wiper. Some handling advances followed modifications, but unpleasant high speed phenomena appeared at the lower Mach of 0.805 in 1953. Radios and the four 20 mm guns and the gyro gunsight (GGS Mk 4E(S)) proved satisfactory in 1954. WM500 was spun with the surprising observation that outspin aileron aided recovery. More deck trials on WM510 (Ghost 103) with variable aileron gearing confirmed the need for a two needle ASI followed 1953 deck work on WM503 with the new fin shape, but lacking a widescreen wiper and two needle ASI. WM501 and WM502 (with a wiper) and with all modifications incorporated, completed handling which was marginally

512: Blackburn GR17/45 WB788 in June 1950 with dummy jet exhaust. The rudder and elevator each have balance and trim tabs, the ailerons fixed and trim tabs (on both sides, apparently) and the elevator also has a horn balance. The hook is stowed in the tail bumper. Deck landing trials preceded handling, and only during the latter were serious deficiencies revealed. © Crown Copyright

513: Blackburn GR17/45 WB788 showing a small aerodynamic "fix" under the tailplane which almost cured rudder tramping. © Crown Copyright

514: *Sea Venom FAW.21 WM568 in late 1954 with the latest style of fin and rudder, and with the hook and mass balances of the elevator in evidence.* © Crown Copyright

515: *Sea Venom FAW.20 WK376 in June 1952 with tip tanks.*

516: *Sea Venom FAW.21. One of three aircraft dedicated to Firestreak development flying; missile equipment replaced guns and used the wiring for rockets and a G45 camera.* © Crown Copyright

293

517: Gannet prototype VR546 probably in May 1952. Its first trials, as usual with carrier aircraft, were on the deck where its suitability from the first was amply demonstrated. One event recorded was the tipping up when the brakes were applied while going backwards! © *Crown Copyright*

518: Gannet prototype VR557 without a third cockpit, but with the radar "dustbin" extended and bomb doors open. All the early armament was cleared on this aeroplane. © *Crown Copyright*

519 : Gannet AEW.3 XJ440 in December 1958 about to blow its top in the blower tunnel. The net for catching the errant canopy is barely visible. © *Crown Copyright*

acceptable, although the limit for successful gun firing was determined as 0.78M. Engineering evaluation, probably of WK385, was followed by the recommendation, *inter alia*, of a wing folding interlock. Updated radio and radar were satisfactory in WM504, and only minor snags were found in the navigation fit of WM508. Firing of 3 in rockets at speeds up to 500 kt was approved on WM507 in 1954, and extended to a pair of 5 in HVAR the following year on WM510.

FAW Mark 21. Deck trials received the priority, as usual on a new version, and XA532 (Ghost 104) with powered ailerons and anti-skid brakes proved great advances in August 1954; the need for a two needle ASI was reinforced. Powered ailerons also assisted rocket firing from XA539 and WM571, but were found too sensitive at altitude. WM568 needed better cockpit lighting, but new IFF in WW211 functioned adequately, both in 1955; information is scant on WM570 on radar/guns/deck tests in 1955–6, WM573 on rockets and deck work in 1955, WM574 CATS (5hr flying) and WW296 (Ghost 105) on hot weather investigation at Idris in 1956. WM575 was unserviceable at the end of 1955, but eventually made acceptable take offs using rocket assistance. Three aircraft (XG607, XG612 and XG622) had the RP wiring replaced by Blue Jay (renamed Firestreak) missile wiring, and flew for the JSTU on trials of the new weapon. A target Meteor adjusted throttle settings to produce 500°C jpts; eight missiles were later fired in the Aberporth range. XG662 came in November 1957 for missile development.

FAW Mark 22. In 1960, WW220 tested Violet Picture, an emergency homing aid for survivors, following a previous trial of a new UHF radio.

FAW Mark 53. This night fighting version for Australia involved WZ893 (Ghost 104) and WZ944 on tests of radio, radar (AI 17) and armament; many minor criticisms followed. Brief gun firing from WZ941 in late 1955 caused damage to the fabric covering of the wooden fuselage, and WZ894 went to Idris twice in 1955.

Aquilon. Two French Naval Aquilons (Sea Venoms), flew to Boscombe in 1951 where C Squadron assisted in operational training, and later included deck work on *HMS Bulwark*.

Fairey Gannet

Prototype and AS Mark 1. VR546 (Double Mamba 204) started trials by launching straight into 25 deck landings in June 1950 on *HMS Illustrious* where its potential was spoilt by poor elevator and aileron response at low speed. With a two position tailplane interlinked to the flaps of reduced span, trim changes became small, and after more deck work the aeroplane was described as, "exceptionally well suited ... to the deck." Of general handling, the large trim change with flap retraction and complicated engine handling were the only significant criticisms; loitering in its anti submarine role on one engine alone could be achieved up to the maximum weight of 20,000 lb. The extra drag of the new, third canopy, radar dustbin, and "finlets" reduced the single engine loitering weight to 19,000 lb, but gave no problems on another set of carrier landings, and, with a modified leading edge to the tailplane, further improved handling. Flying with the canopies removed was tried with no adverse comment, but even with full protection, the pilot needed a more comfortable seat for long sorties. VR557 joined in December 1950 to confirm the excellent handling; instrument layout was somewhat haphazard in the spacious cockpit, but the view good. RPs, in four double tiers, and flare containers were cleared after AAEE modifications in 1952. WN339, WN340 and WN341 arrived in October 1953; the first two collided when WN339's brakes failed taxying, but repairs minimised the delay to the engineering evaluation; improvements to wing folding and engine starting were recommended. Radar (ASV 19b) and radio trials on WN342 were soon completed in 1954, but it took three years of concentrated ground and air testing to clear the nine operational and ten training loads of offensive weapons in WN341 and XA401. WN357 (3 in rockets on the RP Mk 8 Type 24 installation) extended the variety of stores cleared for use, as did WN393 (Uncle Tom rockets), and XA401, returning in late 1957 with the first RP Mk 12 installation capable of firing 5 in HVAR and French T10 rockets. The Autopilot Mk 11 of WN374 worked well at all speeds, but the possibility of a catastrophic runaway limited the recommended use to 200 kt. WN372 went to Khartoum in 1955, and WN393 to Idris in 1956 as part of an extensive evaluation of the Blue Silk/Doppler/GPI 5 navigation suite—reliability was poor. WN352 flew for five months from November 1958 on unknown duties, and WN355 stayed on the ground at the end of 1957 for electrical assessment.

T Mark 2. Pilot training needs gave rise to this version; cockpit canopies, with a periscope for the instructor, jettisoned well from XA518 in the blower tunnel, in marked contrast to the many canopies used to achieve a satisfactory clearance on the Mark 1. WN365 needed a brief period for radio and IFF trials in 1954, and Green Salad homer in 1956. Between these dates XA515 and XA528 made gunsight trials; rear seat alignment proved very difficult, and only the front seat could be used for RP firing.

AEW Mark 3. No handling report has been found of this extensive redesign for early warning and carrying a large radome but XJ440 spent a month at AAEE in mid-1959. Clearance trials of the extensive radio and radar fit[1]

---

[1] The kit was: AN/APS 20F radar, AN/APX 7 homer, Blue Silk doppler, AN/ART 28 radio relay, Radio altimeter 5, IFF 10 and interrogator, intercom, TACAN navigation aid, Violet Picture homer, HF and UHF communications, and later, SSB radio.

520: *Gannet AS.1 WN340 with very few differences from the protoype. The rear cockpit has a wind shield, the radio mast on the canopy is new and the entrance steps on the far side led "forever upwards" in the words of one wag.* © *Crown Copyright*

521 left: *Gannet prototype VR546 with an interim standard of finlets on the tailplane; the pilot's foot step is extended.*

522 below: *Gannet AEW.3 XL452—probably in 1961, with an unknown missile under the starboard wing. The ground crew display the current sartorial fashion without ear defenders.* © *Crown Copyright*

used XL449, XL450, and XL451, lasted a year from April 1959 at Boscombe and White Waltham. The outstanding concern, that of the effect of anti-icing, proved unfounded in late 1962. By 1966, the Navy required a clearance to operate the Mark 3 at weights above the previous limit of 24,400 lb; an acceleration of over 1.5 kt/sec was specified. Shore trials using the catapult at Bedford for XL449 and XL450 (at 26,000 lb) were successful, and two squadron aircraft borrowed for ship launches from *HMS Victorious* in the hot air (28° C). It was found that full flap, previously the standard technique, reduced acceleration to 0.5 kt/sec, and that a small reduction in flap setting gave an acceptable 1.5 kt/sec. The Gannet retained its excellent launch characteristics at the new weight. In 1963, XL503 blew its top in the blower tunnel, smoke floats fell cleanly from XL452 in 1965, and, in 1968, XR433 (the last of many thousands of Fairey aeroplanes for the Royal Navy) had a new radar amplifier, and XL456 new passive Electronic Counter Measures (ECM). Electro Magnetic Compatibility (EMC)—confusingly—employed XL497 in 1965 and XP226 in 1966 on brief but comprehensive ground trials; advanced radar modifications to distinguish moving targets were tested on XL497 in 1974.

AS and COD Mark 4. WN372 with more powerful engines returned as a Mark 4 for hunting submarines, and visited Idris in Libya in 1956; XG827 flew nine hours with C Squadron in 1957. XA470, a Carrier On-board Delivery aircraft, needed only a week's EMC testing in 1966.

T Mark 5. The prototype, XG873, appears to have done deck trials on *HMS Victorious* in 1959.

de Havilland Type 110 and Sea Vixen

Designed to meet the same specification as the Javelin, the RAF had decided against the DH110 before AAEE trials began. Relatively few aerodynamic changes were needed, and the large number of Sea Vixens at Boscombe is attributable to the wide range of armament to be cleared for shipborne use by the Fleet Air Arm. Some important reports have not been found.

Type 110. The preview at deHavilland's airfield on 26 August 1954 using WG240 (two Avon RA7) showed the type's good performance and docile transonic characteristics. Buffeting at 2.5g above 0.85M and at 0.97M in unaccelerated flight limited use as a weapon platform; breakout forces for the flying tailplane became irksome in the cruise. In late 1955 at Boscombe, modifications to the longitudinal control system reduced the breakout forces and produced pleasant handling. Contemporary trials on XF828 (two Avon RA28) without the modifications, retained, by contrast, poor feel, control and trim systems. The type needed changes to the aileron gearing, a strengthened undercarriage and raising of the speed limit for flap operation. Equipped with a hook and a strengthened undercarriage, but lacking folding wings, XF828 made 32 landings (22 by AAEE pilots) on *HMS Ark Royal* in March 1956 at weights up to 27,950 lb. Deck landings were described as pleasant and the audio airspeed device was liked; catapult launches were straightforward. One year later further deck trials by XF828 (engines now designated Avon 203) together with XJ474 (Avon 208) included successful landings at 30,000 lb—the limit of the Mk 13 arrester gear. The pilot's view of the starboard landing mirror was blocked by the nose, and strong criticism was made of the crew escape facilities. Handling after airfield take offs at 33,390 lb remained unaltered carrying two Firestreak missiles, although the three pitot-static systems (two sensors at the wing tips and on the nose) had significant discrepancies.

Sea Vixen FAW Mark 1. Armament trials got underway with wing mounted rockets on XJ477 from July 1958; three inch and five inch HVARs could be fired up to 600 kt provided the airbrakes remained in above 450 kt. Firing the two inch rocket battery from the fuselage position in the air-to-air mode and in conjunction with the AI 18 radar was limited to 600 kt and 40,000 ft. In 1963, the air/air mode of the pilot's attack sight was claimed as the first trial in the UK of such a system for launching two inch rockets; errors in earlier calculations of the rockets' flight path were revealed. In 1959 emergency clearance of stores under the wings using the Ejector Release Unit No 3 Mk 1 received clearance for naval use. A vulture ended tropical trials in the Sudan when it collided with XJ479 in October 1958 at 100 ft and 450 kt; one crew member received injuries from a malfunctioning ejection seat. A year later, tropical trials of the two rocket firing systems of XJ485 identified the rapid and potentially dangerous temperature rise from high speed; consequently time above 450 kt was limited to seven minutes per flight. The Sea Vixen's resistance to the cold involved XJ482 in a non-flying test in the climatic chamber of Vickers at Weybridge. The Establishment analysed results of de Havilland's tests in 1958 of Firestreak acquisition and slaving using another Sea Vixen as target for XJ478. As a result of the improvements recommended, AAEE's own trials in 1959 with this aircraft and XJ483 went smoothly in both extreme and normal manoeuvres including supersonic, and culminated in two live firings in which two target aircraft were destroyed. Radios and IFF (XJ485), violet picture homing aid (XJ521), practice 1,000 lb bombs with mechanical fusing (XJ492), 1,000 lb bombs with variable timing (XJ526 in UK and El Adem, Libya) received approval in 1959–60, and 25 lb practice bombs on a light store carrier (XJ564) in 1962. In 1961–2, the Bullpup missile was carried and fired throughout the flight envelope, but jettison had to be made below 569 kt; the tests, on XJ582, included 16 release flights. Later tests included Lepus flares and a Mk 2 Reconnaissance Pod,

523: *Sea Vixen FAW.1 XJ477 taxying with apparently empty rocket pods, but having many cameras: on the tailplane, wing tips, boom tips and under the fuselage. © Crown Copyright*

524: *Sea Vixen FAW.1 XJ488 in late 1965 with a Rushton target under the outboard wing and winch on the next pylon, while the starboard wing carries a 200 gal pod. Hydraulic pressure has fallen, allowing the hook and undercarriage door to droop. © Crown Copyright*

525: *Sea Vixen FAW.2 (XN684 on intake blank—XN690 according to report), with two VT fused bombs outboard and four VT fused 540lb bombs inboard. Modifications taking a year were necessary to prevent arming of the bombs on the aircraft in flight. © Crown Copyright*

the latter continuing on XN700. After initial work on aerial refuelling and towing the Rushton Target, XJ488 remained for five years of pilot training until 1972; trials of the Del Mar target system continued on XJ488 in 1962–3. XJ525 was probably concerned with the Ikara and the Mk 31 torpedo at Culdrose. Results of the several trials on XJ516 (Avon 208) between 1959 and 1962 appear to have been lost, but included flight refuelling, auto throttle assessment and carrier work generally. 1963's shorter trials included XJ480 with the TACAN navaid.

C Squadron operated the four aircraft which joined 22 JSTU in 1968 for evaluation of the Martel air-to-ground missile. All four aircraft had done some previous trials work, including pinion fuel tanks (XJ475), Red Top missiles (XJ476), night assessment (XJ481) and elecro magnetic compatibilty checks on *HMS Victorious* (XJ494). XJ475 met its end in November 1970 in a ground accident.

FAW Mark 2. 14 aircraft of this mark feature in surviving maintenance returns; records of their individual work have largely failed to survive. CA Release in 1964 followed two years of trials, mostly carried out by De Havilland and concentrating on systems and armament. AAEE maintained close supervision before recommending world wide clearance, from land and ship bases, of Red Top and Firestreak air-to-air missiles, Bullpup air-to ground missiles and a wide range of bombs and rockets, together with the use of the AI 18R radar. The Establishment's own flying had taken place on the two interim standard aircraft, XJ684 (two Avon 208) from November 1962 and XJ685, both continued Red Top trials until 1966 together with XP919 (including deck trials on *HMS Hermes*) and, XP954 (EMC on *HMS Eagle*). Further Bullpup tests on XP919 followed in 1966 using an F 95 camera to record separation from the aircraft. XP920 completed initial CA Release on *HMS Hermes* in 1964, followed by clearance of many armament loads including Lepus flares and nuclear weapons (WE177); in 1967 XJ609 operated from *HMS Eagle*. as part of a low speed handling investigation. VT fusing of 540lb bombs on XJ608 in 1968–9 followed gunnery and VT fuse tests on XN690 in 1967; XN653 had IFF/SSR in 1969. Between 1970 and 1974, three aircraft were associated with the Martel missile, XJ579 (flew 33 hr in 18 months), XN686 (crashed on an air test in September 1970) and XP956. XN652 spent six months at AAEE in 1972 without flying.

Short Seamew

Only the carrier-based version of this simple submarine hunter reached AAEE before cancellation of both sea and land based versions. XA209 (Mamba 3) arrived in May 1954, but was soon assessed as unsuitable for deck work on account of poor aileron response at low speed, slow deceleration at idle throttle setting (flight fine propeller pitch too coarse), and, most significant, low performance. Modified ailerons remained unacceptable later in 1954, with additional problems from overbalance of the elevator and lack of rudder response. XE170 had unrepresentative navigation equipment in 1956, but acceptable ASV 19B radar and radios. With a Mamba 6 and other improvements, deck trials by XA213 and XE169 took place on *HMS Warrior* in 1956 at weights up to 13,340 lb; 200 deck landings were achieved by AAEE assisted by other pilots. The type proved simple and robust in 107 hr of reliability flying of XE181, while the RP VIII Type 25 rocket installation on XE171 used a Mk 2 reflector sight and gave good results.

XE186 spent two months at Boscombe in 1957 flying 24 hr to give pilots experience on type.

Supermarine Type 525 and Scimitar

Type 525. VX138 (two Avon), also known as the N113D, had scarcely started flying at Boscombe in July 1955 when disaster struck on the pilot's first flight. Preliminary low speed handling was being investigated at 10,000 ft when a spin developed; the reinforced canopy would not jettison, and the pilot was killed after he eventually managed to eject at very low altitude through the unlocked canopy. Redesign of the canopy was followed by extensive tests in the blower tunnel at the end of 1955.

F Mark 1. A dummy fuselage for the Scimitar followed the 525 in the blower tunnel, a few months before WT854 (two Avon 28) went to the deck with double slotted flaps; poor tailplane response and wing rocking added to the difficulty of maintaining an accurate approach speed. Later in 1956 an anhedral in place of a dihedral tailplane and larger fin and rudder gave docile transonic behaviour, but the lack of precision in keeping the wings level needed improvement. A contemporary concern involved roll coupling, ie rapid rolls at high speed leading to complete loss of control. 250 full rolls, including some supersonic, using full aileron and up to 4g led to the conclusion that the risk was small, although the sideslip limit was approached. The moment of inertia in yaw was 112,000 slugs/ft^2, a fact that makes the price of this book a mere snip—what a trivial pursuit question! With blow over the flaps, modified wing fences and audio speed warning, dummy deck landings were made by WW134 (two Avon 24); in July 1957 deck operations by XD215 achieved 148 landings and take offs assisted by the new BS 4 catapult. Four AAEE pilots took part. Back on shore, the best advice for recovery from inadvertent spins, it was considered, involved releasing the stick and applying rudder in opposition to the turn needle. Poor aerial positioning degraded the

526: Sea Vixen FAW.1 XJ478 during the trial September 1958 to October 1959 to clear Blue Jay (Firestreak) missiles for carriage, firing, acquisition, slaving, engineering and safety. © Crown Copyright

527: Seamew AS.1 XE169 with bomb doors open and an anti-spin parachute on the arrester hook in 1956. The pressure head under the port wing appears to be non-standard. © Crown Copyright

528: Seamew prototype XA209 in mid-1954, when the unacceptable ailerons and rudder led to cancellation of planned carrier trials. © Crown Copyright

529: *Vickers N 113D WT854 (as the protoype Scimitar was known) in October 1956. The anhedral tailplane attracted the photographer, but considerable work on the controls remained to be done before satisfaction could be achieved for deck landing. © Crown Copyright*

530: *Scimitar F.1 XD327 with a "buddy" flight refuelling pod under the starboard wing. © Crown Copyright*

531: *Scimitar F.1 XD217 with nose cone containing three F 95 Mk 2 cameras in April 1961. © Crown Copyright*

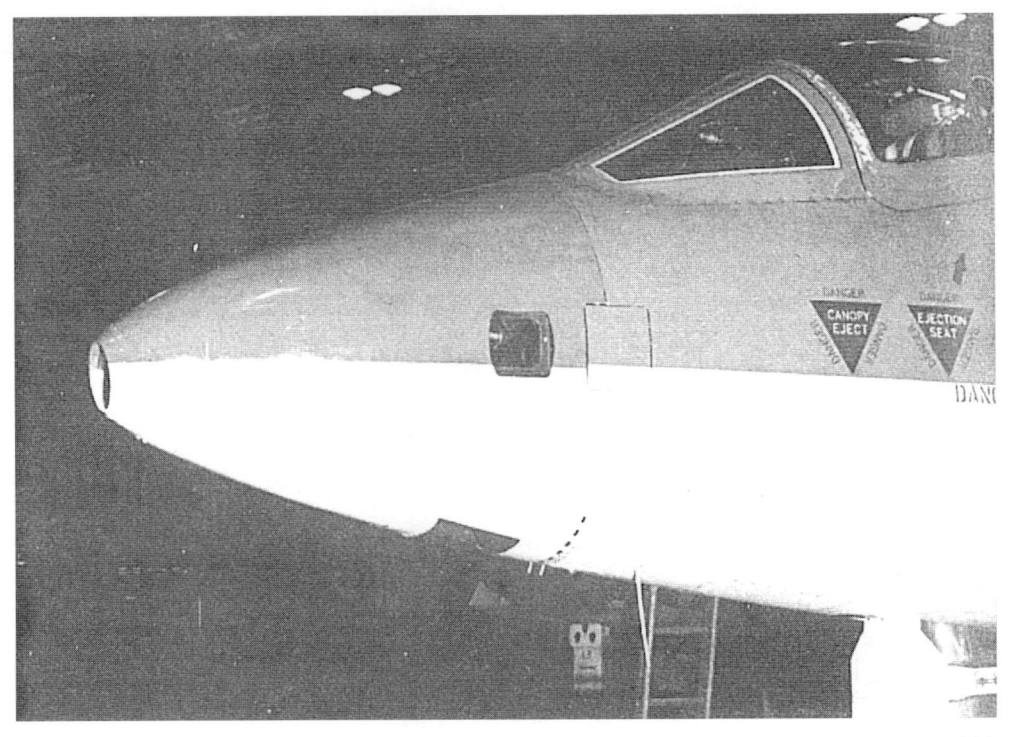

301

532: Scimitar F.1 XD268 in 1961/2 with a pair of Sidewinder Mk 1A missiles and a belly mounted camera pod © Crown Copyright

533: Buccaneer S.1 XK532 in 1963 with a day reconnaissance fit in the bomb bay with one forward looking and two oblique cameras. The "editor" has brushed out details, including the electrical cable just aft of the nosewheel. © Crown Copyright

534: A comparison in August 1974 between the Buccaneer S.1 (background) with a cover over its small engine intake, but carrying a Palouste engine starter, and the S.2 (foreground) XN974. © Crown Copyright

performance of IFF and the radio altimeter in XD217, and the UHF radio needed extra cooling. This aircraft came close to disaster in September 1957 when the fin failed but remained in situ. Blue Silk doppler in place of guns gave few problems in XD219 and XD275 at Idris in 1958. The Dart target gave some interesting flying of XD226 as the technique for pick up involved a slow, low approach with the special hook exposed, and immediately before engagement, applying full power and climbing at 160 kt. AAEE observers later watched 803 Squadron perform this trick from a deck at sea. The year 1958 also saw eight hours flying of WT859, XD214 in Bahrein, four weeks work on XD229 and unknown tests on XD241. The next year XD275 went to Idris and, in 1961, the Establishment checked the firm's performance figures on XD232.

All remaining reports feature armament tests. Four 30 mm Aden Mk 4 guns fired 38,705 rounds from XD213; pitch down was overcome by extra deflectors on the blast tubes, and the installation cleared for firing between 200 and 640 kt. In tropical conditions, an extra limitation was imposed as it took two hours for the guns to cool below 71°C after shooting. XD216 and XD268 cleared the Sidewinder Mk 1A missile in 1961–2, plus the Mk 26 target rocket, both simple and reliable, while XD268 also had four of the air-to-ground Bullpup missiles, successfully carried and fired. The "Fighter" designation was something of a misnomer since many types of bomb required clearance, as follows: on XD228, 25 lb practice and 1,000 lb bombs in 1958, and with modified pylons in 1960, 500 lb bombs in 1961, 24 three inch rockets and HVAR in 1960 and two inch rocket pods on four pylons, also in 1960 and finally four 100 gal napalm tanks in 1965, on XD327 various fusing in 1960; on XD246, Low Altitude Bombing System (LABS) in 1960–1, and, in 1969, triple ejector carriers on XD224 for application to the Phantom. The report on the associated tests of the nuclear store is missing. F95 Mk 2 cameras in a fan of three in the nose needed better heating after tests on XD217 in April 1961. Aerial refuelling tests involved XD212 and XD227 in late 1960/early 1961,

Blackburn Buccaneer

Designed to a very ambitious operational requirement for a Naval strike aircraft, the Buccaneer was the first type developed to the Weapon System concept. Of the 20 development batch aircraft, the majority appeared at AAEE where testing of the Mk 1 reached its culmination with the third issue of the CA Release in November 1963, some five years after the type's first flight.

Development and S Mark 1. From the limited preview flying of XK486 (Gyron Junior Phase 1A) in October 1958 the good low level handling became apparent, but major shortcomings included poor lateral and directional characteristics, particularly for deck landings, undesirable control and feel systems, low manoeuvre boundary, large trim change with extension of the airbrakes, and, above all, low engine power. Modifications tested some six months later showed that vortex generators and revised wing leading edge had improved the buffet boundary, strakes had reduced the trim change with airbrake selection, but a roll damper had scarcely affected the lateral behaviour. XK489 and XK523 made arrivals on *HMS Hermes* in January 1960 from approaches described as very difficult due to poor control and engine response; woeful thrust led to slow acceleration after launch and the need for very careful handling. XK526 and XK527 made a further carrier assesment one year later on *HMS Ark Royal*. In August 1961, tests were underway on *HMS Hermes* to determine the optimum tailplane settings for a hands-off launch when XK529 pitched up and crashed fatally. In 1963, the tests of XN959 *HMS Victorious* were concerned with the electro magnetic environment for the range of weapons recently cleared for naval use, including 2,000lb nuclear bomb, Bullpup missiles and rockets. Up to eight 1,000 lb bombs (four in the bay and four under the wings) received approval after 39 flights at West Freugh of XK528, following successful dropping of 25 lb practice bombs on flights from Boscombe. Asymmetric bomb load (one 1,000 lb under the starboard wing) trials terminated when XN922 crashed on take off into D Squadron hangar; the observer and a supervisor were killed. Failure of the boundary layer blowing system was the most likely cause; prior to this accident the system had worked well at AAEE. Seven release flights of Bullpups from XN959 cleared the installation up to 350 kt, 0.93M and dive angles up to 45°; XK530 made the EMC checks of the missiles. In 1964, dummy 2,000 lb nuclear stores were dropped from XK525 and XK528 using the long toss mode of the low altitude system; an average (CEP) error of 600 ft using a radar offset was considered creditable. Two years previously, the erratic errors of the Blue Jacket doppler, and the poor performance of the master reference gyro (MRG) in XK528 and XK533 would have precluded such results. Improved alignment procedures for the whole weapon system, developed on XN934 and proved in Singapore on XN931, helped to remedy the situation. The long serving XN923, after dropping numerous 250 gal under wing tanks, went to sea where alignment of the Sperry MRG could be made accurate to within 0.9°. 128 flights at the end of 1963 in Aden and Singapore, probably using XN931, served to emphasise the inadequacy of the cooling of the radio and bomb bays. Day photography was added to the Buccaneer's repertoire by an F95 Mk 4 camera in the bomb bay of XK532; good snaps could be obtained between 300 and 550 kt up to 10,000 ft. Auto pilot performance including the height lock occupied XK491 in 1962–3, and two months of trials on XK524 in 1963–4 centred on flight refuelling and optimising the position of the probe. XK531 performed in July 1961, and

535: Buccaneer S.1 XK486 in October 1958 during the preview. The early, unsatisfactory, form of strakes can be seen on the airbrakes and the later vortex generators are absent from the upper surfaces of the wings. © Crown Copyright

536: Buccaneer S.2 XK526 with the new tanks with inner wing and tank painted black with tufts to visualise flow on the port side in July 1967. © Crown Copyright

537: Buccaneer S.2D appearing as a Lossiemouth inhabitant landing in the hands of Lt John Leng on HMS Ark Royal in July 1974 and carrying two Martel missiles. © Crown Copyright

538: Buccaneer S.2 XK527 in July 1964 with the infinitely variable airbrakes opened below a trailing static head. © Crown Copyright

XK536 flew onto *HMS Hermes* and *HMS Ark Royal* in 1962, and *HMS Victorious* in 1963 followed by assessment of the bomb bay fuel tank in 1964. XK968 made another deck trial on *HMS Hermes* in 1964 while XK973 checked EMC without flying on *HMS Eagle*; XK955 flew bombs with VT fuses from *HMS Hermes* in 1967.

S Mark 2. Immediately on arrival in August 1964, XN974 (Spey 101) flew onto *HMS Eagle*, and, six months later, XN975 similarly went to *HMS Ark Royal*. Limited to 50,000 lb all up weight at launch due to the strength of the decks, and to 35,000 lb for landing due to the strength of the undercarriage, the existing configurations were nevertheless assessed, minimum launch speeds established, and single engine and boundary layer "blow off" approaches flown successfully. In mid-1965 XK527 (converted from Mark 1), XN974 and XN976 together went to Florida for engine handling; the only two significant problems were a tendency to surge on throttle opening above 35,000 ft, and a slow relight at height. The avionics suffered in the heat, and a maximum speed of 550 kt imposed at 40°C, and 580 kt at 35°C; similar over heating was detected in the instrumented bomb bay of XK527, at Idris. In 1973, as part of a trial investigating the implications of a double electrical failure, the long suffering XK527 made approaches to land without benefit of boundary layer blow; the higher speeds necessary gave few difficulties on runways.

While in Florida XN974 and XN976, modified with a longer hook, engaged the arrester wires of *USS Lexington*; launches up to the new maximum of 53,500 lb proved feasible at speeds lower by six knots than those recently extrapolated and based on increasing launch speeds by 4 kt per 10°C above standard. Throttle sensitivity was reduced, because previously retarding the throttle by slightly more than intended could significantly lower the boundary layer blowing and seriously damage the approach. Trim settings for take offs with asymmetric wing stores were established at RAE Bedford; a single 1,000 lb bomb on an outboard pylon was recommended for the ensuing launches from *HMS Hermes*. In 1966–7 a further investigation was made into the feasibility of reducing launch speeds and thus to maximise loads in conditions of low wind; a reduction of 3 kt was suggested except when carrying 250 gal tanks. During the course of this trial in October 1966, XV153 (a Naval squadron aircraft) pitched up and crashed on launch damaging the pilot on ejection. As a result of much further work from two carriers, and involving XN974, XN976, XT279, XT280, XV164 and XV165 of the AAEE plus a squadron aircraft, the original speeds were reinstated. With a modified shape to the under wing tanks on XK526 (modified from Mark 1), stability at high incidence was improved, but 1968 deck trials on *HMS Hermes* by XN983 and XN975 showed no benefit. With the CG moved aft by the installation of the Martel missile, XV863 flew to the deck of the long suffering *HMS Hermes* in 1969. Tests of the Sidewinder

539: Buccaneer S.1 XK528 in mid-1963 with four 1,000lb bombs visible in the bomb bay; later another four bombs were also mounted on the wing stations. © Crown Copyright

540 and 541: Two, slightly different, underwing tanks on Buccaneer S.2 XK526. The tank above shows the original tank which was accompanied by marked loss of stability at high angles of attack, and the one on the right, the new tank, which gave slightly better handling on catapult launches. © Crown Copyright

542: Phantom FG 1 XT860 in May 1968 attracting a crowd of "goofers" on an early visit to Boscombe, On one occasion (possibly the one depicted) ground refuelling was made without shutting down the engines— a procedure new to the Establishment. © Crown Copyright

1A air-to-air missile were brief; XN974 had malfunctions in April 1967, but XN976 achieved success in mid-1968. XN974 continued trials until 1974 with radar ranging for automatic release of retarded stores, calibration of incidence indicator and updated Blue Jay doppler and ground position indicator. XV352, a Mark 2B, cleared the anti radar Martel missile for training in the S band, although some errors prior to release became apparent due to reflections from the fuselage; later, using a Mark 2B, XW529, the effect of the reflections was defined, and some over heating of the anti radar unit discovered. The television version of Martel suffered some interference from the TACAN navaid, and considerable flying until 1974 was devoted to increasing the number of possible manoeuvres following release. In 1969 XV352 tested the IFF/SSR and voice recorder while XN976 had good results with passive ECM in S and X bands. Mark 2B XW540 with a bomb bay fuel tank had no difficulty with minus 20°C at Fort Churchill in Canada, nor did XV350 (following four years of Martel and bomb bay tests), at Yuma in the USA desert in 1973, apart from some tyre and bomb bay hot spots. Flying from Yuma included investigation of the round-the corner (RTC) escape manoeuvre after tossing off a nuclear weapon; limiting parameters were the angle of attack (maximum of 20 ADD units) and weight (57,000 lb or less). XV337 arrived in December 1974 for several years of miscellaneous work including training. Another long serving trials aircraft, Mark 2B XW525, concentrated in 1970 and 1971 on armament—SNEB rockets and 600 lb nuclear weapons. Naval Mark 2Ds, XV866 and XV869 included sea trials in1974 on *HMS Ark Royal* in their Martel programme; XV168 (EMC in 1967), XV334 (rudder trim and EMC in 1967) and XV353 (ground tests in 1968) also featured.

McDonnell Phantom

See Chapter 6.

543: Victor K.1 XA918 refuels Buccaneer S.2 XN976 and Sea Vixen FAW.2 XN685 in late 1965. The two Naval craft have C Squadron badges on their fins. © Crown Copyright

APPENDICES

APPENDIX 1: Commandants, Chief Superintendents, Superintendents and Establishment Secretaries—1945 to 1975

Commandants (all Air Commodore)
- Jun 1945   H P Fraser CBE AFC
- 16 Dec 1946   C B R Pelly CBE MC
- 26 Jul 1948   H L Patch CBE
- 2 Jan 1950   A W B McDonald CB AFC
- 23 Aug 1952   A H Wheeler OBE
- 7 Apr 1955   *R A Ramsay Rae OBE
- 27 May 1957   A E Clouston CB DSO DFC AFC
- 10 Mar 1960   J F Roulston CBE DSO DFC
- 10 Dec 1964   F R Bird DSO DFC AFC
- 16 Feb 1968   C D A Browne DFC
- 1 Sep 1970   R L Topp AFC
- 12 Aug 1972   G C Cairns CBE AFC
- 12 Oct 1974   A D Dick CBE AFC
- 6 Sep 1975   H A Merriman CBE AFC

* Shewn in the Air Force List as R A R Rae

Chief Superintendents
- (1938)   Mr E T Jones
- 1947–50   Mr I Bowen
- 1950–52   Mr J Hanson
- 1952–55   Mr H Davies
- 1955   Mr J Hanson
- 1956–59   Dr D E Morris
- 1959–62   Dr D Cameron
- 1962–66   Mr E A Poulton
- 1966–71   Mr R J Atkinson
- 1971–74   Mr F G J Brown
- 1974–75   Mr H W Turner

Superintendents of Performance
- 1944–46   Mr S Scott-Hall
- 1946–53   Mr P A Hufton
- 1953–61   Mr R P Dickinson
- 1961–64   Mr J Poole
- 1964–66   Mr D J Higton
- 1966–69   Mr J C Morrall
- 1969–74   Mr D A Lang
- 1974   Mr J Andrews

Superintendents of Armament (All Group Captains)
- 1945   E S Dru-Drury AFC
- 1945–47   C F S Fraser
- 1947–48   S P A Patmore OBE
- 1948–51   E M T Howell
- 1951–52   R J P Morris
- 1952–53   D S Kite
- 1953–57   W A Theed
- 1957–60   W D G Watkins DSO DFC DFM
- 1960–61   I J Lightfoot
- 1961–64   C R C Howlett
- 1964–66   A H Bullock OBE
- 1966–69   A W Ayre
- 1969–71   G J Aylett OBE
- 1971–74   R K Hooks
- 1974–(76)   B A Ward

Superintendents of Engineering
- 1944–47   Mr B D Clark
- 1947–66   Mr F H Beer
- 1966–69   Mr C S Wills
- 1969–(78)   Mr H Plascott

Superintendents of Navigation and Radio
- 1956–74   Mr H A Popham
- 1974–after 75   Mr J McIver

Superintendent of Airborne Experiments/Airborne and Helicopter
- 1950–61   Mr W A Jennings

Superintendents of Photographic
- 1954–73   Mr G MacLaren-Humphreys
- 1974–after 75   Mr R T Shields

Superintendents of Weapon Systems/Trials Management
- 1961–65   Mr R P Dickinson
- 1965–68   Mr F G J Brown
- 1968–69   Mr H W Turner
- 1969–73   Mr J Lambie
- 1973–(76)   Mr B Ramsdale

Superintendent of Technical Services
- 1958–75   Mr J D Bennett

Superintendents of Flying (All Group Captain)
- 1945–46   G Silyn-Roberts AFC
- 1946   S Wroath AFC
- 1946–48   R C Dawkins
- 1948–49   T B Cooper OBE DFC (killed 5 Mar 49)
- 1949–51   H P Broad CBE DFC
- 1951–53   G A V Clayton DFC
- 1953–56   S L Ring DFC
- 1957–59   G H Goodman DSO DFC
- 1959–62   I N M MacDonald AFC
- 1963–65   K C M Giddings DFC AFC
- 1965–67   A D Dick AFC
- 1968–70   G C Cairns AFC
- 1971–73   V R L Evans AFC
- 1973–75   J Wilkinson AFC

Senior Administration Officers and Establishment Secretaries
- (1942)–49   Mr T W Marsden
- 1949–54   Mr K P Varney
- 1954–57   Mr J Watson
- 1957–61   Mr S G Surman
- 1961–(78)   Mr K J Hodges

APPENDIX 2: Roll of Honour

Those killed while flying on AAEE duty, August 1945 to end 1975
(NB: Omits Handling Squadron, ETPS and firms)

Rank	Initials	Name	Aircraft	Date
Sqn Ldr	MR	Alston	Canberra WT328	7 May 56
Flt Lt	B	Bastable	Marathon G-AGPD	28 May 48
Flt Lt	RL	Beeson	Hunter XL611	14 May 68
Flt Lt	IP	Bishop	Hastings TG499	26 Sep 49
Mr	M	Booth	Whirlwind XJ395	30 Apr 56
Flt Lt	AG	Bradfield	Lincoln RF560	2 Jul 48
Lt Cdr	O	Brown	Buccaneer XK529	31 Aug 61
Fg Off	P	Chilton	Vulcan XH535	11 May 64
M Sig	L	Christian	Vulcan XH535	11 May 64
Sqn Ldr	CG	Clark	Venom WE258	25 Nov 52
Fg Off	JMV	Coates*	Javelin XH714	26 Feb 58
Gp Capt	TB	Cooper	Meteor RA382	5 Mar 49
Sqn Ldr	DW	Colquhoun	Sea Hawk WF149	27 Jun 53
Flt Lt	J	Dingley	Vulcan XH535	11 May 64
Lt		Dunn	Buccaneer XK529	31 Aug 61
Miss	BR	Edmunds	Marathon G-AGPD	28 May 48
Sqn Ldr	PG	Evans	Hastings TG499	26 Sep 49
Sub Lt	KWA	Fehler	Monitor NP409	31 Aug 45
Flt Lt	GWE	Foster	Canberra WJ632	1 May 70
Lt	LRV	Habgood	Monitor NP409	31 Aug 45
Flt Lt	VD	Hall	Canberra WT328	7 May 56
Flt Lt	RJ	Hannaford	Victor XH668	20 Aug 59
Lt Cdr	DK	Hanson	Wyvern VW869	8 Jun 51
Flt Lt	IJ	Hartley	Brigand RH752	19 Jul 47
Sgt	LD	Hicks	(parachute)	17 Dec 70
Fg Off	R	Hodge	Hastings TG499	26 Sep 49
Mr	PW	Howes	Lincoln RF560	2 Jul 48
Flt Lt	IK	Johnston	Harvard FX371	12 Jun 52
Lt	GWN	Jones	Buccaneer XN922	5 Jul 62
Lt	TJA	King-Joyce	Attacker TS413	22 Jun 48
Sqn Ldr	NED	Lewis	Swift WJ965	10 Nov 53
Mr	JW	Lowman	Whirlwind XJ395	30 Apr 56
Sqn Ldr	AR	Majcherczyk	Meteor EE312	2 Jul 46
Flt Lt	RS	May	Javelin XH714	26 Feb 58
Sqn Ldr	MJPH	Mercer	Hunter XL611	14 May 68
Sqn Ldr	RJ	Morgan	Victor XH668	20 Aug 59
Flt Lt	TWG	Morren	Brigand RH752	19 Jul 47
Lt Cdr	RM	Orr-Ewing	Attacker WA485	5 Feb 52
Lt Cdr	RB	Pearson	Sea Otter RD869	19 Jul 46
Mr	DE	Purse	Brigand RH753	2 Jul 52
Lt Cdr	TA	Rickell	S'marine 525 VX138	6 Jul 55
Sqn Ldr	EJ	Roberts	Gnat XK767	15 Oct 58
Sqn Ldr	GB	Stockman	Victor XH668	20 Aug 59
Sqn Ldr	A	Tooth	Lincoln RF560	2 Jul 48
Miss	GM	Warman	Whirlwind XJ395	30 Apr 56
Maj	JR	Weaver**	Canberra WJ632	1 May 70
Mr	RJ	Whatley	Harvard FX371	12 Jun 52
Fg Off	GW	Williams	Lincoln RF560	2 Jul 48
Flt Lt	LN	Williams	Victor XH668	20 Aug 59
Mr	R	Williams***	Victor XH668	20 Aug 59
Flt Lt	G	Wood-Smith	Brigand RH753	2 Jul 52
Flt Lt	FA	Young	Vulcan XH535	11 May 64

* No 23 Squadron   ** USAF   *** Handley Page

APPENDIX 3: First Flights from Boscombe Down 1945–75
and types tested in blower tunnel only

Supermarine Attacker (E.10/44)	TS409	27 Jul 46	J K Quill
Westland Wyvern	TS371	12 Dec 46	H J Penrose
Hawker P1040	VP401	2 Sep 47	W Humble
Armstrong Whitworth AW52	TG363	13 Nov 47	E G Franklin
Gloster E.1/44	TX145	9 Mar 48	W A Waterton
Hawker P1052	VX272	19 Nov 48	T S Wade
Supermarine 510	VV106	29 Dec 48	M J Lithgow
Avro 707	VX784	4 Sep 49	S E Esler
Supermarine 528	VV119	27 Mar 50	M J Lithgow
Supermarine 535	VV119	23 Aug 50	M J Lithgow
Hawker P1081	VX279	19 Jun 50	T S Wade
Avro 707B	VX790	6 Sep 50	R J Falk
Boulton Paul BP111	VT935	10 Oct 50	R H Smythe
Fairey FD 1 (*also blower tunnel*)	VX350	12 Mar 51	R G Slade
Avro 707A	WD280	14 Jun 51	R J Falk
Hawker Hunter	WB188	20 Jul 51	N Duke
Supermarine Swift	WJ960	1 Aug 51	M J Lithgow
Supermarine 508	VX133	31 Aug 51	M J Lithgow
Boulton Paul BP120	VT951	6 Aug 52	A E Gunn
Shorts SB 5 (*also blower tunnel*)	WG768	2 Dec 52	T W Brooke-Smith
Handley Page Victor	WB771	24 Dec 52	H G Hazelden
Avro 707C	WZ744	1 Jul 53	R J Falk
Supermarine 525	VX138	27 Apr 54	M J Lithgow
English Electric P 1	WG760	4 Aug 54	R P Beamont
Folland Midge	G-39-1	11 Aug 54	E A Tennant
Fairey FD 2 (*also blower tunnel*)	WG774	6 Oct 54	L P Twiss
Folland Gnat	G-39-2	18 Jul 55	E A Tennant
Supermarine Scimitar	WT854	19 Jan 56	M J Lithgow
Shorts SC 1 (*also blower tunnel*)	XG900	2 Apr 57	T W Brooke-Smith
Saunders Roe SR 53 (*also blower tunnel*)	XD145	20 May 57	J S Booth*
BAC TSR 2	XR219	27 Sep 64	R P Beamont

* Killed on 5 June 1958 when SR 53 XD151 crashed at Boscombe

Tests of the following were made in the blower tunnel:
Short B.14/46 (Sperrin) The upper escape hatch always fouled the tailplane, and was recommended to be used in dire emergency only.
Dassault Mystere 2. Tip and underwing tanks jettisoned unremarkably in July 1953
Piaggio P148. MM53587 received wind speeds up to only 80 kt in March 1954.
Hunting H 126 XN714 came in October 1964
BAC 221 fuselage may have been tested in the blower tunnel.

Other events
The Bristol 188 landed at Boscombe after its first flight on 14 April 1962, and made 19 flights before departure.

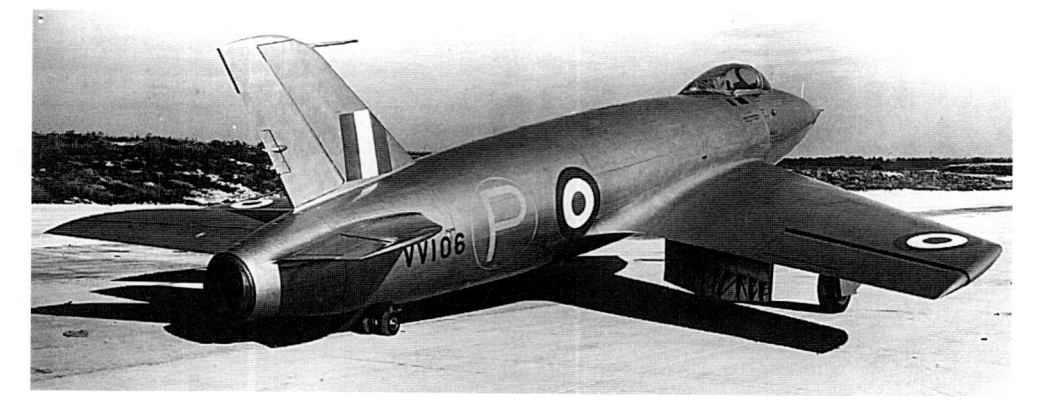

544: *Swift prototype (as the Supermarine Type 510 VV106 is referred to in the report) in October 1949 with the original intakes which caused vibrations and rumblings. One year later this aeroplane made the first deck landing by a swept-wing aeroplane. Deck take-offs (no catapult) all required rocket assistance.* © *Crown Copyright*

APPENDIX 4: Flying Hours

1946(5 mo)	1,359	1951	5,885	1956	7,500	1961	9,716	1966	8,812	1971	7,332**
1947	3,129	1952	6,928	1957	7,700	1962	10,362	1967	9,038	1972	7,132**
1948	5,257	1953	6,900	1958	9,300	1963	8,444	1968	10,821*	1973	7,666**
1949	5,031	1954	7,850	1959	9,150	1964	9,689	1969	11,483*	1974	6,957**
1950	4,443	1955	7,650	1960	8,683	1965	10,445	1970	8,331**	1975	6,281**

* includes ETPS and Handling Squadron
** includes Handling Squadron (1954—68 inclusive probably include Handling Sqn)

NB. Between 20 Jun 55 and 31 Dec 65, Air Transport Flight flew 15,442 hr.

APPENDIX 5: Electromagnetic Compatability (EMC)

An example of the range of equipment and armament tested in the AAEE Radio Electromagnetic Simulator (REG) in 1970

PHANTOM FG 1 AND FGR 2
a Sparrow III AIM-7E
b Sidewinder 1C AIM-9D
c Bomb Practice 28lb No 1 Mk 1
d Bomb Aircraft 1,000lb with nose and tail fusing
e Bomb Aircraft 540lb with nose and tail fusing
f Bomb Aircraft HE 2,100lb HC (FGR 2 only)
g Bomb Aircraft HE 550lb MC (FGR 2 only)
h Flare Aircraft Reconnaissance 8 in No 2 Mk 2
j Rocket 2 in No 2 Mk 2 in 36 tube launcher
k Rocket 68 mm SNEB in 155 launcher (FGR 2 only)
l Firebomb (NASR 1209) with fuse 949
m Bomb Cluster HE 600 lb No 1 Mk 1 (BL755) (FGR 2 only)
n Launcher AERO-27A with Cartridge No 200, 201, 204 or 205
o Launcher AERO-7A with Cartridge No 203
p Carrier Bomb Triple Ejection (CBTE) No 1 Mk 2
q Carrier Bomb Triple Ejection (CBTE) No 2 Mk 2
r Carrier Bomb Light Stores (CBLS) No 100
s Outboard Pylon with Cartridge Mk 9
t Inboard Pylon with Cartridge Mk 67
u Sergeant Fletcher Fuel Tank with Cartridge Mk 9
v SUU23 Gun Pod with HEI M56A3 and M55A2 20 mm ammunition (FGR 2 only)

*545: Seagull prototype PA147 on its land wheels showing the large flap and drooped aileron area giving a slow approach. The aileron control did not suffice for the low speed of carrier approaches.
© Crown Copyright*

APPENDIX 6: Abbreviations and Acronyms

abseiling	descending by rope (here, from helicopters)
AFCS	automatic flight control system
AFEE	Airborne Forces Experimental Esrablishment
AI	airborne interception (radar)
anmpg	air nautical miles per gallon
APU	auxiliary power unit
ARB	Air Registration Board
ARI	Air Radio Installation
ASDIC	Anti-Submarine Detection Investigation Committee (from WWI)
ASE	automatic stability equipment
ASI	air speed indicator
ASR	air/sea rescue
ASV	air/surface vessel (radar)
avionics	aviation electronics
AVTAG	aviation turbine gasolene
AVTUR	aviation turbine kerosene
BCAR	British Civil Airworthiness Requirements
BEAC	British European Airways Corporation
BOAC	British Overseas Airways Corporation
C of A	Certificate of Airworthiness
CA	Controller (Aircraft)
CAA	Civil Aviation Authority
CATS	Civil Aircraft Testing Section
CEP	circular error of probability (bombing)
CG	centre of gravity
CinC	Commander in Chief
C_L	coefficient of lift
C_{Lmax}	greatest C_L for given aerofoil
CLE	Central Landing Establishment
CO	Commanding Officer/ Carbon monoxide
CS(A)	Controller of Supplies (Air)
DECTRA	Decca Transatlatic (navigation aid)
DR	dead reckoning
ECM	electronic counter measures
ECU	engine change unit
Ekco	E K Coles (avionic company)
EMC	electromagnetic compatibility
ETPS	Empire Test Pilots' School
FAA	Fleet Air Arm
ft	feet or foot (1ft = 0.305 metre)
ft/min	feet per minute
FTO	Flight Test Observer
g	gravity or acceleration of 32 ft/sec/sec
gal	Imperial gallon
GCA	ground controlled approach
Gee-H	hyperbolic navigation and bombing aid
GGS	gyoscopic gun sight
GPI	ground position indicator
HF	high frequency (radio)
HQ	headquarters
hr	hour
HVAR	high velocity aircraft rocket
IFF	Identification—friend or foe
ILS	instrument landing system
IN	inertial navigator
IPN	iso-propyl nitrate (mono fuel)
jpt	jet pipe temperature
JSTU	Joint Services Trials Unit
kt	knot
LABS	low altitude bombing system
lb	imperial pound (1lb = 0.454 kilogram)
LORAK	long range hyperbolic navigation aid
M	Mach (decimal fraction of speed of sound)
m	metre
MAD	magnetic anomaly detector
MAT	(torpedo air tail)
min	minute
MoA/MoS	Ministry of Aviation / Supply
mm	millimetre-
mph	miles per hour (1 mph = 0.447 m/sec)
MRG	master reference gyroscope
navaid	navigation aid
NBS	navigation and bombing sysem
nm	nautical mile
OCU	operational conversion unit
OR	Operational Requirements (branch of Air Ministry/MoD)
PAS	Pilot Attack Sight
PE	pressure error
PEC	pressure error correction
PPL	private pilot's licence
psi	pounds per square inch (1 psi = 0.07 bar)
RAE	Royal Aircraft Establishment
RAF	Royal Air Force
RATO/G	rocket assisted take off/gear
Rebecca	aircraft distance and bearing measuring equipment
REG	Radio Environment simulator
RN	Royal Navy
roping	*see abseiling*
RP	rocket projectile
rpm	revolutions per minute
RRE	Royal Radar Establishment
SARAH	Search And Rescue And Homing
SAS	stability augmentation system
SEAC	South East Asia Command
sec	second
sfg	stick force (in pounds) per g
sg	specific gravity
slug/sq ft	slugs per square foot (1 slug/ft^2 = 1.356 kg/m^2)
SRIM	service radio installation modification
SSR	(advanced feature of *IFF qv*)
TACAN	tactical air navigation
TRE	Telecommunications Research Establishment
UHF	ultra high frequency (radio)
VHF	very high frequency (radio)
VOR	VHF omni range (navaid)
VT	variable timing (bomb fuse)
w	watt
yd	yard (1 yd = 0.915 metre)
ZABRA	(one off avionic equipment on a Canberra)

INDEX OF AIRCRAFT

This list contains all aircraft known to have been at Boscombe Down for AAEE purposes, and those flown elsewhere for trials. Aircraft used exlusively by Handling Squadron and ETPS are omitted. Dates generally are for the first arrival at Boscombe; Ministry records differ both from those maintained officially at Boscombe and from those kept by individuals. The discrepancies in dates are usually small. Other differences between existing records are accounted for by a firm servicing and/or flying the machine at Boscombe when there may be no mention in records of the AAEE maintenance organisation. There are other minor anomolies, but the purpose of the list is to serve as an index to the whereabouts of individual aircraft in the book and to indicate the page on which its illustration appears. Brackets round dates indicate tests at locations other than Boscombe.

Aircraft shown in **bold** are illustrated in the colour profile section. Photographs are indicated by **bold** page numbers.

Type	Serial	Arrived	Page	Type	Serial	Arrived	Page
AH-1G	64-7015		187	Argosy	XN815	06.06.61	213
Albermarle	V1743	Wartime	72	Argosy	XN816	06.09.61	213, **214**
Alouette	XJ378	05.06.61	181, **182**	Argosy	XN817	27.04.61	215, **245**
Alouette	XR232	04.09.64	181, **247**	Argosy	XN818	28.08.61	215
Ambassador	G-AGUA	22.02.49	203	Argosy	XN819	11.10.62	215
Andover	H-1176	(1972)	215	Argosy	XN855	01.12.70	215
Andover	G-ARRV	20.02.65	**214**, 215	Argosy	XN856	22.11.62	215
Andover	XS594	02.12.65	215	Argosy	XR105	26.06.63	215, **215**, 218
Andover	XS595	25.01.66	**214**, 215	Arsenal (V-1)	69		**12**, 117
Andover	XS596	01.06.66	215	Ashton	WB490	01.09.50	223, **226**
Andover	XS597	01.04.66	215, **216**	Ashton	WE670	1952	223, **226**
Andover	XS606	02.11.66	215	Athena	VM125	24.11.48	**237**, 239
Andover	XS611	18.10.73	215	Athena	VR567	17.10.50	239
Andover	XS613	22.03.71	215	Athena	VR568	11.05.50	239
Andover	XS640	02.02.68	215	Athena	VW890	20.04.49	**238**, 239
Andover	XS647	22.03.68	215	Athena	VW891	30.06.49	**30**, **238**, 239
Andover	XS789	04.06.64	215, **218**	Athena	VW892	21.11.49	239
Andover	XS791	23.11.64	215	Attacker	TS409	09.06.47	**282**, 283
Andover	XS794	09.07.65	215	Attacker	TS413	27.08.47	**282**, 283
Anson	G-AGUD	07.03.49	190, **192**	Attacker	TS416	1950	283
Anson	G-AKUD	05.05.48	190	Attacker	WA469	01.08.50	**282**, 283
Anson	LT764	Wartime	190	Attacker	WA471	12.01.51	285
Anson	NK500	02.05.47	190	Attacker	WA472	20.02.50?	285
Anson	NL141	Wartime	190	Attacker	WA485	02.52	285
Anson	NL171	Wartime	190	Attacker	WA525	05.05.53	285
Anson	NL172	24.04.46	190	Attacker	WA535	31.03.52	285
Anson	NL200	08.04.49	190	Attacker	WK319	07.10.52	**284**, 285
Anson	PH775	03.08.50	190	Auster	G-AJIZ	03.11.48	225
Anson	VL301	10.03.53	190	Auster	NJ630	Wartime	225
Anson	VM305	31.12.47	191, **192**	Auster	NJ631	Wartime	225
Anson	VM306	20.04.48	191	Auster	TJ645	04.12.50	225
Anson	VM360	01.09.47	190	Auster	TJ707	06.12.45	225
Anson	VM371	05.12.61	190	Auster	TW384	12.09.46	225
Anson	VM373	05.05.48	190	Auster	TW513	04.01.46	225
Anson	VM411	03.02.48	191	Auster	TW519	18.01.46	225
Anson	VP509	05.03.51	191	Auster	VF518	12.05.48	225
Anson	VS505	28.11.53	191	Auster	VF665	18.08.50	225, **227**
Anson	VS562	1956	191, **192**	Auster	VX125	31.10.50	225
Anson	VV884	26.10.59	191	Auster	WE555	11.11.59	225
Anson	VV973	17.09.59	191	Auster	WE566	31.08.51	225
Anson	WD402	18.09.50	191, **191**	Auster	WJ316	09.04.51	225, **226**
Apollo	VX220	24.09.52	**204**, 207	Auster	WZ662	30.06.54	225
Apollo	VX224	15.10.53	207	Auster	WZ663	10.12.54	**221**, 225, **226**
Argosy	XN814	29.06.64	**23**, **214**, 215	Auster	WZ672	07.03.56	225, **227**

313

Type	Serial	Arrived	Page	Type	Serial	Arrived	Page
Auster	WZ677	04.05.55	225	Beaufighter	JL955	Wartime	221
Auster	WZ702	03.57	225	Beaufighter	RD834	29.07.46	221
Auster	XJ941	14.03.55	225	Beaufighter	RD854	1959	221, **224**
Auster	XK376	03.08.56	225	Beaver	G-AMVU	29.01.53	230
Auster	XP254	07.11.61	225, **228**	Beaver	XP769	02.01.61	**229**, 230
Auster A.2/45	VL522	09.05.49	225, **228**	Beaver	XP775	(06.62)	230
Auster B4	XA177	16.04.52	225, **228**	Beaver	XP822	20.04.67	230
Avenger	53358	06.07.53	277	Beaver	XV270	31.10.67	230
Avenger	JZ625	06.12.45	277	Beaver	XV271	21.12.70	230
Avenger	JZ635	Wartime	277	Belfast	XR363	19.06.64	216
Avenger	JZ689	03.12.45	277	Belfast	XR364	30.06.66	216
Avenger	KE439	16.04.47	277	Belfast	XR365	06.05.65	216
Avenger	XB355	11.09.53	277, **280**	Belfast	XR366	07.09.65	216, **217**
Avenger	XB358	16.03.54	277	Belfast	XR371	24.07.67	216
Avro 707	VX790	09.50	310	Bell 47B	G-AKFB	08.50	**161**, 162
Avro 707C	WZ744	23.09.53	**229**, 230	Bell 204	I-AGUG	06.65	184, **186**
AW52G	RG324	09.50	230	Bell 205	MM80474	07.65	184, **186**
Balliol	VL892	11.12.47	235, **236**	Belvedere	XF785	11.12.53	171, **173**
Balliol	VL935	04.01.50	235	Belvedere	XG449		**175**
Balliol	VR590	04.03.52	239	Belvedere	XG451	22.04.60	171
Balliol	VR591	12.50	239	Belvedere	XG452	27.05.60	171, **173**, 174
Balliol	VR592	03.10.49	239	Belvedere	XG457	03.03.61	171
Balliol	VR593	1949	239	Belvedere	XG460	30.08.61	171
Balliol	VR595	01.50	239	Belvedere	XG468	21.09.62	174
Balliol	VR596	08.11.50	239	Belvedere	XG475	(1962)	174
Balliol	VR597	17.10.50	239	Beverley	WF320	07.07.52	**208**, 209
Balliol	VR598	02.11.50	239	Beverley	WZ889	17.03.54	**190**, 209
Balliol	VR599	20.06.50	**236**, 237 **239**	Beverley	XB259	10.08.55	209
Balliol	VW898	25.02.49	235, **237**	Beverley	XB261	27.01.56	209, **245**
Balliol	VW899	13.06.51	239	Beverley	XB262	02.08.55	209
Balliol	VW900	31.05.49	235	Beverley	XB263	24.05.56	209
Balliol	WF989	23.05.52	239	Beverley	XB266	25.06.56	209
Balliol	WL716	09.53	239	Beverley	XB269	11.05.64	209
Balliol	WL732	09.53	**22**, 239	Beverley	XB284	24.05.61	209
Balliol	WN526	11.01.57	**18**, 239	Beverley	XB285	21.08.63	209
Balliol	WP328	26.06.57	239	Beverley	XL150	07.08.59	209
Balliol	WP333	09.12.54	**235**, 239	Beverley	XM111	09.06.61	209
Barracuda	LS837	05.09.45	269	Blackhawk	N8715A	(02.72)	189
Barracuda	PM940	Wartime	269	Blackburn GR17	WB781	15.12.49	291
Barracuda	PM941	17.09.45	269	Blackburn GR17	WB788	06.06.50	291, **292**
Barracuda	RJ769	02.04.49	269	Blackburn GR17	WB797	11.50	291
Barracuda	RJ781	1952	269	Bolkow 105		(05.70)	184
Barracuda	RJ916	20.07.51	269, **270**	Boston	BZ274	Wartime	76
Barracuda	RJ919	11.49	269	Boston	BZ286	27.08.45	76
Barracuda	RK531	20.12.45	269	Boston	BZ315	Wartime	76
Barracuda	RK533	24.04.46	269	Boston	BZ320	Wartime	76
Barracuda	RK535	21.08.46	269, **270**	Boston	W8315	Wartime	76
Basset	G-ATYE	01.11.66	217	Brantly B-2	XS681	26.06.63	184, **185**
Basset	XS742	15.07.64	216, **248**	Brantly B-2	XS683	26.06.63	184
Basset	XS743	14.01.65	216, 217, **218**	Brigand	MX991	(13.12.45)	80, **81**
Basset	XS765	04.08.65	217	Brigand	MX994	02.09.46	80
Basset	XS769	06.08.65	217	Brigand	RH742	01.04.47	80
Basset	XS770	17.01.75	217	Brigand	RH745	28.10.46	80
Basset	XS772	02.08.71	217	Brigand	RH746	18.06.46	80, **81**
Basset	XS774	23.11.66	217	Brigand	RH750	29.11.46	80
Basset	XS781	06.02.70	217	Brigand	RH752	13.11.46	80
Beaufighter	V8319	08.09.45	221	Brigand	RH753	17.06.47	80
Beaufighter	X7574	Wartime	221	Brigand	RH754	12.05.47	80, **81**

Type	Serial	Arrived	Page	Type	Serial	Arrived	Page
Brigand	RH763	26.02.48	80	Buccaneer	XV869	06.04.72	305
Brigand	RH773	08.05.47	80	Buccaneer	XW525	04.05.70	307
Brigand	RH796	05.08.47	80	Buccaneer	XW529	29.10.70	307
Brigand	RH798	21.05.48	**41**, **79**, 80, 82	Buccaneer	XW540	21.12.71	307
Brigand	RH800	08.48	80	Buckmaster	RP137	02.06.45	235
Brigand	VS818	12.10.48	80	Buckmaster	TJ717	(02.46)	235
Brigand	VS860	29.12.49	80	Buffalo	9456	02.09.69	217
Brigand	WA565	20.02.54	82	Bulldog	G-AXEH	(12.69)	267
Bristol Freighter	VR380	28.09.46	199, **200**	Bulldog	XX513	21.02.73	267
Bristol Freighter	WJ320	04.06.51	199	Bulldog	XX514	06.03.73	**264**, 267
Bristol Freighter	XJ470	18.02.55	199	Bulldog	XX522	25.06.74	267
Bristol Freighter	VR382	(1948)	199	Bulldog/Pup	G-AVLN	15.10.68	**264**, 267
Britannia	XL635	(1959)	213	Bulldog/Pup	G-AXIG	26.10.71	267
Britannia	XM518	1964	213	C-119 Boxcar	53-3182	(1955)	211
Britannia	XX367	03.05.72	**212**, 213	Cadet	TS291	10.04.53	263
Buccaneer	XK486	10.68	303, **304**	Canadair 4	G-ALHD	30.04.49	207
Buccaneer	XK489	21.05.60	303	Canadair 4	G-ALHY	11.12.67	207
Buccaneer	XK491	21.02.61	303	Canberra	VN799	26.10.49	82
Buccaneer	XK523	14.09.60	**38**, **241**, 303	Canberra	VX165	08.11.50	82, **83**
Buccaneer	XK524	13.12.63	303	Canberra	VX169	28.03.51	50, **82**
Buccaneer	XK525	02.06.64	303	Canberra	VX181	06.11.51	**17**, 84, 85, **248**
Buccaneer	XK526	15.11.60	303, **304**, 305, 306	Canberra	VX185	04.05.55	86
Buccaneer	XK527	22.10.60	303, 304, **305**	Canberra	WD932	(02.51)	**26**, 82
Buccaneer	XK528	23.01.61	303, **304**	Canberra	WD937	17.12.54	84
Buccaneer	XK529	23.08.61	303	Canberra	WD945	18.12.51	82
Buccaneer	XK530	17.08.61	303	Canberra	WD954	14.05.52	**71**, 84
Buccaneer	XK531	27.06.61	303	Canberra	WD956	(12.51)	82
Buccaneer	XK532	11.62	**302**, 303	Canberra	WD958	26.08.52	84
Buccaneer	XK533	28.09.62	303	Canberra	WD959	19.09.52	84
Buccaneer	XK536	07.05.62	305	Canberra	WE121	01.07.69	84
Buccaneer	XN922	29.06.62	303	Canberra	WE135	15.02.53	85
Buccaneer	XN923	20.07.62	303	Canberra	WE137	03.12.52	85, **87**
Buccaneer	XN924	26.10.62	**19**	Canberra	WE146	14.08.57	85
Buccaneer	XN931	(08.64)	303	Canberra	WE167	28.06.56	85
Buccaneer	XN934	(1962)	303	Canberra	WE173	17.12.59	85
Buccaneer	XN955	14.07.67		Canberra	WE174	28.06.56	85
Buccaneer	XN959	10.06.63	303	Canberra	WE190	29.10.59	90, **91**
Buccaneer	XN968	23.01.64		Canberra	WF916	03.08.70	90
Buccaneer	XN973	03.07.64		Canberra	WF922	11.06.68	85
Buccaneer	XN974	10.08.64	**22**, **302**, 305, 307	Canberra	WH638	09.06.53	84
				Canberra	WH640	01.53	84
Buccaneer	XN975	12.10.64	305	Canberra	WH715	12.11.54	82
Buccaneer	XN976	17.09.64	**37**, 305, **307**	Canberra	WH718	04.10.68	90
Buccaneer	XN983	03.03.67	305	Canberra	WH775	11.01.54	85
Buccaneer	XT279	02.11.66	305	Canberra	WH780	24.04.58	85
Buccaneer	XT280	26.10.66	305	Canberra	WH792	03.08.54	85
Buccaneer	XV153	(10.66)	305	Canberra	WH793	07.56	85, **88**
Buccaneer	XV164	07.11.66	305	Canberra	WH840	13.10.65	90
Buccaneer	XV165	05.11.66	305	Canberra	WH841	22.09.67	90
Buccaneer	XV168	13.06.67	307	Canberra	WH844	19.01.60	90
Buccaneer	XV334	24.07.67	307	Canberra	WH854	04.12.67	90, **248**
Buccaneer	XV337	23.12.74	**241**, 307	Canberra	WH863	08.04.65	90
Buccaneer	XV350	17.06.69	307	Canberra	WH876	25.09.63	**29**, 84, **108**, **248**
Buccaneer	XV352	17.09.68	307				
Buccaneer	XV353	29.10.68	307	Canberra	WH919	27.02.61	84
Buccaneer	XV863	20.05.69	305	Canberra	WH952	02.02.55	**56**, 84, **89**
Buccaneer	XV866	26.03.74	305	Canberra	WH966	08.07.66	86

Type	Serial	Arrived	Page	Type	Serial	Arrived	Page
Canberra	WH967	14.10.60	**46**, **53**, **83**, 86	Canberra	XH135	09.08.60	85
Canberra	WH972	27.05.70	86	Canberra	XH164	15.06.61	86
Canberra	WJ565	11.04.53	84	Canberra	XH174	08.05.68	86
Canberra	WJ567	22.07.68	84	Canberra	XH175	17.12.68	86
Canberra	WJ611	05.10.61	84	Canberra	XH176	09.02.65	86
Canberra	WJ632	22.11.66	**59**, 90, **248**	Canberra	XH209	18.02.63	86
Canberra	WJ638	27.06.62	84, **247**, **248**	Canberra	XH232	05.57	90
Canberra	WJ639	08.07.71	90	Canberra	XK952	27.03.63	86
Canberra	WJ643	13.11.58	84	Canberra	XM245	01.09.59	86
Canberra	WJ678	27.11.56	84	Canberra	XM265	19.10.64	86
Canberra	WJ723	02.12.59	84	Canberra	XM272	16.07.63	86
Canberra	WJ730	18.08.54	84	Canberra	XM275	04.07.63	86
Canberra	WJ734	21.05.58	90	Caproni RF5	MM553	(1953)	**262**, 263
Canberra	WJ754	06.04.54	84	CH-47C	632	(02.71)	189
Canberra	WJ755	04.05.54	84	CH-53D	—	(02.71)	189
Canberra	WJ764	06.74	84	Chipmunk	G-AJVD	04.11.48	257
Canberra	WJ815	(07.75)	85	Chipmunk	G-AKDN	29.06.48	**240**, 257
Canberra	WJ867	(22.01.68)	90	Chipmunk	WB549	18.11.49	**240**, 257
Canberra	WJ878	09.05.56	90	Chipmunk	WB550	18.11.49	257
Canberra	WJ880	25.09.62	90	Chipmunk	WG307	14.01.69	257
Canberra	WJ977	06.05.66	**87**, **88**, 90	Chipmunk	WG407	26.03.63	257
Canberra	WK121	15.02.60	**83**, 84, **248**	Chipmunk	WG419	03.07.67	257
Canberra	WK122	04.04.68	90	Chipmunk	WG466	13.04.54	257
Canberra	WK123	14.06.56	84	Chipmunk	WK634	10.06.74	257
Canberra	WK164	09.12.59	84, **89**	Chipmunk	WP804	25.04.58	257
Canberra	WN467	11.11.52	90	Chipmunk	WP903	26.04.61	257
Canberra	WT205	19.04.63	86, **248**	Chipmunk	WP930	27.01.53	257
Canberra	WT210	14.12.64	86	Comet	G-AMXD	09.12.58	211
Canberra	WT302	29.05.61	90	Comet	XK655	20.04.59	211, **212**
Canberra	WT305	18.12.74	84, **91**	Comet	XK671	22.08.56	**210**, 211
Canberra	WT307	12.07.55	86	Comet	XK697	22.04.59	211
Canberra	WT311	27.11.62	86	Comet	XK699	11.61	211
Canberra	WT312	09.10.58	86	Comet	XM829	11.09.58	**210**, 211
Canberra	WT319	14.10.60	86	Comet	XR395	16.01.61	211
Canberra	WT322	28.05.59	86	Comet	XS235	02.12.63	**210**, 211
Canberra	WT326	07.11.55	86	Comet	XW626	17.07.72	211
Canberra	WT328	06.02.56	86	Commander	N9203N	02.08.71	**266**, 267
Canberra	WT329	13.04.59	86	Corsair	JT406	Wartime	277
Canberra	WT330	04.05.62	86	Corsair	KD835	Wartime	277
Canberra	WT333	23.03.59	86	Corsair	KD903	Wartime	277
Canberra	WT338	(1957)	90	Cub	VM286	Wartime	223
Canberra	WT346	21.06.62	86	Dakota	FZ564	17.09.45	191
Canberra	WT347	09.03.59	**54**, 86	Dakota	KJ829	16.04.50	**193**, 194
Canberra	WT364	28.09.56	86	Dakota	KJ881	23.09.52	194
Canberra	WT370	26.09.58	84	Dakota	KJ945	02.02.54	194
Canberra	WT503	20.03.61	85	Dakota	KK127	09.50	194
Canberra	WT507	17.12.57	85	Dakota	KN407	27.10.45	194
Canberra	WT509	12.11.74	**68**, 85	Dakota	KN645	20.09.67	194
Canberra	WT510	30.08.73	**88**, 90	Dassault 450	02	(07.50)	**59**, 134
Canberra	WT519	10.07.73	85	Desford	G-AGOS	1946	**222**, 223
Canberra	WT527	15.03.66	85	Devon	VP952	20.05.55	209
Canberra	WV787	10.11.66	**83**, 84, **87**, **248**	Devon	VP961	09.04.69	209
Canberra	XH130	01.07.59	85	Devon	VP971	22.07.66	209
Canberra	XH131	11.59	85	Devon	VP973	04.01.72	209
Canberra	XH132	2.60	85	Devon	VP979	23.09.59	209
Canberra	XH133	06.11.59	85	Devon	WB530	14.06.67	209
Canberra	XH134	10.59	85, 86, **89**	Devon	WB531	30.01.62	**208**, 209
				Devon	XA880	20.05.54	209

Type	Serial	Arrived	Page	Type	Serial	Arrived	Page
Devon	XJ321	22.04.55	209	Firefly	Z2118	12.01.46	271
Devon	XJ350	18.11.68	209	Firefly	DK550	22.09.52	271
Dominie	R2487	18.09.45	191	Firefly	DT985	Wartime	271
Dominie	R9545	Wartime	191	Firefly	MB465	Wartime	271
Dominie	X7353	1945	191	Firefly	MB520	14.11.49	271
Dominie	X7381	29.11.45	191	Firefly	MB621	08.07.47	271
Dominie	X7411	27.11.45	191	Firefly	MB647	Wartime	271
Dominie	XS709	30.03.65	**264**, 265	Firefly	MB649	16.12.49	271
Dominie	XS710	23.04.65	265	Firefly	MB750	30.08.46	**270**, 271
Dominie	XS711	06.05.68	265	Firefly	MB757	04.10.49	**273**, 275
Dominie	XS714	03.01.67	265	Firefly	PP391	08.08.47	271
Dominie	XS726	15.05.71	265	Firefly	PP427	09.02.46	271
Dove	G-AGPJ	13.10.49	**206**, 207	Firefly	PP468	10.05.46	271
Dragonfly	VW209	15.09.50	165	Firefly	PP482	02.48	271
Dragonfly	VX595	09.50	165	Firefly	PP562	22.08.52	271
Dragonfly	WB810	13.06.49	165	Firefly	PP605	17.07.47	271
Dragonfly	WG661	26.03.52	165	Firefly	PP639	25.07.51	271
Dragonfly	WG662	27.02.52	**164**, 165	Firefly	TW689	25.03.47	271
Dragonfly	WG663	22.04.52	165	Firefly	TW690	28.08.47	271
Dragonfly	WG666	04.06.52	165	Firefly	TW693	11.04.47	271, **272**
Dragonfly	WG667	12.07.60	165	Firefly	TW694	18.11.47	271
Dragonfly	WG714	21.12.50	165	Firefly	TW718	06.12.48	271
Dragonfly	WG725	12.01.53	165	Firefly	TW722	25.08.47	271
Dragonfly	WN493	12.06.53	**164**, 165	Firefly	TW735	11.49	271
Dragonfly	XB251	(1953)	165	Firefly	TW746	06.48	271
Dragonfly	G-ALIK	02.51	**163**, 165	Firefly	VG964	23.01.51	271
EP9	XM797	23.04.58	232	Firefly	VH143		271
EP9	XM819	09.05.58	**231**, 232	Firefly	VT393	02.07.48	**60**, 271
Ercoupe	G-AKFC /			Firefly	VT428	04.01.51	271
	VX147	26.05.47	**240**, 257	Firefly	VT477	31.12.48	**58**, 271
F-15	71-291	1975	**156**, 157	Firefly	WB343	11.04.51	271
Fairey Primer	G-6-5	08.11.48	**238**, 239	Firefly	WB381	01.03.50	271
Fairey Primer	OO-POM	03.48	239	Firefly	WB402	24.10.51	271
FD1	VX350	1951	310	Firefly	WB406	05.10.50	271, **272**
FD2	WG774	1954	40	Firefly	WD845	07.01.53	271
Fiat G-82	1 P	(11.54)	265	Firefly	WD848	23.02.54	275
Fiat G-82	2 P	(04.55)	265	Firefly	WD882	30.04.52	275
Firebrand	DK392	Wartime	277	Firefly	WD886	25.01.52	275
Firebrand	DK393	Wartime	277	Firefly	WD918	18.05.54	**273**, 275
Firebrand	DK394	12.45	277	Firefly	WH629	25.01.52	275
Firebrand	DK408	Wartime	277	Firefly	WJ146	25.07.52	275
Firebrand	EK602	Wartime	277	Firefly	WJ148	28.07.52	275
Firebrand	EK605	Wartime	277, **278**	Firefly	WJ194	1958	275
Firebrand	EK616	19.12.45	277	Firefly	WJ215	09.07.51	**274**, 275
Firebrand	EK630	21.08.46	277	Firefly	WJ216	28.11.51	275
Firebrand	EK655	28.03.51	277	Firefly	WK367	27.08.53	275
Firebrand	EK691	10.03.50	277	Fokker S14	K-1	(05.52)	**261**, 263
Firebrand	EK692	15.01.46	**276**, 277	Fokker S14	L-1	1955	263
Firebrand	EK732	08.45	277	Fortress	KL835	Wartime	76
Firebrand	EK736	18.07.46	277	Fouga CM170	03	(mid 1953)	263
Firebrand	EK742	14.05.47	277	Fournier RF5	G-AYZX	24.06.71	**266**, 267
Firebrand	EK743	21.11.47	277	Gannet	VR546	05.06.50	**294**, 295, **296**
Firebrand	EK778	22.08.52	277	Gannet	VR557	01.12.50	**294**, 295
Firebrand	EK844	27.06.49	277	Gannet	WN339	05.10.53	295
Firebrand	EK848	04.05.48	277	Gannet	WN340	05.10.53	295, **296**
Firefly	Z1835	13.06.46	271	Gannet	WN341	08.10.53	295
Firefly	Z1909	Wartime	271	Gannet	WN342	14.07.54	295
Firefly	Z2033	16.09.47	271	Gannet	WN352	18.11.58	295

Type	Serial	Arrived	Page	Type	Serial	Arrived	Page
Gannet	WN355	19.09.57	295	Halifax	NP849	05.11.45	72
Gannet	WN357	28.08.54	295	Halifax	NP924	Wartime	72
Gannet	WN365	11.12.54	295	Harrier	XV277	15.03.68	151, 152
Gannet	WN372	02.08.55	295, 297	Harrier	XV278	24.05.73	151, 152
Gannet	WN374	02.05.55	295	Harrier	XV279	04.10.71	152, **153**
Gannet	WN393	23.01.55	295	Harrier	XV281	02.05.68	**150**, 151, 152, **153**
Gannet	XA401	02.03.56	295				
Gannet	XA470	06.12.66	297	Harrier	XV738	31.01.72	152
Gannet	XA515	30.08.55	295	Harrier	XV740	23.07.68	152
Gannet	XA518	07.55	295	Harrier	XV741	16.08.68	152, **245**
Gannet	XG827	02.05.57	297	Harrier	XV742	06.03.72	152
Gannet	XJ440	09.06.59	**294**, 295	Harrier	XV744	09.04.69	152
Gannet	XL449	24.11.59	297	Harrier	XV788	04.09.75	154
Gannet	XL450	08.06.60	297	Harrier	XW175	10.01.74	154
Gannet	XL451	(1959)	297	Harrier	XW264	(1970)	152
Gannet	XL452	06.10.59	**296**, 297	Harrier	XW265	21.05.70	**108**, 152, 154
Gannet	XL456	31.10.68	297	Harrier	XW934	16.04.74	154
Gannet	XL497	02.11.65	297	Harvard	FT375	21.11.54	233
Gannet	XL503	07.07.64	297	Harvard	FX216	09.05.50	233
Gannet	XP226	03.10.66	297	Harvard	FX278	15.09.50	233
Gannet	XR433	18.06.68	297	Harvard	FX371	15.09.50	233
Gazelle	340-001	(1969)	189	Harvard	FX373	03.10.49	233
Gazelle	340-02	(05.68)	189	Harvard	FX402	22.10.48	233
Gazelle	341-01	(1969)	189	Harvard	KF183	30.01.53	**51**, 233, **248**
Gazelle	341-04	(1970)	189	Harvard	KF314	10.02.49	233, **248**
Gazelle	XW276	08.02.71	189	Harvard	KF562	08.09.49	233
Gazelle	XW842	11.08.72	189	Hastings	TE580	18.06.46	199
Gazelle	XW843	17.10.72	189	Hastings	TE583	17.01.47	199, **201**
Gazelle	XW845	14.09.73	189	Hastings	TG499	15.09.49	201
Gazelle	XW846	15.12.72	189, **246**	Hastings	TG500	27.04.48	**19**, **54**, **60**, **64**, 201, **202**
Gazelle	XW848	(06.73)	189				
Gazelle	XW851	17.11.75	189	Hastings	TG501	10.11.47	199
Gazelle	XW856	08.10.73	189	Hastings	TG502	15.09.50	**19**, 199, 201
Gazelle	XW901	18.06.74	189	Hastings	TG503	24.05.49	199, 203
Gazelle	XW907	25.07.74	189	Hastings	TG505	12.59	203
Gnat	IE1060	08.58	265	Hastings	TG509	10.48	**26**, 199, 201
Gnat	IE1071	09.03.62	265	Hastings	TG524	02.05.60	201
Gnat	G-39-6	1958	265	Hastings	TG527	16.05.60	201
Gnat	XK739	(01.57)	265	Hastings	TG565	27.06.63	201
Gnat	XK741	1959?	**262**, 265	Hastings	TG568	15.05.59	201
Gnat	XK767	(1958)	265	Hastings	TG620	10.50	201
Gnat	XM691	21.03.60	265	Hastings	TG622	15.01.50	199
Gnat	XM692	12.03.63	265	Hastings	TG623	18.07.58	201
Gnat	XM693	08.03.61	265	Hastings	WD475	09.01.51	201
Gnat	XM696	10.62	265	Hastings	WD476	14.03.51	**200**, 201
Gnat	XM697	16.10.61	265	Hastings	WD477	02.60	203
Gnat	XM698	27.04.61	265	Hastings	WD493	12.59	203
Gnat	XM704	30.11.61	265	Hastings	WD496	27.03.53	**19**, **202**, 203
Gnat	XM705	16.10.61	265	Hastings	WD498	27.07.61	203
Gnat	XN122	1958	265	Hastings	WD500	01.10.51	**200**, 203
Gnat	XP500	23.09.74	265	Hastings	WJ325	10.56	203
Gnat	XP505	06.12.68	265	Hastings	WJ328	12.07.62	203
Gnat	XR540	24.09.64	265	Hastings	WJ336	18.02.63	203
Gnat	XR543	27.09.63	265	Hastings	WJ337	12.02.59	203
Gnat	XS110	04.11.75	265	Hawk	XX154		**155**, 268
Halifax	HX246	05.49	72	Hawk	XX159	30.07.75	268
Halifax	LV838	Wartime	**60**, 72	Hawker 1052	VX272	11.48	310
Halifax	LV999	Wartime	72	Hawker 1052	VX279	11.48	225, **229**

Type	Serial	Arrived	Page	Type	Serial	Arrived	Page
Hellcat	JX901	Wartime	269	Hoverfly	KN841	15.09.50	158
Hellcat	JX998	20.07.45	269	Hoverfly	KN846	15.09.50	158
Hercules	XV177	23.02.67	**219**, 220	Hoverfly	KN862	15.09.50	158
Hercules	XV178	21.03.67	**62**, 220, **248**	HP T16/48	WE496	07.12.50	**258**, 259
Hercules	XV191	18.12.73	220	HP T16/48	WE505	30.10.50	257, **260**
Hercules	XV196	20.10.75	220	Hudson	AM553	31.08.45	221
Hercules	XV206	01.02.71	220	Hughes 269	XS684	25.16.63	**183**, 184
Hercules	XV207	22.06.71	220	Hughes 269	XS685	25.06.63	184
Hercules	XV208	12.06.73	220	Hughes 300	N9302F	29.01.64	184, **185**
Hercules	XV218	24.10.72	220	Hunter	WB195	05.12.52	136
Hermes	G-AGUB	15.07.48	**202**, 203	Hunter	WN888	16.03.54	136
Hermes	G-AKFP	19.04.49	203, **204**	Hunter	WN890	17.12.54	136
Hermes	G-ALEU	1951???	203	Hunter	WN892	15.07.54	136
Hermes	G-ALEV	02.02.51	203, **204**	Hunter	WN954	30.11.54	138
Heron	XH375	06.04.55	**208**, 211	Hunter	WN955	07.01.57	138
Heron	XM296	10.08.62	211	Hunter	WN958	19.06.56	138, **139**
Heron, Sea	XR444	18.12.62	211	Hunter	WT555	30.10.53	136, **137**
Heron, Sea	XR445	07.05.68	211	Hunter	WT556	27.02.56	**18**, 136
Heston A2/45	VL529	13.05.48	223, **224**	Hunter	WT557	10.02.55	136
Hiller	XB513	20.10.53	174, **175**	Hunter	WT558	19.05.54	136
Hornet	PX211	Wartime	126	Hunter	WT559	20.11.53	136
Hornet	PX217	Wartime	126	Hunter	WT562	19.01.55	136
Hornet	PX218	Wartime	126	Hunter	WT564	13.06.55	136
Hornet	PX219	03.03.47	**129**, 277, **280**	Hunter	WT567	22.03.54	136, **139**
Hornet/Sea	PX220	29.01.46	126	Hunter	WT568	01.09.55	136
Hornet	PX221	Wartime	126	Hunter	WT569	15.07.54	136, **137**
Hornet	PX222	18.12.46	126	Hunter	WT570	27.07.54	136
Hornet	PX223	09.11.45	126	Hunter	WT573	20.04.54	136
Hornet/Sea	PX230	24.04.47	279	Hunter	WT576	03.06.54	136
Hornet	PX239	04.48	279, **280**	Hunter	WT612	05.06.56	136
Hornet	PX312	30.06.47	126	Hunter	WT616	19.01.55	136
Hornet	PX336	26.07.51	128	Hunter	WT702	11.09.56	138
Hornet	PX340	13.02.50	128	Hunter	WT703	03.06.55	138, **140**
Hornet	PX347	01.09.50	128	Hunter	WT704	06.12.56	138
Hornet	PX348	24.10.46	126	Hunter	WT705	24.05.55	138
Hornet	PX383	28.06.48	**127**, 128	Hunter	WT721	21.12.62	**19**, 142
Hornet	PX385	27.07.51	128	Hunter	WT735	17.09.58	138
Hornet	PX386	08.07.47	126	Hunter	WT736	04.01.56	138
Hornet	PX393	01.07.49	126, **127**	Hunter	WT739	(01.56)	138
Hornet	PX395	11.05.50	128	Hunter	WT751	28.06.62	138, **140**
Hornet/Sea	TT186	04.07.49	279	Hunter	WT775	10.55	138
Hornet/Sea	TT187	07.48	279	Hunter	WT798	02.56	138
Hornet/Sea	TT188	07.05.47	279	Hunter	WT808	26.04.66	142, **143**
Hornet/Sea	TT189	Early 49	279	Hunter	WT810	04.05.62	142
Hornet/Sea	TT190	15.02.49	279	Hunter	WV276	13.06.56	138
Hornet/Sea	TT191	21.10.48	277	Hunter	WV318	16.07.63	141, **143**
Hornet/Sea	TT195	28.05.47	279	Hunter	WV325	07.03.61	138
Hornet/Sea	TT205	18.08.47	279	Hunter	WV330	06.03.56	138
Hornet/Sea	TT248	09.10.47	**127**, 279	Hunter	WV363	17.05.63	141
Hornet/Sea	VV430	21.10.48	279	Hunter	WV375	06.12.57	138
Hornet/Sea	VW930	(04.51)	279	Hunter	WW592	16.08.55	138
Hornet/Sea	VV959	22.02.51	279	Hunter	WW605	24.07.61	136
Hornet/Sea	WF954	29.11.51	128	Hunter	WW642	08.56	136, **137**
Horsa	TK994	09.50	223	Hunter	WW664	06.05.58	**139**, 141
Hoverfly	KK985	15.09.50	**159**	Hunter	XE531	12.02.55	141
Hoverfly	KK989	09.01.51	158	Hunter	XE543	1957	141
Hoverfly	KK990	28.11.50	158	Hunter	XE551	(01.57)	141
Hoverfly	KL108	28.11.50	158	Hunter	XE558	11.04.56	141

Type	Serial	Arrived	Page	Type	Serial	Arrived	Page
Hunter	XE587	19.09.58	141	Jaguar	XX720	07.06.74	157
Hunter	XE588	11.57	141	Jaguar	XX731	17.10.74	157
Hunter	XE598	12.05.46	141	Jaguar	XX744	05.12.74	157
Hunter	XE600	15.05.56	141	Javelin	WT827	20.07.55	142, **145**
Hunter	XE601	10.08.59	**70, 109**, 141, **242**	Javelin	WT830	(03.54)	142
				Javelin	XA544	20.07.55	142
Hunter	XE605	03.12.56	141	Javelin	XA547	07.04.55	142, **144**
Hunter	XE617	07.07.61	**138**	Javelin	XA548	1955	142
Hunter	XE621	02.09.60	141	Javelin	XA549	20.07.55	142
Hunter	XE707	23.10.68	142	Javelin	XA551	1956	142
Hunter	XE712	06.04.62	142	Javelin	XA554	28.07.55	142
Hunter	XF310	28.08.68	141	Javelin	XA558	20.07.55	142
Hunter	XF376	1956	141	Javelin	XA559	05.12.55	142
Hunter	XF377	18.01.56	141	Javelin	XA561	1956	**34**, 142
Hunter	XF378	21.10.57	141	Javelin	XA563	1955	142
Hunter	XF380	01.03.56	138	Javelin	XA623	18.01.56	142
Hunter	XF381	23.09.55	141	Javelin	XA631	02.06.56	142
Hunter	XF426	21.04.65	**21**, 142	Javelin	XA641	15.01.57	145
Hunter	XF429	27.02.58	141	Javelin	XA711	25.11.60	145
Hunter	XF442	05.12.61	**140**, 141	Javelin	XA720	06.06.56	142, 145
Hunter	XF452	06.04.56	141	Javelin	XA721	10.07.56	145
Hunter	XF833	08.02.54	138	Javelin	XA723	1957	145
Hunter	XF970	06.06.56	138	Javelin	XA725	02.01.58	**70**, 145
Hunter	XG161	05.08.69	141	Javelin	XA760	07.02.62	145
Hunter	XG168	11.11.60	142	Javelin	XA769	14.02.57	142
Hunter	XG207	03.07.64	141	Javelin	XA770	11.02.57	142
Hunter	XG210	08.06.64	141	Javelin	XA771	31.07.58	142
Hunter	XG232	31.07.64	141	Javelin	XA778	01.03.61	**21**, 142, **144**
Hunter	XG290	12.02.57	141	Javelin	XA821	14.05.59	145
Hunter	XJ615	(1956)	141	Javelin	XD158	10.05.56	142
Hunter	XJ627	06.12.57	141	Javelin	XH390	30.05.58	142
Hunter	XJ714	15.05.57	141	Javelin	XH433	09.05.63	142
Hunter	XK140	31.05.57	141	Javelin	XH704	01.05.57	145, **146**
Hunter	XL563	19.12.57	141	Javelin	XH705	30.12.58	145
Hunter	XL564	09.03.60	141	Javelin	XH706	05.01.60	145
Hunter	XL566	23.05.58	141	Javelin	XH708	11.07.57	147
Hunter	XL574	16.10.58	141	Javelin	XH710	13.11.57	145
Hunter	XL596	12.01.72	141	Javelin	XH711	26.07.58	147
Hunter	XL611	24.10.66	141	Javelin	XH712	17.08.57	145
Hunter	XL612	09.11.66	141	Javelin	XH713	18.06.58	145
Hunter	XL616	11.10.66	141, **245**	Javelin	XH714	30.10.57	145
Hurricane	KZ379	Wartime	109	Javelin	XH722	10.02.59	145
Hurricane	LB743	Wartime	109	Javelin	XH746	11.04.62	145
Hurricane	LS587	1945	109	Javelin	XH753	19.01.59	147
Hurricane	PG489	14.01.46	109	Javelin	XH757	15.06.58	145
Islander	G-51-243	10.05.71	220	Javelin	XH759	02.09.60	147
Islander	G-AYCU	03.07.70	220	Javelin	XH762	01.02.65	147
Islander	G-AYRU		220	Javelin	XH783	31.12.59	145
Jaguar	F-ZWRC	22.12.71	154	Javelin	XH891	10.08.67	147
Jaguar	XW560	17.03.71	154, **156**	Javelin	XH896	22.10.63	147
Jaguar	XW563	28.09.73	154	Javelin	XH897	19.01.67	**109, 143**
Jaguar	XW566	12.09.73	157	Javelin	XH964	29.03.61	147
Jaguar	XX108	01.05.73	157	Javelin	XH965	04.12.59	147
Jaguar	XX109	27.04.73	157, **244**	Javelin	XH966	10.03.60	147
Jaguar	XX110	26.04.74	157	Javelin	XH967	28.04.59	147
Jaguar	XX112	17.09.73	157	Javelin	XH968	24.07.59	147
Jaguar	XX113	08.10.73	157	Javelin	XH969	14.06.60	147
Jaguar	XX136	23.05.73	**156**, 157	Javelin	XH970	21.03.63	147

Type	Serial	Arrived	Page	Type	Serial	Arrived	Page
Javelin	XK577	24.04.58	142	Lightning	XG310	21.12.59	**4**, 149
Jet Provost	G-23-1	04.58	259	Lightning	XG311	26.01.60	149
Jet Provost	XD674	05.11.54	259	Lightning	XG313	21.12.60	**21**, **146**, 147
Jet Provost	XD675	07.05.55	259	Lightning	XG325	05.01.60	149
Jet Provost	XD676	12.05.55	259	Lightning	XG326	31.05.60	149
Jet Provost	XD694	09.55	259, **260**	Lightning	XG327	14.09.59	149
Jet Provost	XM346	20.04.59	**233**, 259	Lightning	XG329	13.04.61	**21**, 149
Jet Provost	XM347	19.12.58	259	Lightning	XG330	13.10.61	149
Jet Provost	XM349	31.10.58	259	Lightning	XG331	23.12.59	149
Jet Provost	XM350	29.01.59	259	Lightning	XG333	14.05.60	149
Jet Provost	XM352	05.01.65	**21**, 263	Lightning	XG335	27.10.60	149
Jet Provost	XM354	01.05.59	259	Lightning	XG336	03.11.60	**21**, 149
Jet Provost	XM365	11.09.59	259	Lightning	XG337	26.08.60	149
Jet Provost	XM383	01.11.60	259	Lightning	XL629	05.05.61	149, **244**
Jet Provost	XM456	(08.62)	263	Lightning	XM134	31.03.60	149
Jet Provost	XN463	29.09.60	259	Lightning	XM169	27.07.61	149
Jet Provost	XN467	08.02.61	259	Lightning	XM174	24.01.61	149
Jet Provost	XN468	27.06.61	259	Lightning	XM966	16.03.61	151
Jet Provost	XN503	22.11.60	263	Lightning	XN723	06.02.62	149
Jet Provost	XP547	11.10.61	263	Lightning	XN728	24.06.69	149
Jet Provost	XR701		263	Lightning	XN729	14.08.64	149, **150**
Jet Provost	XS230	07.06.68	263	Lightning	XN734	16.05.63	149
Jet Provost	XS231	28.01.69	**260**, 263	Lightning	XN772	01.11.63	147
Jet Provost	XW314	29.07.70	263	Lightning	XN789	(1963)	149
Jet Ranger	N8590F	1967	**186**, 187	Lightning	XN795	12.1.68	149
Jetstream	G-AXFV	09.08.71	**266**, 267	Lightning	XP693	24.05.63	149, 151, **247**
Jetstream	XX475	27.07.73	**266**, 267	Lightning	XP694	01.08.63	149
Jetstream	XX476	21.07.73	267	Lightning	XP696	16.02.66	149
Jetstream	XX479	12.02.74	267	Lightning	XP697	02.11.64	151
Jetstream	XX489	12.02.74	267	Lightning	XP698	19.12.63	149
Junkers 88	622138	05.46	223	Lightning	XP699	13.04.64	149
Junkers 188	280032	05.46	223	Lightning	XP701	01.07.64	149
Junior F	OO-TIT	20.10.49	239	Lightning	XP752	02.02.70	149
Junior	OO-ULA		239	Lightning	XP757	13.12.67	149
P1127	XP980	27.01.66	**21**, **150**, 151	Lightning	XR717	29.03.72	151
P1127	XP984	(11.65)	151	Lightning	XR769	12.09.66	**148**, 151
Kestrel	XS689	(1964)	151	Lightning	XS417	29.09.64	151
Kestrel	XS690	(1964)	151	Lightning	XS454	18.10.68	151
Kestrel	XS692	(1964)	151	Lincoln	RE227	Wartime	76, **78**
Kestrel	XS693	(1964)	151	Lincoln	RE232	Wartime	76
Kestrel	XS695	30.03.66	151, **244**	Lincoln	RF329	01.11.50	80
Lancaster	HK543	Wartime	73	Lincoln	RF337	Wartime	76
Lancaster	LL619	Wartime	76	Lincoln	RF354	04.11.48	80
Lancaster	LL813	31.08.45	73	Lincoln	RF368	10.11.45	80
Lancaster	ME570	05.12.45	73	Lincoln	RF370	17.10.45	80
Lancaster	ND899	29.01.46	73	Lincoln	RF383	20.07.46	80
Lancaster	NG384	1945	73	Lincoln	RF401	19.07.46	80
Lancaster	NN801	Wartime	76	Lincoln	RF504	11.48	80
Lancaster	PA367	23.05.49	76	Lincoln	RF519	11.05.50	80
Lancaster	RE206	05.07.51	76, **77**	Lincoln	RF554	18.10.55	80
Lancaster	RF147	06.09.45	76	Lincoln	RF560	14.05.48	80
Lancaster	SW289	26.11.45	**72**, 76	Lincoln	RF561	09.03.49	**77**, 80
Lancaster	TW923	28.01.49	76	Lincoln	RF564	17.10.55	80
Liberator	EW126	Wartime	76	Lincoln	WD123	28.06.50	**79**, 80
Liberator	KL632	Wartime	76	Lockheed 286		(12.68)	184
Lightning	XG307	24.02.64	**21**, 149	Lynx	XW835	26.07.73	189
Lightning	XG308	15.09.59	147, 149	Lynx	XW836	(03.73)	189
Lightning	XG309	12.02.60	149	Lynx	XW837	(02.72)	189

Type	Serial	Arrived	Page	Type	Serial	Arrived	Page
Lynx	XW838	(03.73)	189	Meteor	VW418	18.07.57	116
Lynx	XX153	06.08.75	189	Meteor	VW451	14.07.49	116
Lynx	XX510	25.04.75	**188**, 189	Meteor	VW453	18.03.57	116
Lynx	XX910	08.05.75	189	Meteor	VW780	Early 48	113
Magister	L8253	Wartime	233	Meteor	VW790	09.05.50	113
Magister	N3782	Wartime	233	Meteor	VZ442	30.10.51	116
Magister	BB666	13.08.46	233	Meteor	VZ460	11.12.50	**112**, 116, **119**
Magister	BB667	03.06.46	233	Meteor	VZ467	10.03.50	**55**, 116
Marathon	G-AGPD	26.08.46	197	Meteor	VZ473	25.04.50	116
Marathon	G-AILH	19.10.49	197	Meteor	VZ500	15.11.51	116
Marathon	G-ALVW	26.05.50	197	Meteor	VZ501	23.05.50	116
Marathon	G-AMDH	14.11.50	199	Meteor	VZ506	19.05.50	116
Marathon	VX229	23.06.52	199	Meteor	WA546	17.01.51	116
Marathon	XA250	24.08.53	199	Meteor	WA547	17.01.51	117
Marathon	XA260	02.09.53	**198**, 199	Meteor	WA634	17.04.51	116
Marathon	XA270	14.12.53	199	Meteor	WA690	19.09.51	**57**, 116, **242**
Martinet	HP413	13.12.45	221, **222**	Meteor	WA709	16.01.53	116
MB5	R2496	03.46	128, **129**	Meteor	WA775	05.08.52	116
Meteor	EE212	Wartime	113	Meteor	WA857	20.04.51	116
Meteor	EE230	19.03.46	113	Meteor	WA904	09.07.52	116
Meteor	EE282	04.06.48	113	Meteor	WA982	(1952)	**115**, 116
Meteor	EE312	07.05.46	113	Meteor	WB134	09.06.53	117
Meteor	EE336	(09.45)	**30**, 113	Meteor	WB160	16.04.51	117
Meteor	EE337	06.48	113	Meteor	WB164	15.02.55	117
Meteor	EE351	08.04.46	113, **114**	Meteor	WB181	29.08.51	117
Meteor	EE387	04.48	113, **121**	Meteor	WD587	11.06.52	117
Meteor	EE394	05.06.46	113, **118**	Meteor	WD589	09.07.51	117, **121**
Meteor	EE455	26.06.46	113	Meteor	WD593	28.03.51	117
Meteor	EE460	13.11.46	113	Meteor	WD595	04.51	117
Meteor	EE492	09.10.46	113	Meteor	WD596	19.11.51	117
Meteor	EE517	28.06.51	113	Meteor	WD604	25.02.52	117, **119**
Meteor	EE520	10.07.46	113	Meteor	WD641	07.01.65	**118**, 120
Meteor	EE525	11.01.49	113	Meteor	WD656	09.04.54	117
Meteor	EE530	07.48	116, **118**	Meteor	WD670	10.06.52	117
Meteor	EE531	10.03.50	113	Meteor	WD687	28.01.53	117
Meteor	EE598	06.05.47	113	Meteor	WD706	11.07.62	**52**, 120
Meteor	EG150	09.07.52	116	Meteor	WD721	18.07.52	117
Meteor	RA382	05.05.48	113	Meteor	WD767	17.06.57	**115**, 120
Meteor	RA397	08.07.47	113	Meteor	WD797	02.10.52	117
Meteor	RA417	08.12.47	113	Meteor	WF716	12.11.52	116
Meteor	RA420	08.04.48	113	Meteor	WF822	24.01.56	116
Meteor	RA438	01.12.47	113, **115**	Meteor	WG996	05.11.57	116
Meteor	RA484	20.09.48	113	Meteor	WH284	(03.05.60)	117
Meteor	RA486	09.12.47	113	Meteor	WH420	04.09.70	117
Meteor	VS968	14.07.50	**112**, 117	Meteor	WH447	23.09.55	116
Meteor	VS969	13.08.51	117	Meteor	WH483	17.12.51	116
Meteor	VT110	11.57	117	Meteor	WK648	17.10.52	116
Meteor	VT150	11.08.49	116	Meteor	WL353	01.60	116
Meteor	VT232	10.11.49	113	Meteor	WL377	15.06.55	116
Meteor	VT241	09.10.50	113	Meteor	WL472	27.04.60	116
Meteor	VT259	14.04.50	113	Meteor	WL488	11.04.56	116
Meteor	VW293	01.12.50	113	Meteor	WM147	30.12.57	120
Meteor	VW360	14.07.50	116	Meteor	WM151	27.01.69	120
Meteor	VW362	31.07.50	117	Meteor	WM167	01.02.62	120
Meteor	VW410	23.05.50	116	Meteor	WM242	06.59	120
Meteor	VW411	16.12.48	116	Meteor	WM261	27.08.53	**114**, 117
Meteor	VW412	19.10.49	116	Meteor	WM331	23.06.53	117, **121**
Meteor	VW413	16.09.49	117	Meteor	WM366	06.07.54	117

Type	Serial	Arrived	Page	Type	Serial	Arrived	Page
Meteor	WM367	19.10.54	117, **157**	MRCA		(1975)	157
Meteor	WS110	16.11.54	116	M-S 755	F-ZWRS	(1953)	263
Meteor	WS805	16.06.59	117	Mustang	KH656	Wartime	110
Meteor	WS832	26.06.63	117	Mustang	KH766	Wartime	110
Meteor	WS838	07.03.63	117	Mustang	TK586	Wartime	110
Meteor	WS843	12.12.60	117	Mystere II	NIL?	07.53	310
Meteor	WS844	24.01.55	117	Mystere IVA	10	(10.55)	147
Meteor	XF274	05.12.55	**18**, 116, **242**	Mystere IVA	37	(10.55)	147
Meteor	I-128	07.07.52	**114**, 116	Neptune	WX502	07.54	**104**, 105
Meteor	G-7-1	08.52	116	Neptune	WX507	02.56	105
Midge	G-39-1	09.54	**262**, 265	Nimrod	XV148	24.05.68	106, **107**
Mirage IIIA	01	(01.60)	154, **155**	Nimrod	XV226	15.07.68	106
Mirage IIIA	08	(01.60)	154	Nimrod	XV227	19.02.69	106
Mirage IVA	01	(1965)	105	Nimrod	XV228	05.05.69	106, 108
Mitchell	FV984	Wartime	76	Nimrod	XV229	09.06.69	108
Mitchell	FW151	Wartime	76	Nimrod	XW665	06.06.72	108
Mitchell	HD347	Wartime	76	Nomad	VH-SUR	09.72	220
ML Utility	XK776	25.06.57	230, **231**	Oxford	V4026	13.03.46	233
ML Utility	XK781	14.03.58	**230**, 232	Oxford	AS504	30.03.54	233
ML Utility	XK784	1958	232	Oxford	EB811	09.50	233
Monitor	NP406	Wartime	223	Oxford	HN379	29.08.47	233
Monitor	NP408	13.01.47	223	Oxford	NM331	18.10.48	233
Monitor	NP409	Wartime	223	Oxford	NM528	24.04.52	233
Monitor	NP410	12.10.45	223	Oxford	NM692	11.07.50	233
Monitor	NP411	16.11.45	223	Oxford	PH412	10.07.53	233
Mosquito	KA104	10.10.45	73	Oxford	RR345	06.07.49	233, **234**
Mosquito	KA201	02.10.45	73	Oxford	UB339	13.10.49	233
Mosquito	LR387	Wartime	73	P1	WG760	08.54	**146**, 147
Mosquito	ML994	Wartime	73	P1	WG763		147
Mosquito	NS624	Wartime	73	P1	XA847	13.07.60	147, **148**
Mosquito	PF489	1949	73	P1	XA853	12.05.61	147
Mosquito	PF606	24.11.48	73, **77**	Pembroke	WV698	10.03.53	209
Mosquito	RG176	Wartime	73	Pembroke	WV699	23.09.53	209
Mosquito	RG182	Wartime	73	Pembroke	WV700	(03.54)	209
Mosquito	RG183	Wartime	73	Pembroke	WV701	18.09.53	209
Mosquito	RG231	24.04.47	73	Pembroke	WV706	12.04.62	209
Mosquito	RL114	1949	73	Pembroke	WV733	03.05.62	209
Mosquito	RL136	18.08.49	73, **74**	Pembroke	WV735	31.08.55	209
Mosquito	RS719	21.06.51	73, **77**	Pembroke	WV739	15.02.55	209
Mosquito	RV300	18.10.46	73	Pembroke	WV740	15.02.65	209
Mosquito	TA501	14.10.45	73	Pembroke	XK884	12.06.74	209
Mosquito	TA547	Wartime	73	Pembroke	XK885	12.04.72	209
Mosquito	TA638	Wartime	73	Pembroke	XL956	05.04.68	209, **211**
Mosquito	TK615	30.03.51	73	Phantom	XT597	17.12.69	154
Mosquito	TK634	09.50	73	Phantom	XT598	06.02.69	154
Mosquito	TK650	27.10.48	73	Phantom	XT852	15.06.71	154
Mosquito	TS444	12.02.46	**51**, 73, **75**	Phantom	XT853	03.12.73	154
Mosquito	TS449	17.11.47	73	Phantom	XT857	03.03.69	154
Mosquito	TW227	16.11.45	73	Phantom	XT858	02.12.69	154
Mosquito	TW229	05.12.45	73	Phantom	XT859	(1968)	154, **155**
Mosquito	TW240	31.12.46	73, **75**	Phantom	XT865	17.02.69	154
Mosquito	VL623	03.04.46	73	Phantom	XT872	21.11.68	154
Mosquito	VR793	16.02.53	73	Phantom	XT873	16.05.73	154
Mosquito	VT651	24.02.48	73	Phantom	XT898	28.03.69	154
Mosquito	VT654	13.05.48	73, **75**	Phantom	XT900	05.12.69	154
Mosquito	VT657	21.02.50	73	Phantom	XT928	1971	154
Mosquito	VT658	08.49	73	Phantom	XV406	16.01.70	154, **243**
Mosquito	VT706	31.08.49	73, **74**	Phantom	XV410	05.03.69	154

Type	Serial	Arrived	Page	Type	Serial	Arrived	Page
Phantom	XV415	25.09.69	**109**, 154	Scimitar	WT859	21.03.58	303
Phantom	XV427	18.06.70	154	Scimitar	WW134	12.07.57	299
Phantom	XV442	12.06.69	154	Scimitar	XD212	22.11.60	303
Phantom	XV567	05.03.70	154	Scimitar	XD213	28.04.58	303
Phantom	XV574	09.05.69	154	Scimitar	XD214	09.06.58	303
Phantom	XV587	25.02.70	154	Scimitar	XD215	10.07.57	299
Piaggio P148	MM53587	(03.54)	310	Scimitar	XD216	12.08.57	303
Pioneer	G-31-1 /			Scimitar	XD217	11.09.57	**301**, 303
	VL515	10.01.49	203, **205**	Scimitar	XD219	17.08.57	303
Pioneer	G-ANAZ	09.53	207	Scimitar	XD224	30.04.68	303
Pioneer	XL664	20.11.58	**205**, 207	Scimitar	XD226	20.01.58	303
Pioneer	XL666	04.06.59	207	Scimitar	XD227	01.05.59	303
Pioneer	XL700	05.11.56	207	Scimitar	XD228	20.03.58	303
Pioneer	XL702	22.10.63	207	Scimitar	XD229	13.03.58	303
Porter	HB-FDP	10.68	220	Scimitar	XD232	06.09.61	303
Prentice	HV903	17.11.50	**234**, 235	Scimitar	XD241	05.09.58	303
Prentice	TV163	24.04.47	**234**, 235	Scimitar	XD246	19.01.59	303
Prentice	TV166	16.06.47	235	Scimitar	XD268	21.03.61	**302**, 303
Prentice	TV168	01.05.47	235	Scimitar	XD275	20.07.59	303
Prentice	TV172	09.07.47	235	Scimitar	XD327	08.06.60	**301**, 303
Prentice	VN684	22.01.48	235, **236**	Scout	XP165	11.60	179
Prentice	VR190	20.08.47	235	Scout	XP166	16.08.63	181
Prentice	VR191	08.09.47	235	Scout	XP189	02.05.67	179, 181
Prentice	VR211	17.01.51	235	Scout	XP190	18.12.61	181
Proctor	G-AGLN	06.03.48	221	Scout	XP192	01.03.62	179
Provost	WE522	24.08.50	259	Scout	XP846	22.10.63	179, 181
Provost	WE530	14.09.50	259	Scout	XP847	21.09.62	181, **182**
Provost	WG503	28.04.51	259	Scout	XP848	11.10.62	179
Provost	WV418	27.02.53	259	Scout	XP849	01.12.62	179
Provost	WV421	30.03.53	259	Scout	XP850	28.06.62	181
Provost	WV422	30.03.53	259	Scout	XP851	08.02.62	181
Provost	WV425	10.06.59	259	Scout	XP857	17.08.64	181
Provost	WV508	22.12.53	259	Scout	XP889	03.10.63	181
Provsot	WV510	25.09.61	259	Scout	XP903	06.66	181
Provost	WV577	25.03.55	259	Scout	XP908	15.06.64	181
Provost	WV614	11.06.54	259, **260**	Scout	XR635	14.10.75	181
Provost	WV686	26.10.60	259	Scout	XR637	22.12.64	179
Provost	WW452	03.11.60	259	Scout	XR640	25.08.65	181
Puma	F-ZWWO	(04.66)	187, **188**	Scout	XT624	12.12.66	181
Puma	XW198	15.12.70	187	Scout	XT626	17.07.72	181
Puma	XW202	05.05.75	187	Scout	XT634	09.09.74	181
Puma	XW213	08.05.72	187	Scout	XT639	11.09.75	181
Puma	XW216	04.05.72	187	Scout	XW280	10.04.70	181
Puma	XW227	29.04.74	187	Sea Fury	SR661	26.11.45	279
Puma	XW230	11.07.73	187	Sea Fury	SR666	09.01.46	279
Puma	XW231	24.10.72	187	Sea Fury	TF895	04.12.46	279
Puma	XW233	01.74	187	Sea Fury	TF896	01.04.47	279
Puma	XW237	28.02.74	187	Sea Fury	TF897	04.48	279
Puma	XW241	20.02.70	187	Sea Fury	TF898	28.11.47	279
Reliant	FK818	Wartime	221	Sea Fury	TF900	29.09.47	279
Reliant	FK894	Wartime	221	Sea Fury	TF902	30.07.47	279
Sabre	49-1279	01.03.51	134, **135**	Sea Fury	TF908	04.06.47	279
Sabre	49-1296	01.03.51	134	Sea Fury	TF922	14.12.48	279
Sabre	XB733	22.07.53	136	Sea Fury	TF950	29.09.47	279
Sabre	XB992	31.08.54	136	Sea Fury	TF958	08.48	279
SB5	WG768	10.52	**59**	Sea Fury	TF962	12.47	279, 283
Scimitar	VX138	07.55	299	Sea Fury	TF986	03.03.49	279
Scimitar	WT854	03.56	299, **301**	Sea Fury	VR920	21.01.49	283

Type	Serial	Arrived	Page	Type	Serial	Arrived	Page
Sea Fury	VW226	07.11.50	**281**, 283	Sea Venom	XG622		295
Sea Fury	VW228	06.06.52	283	Sea Venom	XG662	06.11.57	295
Sea Fury	VW588	17.08.50	279, 283	Sea Vixen	WG240	(08.54)	297
Sea Fury	VX298	16.02.50	283	Sea Vixen	XF828	06.3.56	297
Sea Fury	VX818	11.03.49	**281**, 283	Sea Vixen	XJ474	1957	297
Sea Fury	VZ345	15.10.74	**241**, 283	Sea Vixen	XJ475	02.02.60	299
Sea Fury	WG656	27.02.52	283	Sea Vixen	XJ476	17.07.58	299
Sea King	XV370	24.07.68	187, **188**	Sea Vixen	XJ477	22.07.58	297, **298**
Sea King	XV371	13.02.69	187	Sea Vixen	XJ478	01.12.58	297, **300**
Sea King	XV373	08.05.69	187	Sea Vixen	XJ479	22.07.58	297
Sea King	XV642	30.10.69	187	Sea Vixen	XJ480	03.11.58	**241**, 299
Sea King	XV643	08.07.69	187	Sea Vixen	XJ481	12.11.68	299
Sea King	XV647	26.09.69	187	Sea Vixen	XJ482	(07.59)	297
Sea King	XV651	10.06.70	187	Sea Vixen	XJ483	15.12.58	297
Sea King	XV656	06.07.73	187	Sea Vixen	XJ485	13.03.59	297
Sea King	XV671	21.07.75	187	Sea Vixen	XJ488	25.01.61	**69**, **298**, 299
Sea Otter	JM909	17.11.50	221	Sea Vixen	XJ492	18.08.59	297
Sea Otter	JM913	Wartime	221	Sea Vixen	XJ494	18.08.71	299
Sea Otter	RD869	09.03.46	221	Sea Vixen	XJ516	10.10.59	299
Sea Otter	RD875	27.10.45	221	Sea Vixen	XJ521	07.10.59	297
Sea Otter	RD876	03.05.46	221, **222**	Sea Vixen	XJ525	05.06.68	299
Sea Prince	G-ALCM	15.02.51	207	Sea Vixen	XJ526	02.12.59	**55**, 297
Sea Prince	WF118	18.09.51	207	Sea Vixen	XJ560	06.03.63	**19**
Sea Prince	WF119	25.10.51	**206**, 207	Sea Vixen	XJ564	12.10.60	297
Sea Prince	WF128	11.01.74	207	Sea Vixen	XJ579	11.07.72	299
Sea Prince	WF136	24.03.50	207	Sea Vixen	XJ582	15.11.61	**22**, 297
Sea Prince	WF137	1951	207	Sea Vixen	XJ608	11.06.68	299
Sea Prince	WJ350	03.04.68	207	Sea Vixen	XJ609	17.03.67	299
Sea Prince	WM735	30.08.55	207	Sea Vixen	XN652	08.01.69	299
Sea Prince	WM756	29.04.53	207	Sea Vixen	XN653	14.01.69	299
Sea Prince	WP310	15.04.53	207	Sea Vixen	XN684	21.11.62	298
Sea Venom	WK376	06.51	291, **293**	Sea Vixen	XN685	17.04.64	**23, 150, 307**
Sea Venom	WK379	13.02.53	291	Sea Vixen	XN686	08.70	299
Sea Venom	WK385	25.06.53	295	Sea Vixen	XN690	21.04.67	**298**, 299
Sea Venom	WM500	28.04.54	291	Sea Vixen	XN700	03.63	**19**, 299
Sea Venom	WM501	22.12.53	291	Sea Vixen	XP919	09.01.64	299
Sea Venom	WM502	29.12.53	291	Sea Vixen	XP920	24.01.64	299
Sea Venom	WM504	08.10.53	295	Sea Vixen	XP954	25.08.64	299
Sea Venom	WM507	24.10.53	**269**, 295	Sea Vixen	XP956	10.04.71	299
Sea Venom	WM508	03.02.54	295	Seafang	VB895	27.07.48	289
Sea Venom	WM510	23.06.54	291, 295	Seafang	VG474	10.05.46	289
Sea Venom	WM568	27.08.54	**293**, 295	Seafire	LA443	Wartime	**274**, 275
Sea Venom	WM570	08.01.55	295	Seafire	LA446	12.11.45	275
Sea Venom	WM571	02.55	295	Seafire	LA498	29.12.45	275
Sea Venom	WM573	18.02.55	295	Seafire	LA541	25.03.46	**274**, 275
Sea Venom	WM574	18.11.58	295	Seafire	LA552	30.12.46	275
Sea Venom	WM575	22.06.55	295	Seafire	LA564	16.08.46	275
Sea Venom	WW211	15.09.55	295	Seafire	NM938	18.04.47	275
Sea Venom	WW220	05.09.60	295	Seafire	PR314	Wartime	275
Sea Venom	WW296	27.06.56	295	Seafire	PS952	27.08.47	275
Sea Venom	WZ893	01.03.55	295	Seafire	PS944	26.11.46	275
Sea Venom	WZ894	17.03.55	295	Seafire	PS946	10.04.47	275, **276**
Sea Venom	WZ941	02.11.55	295	Seafire	PS948	1947	275
Sea Venom	WZ944	22.01.56	295	Seafire	PS949	20.09.47	275
Sea Venom	XA532	08.54	295	Seafire	PS954	18.11.47	275
Sea Venom	XA539	09.06.54	295	Seafire	PX921	09.04.45	275
Sea Venom	XG607		295	Seafire	RX338	07.45	275
Sea Venom	XG612		295	Seafire	SP182	31.08.45	275

Type	Serial	Arrived	Page	Type	Serial	Arrived	Page
Seafire	SP324	03.09.51	275	Shackleton	VP258	22.01.57	95
Seafire	SR490	1945	275	Shackleton	VP259	(03.51)	94
Seafire	SW793	03.07.45	275	Shackleton	VP261	20.02.51	94
Seafire	SW813	25.09.56	275	Shackleton	VP263	20.07.51	94
Seafire	SX121	16.10.45	275	Shackleton	VP285	09.09.54	94
Seafire	SX153	11.10.45	275	Shackleton	VP293	22.07.59	95
Seafire	SX157	18.01.46	275	Shackleton	VW126	30.03.50	90, **92**, 94
Seafire	SX272	24.06.46	275	Shackleton	VW131	13.02.50	90, **91**, 94
Seafire	SX297	26.06.46	275	Shackleton	VW135	04.07.50	94
Seafire	SX360	30.10.46	275	Shackleton	WB833	23.07.52	**92**, 94
Seafire	SX361	13.11.46	275	Shackleton	WB835	25.09.52	94
Seafire	SX389	07.48	275	Shackleton	WB858	26.08.59	95
Seafire	TM383	09.45	275	Shackleton	WG530	25.09.52	**56**, 94
Seafire	VP437	14.09.49	275	Shackleton	WG556	14.09.65	94
Seafire	VP449	05.48	275	Shackleton	WG558	11.08.61	94
Seafire	VP463	22.02.49	**274**, 275	Shackleton	WL737	05.01.66	94
Seagull	PA147	10.10.47	223, **224**, 311	Shackleton	WL738	17.03.67	94
Seahawk	VP401	06.48	289	Shackleton	WL745	05.04.72	95
Seahawk	VP413	14.02.49	**288**, 289	Shackleton	WL757	07.12.73	95
Seahawk	VP422	17.01.50	289	Shackleton	WL759	22.05.63	94
Seahawk	WF143	16.12.53	289	Shackleton	WL785	12.04.65	94
Seahawk	WF144	18.09.52	289	Shackleton	WL793	16.08.73	**93**, 95
Seahawk	WF145	22.04.52	289	Shackleton	WR953	02.63	94
Seahawk	WF147	06.11.53	291	Shackleton	WR955	30.03.71	94
Seahawk	WF149	10.03.53	289	Shackleton	WR960	15.12.65	94, **242**
Seahawk	WF151	06.10.52	289	Shackleton	WR962	25.02.59	94
Seahawk	WF157	09.06.53	291	Shackleton	WR964	14.04.54	94
Seahawk	WF180	20.05.53	289	Shackleton	WR965	30.03.62	94
Seahawk	WF196	21.02.57	289	Shackleton	WR968	20.02.59	94
Seahawk	WF218	27.07.54	289	Shackleton	WR970	07.09.56	**92**, 95
Seahawk	WF240	20.04.56	291	Shackleton	WR971	14.12.56	95
Seahawk	WF241	09.07.54	291	Shackleton	WR972	31.12.56	95
Seahawk	WF251	17.03.54	291	Shackleton	WR973	10.07.57	**93**, 95
Seahawk	WF280	31.03.54	291	Shackleton	WR974	02.07.57	95
Seahawk	WF284	14.09.54	**51**, 291	Shackleton	WR982	14.04.64	95
Seahawk	WF295	20.07.54	291	Shackleton	WR985	03.04.59	95
Seahwak	WF302	13.01.56	291	Shackleton	WR989	08.04.68	**93**
Seahawk	WM901	18.06.53	289	Shackleton	XF701	18.05.62	95
Seahawk	WM983	15.07.54	**290**, 291	Shackleton	XF702	15.01.65	95
Seahawk	WM992	03.08.55	291	Shackleton	XF703	02.08.68	95
Seahawk	WV828	13.01.55	291	Shackleton	XF705	11.06.69	95
Seahawk	WV840	07.05.57	**290**, 291	Shackleton	XF711	17.07.64	95
Seahawk	WV904	12.58	291	Short SC 1	DUMMY	06.56	310
Seahawk	WV922	27.02.59	291	Sioux	XT127	11.03.65	162
Seahawk	XE327	03.03.55	291	Sioux	XT155	26.04.66	162, **163**
Seahawk	XE328	12.58	291	Sioux	XT250	14.02.67	**162**
Seahawk	XE369	19.04.55	291	Sioux	XT506	06.12.66	162, **163**
Seahawk	XE445	09.09.55	**288**, 291	Sioux	XV310	04.08.67	162
Seamew	XA209	04.05.54	299, **300**	Sioux	XV312	07.11.67	162
Seamew	XA213	04.07.55	299	Sioux	XV320	18.05.71	162
Seamew	XE169	03.01.56	299, **300**	SIPA 200	F-BGVB	(06.54)	**262**, 263
Seamew	XE170	06.01.56	299	Skeeter	WF113	(03.53)	171
Seamew	XE171	23.08.56	299	Skeeter	XG303	02.03.54	171
Seamew	XE181	01.11.56	299	Skeeter	XJ355	24.02.55	171, **172**
Seamew	XE186	17.01.57	**16**, 299	Skeeter	XK482	26.06.58	171
Sedburgh	WB933	31.03.53	**52**, 265	Skeeter	XK773	1955	171
Shackleton	VP254	06.02.56	94	Skeeter	XL734	04.11.60	171
Shackleton	VP255	30.10.50	94	Skeeter	XL739	09.09.58	171

Type	Serial	Arrived	Page	Type	Serial	Arrived	Page
Skeeter	XL764	03.01.64	171	Sunderland	PP127	(1956)	76
Skeeter	XL807	14.01.59	171, **172**	Swift	VV106	19.09.49	131, **310**
Skeeter	XL813	26.06.61	171	Swift	VV119	25.05.51	131
Skeeter	XM528	07.07.59	171	Swift	WJ965	22.06.50	131, **132**
Skyvan	G-AWWS	22.04.69	**219**, 220	Swift	WK194	04.06.53	132
Spearfish	RA356	12.12.46	277, **280**	Swift	WK195	13.07.53	131
Sperrin	DUMMY	1952	310	Swift	WK196	04.06.53	131
Spiteful	NN667	01.02.46	128	Swift	WK197	03.07.53	131
Spiteful	RB517	29.05.46	128, **129**	Swift	WK200	10.07.53	131, 134
Spitfire	EN314	10.10.45	109	Swift	WK201	1953	133
Spitfire	EN397	Wartime	109	Swift	WK202	29.12.53	133
Spitfire	G-AIDN	18.01.47	109, **111**	Swift	WK214	05.03.54	133
Spitfire	LA187	Wartime	110	Swift	WK216	29.05.54	133
Spitfire	LA219	05.09.45	110	Swift	WK219	28.03.55	133
Spitfire	LA220	Wartime	110	Swift	WK220	30.01.55	133, **134**
Spitfire	LA317	15.02.49	110	Swift	WK244	25.10.54	133
Spitfire	LA326	1945	110	Swift	WK248	27.10.54	133
Spitfire	LV674	Wartime	109	Swift	WK272	16.04.55	133
Spitfire	MD114	Wartime	109	Swift	WK275	26.08.57	133
Spitfire	MD124	Wartime	109	Swift	WK279	21.11.55	133, 134
Spitfire	MD189	27.10.45	109	Swift	WK291	17.08.56	134
Spitfire	MD190	Wartime	109	Swift	WK294	06.06.56	134
Spitfire	MH828	01.10.47	109	Swift	XD903	15.06.55	134, **135**
Spitfire	MT847	13.12.45	110	Swift	XD904	31.08.56	134
Spitfire	NH707	03.07.46	109	Swift	XD917	01.02.56	134
Spitfire	NH872	28.07.45	110	Swift	XF113	03.12.56	134
Spitfire	PK312	29.11.45	110	Swift	XF114	14.03.57	134
Spitfire	PK320	14.10.46	110, **112**	Swift	XF774	13.08.56	134, **135**
Spitfire	PK408	05.02.47	110	Swift	XF780	08.10.56	134
Spitfire	PK515	05.04.46	110	Swordfish	LS364	Wartime	269
Spitfire	PK547	21.01.46	110	Sycamore	VL958	05.49	158
Spitfire	PM630	27.11.45	110	Sycamore	VW905	02.04.51	158
Spitfire	RB146	Wartime	109	Sycamore	WA576	18.02.58	159
Spitfire	RM790	15.04.46	110	Sycamore	WA577	15.03.51	158, **161**
Spitfire	RR238	Wartime	109	Sycamore	WA578	29.08.51	159, **160**
Spitfire	SL745	02.10.45	110	Sycamore	WT924	22.11.51	159
Spitfire	SW777	Wartime	110	Sycamore	WT933	23.05.51	158
Spitfire	TA822	Wartime	109	Sycamore	WT939	28.02.53	158, 159
Spitfire	TB757	Wartime	110, **111**	Sycamore	WV783	14.10.52	159
Spitfire	TE241	04.06.48	110	Sycamore	WV784	22.06.53	159, **161**
Spitfire	TP240	14.11.45	109	Sycamore	XA219	30.10.52	159
Spitfire	TP279	17.09.45	110	Sycamore	XD653	26.11.53	**160**, 162
Spitfire	TP423	16.09.47	110	Sycamore	XD654	01.03.54	162
Spitfire	VN302	03.01.47	110	Sycamore	XE306	20.11.53	159
Spitfire	VN315	09.07.46	110, **111**	Sycamore	XE307	31.03.54	159, **160**
Spitfire	VN324	08.01.47	110	Sycamore	XE308	20.11.53	159, **160**
Spitfire	VN329	26.10.46	110	Sycamore	XG502	16.11.67	159
SR 53	DUMMY	01.56	310	Sycamore	XJ380	29.11.60	159
SRN 6	XV616		232	Sycamore	XJ918	31.07.59	159
Stirling	EF517	Wartime	72	Tempest	EJ891	Wartime	110
Stirling	PK136	15.09.45	72	Tempest	JN740	Wartime	110
Storch	VG919	Wartime	223	Tempest	JN798	Wartime	110
Strikemaster	G27-9	1968	**261**, 263	Tempest	JN799	Wartime	110
Student	XS941	08.68	267	Tempest	MW736	Wartime	110
Sturgeon	RK787	08.05.47	283	Tempest	MW741	Wartime	110
Sturgeon	TS475	11.05.50	283	Tempest	MW762	23.09.46	110
Sturgeon	VR363	20.01.50	**281**, 283	Tempest	NV732	Wartime	110
Sturgeon	VR371	1950	283	Tempest	NV773	03.11.47	110

Type	Serial	Arrived	Page	Type	Serial	Arrived	Page
Tempest	NX119	05.12.45	110	Valetta	VX580	07.02.62	197
Tempest	NX133	11.04.46	110	Valetta	WD157	03.11.65	197
Tempest	NX288	25.09.47	110	Valetta	WD171	26.04.55	197
Tempest	PR533	05.09.45	110	Valetta	WG256	12.10.61	197
Tempest	PR550	30.04.48	110	Valetta	WG266	06.01.64	197
Tempest	PR599	10.01.46	110	Valetta	WJ465	29.03.55	197
Tempest	PR622	08.04.46	110	Valetta	WJ491	09.02.61	**195**, 197
Tempest	PR806	14.10.46	110	Valetta	WJ499	01.09.61	197
Tempest	PR903	14.03.46	110	Valiant	WB210	(09.51)	95, **96**
Tempest	SN219	Wartime	110	Valiant	WB215	08.07.54	95
Tempest	SN329	09.50	110	Valiant	WP199	18.12.54	**96**, 98
Tempest	SN352	13.12.45	110, **112**	Valiant	WP202	28.03.55	98
Tempest	SN354	06.12.45	110	Valiant	WP203	11.07.58	98
Thunderbolt	FL849	Wartime	113	Valiant	WP204	(1954)	98
Thunderbolt	KJ298	03.08.45	113	Valiant	WP205	13.09.55	**97**, 98
Tiger Moth	T5895	01.01.47	233	Valiant	WP208	29.11.56	98
Tiger Moth	T6859	17.12.46	233	Valiant	WP209	15.03.63	98
Tiger Moth	T7340	05.05.53	**52**, 233	Valiant	WP210	01.04.55	98
Tiger Moth	DE249	16.12.48	233	Valiant	WP214	29.12.58	98
Tigercat	TT349	Wartime	277	Valiant	WP219	25.11.63	98
Traveller	FT461	Wartime	221	Valiant	WZ367	(1956)	98
Traveller	FT466	Wartime	221	Valiant	WZ373	22.10.56	98
TSR2	XR220	1965	**15**, 21, 105	Valiant	WZ376	09.06.59	**5**, **96**, 98
Tudor	G-AGPF	25.04.46	197, **198**	Valiant	WZ379	21.07.64	98
Tudor	G-AGRD	11.03.47	197	Valiant	WZ383	22.06.61	98
Tudor	G-AGRI	25.03.47	197	Valiant	XD814	05.06.64	98
Tudor	G-AGRK	02.48	197	Valiant	XD872	08.07.57	98
Tudor	G-AGRX	(22.05.47)	197	Vampire	LZ551	09.02.46	126
Tudor	G-AGSU	23.07.46	197, **198**	Vampire	TG274	Wartime	120
Tudor	G-AHNJ	28.06.47	197	Vampire	TG275	22.04.47	120, **123**
Tudor	G-AHNK	02.10.48	197	Vampire	TG276	13.11.46	120, **122**
Tudor	G-AHNN	24.03.48	197	Vampire	TG280	20.12.46	120
Tudor	VX195	10.11.48	197	Vampire	TG284	01.02.46	120
Tudor	VX199	04.12.48	197	Vampire	TG314	05.06.50	120
Tudor	VX202	20.05.48	197	Vampire	TG330	27.02.46	120
Twin Pioneer	XL966	06.02.58	**213**	Vampire	TG338	01.47	120
Twin Pioneer	XL967	02.04.58	213	Vampire	TG381	21.06.46	120
Twin Pioneer	XL968	16.05.58	213	Vampire	TG386	25.03.47	120, **124**
Twin Pioneer	XL969	20.05.58	213	Vampire	TG428	03.12.46	120
Twin Pioneer	XM940	21.03.60	**212**, 213	Vampire	TG446	1948	120
Twin Pioneer	XM957	08.03.66	213	Vampire	TG447	31.07.46	120
Twin Pioneer	XP294	15.11.61	213	Vampire	TX807	09.10.47	120, **124**
Twin Pioneer	XP295	07.12.65	213	Vampire	VF306	08.09.48	120
Typhoon	MN861	Wartime	110	Vampire	VF314	10.47	120
U-120D	XE725	1955	**52**, 230	Vampire	VF317	26.11.47	120, **122**
Valetta	VL249	08.47	194, **195**, **196**	Vampire	VF343	07.08.47	120
Valetta	VL262	04.48	194	Vampire	VT818	15.09.48	120
Valetta	VL263	04.48	194	Vampire	VV136	05.10.48	**124**, 126
Valetta	VL264	22.09.58	194	Vampire/Sea	VV138	1949	126
Valetta	VL267	06.48	194	Vampire	VV190	22.07.48	120
Valetta	VL270	20.05.49	194	Vampire	VV200	27.04.48	120
Valetta	VW140	23.09.48	194	Vampire	VV215	22.07.48	120
Valetta	VW198	27.02.61	194	Vampire	VV216	24.07.48	**122**, 125
Valetta	VW203	11.52	197	Vampire	VV218	10.01.49	125
Valetta	VW802	16.03.55	194	Vampire	VV220	30.08.48	125
Valetta	VW824	09.08.49	194	Vampire	VV475	19.11.48	125
Valetta	VW838	09.03.56	194	Vampire	VV528	21.04.50	125
Valetta	VX564	17.01.51	194, **196**	Vampire	VV568	14.12.49	126

Type	Serial	Arrived	Page	Type	Serial	Arrived	Page
Vampire	VV675	25.04.50	125	Venom	WE260	25.04.52	128
Vampire	VX985	10.03.52	125	Venom	WE267	03.11.54	128
Vampire	VZ116	21.01.57	125	Venom	WE269	11.09.52	128
Vampire	VZ208	09.49	125	Venom	WE272	01.09.52	128, **130**
Vampire	VZ216	05.05.50	**10**, 125	Venom	WE280	27.01.53	128
Vampire	VZ324	08.12.50	125	Venom	WE288	12.06.54	128
Vampire	VZ808	1948	125	Venom	WE361	27.07.54	128
Vampire	WA201	29.08.51	125	Venom	WE381	18.05.54	131
Vampire	WM711	22.05.53	126	Venom	WE468	20.01.54	128
Vampire	WP232	30.03.51	125	Venom	WE479	27.05.54	128
Vampire	WP243	31.01.52	126	Venom	WK422	14.06.54	128
Vampire	WP249	23.08.51	125	Venom	WL806	11.09.52	131
Vampire	WW458	05.02.52	126	Venom	WL807	13.05.53	131, **132**
Vampire	WZ414	01.06.54	126	Venom	WL808	25.02.53	131
Vampire	WZ415	13.03.52	126	Venom	WL809	05.01.53	131
Vampire	WZ417	30.04.52	126	Venom	WL811	20.04.53	131
Vampire	WZ419	29.11.52	**125**, 126	Venom	WL814	10.06.53	131
Vampire	WZ420	19.08.52	126	Venom	WL857	10.09.53	**70**, 131, **132**
Vampire	WZ421	03.09.52	126	Venom	WP227	05.04.51	131, **132**
Vampire	WZ448	27.01.53	126	Venom	WR288	09.06.54	128
Vampire	WZ466	12.02.53	126	Venom	WR370	14.02.55	128
Vampire	WZ549	22.05.53	126	Venom	WR406	06.10.54	131
Vampire/Sea	XA100	31.12.53	**124**, 126	Venom	WX785	03.06.54	131
Vampire/Sea	XA101	10.08.53	126	Venom	WX786	04.54	131
Vampire/Sea	XA169	01.06.60	126	Venom	WX787	24.06.54	131
Vampire	XD627	13.01.56	126	Venom	WX788	09.04.53	**130**, 131
Vampire/Sea	XG743	11.03.68	126	Venom	WX790	09.11.54	131
Vampire	XK624	18.05.61	126	Venom	G-5-3	10.50	131
Vampire	XK633	25.05.60	126	Venture	XW983	27.05.71	268
Vampire	J1004	22.11.46	120, **123**	Victor	WB775	03.55	101
Vampire	G-5-2	08.12.49	**123**, 125	Victor	XA917	12.04.60	10
Vampire	G-5-5	14.02.51	125	Victor	XA918	12.04.65	**29**, 103, **150,**
Vampire	G-5-7	03.07.51	**122**, 126				**153, 307**
Varsity	VX828	21.08.50	257	Victor	XA919	28.03.57	103
Varsity	VX835	27.06.50	257, **258**	Victor	XA920	25.10.57	101, 103
Varsity	WF326	31.8.51	257	Victor	XA921	17.09.57	103
Varsity	WF327	17.09.51	257	Victor	XA922	1957	103
Varsity	WF328	18.02.60	257	Victor	XA930	14.11.57	**5**, 103
Varsity	WF374	02.10.67	257	Victor	XA932	18.12.64	103
Varsity	WF417	24.06.52	257	Victor	XA933	27.08.64	103
Varsity	WJ887	05.10.61	257	Victor	XA937	14.01.66	103
Varsity	WJ908	12.10.61	257	Victor	XH587	19.08.60	103
Varsity	WJ918	31.12.68	257	Victor	XH614	26.09.67	103
Varsity	WJ939	01.07.60	257	Victor	XH618	12.12.63	103
Varsity	WJ940	24.04.63	257	Victor	XH620	04.12.67	103
Varsity	WJ944	1969	257	Victor	XH667	21.08.69	103
Varsity	WJ947	16.03.62	257	Victor	XH668	08.59	103
Varsity	WL641	31.08.62	257	Victor	XH670	19.08.64	**102**, 105
Varsity	WL684	01.09.64	257	Victor	XH671	17.01.61	105
VC-10	XR806	19.05.66	217	Victor	XH672	11.04.61	103
VC-10	XR807	26.05.66	217	Victor	XH673	27.10.61	105
Venom	VV612	01.05.50	128, **130**	Victor	XH674	02.09.60	103, 105
Venom	VV613	03.04.51	128	Victor	XH675	14.02.62	**69**, 103, 105
Venom	WE255	26.06.51	128	Victor	XL158	19.04.61	103
Venom	WE256	16.09.52	128	Victor	XL159	—	103
Venom	WE257	09.01.52	128	Victor	XL162	30.11.61	105
Venom	WE258	22.02.52	128, **130**	Victor	XL163	—	**104**
Venom	WE259	09.01.52	128	Victor	XL164	08.11.63	105

Type	Serial	Arrived	Page	Type	Serial	Arrived	Page
Victor	XL165	15.07.65	**102**, 105	Wasp	XT417	13.01.67	**183**, 184
Victor	XL188	02.01.69	105	Wasp	XT423	20.09.68	184
Victor	XL231	21.07.73	105	Wasp	XT435	13.10.65	184
Victor	XL232	03.05.73	**104**, 105	Wasp	XT778	30.06.66	184
Victor	XL233	20.05.63	**102**, 103	Wasp	XT793	30.05.75	184
Victor	XL511	(1963)	105	Welkin	P17	05.01.49	120
Victor	XM718	07.09.65	105	Wellington	DF609	05.09.45	72
Viking	G-AGOK	05.01.46	194	Wellington	NA724	Wartime	72
Viking	G-AIJE			Wellington	PG420	(03.50)	72
	(VL226)	19.11.48	**193**, 194	Wellington	RP589	03.07.48	72, **74**
Viking	VL228	17.11.47	**193**, 194	Wessex	XL728	1962	174
Viking	VL229	01.08.47	194	Wessex	XM300	02.02.60	174
Viking	VL232	29.10.47	194	Wessex	XM301	02.02.60	174, **175**
Viking	VL233	07.11.47	194	Wessex	XM326	17.05.61	174, **176**
Viking	VW214	19.08.57	194	Wessex	XM327	31.01.61	174
Viking	VX856	17.06.49	194, **196**	Wessex	XM328	02.60	174
Viscount	G-AHRF	13.01.50	207	Wessex	XM329	15.09.68	174
Vulcan	VX777	30.03.55	**97**, 100	Wessex	XM330	09.06.60	174, **176**
Vulcan	XA889	15.03.56	100	Wessex	XM331	11.10.61	174, **177**, 178
Vulcan	XA890	27.04.56	100	Wessex	XM834	23.12.66	178
Vulcan	XA892	28.11.56	100	Wessex	XM836	17.11.66	178
Vulcan	XA894	29.03.57	100	Wessex	XM837	19.09.60	174
Vulcan	XA895	27.09.60	100	Wessex	XM838	07.09.61	174
Vulcan	XA896	23.06.58	100	Wessex	XM871	14.06.66	**178**
Vulcan	XA899	15.05.58	100	Wessex	XM874	20.12.62	174
Vulcan	XA903	09.02.76	100	Wessex	XM919	05.05.67	178
Vulcan	XH475	03.04.63	100	Wessex	XM923	03.10.68	179
Vulcan	XH478	09.10.58	**47, 83**, 100	Wessex	XP137	07.01.70	179
Vulcan	XH499	18.09.63	100	Wessex	XR494	1964	178
Vulcan	XH533	19.04.63	**99**, 100	Wessex	XR497	24.05.63	178
Vulcan	XH534	11.12.61	**54**, 100	Wessex	XR498	10.07.63	174
Vulcan	XH535	27.02.61	101	Wessex	XR503	29.07.64	**66, 176**, 178
Vulcan	XH536	26.01.60	100	Wessex	XR505	18.10.63	176
Vulcan	XH537	31.10.60	101	Wessex	XR588	06.05.63	174, **177**, 178
Vulcan	XH538	31.01.61	**36**, 101	Wessex	XS121	24.08.65	174
Vulcan	XH539	13.12.67	100, 101	Wessex	XS127	27.02.69	179
Vulcan	XH563	08.04.69	101	Wessex	XS241	31.10.63	179
Vulcan	XJ784	25.11.64	101	Wessex	XS482	31.10.68	179
Vulcan	XL317	27.10.61	100	Wessex	XS484	23.04.68	179
Vulcan	XL320	26.03.62	100	Wessex	XS485	1967	179
Vulcan	XL361	16.12.74	**12**, 101	Wessex	XS506	28.10.64	179
Vulcan	XL391	10.02.64	101	Wessex	XS679	20.12.65	178
Vulcan	XM597	04.10.72	101	Wessex	XS863	21.05.71	174
Vulcan	XM606	24.02.66	**99**, 101	Wessex	XT255	19.07.65	178
Vulcan	XM612	05.03.68	101	Wessex	XT256	16.05.66	178
Vulcan	XM649	02.12.69	101	Wessex	XT257	18.07.66	178, **180**
Warwick	HG362	Wartime	76, **79**	Wessex	XT457	02.11.65	179
Warwick	LM777	Wartime	76	Wessex	XT458	02.05.66	179
Warwick	PN760	30.10.45	76	Wessex	XT460	05.02.71	179
Wasp	XN332		**182**	Wessex	XT667	05.11.71	179
Wasp	XS463	21.02.63	179	Wessex	XT762	06.12.72	179
Wasp	XS476	12.06.63	184	Wessex	XT774	29.09.67	**177**, 179
Wasp	XS527	15.07.63	**181**, 184	Wessex	XV727	06.11.68	178
Wasp	XS528	25.06.63	181, **183**, 184	Wessex	XV729	26.03.69	178
Wasp	XS530	12.09.63	184	Wessex	XV732	13.05.69	179
Wasp	XS532	20.03.64	184	Wessex	XV733	(1969)	179, **246**
Wasp	XS569	07.04.68	249	Wessex	G-17-1	09.56	174
Wasp	XT414	13.10.64	184	Whirlwind	WW339	10.03.52	165, **168**

Type	Serial	Arrived	Page	Type	Serial	Arrived	Page
Whirlwind	XA863	27.03.54	165, **166**	Wyvern	VW885	13.05.52	285, 289
Whirlwind	XA864	17.10.57	165	Wyvern	VZ745	01.07.52	285
Whirlwind	XA865	06.08.54	165	Wyvern	VZ746	25.03.53	289
Whirlwind	XD163	15.04.64	167	Wyvern	VZ748	11.12.53	289
Whirlwind	XD164	13.07.54	167	Wyvern	VZ750	24.06.53	289
Whirlwind	XG586	31.12.56	167	Wyvern	VZ764	13.07.53	289
Whirlwind	XG589	16.01.64	167, **170**	Wyvern	VZ774	02.10.53	289
Whirlwind	XG590	20.05.57	167	Wyvern	VZ775	17.07.53	**287**, 289
Whirlwind	XG591	10.12.58	167	Wyvern	VZ777	05.10.53	289
Whirlwind	XG593	20.05.57	167, **168**	Wyvern	VZ779	10.08.54	289
Whirlwind	XG594	07.10.68	167	Wyvern	VZ790	28.07.54	**288**, 289
Whirlwind	XG597	1958	167	Wyvern	WL885	04.03.55	**286**, 289
Whirlwind	XJ394	10.10.57	167	York	LV639	12.08.47	191, **193**
Whirlwind	XJ395	24.02.56	167	York	MW112	28.06.49	191
Whirlwind	XJ396	02.07.65	167	York	MW132	18.02.53	191
Whirlwind	XJ397	27.07.55	167	York	MW139	30.06.47	191
Whirlwind	XJ398	23.12.60	167	York	MW179	13.04.53	191
Whirlwind	XJ401	06.06.56	167	York	MW234	19.08.54	191
Whirlwind	XJ409	10.03.71	167	York	MW304	22.10.48	191
Whirlwind	XJ411	02.03.55	167	York	MW313	16.12.46	191
Whirlwind	XJ429	08.02.55	165				
Whirlwind	XJ729	31.05.62	167				
Whirlwind	XJ759	20.08.58	165, **169**				
Whirlwind	XJ764	1965	167				
Whirlwind	XK906	14.06.57	167				
Whirlwind	XK941	22.07.58	167, **169**				
Whirlwind	XL899	17.07.67	167				
Whirlwind	XM666	29.08.69	167, **170**				
Whirlwind	XM687	08.12.59	167				
Whirlwind	XN126	13.08.59	167, **168**				
Whirlwind	XN258	18.09.59	167				
Whirlwind	XN310	1965	167				
Whirlwind	XP299	05.07.61	167				
Whirlwind	XP300	01.02.62	**166**, 167				
Whirlwind	XP301	25.01.62	167, **170**				
Whirlwind	XP303	01.09.61	167				
Whirlwind	XP329	25.01.62	167				
Whirlwind	XP333	15.12.61	167				
Whirlwind	XP351	26.10.71	167				
Whirlwind	XP356	09.12.71	167				
Whirlwind	XP399	08.05.72	167				
Whirlwind	XR486	10.02.64	167				
Widgeon	G-AKTW	12.12.56	165, **166**				
Wildcat	JV875	Wartime	269				
Wyvern	TS375	03.03.49	285				
Wyvern	TS378	04.48	**284**, 285				
Wyvern	TS380	1948	285				
Wyvern	TS387	08.11.48	285				
Wyvern	VP109	08.49	285, **286**				
Wyvern	VR132	07.10.49	285				
Wyvern	VR134	09.03.50	285, **286**				
Wyvern	VW867	14.03.50	285, **287**				
Wyvern	VW869	09.02.51	285, **287**				
Wyvern	VW870	07.53	289				
Wyvern	VW873	27.08.51	285, 289				
Wyvern	VW881	04.03.52	289				
Wyvern	VW883	10.04.53	289				
Wyvern	VW884	25.07.52	285				

GENERAL INDEX
Names and places

A

Abel, Mr G C 45
Adams, Wg Cdr Mike 27
Aden 17, 71, 164, 172, 181, 205
Aldergrove 39
Alf's Tower 63
Allen, M Eng Doug 15
Allington 20
Allum, Flt Lt D W E (Dave) 32
Allwright, Mr H J (John) 42
Alston, Sqn Ldr M R 309
Amesbury 20, 21
Amsterdam 39, 40
Andrews, Flt Lt Graham 21
Andrews, Mr J 308
Anne, HRH The Princess 22
Ashley Walk 49
Aston, Flt Lt B G (Bill) 26
Atkinson, Mr R J 308
Attlee, Mrs 22
Aylett, Gp Capt G J 308
Aynsley, Mr W (Bill) 20
Ayre, Gp Capt A W 308

B

Backhaus, Mr Eric 230
Bailey, Lt Cdr J S 40
Bardon, Flt Lt P J (Peter) 39
Barthropp, Sqn Ldr P P C (Paddy) 28
Baskerville, Warrant Officer A 31
Bastable, Flt Lt Brian 45, 309
Beamont, Mr R P 310
Beaulieu 14, 24, 41, 61
Beazley, Sqn Ldr R H (Roger) 41, 156
RAE Bedford 25, 43
Beeching, Flt Lt M H 33
Beer, Mr F H (Bertie) 32, 53, 308
Beeson, Flt Lt R L 15, 309
Bell, Flt Lt J (John) 15
Bemerton, Salisbury 21
Bennett, Mr J D 27, 308
Betts, Sgt Don 61
Bird, Air Cdre F R 308
Bishop, Flt Lt I P 309
Blackstone, Sqn Ldr M E 27
Blaha, Major John, USAF 29
Bolt, Flt Lt R deV (Bob) 28
Bolter, Ms Mary 31
Booth, Mr J S 310
Booth, Mr M 309
Bovingdon 40
Bowen, Mr I 308
Bowers, Sqn Ldr Ron 17
Boyd, Admiral 40

Brabazon Committee 44
Bradfield, Flt Lt A G 309
Bray, Flt Lt R W (Ray) 32, 39
Braybon, J E H (Jack) 48
Broad, Gp Capt H P 308
Brooke-Smith, Mr T W 310
Brown, Lt Cdr O (Ozzie) 31, 309
Brown, Flt Lt J A 39
Brown, Wg Cdr C D (Cyclops) 29, 33, 39
Brown, Mr F G J 27, 308
Browne, Air Cdre C D A, 308
Bullock, Flt Lt Brian 21
Bullock, Gp Capt A H 48, 308
Bussey, Flt Lt J E (John) 15
Byrne, Dr 48
Bywater, Sqn Ldr D L (David) 15

C

Cadiz, Sgt Tony 69
Cairns, Air Cdre G C 27, 29, 150, 241, 308
Callard, Sqn Ldr A E (Arthur) 26, 39
Cameron, Dr D 308
Cannon, Sqn Ldr G (George) 28
Chilbolton 10
Chilton, Fg Off P 309
Christian, M Sig L 309
Clark, Mr B D 308
Clark, Sqn Ldr C G 309
Clayton, Gp Capt G A V 308
Clouston, Air Cdre A E 308
Coates, Fg Off J M V 33, 309
Cole, Flt Lt Bob 27
Cologne/Wahn 241
Colquhoun, Sqn Ldr D W 309
Cook, Sgt Bill 69
Cooper, Gp Capt T B 28, 33, 308, 309
Coryton, Air Marshal Sir W Alec 9
Cottingham, Flt Lt A S (Tony) 15
Cotton, Mr John 26
Cowan, Flight Sergeant 27
Cranfield 7
Crichel Down 49
Crosley, Cdr R M 25, 31
Cruikshanks, Flt Lt C J (Colin) 27, 34
Cull, Flt Lt M J (Mike) 15
Curtiss, Lettice 44
Cushing, Mr R K (Roger) 14

D

Darlow, Flt Lt L (Les) 15
Davies, Mr Handel 25, 308
Davies, Lt 18
Dawkins, Gp Capt R C 28, 308
Dennis, Wg Cdr D F 33

Dick, Air Cdre A D 15, 34, 36, 308
Dickinson, Mr R P (Reg) 15, 67, 308
Dingley, Flt Lt J 309
Dix, Les 31
Drake, Mr Vince 57
Dru-Drury, Gp Capt E S 308
Duke, Mr N 310
Dunn, Terry 31, 309

E
Eagles, Lt Cdr J D (Dave) 20
Eastleigh 182
Edmunds, Miss Beryl 45, 309
Edwards Air Force Base 16, 17, 156
El Centro
Elliott, Roy 31
Enevoldson, Capt Einar, USAF 21
Enford 49
Esler, Mr S E 310
Evans, Gp Capt V R L 308
Evans, Mr Don 26, 61
Evans, Sqn Ldr P G 309

F
Falk, Mr R J 310
Farnborough 35, 53, 61, 173, 204
Fehler, Sub Lt K W A 309
Felixstowe 15
Fell, M AEOp (Jim) 15
Fisher, Flt Lt Alan 15
Flemons, Wg Cdr H C 48
Fletcher, Wg Cdr G R K (Geoff) 15, 33, 231
Flint, Sgt Gordon 69
Forrester-Addie, Mr R (Robbie) 83
Forster, Flt Lt Tony 27
Fort Churchill 20, 31, 163, 217
Fortes, Mr Ben 26
Foster, Flt Lt Dick 21
Foster, Flt Lt G W E 309
Franklin, Mr E G 310
Fraser, Air Cdre H P 308
Fraser, Gp Capt C F S 308
Fraser, Mr D (Donald) 44
Frieze, Flt Lt Pete 27
Frith, Sqn Ldr E D (Ned) 15, 39, 40

G
Gander 39
Gatwick 39
Gevaux, Flt Lt W G (Bill) 266
Gibson, Wg Cdr 24
Giddings, Gp Capt K C M 308
Gigg, Mr R (Bob) 61
Goodhart, Lt H C N (Nic) 34
Goodman, Gp Capt G H 308
Gregory, Mr J (John) 16
Grocott, Sqn Ldr D F H (Pinky) 65
Gunn, Mr A E 310

H
Habgood, Lt L R V 309
Hagget, Sqn Ldr Norman 69
Haines, Mr Derek 67
Hall, Flt Lt V D 309
Hannaford, Flt Lt R J 309
Hanson, Lt Cdr D K 33, 309
Hanson, Mr J 308
Hare, Sqn Ldr E W F 65
Hargreaves, Flt Lt Robin 21
Hartley, Flt Lt I J 309
Harvey, Mrs Pat 21
Haskett, Flt Lt E A J 26
Hatfield 122
Hazelden, Mr H G 310
Heathrow 43
Hedges, Lt Maurice 18, 35, 230
Heffernan, Mr T H J (Terry) 21
Hibbert, Mr W A 61
Hicks, Sgt L D 309
Hickson, Lt K R (Ken) 33
High Post 7
Higton, Mr Dennis 25, 308
Hindley, Flt Lt Mick 27
Hodge, Fg Off R 309
Hodges, Mr K J 27, 308
Holme, Flt Lt B P (Pidge) 15, 32
Hooks, Gp Capt R K 308
Howell, Gp Capt E M T 308
Howes, Mr P W 309
Howlett, Gp Capt C R C 308
Hufton, Mr P A 308
Humble, Mr W 310
Hurn 45

I
Idris 17, 39, 169, 176, 183, 217
Imber 49
Innes, Flt Lt J W L (John) 26

J
Jackson, Maj J P R 185
Jennings, Mr W G 14, 15, 308
Johnston, Flt Lt I K 309
Jones, Mr E T 8, 308
Jones, Flt Lt Alan 69
Jones, Flt Lt Andy 21
Jones, Lt G W N 309
Julian, Lt 18

K
Kano 34
Keane, Sgt P 40, 69
Keppie, Wg Cdr I H (Ian) 40
Khartoum 17, 26, 30, 39, 114, 137, 196, 200, 237, 238
Khormaksar 17
King Joyce, Lt Cdr T J A 33, 34, 309
Kite, Gp Capt D S 308

L
Lambie, Mr J 308
Lang, Mr D A 27, 308
Langton, Mr G 41
Larkhill 11, 21, 47
Lecky-Thompson, Sqn Ldr T L 39, 40, 245
Leigh, M Sig P (Pete) 15
Leng, Lt John 27, 304
Lewis, Sqn Ldr N E D 309
Lightfoot, Gp Capt I J 308
Lithgow, Mr M J 310
Locke, Cdr L G (George) 16, 40
Lodge, Mr Jack 26
London 29, 39, 40, 173, 245
Loveday, Flt Lt Bert 27
Lowman, Mr J W 309
Lumsden, Sqn Ldr John 27
Lush, Mr K J 44
Lyme Bay 32, 49

M
MacDonald, Gp Capt I N M 308
MacLaren Humphreys, Mr G 67, 308
Maidment, Mr H (Henry) 63
Majcherczyk, Sqn Ldr A R (Tony) 31, 309
Malta 29, 39, 173, 176
Mann, Wg Cdr J C 33
Marsden, Mr T W 308
Martlesham Heath 13, 212
Mason, Flt Lt T (Tim) 12, 15
Matthews, Mr Fred 26
May, Flt Lt R S 33, 309
Mayes, Flt Lt J 31
McDonald, Air Cdre A W B 308
McIver, Mr J 308
Mercer, Sqn Ldr M J P H 309
Merriman, Air Cdre H A 16, 21, 27, 31, 308
Miller, Flt Lt J I (Dusty) 15
Millet, Mr Paul 156
Mills, Sqn Ldr Keith 27
Moakes, Mr John 24
Moore, Flt Lt (Dinty) 15
Moore, Flt Lt G (George) 15
Moreton Valence 118
Morgan, Sqn Ldr R J 309
Morrall, Mr J C 308
Morren, Flt Lt T W G 309
Morris, Dr D E 308
Morris, Gp Capt R J P 308
Mount Kilimanjaro 71
Munday, Flt Lt R F 185

N
Nairobi 17, 204
Namao 20
Neilson, Lt J A (John) 34
New York 40, 245
Newbery, Flt Lt J (Jim) 15
Noble, Flt Lt B J (Bernie) 32, 39, 146

O
Old Sarum 264
Orange 39
Orme, Flt Lt Peter 27
Orr-Ewing, Lt Cdr R M 31, 309
Ottawa 177, 246
Overbury, Lt J R F 39, 40
Oxford, Mr V 21

P
Parker, Lt Cdr D G 40
Parkinson, Sgt Harry 69
Parrot, Sqn Ldr PL (Peter) 26
Parry, Flt Lt Derek 21, 244
Patch, Air Cdre H L 308
Patmore, Gp Capt S P A 308
Patuxent River 16
Pearson, Lt Cdr R B 309
Pelly, Air Cdre C B R 308
Pengelly, Flt Lt Russ 27
Penrose, Mr H J 310
Perkins, Flt Lt Polly 26
Pitton 28
Plascott, Mr Harry 27, 308
Platt, Lt B (Barny) 15
Poole, Mr J 43, 61, 308
Popham, Mr H A (Pop) 27, 65, 308
Port Said 114
Porton Down 23, 31, 33, 49, 242
Potter, M Eng (Gillie) 15
Poulton, Mr E A 308
Pratica di Mare 39
Price, Flt Lt J D 17
Purse, Mr D E 309
Purvis, Gp Capt H A (Bruin) 44

Q
Quill, Mr J K 310
Quinney, Flt Sgt P J 40, 69

R
Radlett 198, 200
"RAF St Pancras" 245
Ramsay Rae, Air Cdre R A 308
Ramsdale, Mr Brian 24, 27, 308
Rayner, Wg Cdr M O 48
Revell, Wg Cdr 65
Reynolds, Lt 18
Rickell, Lt Cdr T A 33, 309
Rigg, Sqn Ldr Hugh 21
Ring, Gp Capt S L 308
Robbins, Lt Cdr D F 39
Roberts, Sqn Ldr E J (Red) 26, 34, 309
Robertson, Flt Lt F (Fergus) 15
Robson, A J R 26
Rollason, Flt Lt Vic 15
Roulston, Air Cdre J F 308
Rustin, Wg Cdr C C (Clive) 34

S

Salisbury 8
Schipol 261
Scott-Hall, Mr S 41, 308
Scouller, Flt Lt D C (David) 28
Sewell, Sqn Ldr K J (Pop) 32
Shields, Mr R T 27, 308
Shipp, Mr J C K 44
Sigonella 152
Silyn-Roberts, Gp Capt G 308
Singapore 17, 217
Singleton, Flt Lt P H R (Pete) 15
Slade, Mr R G 310
Sleeman, Mr Stan 26
Smith, Flt Lt Gordon 29, 39, 160
Smythe, Sqn Ldr R H 310
Sopley 24
Sorley, Air Marshal Sir Ralph 7, 21
Stark, Col W R, USAF 11
Stark, Sqn Ldr L W F 31
Stephenson, Flt Lt (Steve) 15
Stewart, W H (Willie) 34, 44
Stockman, Sqn Ldr G B 309
Stonehenge 247
Stonor, Wg Cdr J B 48
Strachan, Sqn Ldr I (Ian) 268
Surman, Mr S G 308
Sykes, Flt Lt Les 24

T

Tennant, Mr E A 310
Theed, Gp Capt W A 308
Thirtle, Sqn Ldr John 39
Thorne, Sqn Ldr P D (Peter) 25, 40
Tomlinson, Sqn Ldr C A (Tommy) 31
Tooth, Sqn Ldr A 309
Topp, Air Cdre R L 28, 308
Turner, Mr H W (Wason) 14, 24, 308
Twiss, L P (Peter) 40, 310

U

Upavon 23
Uplands 20, 68, 246
USAF Wheelus 17, 31, 32

V

Varney, Mr K P 308
Villacoublay 262

W

Wade, Mr T S 310
Ward, Gp Capt B A 27, 308
Warman, Miss G M 309
Warner, Sqn Ldr Nick 27
Warton 67
Waterton, Mr W A 310
Waterton, Sqn Ldr J (John) 15
Watkins, Gp Capt W D G 308
Watson, Mr J 308
Watts, Sqn Ldr R A (Ray) 26
Watts-Phillips, Flt Lt J (Jim) 15
Weaver, Maj J R 309
Weaver, Mr A K 44
West Freugh 53
Whatley, Mr R J 309
Wheeler, Air Cdre A H 308
White, Sqn Ldr D 31
White, Flt Lt D (Chalky) 26
Whitehead, Lt D J (Block) 18, 287
Wilkinson, Gp Capt J 27, 83, 308
Williams, Sqn Ldr Graham 40
Williams, Fg Off G W 309
Williams, Flt Lt L N 309
Williams, Mr R 309
Wills, Mr C S 308
Wingate, Flt Lt Jock 83
Withers, Mr C (Cyril) 63
Wittington, Flt Lt Dick 39
Wood-Smith, Flt Lt G 309
Woodcock, Flt Lt A D (Alan) 26
Woodford 192, 198
Woods, Flt Lt Guy 27
Wormworth, Capt B J (Jake) 266
Wroath, Gp Capt S 308
Wycherley, Mr Alan 88

Y

Yeovilton 155
Young, Flt Lt F A 309
Yuma 17

Z

Zurakowski, Sqn Ldr J (Jan) 31